THE ELEMENTS OF JURISPRUDENCE

BY

THOMAS ERSKINE HOLLAND, D.C.L.

OF LINCOLN'S INN, BARRISTER-AT-LAW
CHICHELE PROFESSOR OF INTERNATIONAL LAW AND DIPLOMACY
AND FELLOW OF ALL SOULS COLLEGE, OXFORD
HON. LL.D. OF THE UNIVERSITIES OF
BOLOGNA, GLASGOW, AND DUBLIN
HON. PROFESSOR IN THE UNIVERSITY OF PERUGIA
HON. MEMBER OF THE UNIVERSITY OF ST. PETERSBURG AND OF THE
JURIDICAL SOCIETY OF BERLIN

FIRST AMERICAN FROM THE
SEVENTH ENGLISH EDITION

THE LAWBOOK EXCHANGE, LTD.
Clark, New Jersey
2006

ISBN-13: 978-1-58477-632-1
ISBN-10: 1-58477-632-3

Second printing 2008

The quality of this reprint is equivalent to the quality of the original work.

Printed in the United States of America on acid-free paper

THE LAWBOOK EXCHANGE, LTD.
33 Terminal Avenue
Clark, New Jersey 07066-1321

Please see our website for a selection of our other publications and fine facsimile reprints of classic works of legal history:
www.lawbookexchange.com

Library of Congress Cataloging-in-Publication Data

Holland, Thomas Erskine, Sir, 1835-1926.
The elements of jurisprudence / by Thomas Erskine Holland.
p. cm.
Originally published: 1st American ed. from 7th English ed. St. Paul : West Pub. Co., 1896.
Includes bibliographical references and index.
ISBN 1-58477-632-3 (alk. paper)
1. Jurisprudence. I. Title.
K230.H65 2005
340--dc22

2005014289

THE ELEMENTS OF JURISPRUDENCE

BY

THOMAS ERSKINE HOLLAND, D.C.L.

OF LINCOLN'S INN, BARRISTER-AT-LAW
CHICHELE PROFESSOR OF INTERNATIONAL LAW AND DIPLOMACY
AND FELLOW OF ALL SOULS COLLEGE, OXFORD
HON. LL.D. OF THE UNIVERSITIES OF
BOLOGNA, GLASGOW, AND DUBLIN
HON. PROFESSOR IN THE UNIVERSITY OF PERUGIA
HON. MEMBER OF THE UNIVERSITY OF ST. PETERSBURG AND OF THE
JURIDICAL SOCIETY OF BERLIN

FIRST AMERICAN FROM THE
SEVENTH ENGLISH EDITION

ST. PAUL, MINN.
WEST PUBLISHING CO.
1896

iv *Amplissimum Iuris Oceanum ad paucos revocare fontes limpidos rectae rationis.—LEIBNITZ, *Ep. ad Magl.*, xxvii.

Das bedarf heutzutage keiner Bemerkung, dass das System, ebensowenig beim Recht wie bei jedem andern Gegenstande, keine Ordnung sein soll, die man in die Sache hineinbringt, sondern eine solche, die man herausholt.—IHERING, *Geist des R. R.*, i. p. 36.

PUBLISHERS' PREFACE.

This first American edition of Holland's Elements of Jurisprudence is from the seventh English edition, and closely follows that text. The chief variations are, first, that italic lines have been inserted so as to make readily apparent the *frame-work* of the subject; and, second, that the table of contents, which, in the English edition, was merely an enumeration of the chapter titles, has been elaborated to show the analysis of each chapter.

WEST PUBLISHING CO.

PREFACE

TO THE FIRST EDITION.

---

*The legal systems of the continent owe to their common derivation from the law of Rome, not only a uniform legal nomenclature, but also a generally accepted method, which at once assigns any newly developed principle to its proper place, and has greatly facilitated the orderly exposition of those systems in the form of codes.

In England, on the other hand, legal nomenclature is a mosaic of many languages, and the law itself, as expounded by Coke and Blackstone, except so far as it has been deduced with much logical punctiliousness from the theory of feudal tenure, is little more than a collection of isolated rules, strung together, if at all, only by some slender thread of analogy. The practitioner has been content to find his way through it, as best he might, by the help of the
*vi indices of *text-books, or of 'Abridgments,' or so-called 'Digests,' arranged under alphabetical titles.

It was a step in advance when it occurred to Mr. J. W. Smith to publish a series of 'Leading Cases,' selected almost at random, and to group round each a collection of subordinate decisions, in which the rule recognized in the principal case is deviously tracked in its various applications. Of a somewhat similar nature is Dr. Broom's 'Selection of Legal Maxims,' which explains the workings in different departments of law of a string of principles, such as those which are collected in the title of the Digest 'de Regulis Iuris.' It may be remarked that the principles to which reference is made, alike in the 'Leading Cases' and in the 'Maxims,' are but what Bacon would call 'media axiomata,' which neither work attempts to exhibit in their mutual relations, or to deduce from the higher principles of which they are corollaries; also that the search for these principles is an enquiry into the ethical reasons by which English law ought to be moulded, not an analysis and classification of legal categories.

There have been of late years signs of a change in the mental habit of English lawyers. Distaste for comprehensive views, and indifference to foreign modes of thought, can no longer be said to be national characteristics. The change is due partly to a revival of the study of Roman law, partly to a growing familiarity with continental life and literature, partly to such investigations as those of Sir H. Maine into the origin of legal ideas, but chiefly to the writings of Bentham and Austin. To the latter especially most Eng-
*vii lishmen *are indebted for such ideas as they possess of legal
method. The 'Province of Jurisprudence Determined,' is indeed a book which no one can read without improvement. It presents the spectacle of a powerful and conscientious mind struggling with an intractable and rarely handled material, while those distinctions upon which Austin after his somewhat superfluously careful manner bestows most labour are put in so clear a light that they can hardly again be lost sight of.

The defects of the work are even more widely recognized than its merits. It is avowedly fragmentary. The writer is apt to recur with painful iteration to certain topics; and he leaves large tracts of his subject wholly unexplored, while devoting much space to digressions upon questions, such as the psychology of the will, codification, and utilitarianism, which have no necessary connection with his main argument. It may be asserted, without injustice either to Bentham or to Austin, that works upon legal system by English writers have hitherto been singularly unsystematic.

It is long since the author formed the hope of attempting to write a treatise upon legal ideas which should at least be free from this particular fault, and the objects which he proposed to himself differed so considerably from those aimed at in Mr. Justice Markby's 'Elements of Law' that the appearance of that very valuable work did not dissuade him from the prosecution of his design. In carrying it out he has not gained so much assistance as he expected from the legal literature of the continent. He soon discovered *not
*viii only that the name of Austin was unknown in Germany, but
that very little had been written in that country with a direct

bearing upon analytical jurisprudence. The latter fact is not so surprising as it may appear, if it be remembered that the continental jurists find in Roman law a ready-made terminology and a typical method, upon which they are little inclined to innovate. From treatises upon 'Naturrecht,' which may be described as 'Jurisprudence in the air,' he has derived next to nothing; and works upon 'Encyclopädie' and 'Methodologie' are generally too brief, and too much infected with a priori conceptions, to have been consulted with much profit. More help has been found, where it might not at first be looked for, in the numerous works, usually entitled 'Pandekten,' in which the Germans have set forth the Roman law as it has been modified with a view to modern convenience. Foremost among these must be mentioned von Savigny's 'System des heutigen Römischen Rechts.'

Still less has been derived from the other modern literatures; and after a general survey of the subject the author set to work to think it out for himself, resolving to traverse the whole of it, and to hold a straight course through it, turning neither to the right hand nor to the left into any digression however tempting. He now offers the result of his labours, which has been much delayed by other and more pressing engagements, to the indulgence of those who best know the extent and difficulty of the topic of which he has attempted to give a complete and consistent view. T. E. H.

Oxford, March 20, 1880.

PREFACE TO THE SECOND EDITION.

*ix *This edition has been carefully revised, and contains a good deal of new matter. The author has to thank several of his reviewers, whose articles form in themselves valuable contributions to the literature of the subject, especially Mr. A. V. Dicey and Mr. F. Pollock. He is also indebted to previously unknown correspondents, such as Mr. R. Foster of the New York Bar, who have been good enough to favour him with private communications upon points suggested by their reading of the book. He takes this opportunity of explaining, with particular reference to an able article by Mr. A. Tilley, that the method which he has followed, as best exhibiting the scientific order of legal ideas, is not, in his opinion, necessarily that which would be found most convenient for the arrangement of a Code. He has elsewhere pointed out that logical division should be to the codifier what anatomy is to the painter. Without obtruding itself upon the surface, it should underlie and determine the main features of every systematic exposition of law. T. E. H.

Oxford, August 25, 1882.

PREFACE TO THE THIRD EDITION.

In preparing this edition for the press, the author has throughout taken account of the development both of positive law and of legal theory, in this and other countries, during the last three years, so far as he has been able to follow it. He has also worked out in greater detail than before, though it is hoped without detriment to the general proportions of the book, the difficult topics dealt with in Chapter VIII, and what he ventures to think the important question, raised in Chapter XII, as to the necessity of agreement in contract.

Upon many points he has found help in the elaborate reports upon foreign law which some of the governments of the continent are careful to have drawn up before proposing serious legislative changes. No one can consult these reports without wishing that something of the kind were more usual in this country, where a legal principle which has elsewhere long been discussed from every point of view, is not unfrequently treated in Parliament, and even by the Courts, as a novelty. T. E. H.

Oxford, January 31, 1886.

PREFACE TO THE FOURTH EDITION.

*x *In revising the edition, care has been taken to introduce as much illustration as possible from recent English cases, in which one seems to remark a growing tendency towards scientific generalization. The author has reason to be more than ever convinced of the truth of what may perhaps be described as the 'objective' theory of Contract, maintained in Chapter XII. He has seen with pleasure that the method of this work has been followed 'as the most logical and most exact,' by Mr. Stimson in compiling his 'American Statute Law: an Analytical and Compared Digest of the Constitutions and civil public Statutes of all the States and Territories, relating to persons and property;' and that much of its terminology has been adopted in the able treatise of Professor Terry, of Tokio, 'Some Leading Principles of Anglo-American Law, expounded with a view to its Arrangement and Codification.' T. E. H.

Oxford, December 1, 1887.

PREFACE TO THE FIFTH EDITION.

This edition has been revised throughout, and the author ventures to hope that it may be found in some respects a considerable improvement upon its predecessors. He regrets not to have found time to profit as he could have wished by the copious and interesting literature which has been called into existence by the publication of the draft of a Civil Code for the German Empire. T. E. H.

Oxford, October 10, 1890.

PREFACE TO THE SIXTH EDITION.

This edition has undergone careful revision. In compliance with a wish expressed in many quarters, especially by Oriental students, the author has translated the German and Greek definitions which occur in the earlier chapters, though well aware how much of the meaning of the former at any rate must perish in the process.

T. E. H.

Oxford, September 13, 1893.

PREFACE TO THE SEVENTH EDITION.

This edition has been carefully revised and brought up to date.

T. E. H.

Oxford, February 18, 1895.

TABLE OF CONTENTS.

[REFERENCES ARE TO STAR (*) PAGES]

CHAPTER I.

JURISPRUDENCE.

CHAPTER II.

LAW.

[The figures refer to star (*) pages.]

CHAPTER III.

LAWS AS RULES OF HUMAN ACTION.

CHAPTER IV.

POSITIVE LAW.

CHAPTER V.

THE SOURCES OF LAW.

[The figures refer to star (*) pages.]

CHAPTER VI.

THE OBJECT OF LAW.

CHAPTER VII.

RIGHTS.

CHAPTER VIII.

ANALYSIS OF A RIGHT.

[The figures refer to star (*) pages.]

[The figures refer to star (*) pages.]

CHAPTER IX.

THE LEADING CLASSIFICATIONS OF RIGHTS.

[The figures refer to star (*) pages.]

CHAPTER X.

RIGHTS AT REST AND IN MOTION.

CHAPTER XI.

PRIVATE LAW: RIGHTS IN REM.

[The figures refer to star (*) pages.]

[The figures refer to star (*) pages.]

[The figures refer to star (*) pages.]

CHAPTER XII.

PRIVATE LAW: RIGHTS IN PERSONAM.

[The figures refer to star (*) pages.]

[The figures refer to star (*) pages.]

[The figures refer to star (*) pages.]

CHAPTER XIII.

PRIVATE LAW: REMEDIAL RIGHTS.

CHAPTER XIV.

PRIVATE LAW: ABNORMAL.

[The figures refer to star (*) pages.]

CHAPTER XV.

PRIVATE LAW: ADJECTIVE.

[The figures refer to star (*) pages.]

CHAPTER XVI.

PUBLIC LAW.

[The figures refer to star (*) pages.]

CHAPTER XVII.

INTERNATIONAL LAW.

CHAPTER XVIII.

THE APPLICATION OF LAW.

[The figures refer to star (*) pages.]

TABLE OF CASES

ENGLISH, SCOTCH, AND AMERICAN.

[THE FIGURES REFER TO THE STAR (*) PAGES.]

[The figures refer to star (*) pages.]

[The figures refer to star (*) pages.]

[The figures refer to star (*) pages.]

[The figures refer to star (*) pages.]

ELEMENTS OF JURISPRUDENCE.

*1 ## *CHAPTER I.

JURISPRUDENCE.

The need of a science of Law.

The present treatise is an attempt to set forth and explain those comparatively few and simple ideas which underlie the infinite variety of legal rules.

The search for these ideas is not merely a matter of scientific curiosity. The ever-renewed complexity of human relations calls for an increasing complexity of legal detail, till a merely empirical knowledge of law becomes impossible. The evil has been partially remedied by the formation of Codes, in which legislators, more or less imbued with legal principles, have grouped the legal chaos under genera and species. But an uncodified system of law can be mastered only by the student whose scientific equipment enables him to cut a path for himself through the tangled growth of enactment and precedent, and so to codify for his own purposes. In this department of knowledge, as in others, the difficulty of the subject is due less to the multiplicity of its details than to the
*2 absence of general principles under *which those details may be grouped. In other words, while legal science is capable of being intelligently learnt, isolated legal facts are capable only of being committed to memory.

The name Jurisprudence.

For the beginnings of the science which reduces legal phenomena to order and coherence the world is indebted to the Romans. It is also from their language that the science derives its name.

'Iurisprudentia,' in its original use, was merely one among several phrases signifying a knowledge of the law, just as 'rei militaris prudentia' signified a knowledge of the conduct of warfare[1]. The sort of knowledge which the term denoted may be gathered from Cicero's description of a jurisconsult as one who must be 'skilled in the laws, and in the usages current among private citizens, and in giving opinions and bringing actions and guiding his clients aright[2].'

From this thoroughly practical conception of legal knowledge the Roman jurists subsequently rose to a far higher one. The rudiments of this may already be traced in the writings of Cicero, who enumerates the civil law, along with astronomy, geometry, and dialectic, among the arts which have to do with the pursuit of truth[3]. He tells us that the study of law must be derived
*3 from the depths of *philosophy, and that, by an examination of the human mind and of human society, principles may be discovered in comparison with which the rules of positive law are of but trivial importance[4].

Thus the way was prepared for Ulpian's well-known definition of jurisprudence as 'the knowledge of things human and divine, the science of the just and unjust[5].' Jurisprudence was conceived of as a branch of philosophy; and such an elevation of the idea of

[1] 'Habebat enim magnam prudentiam, tum iuris civilis tum rei militaris.' Nep. Cim. 2. The following terms are used synonymously with 'iurisprudentia': 'legum prudentia,' Cic. Rep. ii. 36; 'legum scientia,' Inst. Prooem. 3; 'legitima scientia,' ib. 2; 'iuris notitia,' Tac. Orat. 31; 'cognitio iuris,' Cic. de Orat. i. 44; 'iuris scientia,' ib. 55, Tac. u. s., Pompon. Dig. i. 2. 2. 40; 'civilis scientia,' Cic. de Orat. i. 43; 'iuris peritia,' Ulp. Dig. i. 1, 1. Knowledge of a particular department of law is described by such phrases as 'iuris civilis cognitio,' Cic. de Orat. i. 59; 'iuris publici prudentia,' ib. 60.

[2] Cic. de Orat. i. 48. The same persons who were called 'iurisconsulti' or 'iure periti' were also described as 'prudentes in iure civili,' Cic. Amic. 2; more briefly as 'prudentes,' Gai. i. 7. The phrase 'iuris prudens' is employed by Pomponius (Dig. xxxviii. 15. 2). 'Legum prudens' occurs in Ennius (Gell. xii. 4) and 'imprudens iuris' in Iust. Inst. iv. 2.

[3] Cic. de Off. i. 6.

[4] Cic. de Leg. i. 5.

[5] 'Iurisprudentia est divinarum atque humanarum rerum notitia, iusti atque iniusti scientia.' Dig. i. 1. 10. This is nearly a translation of the Stoic definition of *σοφία* as being *θείων τε καὶ ἀνθρωπίνων ἐπιστήμη* (Plut. Plac. Phil. i. pr.; cf. Cic. de Off. i. 43), modified by the addition of a clause specifying the particular kind of wisdom intended. The first clause of Ulpian's definition has

legal study was naturally accompanied by a corresponding elevation of its professors. Ulpian claims for himself and his learned brethren that they are 'the priests of Justice, engaged in the pursuit of a philosophy that is truly such and no counterfeit[6].' The Romans had, in fact, attained by this time to the idea of a science of those legal principles which exist independently of the institutions of any particular country. No technical term could be borrowed from the Greek language to denote what was of purely indigenous growth[7], and thus it happened that a phrase which at first had been but one among several signifying, in a homely and quite unscientific sense, a 'knowledge of law,' came at length by an accident of Latin philology to express the new idea of a legal science.

The nations of modern Europe are fortunately in the habit of calling the various branches of knowledge by non-vernacular
*4 names, adopted by common consent from the *classical languages; so that a science is generally known by the same Greek or Latin term wherever Western civilisation extends. It is therefore natural and convenient that most of the European nations should express the idea of a science of law by a word which they have borrowed from the language of those by whom the idea was first conceived [8].

Improper uses of the term Jurisprudence.

But the term is unfortunately also borrowed by the modern languages to express other ideas, which might be much better expressed in the vernacular. Thus, upon the analogy of certain loose expressions of the Roman writers, who sometimes use 'iurisprudentia' to denote a current view of the law[9], there has sprung up

been, with little reason, thought by some to have reference to the distinction between ius sacrum and the other branches of law; see Glück, Pandekten, i. p. 198.

6 Dig. i. 1. 1. 1.

7 Iurisprudentia is represented in the Basilika, ii. 1. 1, and in Harmenopulus, Prompt. i. 1. 18, by *σοφία νόμου*.

8 Even the Germans, who have vernacular names for so many of the sciences, recognise 'Jurisprudenz' as well as 'Rechtswissenschaft.'

9 'Media iuris prudentia,' Iust. Inst. iii. 2. 3.

in French the use of such phrases as 'jurisprudence constante,' 'jurisprudence des arrêts de la Cour de Cassation'; in the sense of the view which the courts are in the habit of taking of certain questions[10].

Still less justifiable is the use, so frequent both in French and in English, of 'Jurisprudence' as the equivalent of 'Law.' The imposing quadrisyllable is constantly introduced into a phrase on grounds of euphony alone. Thus we have books upon 'Equity Jurisprudence,' which are nothing more nor less than treatises upon the law administered by Courts of Equity; and we hear of the Jurisprudence of France or Russia, when nothing else is meant than the law which is in force in those countries respectively[11].
*5 This sacrifice of sense *to sound might more readily be pardoned, had it not misled serious and accurate thinkers.

Jurisprudence is the name of a science.

Bentham, for instance, divides Jurisprudence into 'expository,' which ascertains what the law is, and 'censorial,' which ascertains what it ought to be[12]. Now an exposition of existing law is obviously quite another thing from a science of law, and criticisms upon the law with a view to its amendment are the subject, not of Jurisprudence, but, as Bentham himself states in the next paragraph, of the art of Legislation. Bentham carries the confusion further by proceeding to sub-divide expository Jurisprudence into 'authoritative' and 'unauthoritative[13].' By 'authoritative expository jurisprudence' he means nothing more nor less than law emanating from the legislative power; under 'unauthoritative' he would apparently include both text-books upon the laws of any one coun-

10 'La manière dont un Tribunal juge habituellement telle ou telle question.' Dict. de l'Académie.

11 'A practical Treatise of Architectural Jurisprudence,' by James Elmes, was published in 1827. Perhaps the least pardonable application of the term takes place when a treatise upon such medical facts as may incidentally become important in legal proceedings is described as a book upon 'Medical Jurisprudence' (first, apparently, by Dr. Samuel Farr, London, 1788). Such a work is more properly described as dealing with 'Forensic Medicine,' or 'Médecine légale.'

12 Works, i. p. 148.

13 Ib. i. p. 148.

try, or, as he would say, upon 'local jurisprudence,' and works upon law without special reference to any one country, or, to use his own phrase, upon 'universal jurisprudence.' If we are right in considering that 'censorial jurisprudence' should be called 'the art of legislation,' that 'authoritative jurisprudence' is nothing more nor less than a body of law, and that 'unauthoritative local jurisprudence' is mere commentary, it is obvious that what Bentham makes the sub-department of 'unauthoritative universal jurisprudence' is alone entitled to bear the name of the science; and should bear the name simply, without the addition of epithets intended to distinguish it from departments of the subject which are non-existent. 'Jurisprudence' ought therefore to be used, and used without any qualifying epithet, as the name of a science.

Jurisprudence is a formal science.

We have next to inquire what kind of a science it is; and we shall find that it is a formal, or analytical, as opposed to a material one; that is to say, that it deals rather with the
*6 *various relations which are regulated by legal rules than with the rules themselves which regulate those relations.

This was not indeed the whole scope of the science as conceived of by its founders[14]. There floated also always before the eyes of the later Roman jurists a vision of a 'ius naturale'; a universal code, from which all particular systems are derived, or to which they all tend, at least, to approximate: a set of rules, the matter, or contents, of which is of universal application.

But in point of fact, and in the very pursuit of this material unity, they were led to elaborate a system of formal unity; to catalogue the topics with which every system of law has to deal, however each may differ from the rest in its mode of dealing with them. They performed for Law a service similar to that which

[14] Although we find in Cicero the clearest possible description of an analytical science of law. 'Sunt notanda genera et ad certum numerum paucitatemque revocanda . . . si autem aut mihi facere licuerit quod iam diu cogito, aut alius quispiam aut me impedito occuparit, aut mortuo effecerit, ut primum omne ius civile in genera digerat, quae perpauca sunt, deinde eorum generum quasi quaedam membra dispertiat, tum propriam cuiusque vim definitione declaret, perfectam artem iuris civilis habebitis, magis magnam atque uberem quam difficilem atque obscuram.' De Orat. i. 42.

was rendered to Language by the Greeks of Alexandria, when by observing and tabulating the parts of speech, the inflections, moods and syntax, they invented a Grammar, under the formulae of which all the phenomena of any language find appropriate places[15]. Whether the possessive case of a noun substantive is expressed by a specific modification of its termination, or by prefixing to it a specific preposition, is a question of the matter of language; but that the possessive idea, however variously expressed, yet
*7 finds some expression or other in every family *of human speech, is a proposition which relates to linguistic form.

The assertion that Jurisprudence is a formal science may perhaps be made clearer by an example. If any individual should accumulate a knowledge of every European system of law, holding each apart from the rest in the chambers of his mind, his achievement would be best described as an accurate acquaintance with the legal systems of Europe. If each of these systems were entirely unlike the rest, except when laws had been transferred in the course of history from one to the other, such a distinguished jurist could do no more than endeavor to hold fast, and to avoid confusing, the heterogeneous information of which he had become possessed. Suppose however, as is the case, that the laws of every country contain a common element; that they have been constructed in order to effect similar objects, and involve the assumption of similar moral phenomena as everywhere existing; then such a person might proceed to frame out of his accumulated materials a scheme of the purposes, methods, and ideas common to every system of law. Such a scheme would be a formal science of law; presenting many analogies to Grammar, the science of those ideas of relation which, in greater or less perfection, and often in the most dissimilar ways, are expressed in all the languages of mankind.

To each of these formal sciences there ministers a science which supplies it with materials. Just as similarities and differences in

[15] See Max Müller, Science of Language, edit. 3, p. 90. On the 'Technik des Rechts,' or 'Chemie des Rechts,' as a 'formale juristische Logik,' see Ihering, Geist des R. R. ii. p. 335. Cf. J. S. Mill: 'The facts of which law takes cognisance, though far from being identical in all civilised societies, are sufficiently analogous to enable them to be arranged in the same cadres.' Dissertations, iii. p. 212.

the growth of different languages are collected and arranged by Comparative Philology, and the facts thus collected are the foundation of abstract Grammar[16]; so Comparative Law col-
*8 lects and tabulates the *legal institutions of various countries, and from the results thus prepared, the abstract science of Jurisprudence is enabled to set forth an orderly view of the ideas and methods which have been variously realised in actual systems. It is, for instance, the office of Comparative Law to ascertain what have been at different times and places the periods of prescription, or the requisites of a good marriage. It is for Jurisprudence to elucidate the meaning of prescription, in its relation to ownership and to actions; or to explain the legal aspect of marriage, and its connection with property and the family. We are not indeed to suppose that Jurisprudence is impossible unless it is preceded by Comparative Law. A system of Jurisprudence might conceivably be constructed from the observation of one system of law only, at one epoch of its growth. Such, however, has not been in point of fact the mode of its evolution, which must have been extremely tardy but for the possibility of separating the essential elements of the science from its historial accidents, by comparing together laws enforced in the same country at different epochs, and indigenous laws with the differing, though resembling, laws of foreigners.

Jurisprudence is therefore not the material science of those portions of the law which various nations have in common[17], but the formal science of those relations of mankind which are generally recognised as having legal consequences [18].

[16] It is of course true, as is pointed out by Sir F. Pollock in commenting upon this passage (Essays in Jurisprudence and Ethics, p. 4), that, as a matter of fact, abstract grammar is not taught separately, but 'is given by implication in every systematic grammar of a particular language.' This is probably a subject of regret to most persons who, after mastering one language, find many pages in the grammars of every other language devoted to a reiteration of the now familiar distinctions between a substantive and an adjective, a present and a future tense, direct and oblique narration.

[17] A subject which, under the description of the 'ius gentium,' largely occupied the attention of the Roman jurists.

[18] Prof. Grueber, in his review of this work, prefers to describe the object of Jurisprudence as being 'die Gesammtheit der auf die verschiedenen Ver-

Jurisprudence is a science of positive law, and is progressive.

In the next place, it must be sufficient at present merely
*9 *to state, without further explanation, that Jurisprudence is not a science of legal relations a priori, as they might have been, or should have been, but is abstracted a posteriori from such relations as have been clothed with a legal character in actual systems, that is to say from law which has actually been imposed, or positive law. It follows that Jurisprudence is a progressive science. Its generalisations must keep pace with the movement of systems of actual law. Its broader distinctions, corresponding to deep-seated human characteristics, will no doubt be permanent, but, as time goes on, new distinctions must be constantly developed, with a view to the co-ordination of the ever-increasing variety of legal phenomena[19].

Jurisprudence as general and particular.

We have lastly to consider whether the science is rightly divided into several species, and especially to inquire into the justness of the distinction drawn between 'general' and 'particular' Jurisprudence. 'Particular Jurisprudence,' says Austin, 'is the science of

hältnisse anwendbaren Rechtsvorschriften.' Krit. Vierteljahresschrift für Rechtswissenschaft, 1884, p. 180. But see Windscheid, Pand. i. § 13, n. 2.

19 So Lord Hale: 'It cannot be supposed that humane laws can be wholly exempt from the common fate of humane things. Parliaments have taken off and abridged many of the titles about which the law was concerned: usage and disusage have antiquated others, . . . and it shall not be altogether impertinent to give some instances herein of several great titles in the Law, which upon those occasions are at this day in a great measure antiquated, and some that are much abridged and reduced into a very narrow compass and use' (he mentions, inter alia, tenures by knight-service, descents to take away entry, atturnment), 'and as time and experience and use, and some Acts of Parliament, have abridged some and antiquated other titles, so they have substituted or enlarged other titles: as for instance, action upon the case, devises, ejectione firmae, election, and divers others.' Preface to Rolle's Abridgment, 1668. Cf. the interesting remarks of Sir Henry Maine on the probability that a general adoption of a system of Registration of title would render comparatively unimportant such topics as Possession, Bonitarian ownership, and Usucapio; 'although these have always been recognised as belonging to what may be called the osseous structure of Jurisprudence.' Early Law and Custom, p. 360.

any actual system of law or of any portion of it. The only practical Jurisprudence is particular. . . . The proper subject of
*10 general, or universal, *Jurisprudence is a description of such subjects and ends of laws as are common to all systems, and of those resemblances between different systems which are bottomed in the common nature of man, or correspond to the resembling points in these several portions[20].'

Now 'particular' Jurisprudence may mean either of two things. It may mean: a science derived from an observation of the laws of one country only. If so, the particularity attaches, not to the science itself, which is the same science whencesoever derived, but to the source whence the materials for it are gained. A science of Law might undoubtedly be constructed from a knowledge of the law of England alone, as a science of Geology might be, and in great part was, constructed from an observation of the strata in England only: yet as there is no particular science of Geology, so neither is there a particular science of Law. For a science is a system of generalisations which, though they may be derived from observations extending over a limited area, will nevertheless hold good everywhere; assuming the object-matter of the science to possess everywhere the same characteristics. Principles of Geology elaborated from the observation of England alone hold good all over the globe, in so far as the same substances and forces are everywhere present; and the principles of Jurisprudence, if arrived at entirely from English data, would be true if applied to the particular laws of any other community of human beings; assuming them to resemble in essentials the human beings who inhabit England. The wider the field of observation, the greater, of course, will be the chance of the principles of a science being rightly and completely enunciated; but, so far as they are scientific truths at all, they are always general and of universal application. The phrase may however, and probably does, mean: an acquaint-
*11 ance with the laws of a *particular people; and the impropriety of describing such merely empirical and practical knowledge by a term which should be used only as the name of a science has been already pointed out. In either sense therefore

20 Lectures on Jurisprudence, vol. iii. p. 356. Cf. Bentham, Works, i. p. 149.

the term is a misnomer; and it follows that, the existence of a 'particular Jurisprudence' not being admitted, the employment of the opposed term 'general Jurisprudence' becomes unnecessary. Both expressions should be discarded, and the science should be treated as incapable of being divided into these two branches.

Jurisprudence as historical and philosophical.

A distinction may also be suggested between 'historical' and 'philosophical' Jurisprudence. It may be said that the unity which makes Jurisprudence a science exists only in idea; that while it has a side upon which it is closely allied to Ethics and to Metaphysics, it is, on the other hand, no less intimately connected with Archaeology and History; that its phenomena grow from many independent roots, and are formed and coloured according to the character of the various soils from which they have sprung. But to say this is only to say that the facts from which Jurisprudence generalises are furnished by History, the record of human actions. Identical human needs have been satisfied by various means, and all the means of satisfying each of these needs have not been in simultaneous use in every part of the world and in every age. In the satisfaction of their needs mankind have seldom seen clearly the ends at which they were aiming, and have therefore in reaching after those ends invented a vast variety of perverse complications. The unity, in short, which it is the business of Jurisprudence to exhibit as underlying all the phenomena which it investigates, is the late discovery of an advanced civilisation, and was unperceived during much of the time during which those phenomena were accumulating. The facts can only be presented by History, and History may be studied with the sole view of discovering this class of facts. But this is not the task of Jurisprudence, which only begins when these facts begin to fall into an order other than
*12 the *historical, and arrange themselves in groups which have no relation to the varieties of the human race. The province of Jurisprudence is to observe the wants for the supply of which laws have been invented, and the manner in which those wants have been satisfied. It then digests those actual wants, and the modes in which they have actually been satisfied, irrespectively of their historical or geographical distribution, according to a log-

ical method. One work on Jurisprudence may contain more of historical disquisition, while in another philosophical argument may predominate; but such differences are incidental to the mode of treatment, and afford no ground for a division of the science itself.

But though the science is one, it may have as many heads or departments as there are departments of law. It would therefore be unobjectionable to talk of 'criminal' and 'civil,' 'public' and 'private' Jurisprudence.

Summary—Jurisprudence defined.

To sum up. The term Jurisprudence is wrongly applied to actual systems of law, or to current views of law, or to suggestions for its amendment, but is the name of a science. This science is a formal, or analytical, rather than a material one. It is the science of actual, or positive, law. It is wrongly divided into 'general' and 'particular,' or into 'philosophical' and 'historical.' It may therefore be defined provisionally as 'the formal science of positive law.' The full import of this definition will not be apparent till after the completion of an analysis of the all-important term 'Law.'

*13

*CHAPTER II.

LAW.

Meaning of the term Law.

'Law, or the law,' says Bentham, 'taken indefinitely, is an abstract or collective term, which, when it means anything, can mean neither more nor less than the sum total of a number of individual laws taken together[1].'

This simple statement is in striking contrast with a multitude of assertions upon the subject; which however are less frequently made with reference to the English term Law than to its equivalents in other languages. The terms Ius, Recht, Droit, cannot, in fact, be said to express nothing more than 'the sum total of a number of individual laws taken together.' It so happens that all these terms denote not only the sum total of Laws, but also the sum total of Rights (Iura, Rechte, Droits), and the sum total of all that is just (iustum, recht, droit). When therefore we say that Jurisprudence is the science of Ius, Recht, or Droit, we may mean in each case that it is the science of any one of three things, viz.

(1) of Law,
(2) of Rights,
(3) of Justice;

*14 *and, unless this ambiguity be borne in mind, many expressions having apparent reference to law will be quite unintelligible[2]. But a coherent science cannot be constructed upon an idea which has complex or shifting meanings. One or other meaning must be chosen, and when chosen must be made the sole foundation of the edifice. It is therefore a piece of good fortune that when we say in English that Jurisprudence is the science of law, we are spared the ambiguities which beset the expression of that

1 Works, i. p. 148. Cf., among the meanings of 'Ius' enumerated by Puffendorf, i. i. § 20, 'complexus seu systema legum homogenearum.'

2 So Lord Westbury was at the pains to explain that the word 'ius,' in the maxim 'ignorantia iuris haud excusat,' is used in the sense of 'general law, the ordinary law of the country,' not in the sense of 'a private right.' Cooper v. Phibbs, L. R. 2 H. L. 170.

proposition in Latin, German, and French, and have greatly obscured its exposition in those languages.

Meaning of the term 'a law.'

But if the English abstract term 'Law' is free from any suggestion of the aggregate of Rights, or of the aggregate of just things, it is of course suggestive of all the meanings in which the concrete term 'a law' is employed in our language; and these have unfortunately been so numerous as to involve the abstract idea in considerable obscurity. Hence it is that so many of the definitions which have been given of that mysterious non-entity strike us as being vague or merely eulogistic. Many of them have reference to that divine order which pervades the inanimate universe even more than the actions of rational beings; and those of them which have reference to human action deal quite as often with the voluntarily observed maxims of society as with rules which are supported by the authority of the State.

Heterogeneous however as the senses of the term 'a law' may at first sight appear, the connection between them is not hard to trace; nor is the earliest use widely different from the latest and most accurate.

Same—Its earliest use.

The shepherd who guides his flock, or, on a larger scale, the head of a family who regulates its encampments and employments,
*15 seems to have been the earliest 'lawgiver,' *and his directions, as orders given by one who has power to enforce their observance, are the earliest 'laws[3].' The original, and still the

[3] So Homer says of the Cyclopes, Θεμιστεύει δὲ ἕκαστος παίδων ἠδ' ἀλόχων, Odyss. ix. 114; and Plato, Οὗτοι ἄρα τῶν παλαιῶν ἄριστοι νομοθέται γεγόνασι, νομεῖς τε καὶ ποιμένες ἀνδρῶν, Minos, p. 320 B. It may be worth while to notice that νόμος (as distinguished from νομός) does not occur in Homer. Hesiod uses it twice, both times in the singular number, in the Op. et Dies, 276, 388; and it occurs in the Theogonia. The Homeric word most nearly expressive of laws is θέμιστες, which however really signifies rather decrees made for special cases. Grote, Hist. ii. p. 111; Maine, Ancient Law, ch. i. Cicero derives νόμος 'a suum cuique tribuendo,' De Legg. i. 6. It is surely reversing the order of ideas to suppose that the use of νόμος in the sense of 'a chant' is the original one, as does, e. g., Fustel de Coulanges, La Cité Antique, p. 227.

popular, conception of a 'law,' is a command, disobedience to which will be punished, prescribing a course of action. This conception necessarily implies that of a lawgiver, who has power to enforce his commands[4]. From this vague original use of the term has arisen that large development of uses, some proper, some merely metaphorical, out of which the jurist has to select that which he admits into his science.

Same—Derivative uses.

The strongest intellectual tendency of mankind is the anthropomorphic. If man is a mystery to himself, external nature is a still greater mystery to him, and he explains the more by the less obscure. As he governs his flock and his family, so he supposes that unseen beings govern the waters and the winds. The greater the regularity which he observes in nature, the fewer such beings does he suppose to be at work in her; till at length he rises to the conception of one great being whose laws are obeyed by the whole universe; or it may be that, having thus arrived at the notion of a universe moving according to law, he holds fast to it, even while he loses his hold on the idea of the existence of a supreme lawgiver.

*16 *Men have also almost always believed themselves to be acquainted with certain rules intended for the guidance of their actions, and either directly revealed to them by a superhuman power, or gathered by themselves from such indications of the will of that power as are accessible. They have supposed that they have discovered by self-analysis a master part of themselves, to the dictates of which they owe allegiance. They have observed that, in order that their senses may receive certain impressions from external objects, those objects must be arranged in certain ways, and no other.

It is easy enough, upon consideration of these facts, to account for the existence of such phrases as laws of Nature, laws of God,

[4] Prof. Max Müller appears to think that, among the Hindoos at all events, the order of ideas was the converse, showing that in the Vedic Hymns, *Rita*, from meaning the order of the heavenly movements, became in time the name for moral order and righteousness. Hibbert Lectures, 1878, p. 235.

laws of Morality, laws of Beauty, and others which will at once suggest themselves.

The separation of the sciences.

The employment of the same name to denote things so different may appear to us to imply an extraordinary confusion of the topics appropriate to Theology, to Physics, to Ethics, to Aesthetics, and to Jurisprudence; but the wonder will be less if we remember that the separation of the sciences to which we are accustomed, and which we take for granted, was unknown to remote antiquity. The world with all its varied phenomena was originally studied as a whole. The facts of nature and the doings of man were alike conceived of as ordained by the gods. The constitutions of states and the customs and laws of all the peoples of the earth were as much of divine contrivance as the paths of the planets. The great problem thus presented for the study of mankind was gradually broken up into a number of minor problems. There occurred a division of the sciences. A line was drawn between those which deal with external nature, including Theology and Metaphysics, and those which deal with the actions of men. These latter, the practical,
*17 were thus severed from the theoretical sciences[5]; *and the term law, which had been used ambiguously in the discussion of both sets of topics before their severance, has henceforth two distinct histories. In the theoretical sciences, it is used as the abstract idea of the observed relations of phenomena, be those relations instances of causation or of mere succession and co-existence. In the practical sciences the term is used to express the abstract idea of the rules which regulate human action.

Use of the term Law in the physical sciences.

In the theoretical, or as we should rather say in modern phrase, in the physical sciences, Law is used to denote the method of the phenomena of the universe; a use which would imply, in accordance with the primitive meaning of the term, that this method is imposed upon the phenomena either by the will of God, or by an abstraction called Nature.

[5] They are henceforth connected only by means of religion, and by speculations concerning the faculties of the human mind.

This use of the term may certainly lead to misconceptions. It has long ago been agreed that all we can know of natural phenomena is that they co-exist with, or succeed, one another in a certain order, but whether this order be imposed immediately by a divine will, or mediately through an abstraction called Nature, or through minor abstractions called Gravitation, Electricity, and the like, the phenomena themselves are unable to inform us. It is therefore necessary to realise that when we talk of the laws of Gravity or of Refraction, we mean merely that objects do gravitate and that rays are refracted. We are using the term law merely to convey to our minds the idea of order and method, and we must beware of importing into this idea any of the associations called up by the term when it is employed in the practical sciences.

Use of the term Law in the practical sciences.

Its use in these sciences is, speaking very generally, to express a rule of human action; and the sciences of human action being those in which the term is most used, and indeed is most needed, it is reasonable to say that this is its proper meaning, and that its use in the theoretical sciences is improper, or metaphorical merely. But just as its metaphorical use, as meaning 'order,' is
*18 *sometimes obscured by associations derived from its proper use as signifying 'a rule,' so is its proper use as 'a rule' occasionally confused by an imagined parity between a rule and the invariable order of nature.

The two meanings.

The first step therefore towards clearing the term Law of ambiguity for the purposes of Jurisprudence is to discard the meaning in which it is employed in the physical sciences, where it is used, by a mere metaphor, to express the method or order of phenomena, and to adopt as its proper meaning that which it bears in the practical sciences, where it is employed as the abstract of rules of human action.

The opposition between these two meanings will be best seen by grouping together, under the heads of Order and Rule respectively, a few characteristic specimens of the vague employment of the term Law.

I. Law as the order of the Universe.

Order.

'Law is the King of Kings, far more powerful and rigid than they: nothing can be mightier than law, by whose aid as by that of the highest monarch, even the weak may prevail over the strong.' —The Vedas[6].

Νόμος, ὁ πάντων Βασιλεὺς
θνατῶν τε καὶ ἀθανάτων.—Pindar[7].

'Επεὶ καὶ τὸν ὅλον κόσμον, καὶ τα θεῖα καὶ τὰς καλουμένας ὥρας, νόμος καὶ τάξις, εἰ χρὴ τοῖς δρωμένοις πιστεύειν, διοικεῖν φαίνεται.—Demosthenes[8].

'Ο νόμος ὁ κοινός, ὅσπερ ἐστὶν ὁ ὀρθὸς λόγος διὰ πάντων ἐρχόμενος, ὁ αὐτὸς ὢν τῷ Διὶ καθηγεμόνι τούτῳ τῆς τῶν ὅλων διοικήσεως ὄντι.— Chrysippus[9].

*19 *'Lex vera atque princeps, apta ad iubendum et ad vetandum, ratio est recta summi Iovis.'—Cicero[10].

'Lex aeterna nihil aliud est quam summa ratio divinae sapientiae, secundum quod est directiva omnium actuum et motionum.'—S. Thomas[11].

'Of Law there can be no lesse acknowledged, than that her seate is the bosome of God, her voyce the harmony of the world, all things in Heaven and Earth doe her homage, the very least as feeling her care, and the greatest as not exempted from her power; both angels and men and creatures of what condition soever, though each in different sort and manner, yet all with uniforme

6 Sat. Br. 14. 4, 2. 23; Br. Ar. Up. 1, 4, 14, cited Tagore Lect. 1880, p. 136.

7 'Law, the King of All both mortals and immortals.' Apud Plat. Gorg. 484 B.

8 'Since also the whole world, and things divine, and what we call the Seasons, appear, if we may trust what we see, to be regulated by Law and Order.' Adv. Aristog. B. p. 808.

9 'The common law, which is the right reason moving through all things, identical with Zeus, the supreme administrator of the Universe.' Apud D. Laert. vii. 88.

10 De Leg. ii. 4.

11 1. 2. qu. 93. art. 1.

consent, admiring her as the mother of their peace and joy.'—Hooker[12].

II. Law as a rule of Action.

Rule.

'Lex est recta ratio imperandi atque prohibendi.'—Cicero[13].

'Lex nihil aliud nisi recta et a numine deorum tracta ratio, iubens honesta, prohibens contraria.'—Cicero[14].

'Ius est ars boni et aequi.'—Celsus[15].

'Any kind of rule or canon whereby actions are framed.' . . .

'That which reason in such sort defines to be good that it must be done.'—Hooker[16].

'Der Inbegriff der Bedingungen unter denen die Willkühr des Einen mit der Willkühr des Anderen nach einen allgemeinen Gesetze der Freiheit vereinigt werden kann.'—Kant[17].

'Der abstracte Ausdruck des allgemeinen, an und für sich seienden Willens.'—Hegel[18].

*20 *'Das organische Ganze der äusseren Bedingungen des vernunftgemässen Lebens.'—Krause[19].

'Die Regel wodurch die unsichtbare Gränze bestimmt wird, innerhalb welcher das Daseyn und die Wirksamkeit jedes Einzelnen einen sichern freyen Raum gewinnt.'—Savigny[20].

12 Eccl. Pol. i. c. 18.

13 De Leg. i. 15.

14 Phil. xi. 12.

15 Dig. i. 1. 1.

16 Eccl. Pol. i. c. 3, c. 8.

17 'The sum-total of the conditions under which the personal wishes of one man can be combined with the personal wishes of another man, in accordance with a general law of Freedom.' Rechtslehre, Werke, vii. p. 27.

18 'The abstract expression of the general Will, existing in and for itself.' Propädeutik, Cursus, i. § 26.

19 'The organic whole of the external conditions of life in conformity to reason.' Abriss des Systemes der Philosophie des Rechtes, p. 209.

20 'The rule whereby the invisible border-line is fixed within which the being and the activity of each individual obtains a secure and free space.' System, i. p. 332.

Diversity of rules called laws.

The term Law is employed in Jurisprudence not in the sense of the abstract idea of order, but in that of the abstract idea of rules of conduct. But of these rules only a particular class are 'laws' in the strict sense of the term; so that although the jurist is in no danger of getting entangled in questions of physical science, he is obliged to busy himself in marking the boundary which separates his own department of study from the wider field of morality. His task is so to narrow and deepen the popular conception of 'a law' in the sense of a rule of action, as to fit it for his own purposes. This task will be undertaken in the next chapter; before entering upon which it may perhaps be as well to point out how various in character are those precepts for the guidance of the life and conduct of men to which the term law is with more or less propriety applied.

While some of these precepts are received wherever human beings are gathered together, others are limited to the followers of a particular religion, or to the inhabitants of a definite portion of the earth's surface. While some of them deal with the fundamental institutions of society, others are occupied with the pettiest details of ceremonial or deportment. Some are enforced by the whole power of great empires, whilst others may be violated by any one who is not afraid to encounter the banter of his acquaintance. They possess, however, certain characteristics in common, which must be briefly enumerated.

*21 * *Characteristics common to all rules called laws.*

They all either are, or may be, expressed as distinct propositions. They are, further, propositions addressed to the will of a rational being.

Of the two kinds of propositions which may be so addressed, they are commands; that is to say, precepts in which the cause of obedience depends on the will of him who commands; not counsels, which are precepts in which the reason of obedience is taken from the thing itself which is advised[21]. Being commands, they are accom-

[21] Hobbes, Works, ii. p. 183. On 'Imperium' and 'Consilium,' cf. Thomasius, Fundamenta I. Naturae et G. 1705, p. 133.

panied by a sanction; that is to say, they imply, if they do not express, an intimation that their author will see to their being obeyed; not necessarily by a threat of punishment, as such, but also by a promise of interference to prevent disobedience, or to reinstate things in the position in which they were before the act of disobedience.

Lastly, they are general commands. They relate to courses of conduct, as opposed to special commands, which enjoin only a particular action[22].

Laws, therefore, in the vague sense of rules of human action, are propositions commanding the doing, or abstaining from, certain classes of actions; disobedience to which is followed, or is likely to be followed, by some sort of penalty or inconvenience.

There are many propositions of this kind which no one is likely seriously to mistake for laws. It is generally under-
*22 *stood that such phrases as the laws of honour, or of etiquette, are employed, by way of analogy merely, to indicate rules which, either by their trifling importance, or from the limited circle in which they are recognised, differ widely from precepts which are of such vital moment, either on account of the penalties attached to their violation, or of the general acceptance which they find, as to be more ordinarily talked of as 'laws.'

Uses most likely to be confused with the true one.

The rules of human action which are most often confused with laws proper, are those which are called laws of God, laws of nature, and laws of morality. So closely indeed are these topics connected with those proper to Jurisprudence, that many of the older

[22] Austin, i. p. 11. On the other hand, Blackstone, i. p. 44, makes the generality of a law depend on its being addressed to a class of persons. So Cicero, de Leg. iii. 19, 'legis haec vis est scitum et iussum in omnes.' A. Gellius, x. 20, takes Capito's definition of lex as 'generale iussum' to imply that it must be 'de universis civibus,' as opposed to 'privilegia,' and Ulpian, 'iura non in singulas personas, sed generaliter constituuntur.' Dig. i. 3. 8. Cf. Bentham, Nomography, c. 1, Works, iii. p. 233. Sir H. Maine attributes the 'generality' of law, in both senses, to the great distance at which the force wielded by the Sovereign has to act upon the bulk of the persons exposed to it. Early Hist. of Inst. p. 393. On the advantages and disadvantages of this characteristic of law. cf. Arist. Pol. iii. 15. 5; Liv. 2. 3.

works on the subject are occupied as much with the laws of God, or of nature, as with law proper. Sir Walter Raleigh, for instance, begins a dissertation upon Law, by stating that laws are of three kinds—the eternal or uncreated; the natural or internal; and those which are imposed, or of addition. These last, which are 'explicatory and perfecting to the law of nature,' are either divine or human; both of which kinds are again variously subdivided[23].

It will therefore be necessary to touch briefly on those classes of so-called laws which are occasionally confused with laws properly so called.

[23] Works, iii. p. 101; Hobbes, Works, ii. p. 186. Cf. Hooker, Eccl. Pol. i. c. 15: Locke, Hum. Understanding, ii. § 6.

*23

*CHAPTER III.

LAWS AS RULES OF HUMAN ACTION.

Uses of the term Law in the practical sciences.

The use of the term Law in any but the sciences called practical or moral, that is to say which have to do with the human will, is thus merely metaphorical, and irrelevant to our inquiry [1]. Our only real difficulty is to draw a sharp line between the meaning in which the term is used in Jurisprudence and that in which it is used in the other practical sciences. The task is the more difficult that the line has not at all times been so sharply drawn as it is now possible and desirable to draw it [2].

The common characteristics of the moral sciences, covering as they do collectively the phenomena of human action, using that term in the widest sense, as including all volitions, whether accompanied or not by external movement, may be summed up as follows: They postulate a will; free at any rate so far as
*24 to be influenced by motives presented to it. *They postulate the determination of that will by other causes than the mere sensations of the moment, and, more specifically, by respect for rules of life and conduct. They have many fundamental ideas in common, such as freedom, act, obligation, sanction, command; ideas which they are not bound to analyse exhaustively, but employ in accordance with the usage of ordinary language, and in senses which might be accepted by widely opposed schools of speculation. Each science must define and classify such ideas so far as is necessary for its own purposes, leaving their full and final investigation to Psychology or Metaphysics. Unless the sciences so far respect each other's boundaries, a treatise upon any one of

[1] The reader need hardly be reminded that by a 'practical science' is not meant a body of rules for the government of practice (which would be an art), but the study of the principles upon which, as a matter of fact, human action is governed.

[2] The expression in Greek writers coming nearest to what we mean by Jurisprudence is probably 'Politike.' Aristotle, Eth. Nic. x. 10. 23, divides ἡ περὶ τὰ ἀνθρώπινα φιλοσοφία into Ethike and Politike.

them must be preceded by a sketch of all the rest; and thus it has happened that systems of Jurisprudence have been encumbered with digressions and polemics upon questions lying wholly outside of its appropriate province.

Division of the practical sciences.

The resemblances and differences in the employment of the term 'a law' in the several practical sciences must be explained by the resemblances and differences between the sciences themselves. The grand division of these sciences is between that which deals with states of the will, irrespectively of their outward manifestation in act, and those which deal with states of the will only so far as they are manifested in action[3]. The former regards, while the latter disregard, those internal acts of the will which do not result in outward acts of the body.

The former kind of science is 'Ethic.' The latter kinds possess no received collective name, but may perhaps be provisionally designated 'Nomology.'

The essential difference between them is that Ethic deals not only with the outward results of the determination of that faculty of respect for a rule which is the basis of all the moral sciences, but also, and rather, with the balance of inward forces by
*25 which those results are produced. It looks not *only to the
sort of acts which men do, but also to the sort of men who do them[4]. Nomology, on the other hand, deals entirely with the conformity or non-conformity of outward acts to rules of conduct.

Ethic is the science of the conformity of human character to a type; Nomology, of the conformity of actions to rules.

Ethic is the science mainly of duties; while Nomology looks rather to the definition and preservation of rights. The terms right and duty are of course correlatives, and are common to both Ethic and Nomology; but the former science, in accordance with its more inward nature, looks rather to the duties which are binding on the conscience; the latter looks to the rights which are the elements of social life.

[3] Including therein willed inaction.

[4] So Arist. Eth. Nic. ii. 4. Law commands not ἀνδρείαν, but τὰ τοῦ ἀνδρείου. Ib. iii. 8. 1; v. 1. 14.

Ethic.

Ethic has been well described by Kant as concerned with the laws for which external legislation is impossible.† It is the science of those rules which when known are themselves adopted by the will as its objects or aims. This rightness of will can never be enforced by external legislation, but must be the free choice of the individual. All that external legislation can do is to affect the external expression of the will in act; and this, not by a rectification of the aim itself of the will, but by causing the will to follow out in act another aim.

Nomology or rules of external action.

The science of this office of external regulation is what we have called 'Nomology.' It may be defined as 'the science of the totality of the laws for which an external legislation is possible [5].'

*26 *The moral sciences having thus been grouped under the head of Ethic, in which the object of investigation is the conformity of the will to a rule; and of Nomology, in which the object of investigation is the conformity of acts to a rule, we pass by the former, as foreign to our subject, and confine our attention to the latter.

Nomology, the science of external action, must be divided, according to the authority by which the rules of which it treats are enforced, into—

I. A science of rules enforced by indeterminate authority.

II. A science of rules enforced by determinate authority.

† Tugendlehre, Werke, vii. p. 182.

[5] This definition is applied by Kant, Rechtslehre, ib. p. 27, to the science of Law. He opposes 'Rechtslehre' to 'Tugendlehre,' making these two species exhaust the genus 'Sittenlehre.' Now we have endeavoured to explain that this genus contains the two species 'Ethic,' and what we have called 'Nomology,' which latter, besides Jurisprudence, contains other sub-species. We submit that Kant's definition, as he applies it, is too wide. There are rules of action which can be imposed by external authority, and yet are not laws. His definition should apply, as we have applied it, to a class of sciences, of which Jurisprudence is only one.

I. RULES OF EXTERNAL ACTION ENFORCED BY INDETERMINATE AUTHORITY.

What may be vaguely called 'moral laws' are of very various origin and obligation. Their common characteristic is that, although no definite authority can be appealed to in case of their infraction, yet those who obey them are regarded with favour, and those who disobey them with disfavour, either by society in general or by a section of it. Under this large category may be classed the laws of usage in the pronunciation of words, of fashion in the choice of dress, of social demeanour, of professional etiquette, or of honour between gentlemen, as well as the gravest precepts of morality, specifically so called. All of them possess the common characteristic of being generally received in certain circles of society, while anything done in contravention of them exposes the transgressor to various shades of ridicule, hatred or coercion.

Laws of fashion.

The weakest sort of these rules are undoubtedly those of fashion and etiquette; deviation from which is called eccentricity or vulgarity, and is visited by penalties varying from a smile to ostracism from society.

Laws of honour and morality

A somewhat stronger force may be attributed to the so-called law of honour, deviations from which are in this country stigmatised as 'conduct unbecoming a gentleman.' This however, so far as it exceeds in delicacy the dictates of ordinary morality, is
*27 recognised by a comparatively small *class, and, as has been well observed, regulates only the duties betwixt equals[6]. Far more important are those precepts which are more usually called principles of morality, and the infraction of which is called vice.

As to the origin and authority of the laws of fashion, and of the code of honour, there is no mystery. Every one admits that these are, though in different degrees, conventional, and have grown up

[6] Paley, Mor. Phil. book i. ch. 2. 'The law of Honour is a system of rules constructed by people of fashion, and calculated to facilitate their intercourse with one another, and for no other purpose.' Ibid. Cf. Ihering, Der Kampf um's Recht, p. 25.

in particular circles and states of society to which they were found beneficial. With reference to those wider formulas called moral principles, there is by no means the same consent. This great body of maxims, regulating the relations of man to man in all the intercourse of life, would seem to have grown up partly under the influence of religion, partly out of speculative theories, partly out of the necessities of existence. Which of these ingredients is the essential, or the most essential, element of morality, may well be questioned. It is at any rate certain that morality is not due o the direct interposition of political authority.

Into the battles which are perpetually raging as to the essential quality of virtue in itself, and as to the faculty by which the virtuous quality of actions is discerned[7], it is not the business of the jurist to enter. He is not obliged to decide whether the criterion of virtue be conduciveness to utility, or accordance with nature; nor need he profess his belief, or disbelief, either in an innate moral sense, or in a categorical imperative of the practical reason. These are the hard questions of Metaphysics. The business of the jurist is, in the first place, to accept as an undoubted fact the existence of moral principles in the world, differing in many particulars in different nations and at different epochs, but having certain
*28 broad resemblances; and, in the second *place, to observe
the sort of sanction by which these principles are made effective. He will then be in a position to draw unswervingly the line which divides such moral laws from the laws which are the subjects of his proper science[8].

While the broad resemblance of the moral principles of mankind is universally admitted, the occasional divergencies between them are frequently lost sight of. The truth upon this point is admirably expressed by Paley. 'Moral approbation,' he writes, 'follows the fashions and institutions of the country we live in; which fashions also and institutions themselves have grown out of the

[7] See e. g. Dugald Stewart, Philosophy of the Active and Moral Powers.

[8] Cf. Kant, Tugendlehre, Werke, vii. p. 177. Cf. also the remarks of Seneca: 'Quam angusta innocentia est ad legem bonum esse? Quanto latius officiorum patet quam iuris regula? Quam multa pietas, humanitas, liberalitas, iustitia, fides exigunt, quae omnia extra publicas tabulas sunt?' De Ira, ii. 28.

exigencies, the climate, situation, or local circumstances of the country, or have been set up by the authority of an arbitrary chieftain or the unaccountable caprice of the multitude[9].'

As to the sanction of moral rules, in the wide sense of the term, it was well said by Locke that 'no man escapes the punishment of their censure and dislike who offends against the fashion and opinion of the company he keeps, and would recommend himself to it [10].' Such rules are thus by no means without their appropriate sanction. We cannot therefore, with Thomasius, see in the presence or absence of compulsion the dividing characteristic between morality and Law[11].

Enough has perhaps been said with reference to moral rules generally. One class of these rules has however exercised so
*29 wide an influence, and is so intimately connected *with our
more immediate subject, as to demand a more extended notice.

The Law of Nature.

That portion of morality which supplies the more important and universal rules for the governance of the outward acts of mankind is called the 'Law of Nature.'

This is a plain and, it is submitted, true account of a subject upon which a vast amount of mystical writing has been expended. Such of the received precepts of morality relating to overt acts, and therefore capable of being enforced by a political authority, as either are enforced by such authority or are supposed to be fit so to be enforced, are called 'laws of Nature.' They are precepts obedience to which, whether it be or be not commanded by the State, is insisted upon by a deep-rooted public sentiment. Resting essentially upon public sentiment, they are rules of morality; but having reference only to such outward actions as are thought fit

[9] Mor. Phil. book i. ch. 5. Cf. Herodotus, iii. 38; Arist. Eth. Nic. v. 7; Montaigne, Essais, i. ch. 22; Pascal, Pensées, iii. 8.

[10] Human Understanding. book ii. §§ 1-12, where he scarcely does justice to the effects produced by sympathy with the sentiment of our fellow-creatures.

[11] Fund. I. Nat. ii. c. 6. § 3. Cf. Arist. Eth. Nic. x. 9. 12, ὁ δὲ νόμος ἀναγκαστικὴν ἔχει δυναμιν.

for political enforcement, they form only one class of such rules. After what has been said as to the origin and authority of moral rules in general, it will be unnecessary to discuss at length the origin and authority of such moral rules as are called natural laws. Whatever may be the objective character of those laws[12], whether they should be identified with the will of God, or should be supposed to be in some sort the guides even of that will, it is enough for the jurist that they certainly rest, like other moral rules, upon the support of public sentiment.

While there has been much difference of opinion as to the contents of the Law of Nature, the existence of such a law has been very generally admitted.

At the time when the social were first separated from the physical sciences, speculation recognised in the former nothing but what is variable and arbitrary. Thus Democritus taught that
*30 legal institutions were of human devising, *while atoms and
vacuum exist by Nature[13]. It was the stock sophistical doctrine that moral distinctions, especially Justice, are the creatures of law; which is itself a mere compromise, securing each man against injury on condition that he surrenders the luxury of ill-treating his neighbours[14]. The purely conventional character of morality is also the conclusion drawn by Herodotus from the contradictory views and customs which he found to prevail among different nations[15].

But a contrary view found early expression in literature. Sophocles makes Antigone appeal from the orders of King Kreon to the

ἄγραπτα κἀσφαλῆ θεῶν
Νόμιμα[16].

[12] Whether for instance it be more true to say with Cicero, de Leg. ii. 4, 'Lex vera ratio est recta summi Iovis,' or with Horace, Sat. i. 3. 98, 'Utilitas iusti prope mater et aequi.'

[13] *Ποιητὰ δὲ νόμιμα εἶναι, φύσει δὲ ἀτόμους καὶ κενόν.* Diog. Laert. ix. 45.

[14] *Τὸ δίκαιον* is *ἀλλότριον ἀγαθόν.* Plato, Repub. ii. ad init.; cf. Arist. Eth. Nic. v. 1. 17, Pol. iii. 9. 8; Rousseau, Contr. Social, ii. c. 6.

[15] Herodot. iii. 38. 'J'ai bien peur que cette nature ne soit elle-même qu'une première coutume, comme la coutume est une seconde nature,' says Pascal, Pensées, iii. 19.

[16] 'Unwritten and steadfast customs of the Gods.' Antig. ver. 454; cf. Oedip. R. ver. 838; Xen. Memor. iv. 4. 19; Plato, Legg. pp. 563, 793.

Aristotle fully recognises the existence of a natural as well as of a legal Justice[17]. He mentions as an ordinary device of rhetoric the distinction which may be drawn between the written law, and 'the common law' which is in accordance with Nature and immutable[18].

The Stoics were in the habit of identifying Nature with Law in the higher sense, and of opposing both of these terms to Law which is such by mere human appointment. 'Justice,' they say, 'is by Nature and not by imposition[19].' 'It proceeds
*31 *from Zeus and the common Nature[20].' In a passage already quoted, Chrysippus speaks of 'the common law, which is the right reason, pervading all things, identical with Zeus, the supreme administrator of the Universe[21].'

The same view finds expression in the Roman lawyers. 'Law,' says Cicero, 'is the highest reason, implanted in Nature, which commands those things which ought to be done and prohibits the reverse.' 'The highest law was born in all the ages before any law was written or State was formed[22].' 'Law did not then begin to be when it was put into writing, but when it arose, that is to say at the same moment with the mind of God[23].'

It may be worth while to add a few instances from later writers of the terms in which the law of Nature has been spoken of.

S. Thomas Aquinas says: 'Participatio legis aeternae in rationali creatura lex naturalis dicitur[24].'

[17] *Τοῦ δὲ πολιτικοῦ δικαίου τὸ μὲν φυσικόν ἐστι, τὸ δὲ νομικόν, φυσικὸν μὲν τὸ πανταχοῦ τὴν αὐτὴν ἔχον δύναμιν, καὶ οὐ τῷ δοκεῖν ἢ μή, νομικὸν δὲ ὃ ἐξ ἀρχῆς μὲν οὐθὲν διαφέρει οὕτως ἢ ἄλλως, ὅταν δὲ θῶνται διαφέρει.* He goes on to explain this statement, and to refute the idea that everything which is *φύσει* is wholly *ἀκίνητον*. He uses *συνθήκῃ* as synonymous with *νομικόν*. Eth. Nic. v. 7.

[18] Rhet. i. 16. He also opposes the *ἴδιος νόμος* to that which is *κοινός* or *κατὰ φύσιν*, ib. 14; cf. Demosth. Aristocrat. p. 639.

[19] Stob. Eccl. ii. p. 184.

[20] Chrys. apud Plut de Stoic. Rep. 9.

[21] Chrys. apud Diog. Laert. vii. 88.

[22] De Legib. i. 6; cf. De Inv. ii. 52; Rep. (Mai) iii. 22.

[23] De Legib. ii. 4; cf. the distinction between 'summa lex' and 'lex scripta,' ib. cc. 6. 15; between 'lex Naturae' and 'civilis,' De Off. iii. 17; and between 'summum ius' and 'ius civile,' Rep. v. 3 (Mai).

[24] 1. 2. q. 91. art. 2.

Grotius: 'Ius naturale est dictatum rectae rationis, indicans actui alicui, ex eius convenientia aut disconvenientia cum ipsa Natura rationali ac sociali, inesse moralem turpitudinem aut necessitatem moralem, ac consequenter ab auctore Naturae Deo talem actum aut vetari aut praecipi [25].'

Hobbes: 'Reason suggesteth convenient Articles of Peace, upon which men may be drawn to agreement. These Articles are they which otherwise are called the Lawes of Nature[26].'

Jeremy Taylor: 'The law of nature is the universal law of the world, or the law of mankind, concerning common necessities, to which we are inclined by nature, invited by consent,
*32 *prompted by reason, but is bound upon us only by the command of God [27].'

Cumberland: 'Lex Naturae est propositio naturaliter cognita, actiones indicans effectrices communis boni [28].'

Same—Special uses of term Law of Nature.

The term 'Law of Nature,' besides the sense in which we have just explained it, has been employed in a wider and also in a more restricted sense.

Same—The wider sense.

The wider is that of the well-known 'ius naturale' of Ulpian, which he says prevails among animals as well as men, regulating the nurture of the young and the union of the sexes[29]. It is obvious that the courses of action mentioned by Ulpian are followed in pursuance, not of a precept addressed to a rational will, which alone is properly called a 'law,' but rather of a blind instinct, resembling the forces which sway the inanimate world[30]. Such an employment of the term is, in fact, fully as metaphorical as its use to express the order of the universe. A law for the nurture of offspring is no more intelligible than a law of gravitation.

It is in pursuance of this 'law,' which is supposed to govern the relations of men before they have originated any of those institutions which mark their superiority to the merely animal creation,

25 De I. Bell. et P. i. 1. 10.

26 Leviathan, p. 63.

27 Duct. Dub. ii. c. 1. r. 1.

28 De Lege Nat. v. 1.

29 Iust. Inst. i. 2.

30 Hesiod, Op. et Dies, 276.

that all men are asserted to be equal. 'Iure enim naturali ab initio omnes homines liberi nascebantur'; which is equivalent to saying that before any laws were in existence, no differences between man and man were recognised by law. Ulpian's 'ius naturale' is therefore a merely metaphorical phrase, leading to consequences which, however magniloquently they may be expressed, turn out upon analysis to be dangerous truisms. All legal right and wrong had its origin after human society was put in motion and began to reflect and act. To talk of law and right as applied to mankind at a supposed period anterior to society beginning to think and act is a contradiction in terms [31].

*33 **Same—The narrower sense.**

An employment of the term 'natural law' in a sense as much narrower than that which we have given it as Ulpian's is wider, is its identification with the 'ius gentium.' The 'ius gentium,' in its origin a system of positive law enforced among the Romans and the races with whom they were brought into commercial contact, was conceived of, doubtless as early as the second century B. C.[32], as a body of principles which are found in the laws of all nations, and which therefore point to a similarity in the needs and ideas of all peoples. 'Ius autem gentium omni humano generi commune est; nam usu exigente et humanis necessitatibus gentes humanae quaedam sibi constituerunt. Bella etenim orta sunt et captivitates secutae, et servitutes, quae sunt naturali iuri contrariae[33].' By the introduction of these precepts the narrow and strict law of Rome was gradually enriched and expanded. It was an afterthought to give them a higher authority and a philosophical significance by identifying them with the 'ius naturale'; as is done even by Cice-

[31] Yet writers are not wanting to assure us that the genesis of law preceded even the development of the family. Zocco-Rosa, Principii d'una Preistoria del Diritto, 1885, p. 36.

[32] Cic. de Off. iii. 69. Cf. Voigt, Das Ius Naturale, passim, and Prof. Nettleship, Journal of Philology, xii. p. 169.

[33] Iust. Inst. i. 2. § 2. 'Gentium ius ... ab eo enim nominatum est ... et omnes gentes similiter eo sunt usae; quod enim honestum et iustum est omnium utilitati convenit.' Frag. Vet. I. Cti. Cf. Cic. de Off. iii. 17, Tusc. i. 13; Gai. Inst. iii. 93.

ro[34]; and more explicitly by Gaius when he says: 'Quod vero naturalis ratio inter omnes homines constituit, id apud omnes populos peraeque custoditur, vocaturque ius gentium, quasi quo iure omnes gentes utuntur[35].'

Ulpian's extravagantly wide application of the term never seems to have gained currency. It was, on the other hand, long and generally used in the restricted sense of an equivalent for what the Romans meant by the 'ius gentium.'

Its suitable and convenient use in the sense in which it
*34 *was employed by Aristotle was restored by such writers as Oldendorp, Gentili, and Grotius.

Same —Deductions from the doctrine of ius naturale.

A brief notice must suffice of the various practical conclusions which have been drawn from the doctrine of 'ius naturale.'

1. Acts prohibited by positive law, but not by the so-called natural law, are said to be 'mala prohibita,' not 'mala in se.' Thus a government may find it expedient to forbid certain acts, such as the planting of tobacco[36], which are not regarded as odious by the public sentiment.

2. Positive laws have been said to be invalid when they contradict the law of nature. So Hooker, paraphrasing S. Thomas: 'Human laws are measures in respect of men whose motions they must direct. Howbeit such measures they are as have also their higher rules to be measured by: which rules are two, the law of God, and the law of nature. So that laws must be made according to the general law of nature, and without contradiction to any positive law of scripture; otherwise they are ill made[37].' Grotius: 'Humana iura multa constituere possunt praeter naturam, contra naturam nihil[38].' And Blackstone: 'This law of nature, being co-eval with mankind and dictated by God himself, is of course superior in obligation to any other. It is binding all over the globe

34 'Lege naturae, id est gentium,' De Off. i. 23.

35 Inst. i. 1.

36 12 Ch. II. c. 34. Cf. the lenient view which has been taken by the Courts of evasions of the revenue laws, e. g. Holman v. Johnson, Cowp. 341.

37 Eccl. Pol. iii. c. 9.

38 De I. B. et P. ii. 3. 6.

in all countries and at all times: no human laws are of any validity, if contrary to this; and such of them as are valid derive all their force, and all their authority, mediately or immediately from their original[39].'

*35 *3. Natural law, or natural equity, has been often called in to justify a departure from the strict rules of positive law. With the changing ideas of society cases of course often occurred when the law of the State was found to be in opposition to the views of equity entertained by the people, or by leading minds among them. The opposition would be said in modern language to be between law and morality. But law and morality in early times were not conceived of as distinct. The contrast was therefore treated as existing between a higher and a lower kind of law, the written law which may easily be superseded, and the unwritten but immutable law which is in accordance with Nature.

And this way of talking continues to be practised to the present day. Long after the boundary between law and morality had been clearly perceived, functionaries who were in the habit of altering the law without having authority to legislate found it convenient to disguise the fact that they were appealing from law to morality, by asserting that they were merely administering the law of Nature instead of law positive.

4. In cases for which the law makes no provision, the Courts are sometimes expressly authorised to decide in accordance with the principles of natural law. This is so, for instance, in the Austrian Civil Code[40], and the Commissioners for preparing a body of substantive law for India recommend that the judges should de-

[39] Comm. Introd. p. 43. Cf. Cic. de Legib. ii. 4; Suarez, de Lege et Deo, ii. 14; Raleigh, Works, iii: Coke, I. Inst. 11, 183, 197; 7 Rep. 14; Locke, Civ. Gov. 11. Lord Coke in Bonham's case, 8 Rep. 118, says that 'when an Act of Parliament is against Common Right and Reason, or repugnant, or impossible to be performed, the Common law will control it, and adjudge such Act to be void,' &c.; and Lord Hobart, that 'even an Act of Parliament, made against natural equity, as to make a man a judge in his own case, is void in itself, for iura naturae sunt immutabilia, they are leges legum.' Day v. Savage, Hob. 87. These dicta, though approved of by Lord Holt in London v. Wood, 12 Mod. 687, appear never to have been followed in practice; and see now Lee v. Bude, &c., Ry. Co., L. R. 6 C. P. 582.

[40] 'Nach den natürlichen Grundsätzen,' § 7.

cide such cases 'in the manner they deem most consistent with the principles of justice, equity, and good conscience[41].'

*36 *5. The law of Nature is the foundation, or rather the scaffolding, upon which the modern science of International Law was built up by Gentili and Grotius.

II. RULES OF EXTERNAL ACTION ENFORCED BY DETERMINATE AUTHORITY.

In contrast with the species of rules which we have just been considering, are rules set by a determinate authority.

Divine laws.

Among such rules would no doubt be included rules imposed, or thought to be imposed, upon mankind by a God or Gods. Direct revelations of the will of a supernatural power, or such indirect intimations of that will as each man may find in his own conscience, have alike been described as 'laws of God [42].' It has been believed that infractions of either class of God's laws, generally known as sins, are sooner or later to be redressed; whether, as among the Jews, the redress is to take the shape of temporal reward and punishment, or, as under the Christian dispensation, the readjustment of religious good and evil is postponed to a future state of existence. The laws of God thus resemble in almost every point, other than the essential points of source and sanction, those laws which we shall presently admit to be properly so called. It is however just this difference of source and sanction which withdraws them from the cognisance of Jurisprudence. Laws the author and upholder of which is superhuman are within the province of quite a different science, and the jurist may be warned, in the quaint words of Thomasius, 'not to put his sickle into the field of dread Theology[43].'

[41] First Report, p. 9; Second Report, p. 10.

[42] Austin introduces a new ambiguity into the term 'law of God,' by applying it complimentarily to the conclusions arrived at by the utilitarian philosophy as to the mode of producing the greatest happiness of the greatest number.

[43] 'Ne falcem hic immittamus in campum venerandae Theologiae'; Inst. Iur. Div., lib. i. c. 1. § 163. Elsewhere the same author doubts the truth of the conception of God as a law-giver. The wise man, he says, sees in God

*37 **Human laws.*

Leaving therefore on one side those rules which are set by God, we come to those which are set by a definite human authority, and here we draw the final distinction between the case when such authority is, and the case when it is not, a sovereign political authority. Rules set by such an authority are alone properly called 'laws.'

SUMMARY—DEFINITION OF 'A LAW.'

By a successive narrowing of the rules for human action, we have at length arrived at such of those rules as are laws. A law, in the proper sense of the term, is therefore a general rule of human action, taking cognisance only of external acts, enforced by a determinate authority, which authority is human, and, among human authorities, is that which is paramount in a political society.

More briefly, a general rule of external human action enforced by a sovereign political authority.

All other rules for the guidance of human action are called laws merely by analogy; and any propositions which are not rules for human action are called laws by metaphor only.

rather the teacher of a law of Nature, or a Father; Fund. I. Nat. et Gent. c. 5.

*38

*CHAPTER IV.

POSITIVE LAW.

A law, in the sense in which that term is employed in Jurisprudence, is enforced by a sovereign political authority. It is thus distinguished not only from all rules which, like the principles of morality and the so-called laws of honour and of fashion, are enforced by an indeterminate authority, but also from all rules enforced by a determinate authority, which is either, on the one hand, superhuman, or, on the other hand, politically subordinate.

In order to emphasise the fact that laws, in the strict sense of the term, are thus authoritatively imposed, they are described as 'positive' laws[1].

Definitions of positive law.

It is to such laws that the following definitions will be found to have reference:—

Τοῦτό ἐστι νόμος, ᾧ πάντας ἀνθρώπους προσήκει πείθεσθαι διὰ πολλά, καὶ μά-
λιστα ὅτι πᾶς ἐστὶ νόμος εὕρημα μὲν καὶ δῶρον θεοῦ, δόγμα δὲ ἀνθρώπων
*39 *φρονίμων, ἐπανόρθωμα δὲ τῶν ἑκουσίων* *καὶ *ἀκουσίων ἁμαρτημάτων,*
πόλεως δὲ συνθήκη κοινή, καθ' ἣν ἅπασι προσήκει ζῆν τοῖς ἐν τῇ πόλει.—
Demosthenes[2].

1 'Positive are those which have not been from eternity; but have been made Lawes by the Will of those that have had the Soveraign Power over others.' Hobbes, Leviathan, p. 148. 'Positiva' are opposed to 'naturalia' by Aulus Gellius, as *θέσει* to *φύσει*: 'Naturalia magis quam arbitraria.' Noctes Att. x. 4.

2 'This is Law, to which all men ought to yield obedience for many reasons, and especially because every law is a discovery and gift of God, and at the same time a decision of wise men, and a righting of transgressions, both voluntary and involuntary, and the common covenant of a State, in accordance with which it beseems all men in the State to lead their lives.' Adv. Aristogeit. (p. 774); Dig. i. 3. 2. Cf. the descriptions of *νόμος* as *δόγμα πόλεως*, *δόξα πολιτική*, in Plato's Minos, p. 314 c.

Ὅσα γ' ἂν τὸ κρατοῦν τῆς πόλεως βουλευσάμενον ἃ χρὴ ποιεῖν γράψῃ, νόμος καλεῖται.—Xenophon[3].

Ὁ νόμος ἐστὶ λόγος ὡρισμένος, καθ' ὁμολογίαν κοινὴν πόλεως, μηνύων πῶς δεῖ πραττεῖν ἕκαστα.—Anaximenes[4].

'Lex est generale iussum populi aut plebis, rogante magistratu.' —Atteius Capito[5].

'Lex est commune praeceptum, virorum prudentium consultum, delictorum quae sponte vel ignorantia contrahuntur coercitio, communis reipublicae sponsio.'—Papinianus[6].

'The speech of him who by right commands somewhat to be done or omitted.'—Hobbes[7].

'Voluntas superioris quatenus libertatem coarctat lex dicitur.' —Thomasius[8].

'A portion of discourse by which expression is given to an extensively applying and permanently enduring act or state of the will, of a person or persons in relation to others, in relation to whom he is, or they are, in a state of superiority.'—Bentham[9].

*40 *'Das positive Recht durch die Sprache verkörpert, und mit absoluter Macht versehen, heisst das Gesetz.'—Savigny[10].

'Die von der höchsten Staatsgewalt aufgestellten objectiven Rechtssätze.'—Bruns[11].

3 'Whatsoever the ruling part of the State, after deliberating as to what ought to be done, shall enact, is called a law.' Mem. i. c. 2. 43.

4 'Law is a definite proposition, in pursuance of a common agreement of a State, intimating how everything should be done.' Arist. Rhet. ad Alex. c. 1.

5 Apud A. Gell. x. c. 20.

6 Dig. i. 3. 3.

7 Works, ii. p. 49; cf. iii. p. 251.

8 Iur. Div. i. 84.

9 Works, iii. p. 233.

10 'Positive Right, embodied in language, and invested with absolute power, is called the Law.' System, i. p. 39.

11 'The objective maxims of Right which are set forth by the highest State authority.' Apud Holzendorff, Encyclopädie, i. p. 258.

'Der Inbegriff der in einem Staate geltenden Zwangsnormen.'—Ihering [12].

Most of the terms employed in our definition of positive law have already been sufficiently discussed. It remains however to explain what is meant by 'a sovereign political authority.'

'People'—'State.'

A 'People' is a large number of human beings, united together by a common language, and by similar customs and opinions, resulting usually from common ancestry, religion, and historical circumstances.

A 'State' is a numerous assemblage of human beings[13], generally occupying a certain territory, amongst whom the will of the majority, or of an ascertainable class of persons, is by the strength of such a majority, or class, made to prevail against any of their number who oppose it.

A State may be coextensive with one People[14], as is now the case in France, or may embrace several, as is the case
*41 *with Austria. One People may enter into the composition of several States, as do the Poles and the Jews.

A People, it is truly said, is a natural unit, as contrasted with a State which is an artificial unit [15]. There must doubtless have been Peoples before there were States; that is to say, there must have been groups of human beings united by similarity of language, customs, and opinions, before there arose amongst them an organ-

12 'The totality of the compulsory rules which prevail in a State.' Der Zweck im Recht, i. p. 318. Without the State, says Puchta, 'das Recht nur ein unvollständiges Daseyn hätte.' Without it 'der gemeinsame Wille, auf dem das Recht beruht, mehr ein Wunsch, als ein wirklicher, kräftiger Wille seyn würde.' Inst. § 11.

13 Aristotle, Eth. Nic. ix. 10. 3, denies that a State can be composed of only ten persons, or that 100,000 persons can be comprised in a single State. Cf. Id. Pol. vii. 4; Plato, Legg. p. 737.

14 According to the extreme advocates of the 'doctrine of Nationality,' especially in Italy, this is the only perfect and legitimate State: e. g. Mancini, Della nazionalità come fondamento del diritto delle genti (1851). Prolusioni, Napoli, 1873.

15 Savigny, System, i. p. 22.

isation for enforcing the opinions of the majority, or those of a government acquiesced in by a majority, upon an unwilling minority.

Although scarcely any traces remain in history of the transformation of a People into a State, it is impossible to affirm, with Savigny, that a People, which he calls 'an invisible natural whole,' never exists as such; never, that is to say, without 'its bodily form' the State[16]. Aristotle speaks of the Arcadians as remaining an *ἔθνος* till, by the founding of Megalopolis, they become a *πόλις*[17]. Nor can we follow Savigny in regarding the production of the State as the highest stage in the procreation of Law[18]. Morality may precede, but Law must follow, the organisation of a political society.

Definitions of a State.

Of such a society the following definitions have been given at various periods:—

Ἡ δ' ἐκ πλειόνων κωμῶν κοινωνία τέλειος πόλις ἤδη, πάσης ἔχουσα πέρας τῆς αὐταρκείας, ὡς ἔπος εἰπεῖν, γινομένη μὲν οὖν τοῦ ζῆν ἕνεκεν, οὖσα δὲ τοῦ εὖ ζῆν.— Aristotle[19].

*42 *'Respublica est coetus multitudinis, iuris consensu et utilitatis communione sociatus.'—Cicero[20].

'Civitas nihil aliud est quam hominum multitudo, aliquo societatis vinculo colligata.'—S. Augustine[21].

'Respublica est familiarum rerumque inter ipsas communium summa potestate ac ratione moderata multitudo.'—Bodinus[22].

16 Savigny, System, i. p. 22.

17 Pol. ii. 2. 3.

18 'Die höchste Stufe der Rechtserzeugung.' System, i. p. 22; cf. Liv. Hist. i. c. 8.

19 'The perfect community which arises from several villages is already a City, which achieves, so to say, the fulness of complete self-sufficingness, brought into being by the bare needs of life, but finding its true object in the promotion of a noble life.' Pol. i. 2. 8.

20 De Rep. i. 25.

21 De Civ. Dei, xv. c. 8.

22 De Rep. i. 1.

'Civitas est coetus perfectus liberorum hominum, iuris fruendi et communis utilitatis causa sociatus.'—Grotius[23].

'The Common-wealth is one Person, of whose Acts a great multitude, by mutuall Covenants, one with another, have made themselves every one the Author, to the end he may use the strength and means of them all, as he shall think expedient, for their Peace and Common Defence.'—Hobbes[24].

'Societas hominum communis boni coniunctis viribus promovendi causa contracta civitas est.'—Wolff[25].

'A State is a body of free persons, united together for the common benefit, to enjoy peaceably what is their own, and to do justice to others.'—Supreme Court, U. S.[26].

'Der Staat ist die politisch organisirte Volksperson eines bestimmten Landes.'—Bluntschli[27].

'Der Staat ist die Form der geregelten und gesicherten Ausübung der socialen Zwangsgewalt.'—Ihering[28].

It would be rather within the scope of a professed work upon International Law than of a treatise upon Jurispru-
*43 dence *to explain more fully the characteristics of a true State, and to show how it differs from other societies which in some respects resemble it: as, for instance, the Catholic Church; a great trading corporation, such as the East India Company; a great and permanent league, such as that of the Hanse towns; nomad races; rebels and pirates.

The origin of States.

The origin of States has been a favourite subject of speculation. To the Greeks the organised city government in which they de-

23 I. B. et P. i. c. i. 14.

24 Leviathan, p. 88.

25 Ius Gent. Prol. § 9.

26 Chisholm v. Georgia, 2 Dallas, 456.

27 'The State is the politically organised impersonation of the People of a given country.' Die Lehre vom modernen Staat, i. p. 24.

28 'The State is the form of the regulated and assured exercise of the compulsory force of Society.' Der Zweck im Recht, i. p. 307.

lighted seemed the result of superhuman wisdom. It was a commonplace with their earlier poets and philosophers to ascribe a divine origin to States and to legislation. 'Every law,' says Demosthenes, 'is a gift of God, and a decision of sages[29].'

Later speculators, not content to veil their ignorance under a pious allegory, have explained the rise of political society by the hypothesis of an 'original contract,' the covenants of which they have set out with vast, if misplaced, ingenuity. The hypothesis is clearly, though by no means for the first time, stated by Grotius in the following passage: 'Qui se coetui alicui aggregaverant, aut homini hominibusque subiecerant, hi aut expresse promiserant, aut ex negotii natura tacite promisisse debebant intelligi, secuturos se id quod aut coetus pars maior, aut hi quibus delata potestas erat, constituissent [30].'

Even were the theory of an original contract within the scope of the present treatise, it would be unnecessary to repeat here the arguments by which its untenableness has been almost superfluously demonstrated. Jurisprudence is more concerned with the distinction which we are about to explain.

*44 **Sovereignty.*

Every state is divisible into two parts, one of which is sovereign[31], the other subject.

The sovereign part, called by Bodin 'maiestas,' is defined by him as 'summa in cives ac subditos legibusque soluta potestas [32].' Grotius calls it 'summa potestas,' which he defines as being 'illa cuius actus alterius iuri non subsunt, ita ut alterius voluntatis humanae arbitrio irriti possint reddi [33]'; and so Hobbes defines what he is

29 Adv. Aristogeit. i. (p. 774).

30 I. B. et P. Proleg. 15; so Hooker, Eccl. Pol. i. c. 10; Locke, Civ. Gov. i. c. viii. 99; Rousseau, Contrat Social, i. c. 6. The Sophists taught that Law originates in a bargain, *μήτ' ἀδικεῖν μήτ' ἀδικεῖσθαι*, Plato, Rep. p. 359. Cf. Arist. Pol. iii. 9. 8, *ὁ νόμος συνθήκη.*

31 The term seems only to have come into use in this sense in the time of Louis XIV. It is used by Hobbes, Leviathan, Pt. ii. c. 17.

32 De Rep. i. 8. He continues: 'quam Graeci *ἄκραν ἐξουσίαν, κυρίαν ἀρχήν, κύριον πολίτευμα*, Itali *segnoriam* appellant.'

33 I. B. et P. i. c. 3. 7.

pleased to call a 'City' as 'one person, whose will, by the compact of many men, is to be received for the will of them all; so as he may use all the power and faculties of each particular person to the maintenance of peace and for common defence [34].'

The sovereignty of the ruling part has two aspects. It is 'external,' as independent of all control from without; 'internal,' as paramount over all action within. Austin expresses this its double character by saying that a sovereign power is not in a habit of obedience to any determinate human superior, while it is itself the determinate and common superior to which the bulk of a subject society is in the habit of obedience [35].

External sovereignty.

With reference to each kind of sovereignty, questions arise the nature of which must be briefly indicated. External sovereignty, without the possession of which no State is qualified for membership of the family of Nations, is enjoyed most obviously by what is technically known as a 'Simple State,' i. e. by one which is 'not bound in a permanent manner to any foreign political body.'

States which are not 'simple' are members of a 'System of States,' in which they are combined upon equal or upon unequal
*45 terms. In the former case they compose an 'In*corporate Union,' such as is the United Kingdom of Great Britain and Ireland, or an 'État fédératif,' or 'Bundesstaat,' such as are the United States of America, the Swiss Confederation, or the German Empire. In the latter case the States occupying the inferior position are known as 'misouverains,' and may be 'protected' like the Republics of Andorre and San-Marino, or 'under suzerainty,' as are Bulgaria and Egypt.

When the component states are equally united, their external sovereignty resides in no one of them, but in the government which results from their combination. The external sovereignty of a system of unequally united states is to be looked for usually in the State which is suzerain or protector of the others.

34 The Philosophical Elements of a True Citizen, c. 5, Works, ii. p. 69.

35 Jurisprudence, i. p. 171.

Internal sovereignty.

The questions which arise with reference to internal sovereignty relate to the proportion borne by the sovereign part of the State to the subject part; in other words, to forms of government. These were analysed, with reference to simple states, by the Greek philosophers in a way which left little to be desired. The power may be confided to all members of the State who are not under some disability on account of age, sex, or otherwise; or it may be restricted to one or more of the members. In the former case, the form of polity is a democracy. In the latter, it is an aristocracy or a monarchy, as the case may be. Questions as to the distribution of powers in compound States, and especially in federal governments, have only of late years received an adequate treatment[36].

Whether the ruling power be as widely diffused as possible, or be concentrated in the hands of a despot, makes but little dif-
*46 ference for the purposes of our present inquiry. It is by *the sovereign, be that sovereign one individual or the aggregate of many individuals, that all law is enforced. 'The Lawes of Nature,' says Hobbes, 'are not properly Lawes, but qualities that dispose men to peace, and to obedience. When a Common-wealth is once settled, then are they actually Lawes, and not before; as being then the commands of the Common-wealth [37].' In the words of an eminent living jurist: 'Das Recht existirt erst vermöge der Sanction der Rechtsgemeinschaft des einzelnen Staates [38].'

[36] For a masterly analysis of the structure of a 'Federal Government,' see Professor Dicey's Law of the Constitution, 1886; and for a detailed examination of the questions to which the actual working of the greatest experiment in this form of government has given rise, Mr. Bryce's American Commonwealth, 1888.

[37] Leviathan, p. 138.

[38] 'Law first exists through the sanction afforded by the legal community of the individual State.' Von Bar, Das internationale Privat- und Strafrecht, p. 519. Cf. Sir Henry Maine's remarks on 'the retreat out of sight of the force which is the motive power of law' in the modern world. 'The great difficulty,' he says, 'of the modern analytical jurists has been to recover from its hiding-place the force which gives its sanction to the law.' Early Law and Custom, p. 388.

Difficulties of the theory of sovereignty.

Considerable doubt has of late been thrown upon the doctrine that apart from the existence of a State, and of a sovereign power within it, there can be no Law, because all laws are rules enforced by such a power. Real difficulties in applying the doctrine to the facts of history have been pointed out by Sir Henry Maine, with that fertility of illustration and that cogency of argument for which his writings are so conspicuous. He asks in what sense it is true that the village customs of the Punjaub were enforced by Runjeet Singh, or the laws of the Jews, during their vassalage to Persia, by the Great King at Susa. He denies that Oriental empires, whose main function is the levying of armies and the collection of taxes, busy themselves with making or enforcing legal rules; nor will he concede that it is a serious answer to his objections to say that 'what a government does not forbid it allows.' He would almost restrict to the Roman Empire, and the States which arose out of its ruins, the full applicability of the Austinian conception of positive law. As applied to other political societies, he looks upon it as an ideal or abstraction, related
*47 *to actual phenomena as are the axioms of mathematics to the actual conditions of matter, or the postulates of political economy to the dealings of ordinary life [39].

These remarks are no less valuable than they are interesting. When legal phenomena are explained by the action of an absolute political sovereign, the student of Jurisprudence should always remember, and may no doubt be in danger of forgetting, that the explanation, though true as a general statement, necessarily leaves out of account many other characteristics of such phenomena.

Justification of the theory of sovereignty.

Sir Henry Maine has done good service by pointing out the mistake of supposing that the obligation of law rests everywhere, and at all times, as immediately and obviously upon a sovereign political authority as it does in England at the present day. In guarding against a crude application of the doctrine of sovereignty,

[39] Early History of Institutions, Lect. xiii.

this great jurist has however perhaps hardly done justice to its essential truth. The reply which we would venture to make to his remarks upon this point would be to the following effect.

With reference to the Western nations, we would submit that the dependence of law upon sovereignty was as obvious in Attica and Lacedaemon as it ever was under the Roman Empire. A law as carried by Pericles, or as imagined by Plato, would conform to Austin's definition as completely as would a constitution of Marcus Aurelius.

With reference to the relation of a great Oriental tax-gathering empire to the village customs of its subjects, or to the more distinctly formulated laws of a conquered province, it is necessary to draw a distinction. Disobedience to the village custom or the provincial law may either be forcibly repressed, or it may be acquiesced in, by the local authority. If it be habitually repressed by such local force as may be necessary, it follows that the local force must, if only for the preservation of the peace, be sup-
*48 ported, in *the last resort, by the whole strength of the em-
pire. In this case the humblest village custom is a law which complies with the requirement of being enforced by the sovereign. If, on the other hand, disobedience be habitually acquiesced in, the rules which may thus be broken with impunity are no laws; and, so far as such rules are concerned, the tax-gathering empire is lawless, its organisation consisting merely of an arbitrary force, acting upon a subject mass which is but imperfectly bound together by a network of religious and moral scruples.

It is convenient to recognise as laws only such rules as can reckon on the support of a sovereign political authority, although there are states of society in which it is difficult to ascertain as a fact what rules answer to this description.

*49

*CHAPTER V.

THE SOURCES OF LAW.

Ambiguity of the term 'source.'

The obscurity which has involved the whole subject of the origin of law, and the mutual relations of customary, judge-made, and statute law, is largely due to the ambiguous uses of the term 'Source.' The uses are threefold.

Three senses of the term 'source.'

Sometimes the word is employed to denote the quarter whence we obtain our knowledge of the law, e. g. whether from the Statute-book, the Reports, or esteemed Treatises.

Sometimes to denote the mode in which, or the persons through whom, those rules have been formulated which have acquired the force of law.

Sometimes to denote the authority which gives them that force.

The last two uses are those which are most frequently confused together. Until the State is formed there can be no law, in the strict sense of the term. There may be, and doubtless always have been, morality and customary rules of conduct. After the formation of the State, such rules as receive its sanction and support, whether promulgated for the first time by the governing body, or already in operation among the people, become, in the proper sense of the term, 'laws.'

*50 **But one source of legal character.*

The sole source of laws, in the sense of that which impresses upon them their legal character, is their recognition by the State, which may be given either expressly, through the legislature or the courts, or tacitly, by allowance, followed, in the last resort, by enforcement, as we have seen in the preceding chapter.

Several sources of existence as rules.

The sources of laws, in the sense of the causes to which they owe their existence as rules, are, however, several [1]. These may be distinguished as usage; religion; adjudication; scientific discussion; equity; legislation. Some confusion has arisen from not observing that laws occasionally owe their existence as rules and their validity as laws to one and the same authority.

Custom or usage.

I. Usage, or rather the spontaneous evolution by the popular mind of rules the existence and general acceptance of which is proved by their customary observance, is no doubt the oldest form of law-making. It marks the transition between morality and law. Morality plus a State-organization enforcing the observance of certain parts of it is customary law.

Two questions are much debated with reference to usage. First, as to the mode of its growth as usage. Secondly, as to its transformation into law.

Same—Growth of usage.

Its characteristic is that it is a long and generally observed course of conduct. No one was ever consciously present at the commencement of such a course of conduct, but we can hard-
*51 ly doubt that it originated generally in the conscious *choice of the more convenient of two acts, though sometimes doubtless in the accidental adoption of one of two indifferent alterna-

[1] Cf. Cic. Top. 5; Dig. i. 1, 7; Gai. i. 2. The 'roots' enumerated in the Institutes of Manu (ii. 6) are four: Revelation, or the uttered thoughts of inspired seers; the institutes of revered sages, handed down by word of mouth from generation to generation; the approved and immemorial usages of the people; and that which satisfies our sense of equity, and is acceptable to reason. Tagore Lectures, 1880, p. 137. In Doctor and Student, i. 4, it is said that the 'law of England is grounded on six principal grounds: first, it is grounded on the law of reason; secondly, on the law of God; thirdly, on divers general customs of the realm; fourthly, on divers principles that be called maxims; fifthly, on divers particular customs; sixthly, on divers statutes made in Parliament.'

tives; the choice in either case having been either deliberately or accidentally repeated till it ripened into habit [2].

The best illustration of the formation of such habitual courses of action is the mode in which a path is formed across a common. One man crosses the common, in the direction which is suggested either by the purpose he has in view, or by mere accident. If others follow in the same track, which they are likely to do after it has once been trodden, a path is made.

Before a custom is formed there is no juristic reason for its taking one direction rather than another, though doubtless there was some ground of expediency, of religious scruple, or of accidental suggestion. A habitual course of action once formed gathers strength and sanctity every year. It is a course of action which every one is accustomed to see followed: it is generally believed to be salutary, and any deviation from it is felt to be abnormal, immoral. It has never been enjoined by the organised authority of the State, but it has been unquestioningly obeyed by the individuals of which the State is composed. There can in fact be no doubt that customary rules existed among peoples long before nations or states had come into being. At first no distinction was made between such of these rules as relate to individual character and such as concern society. Morality and customary rules were the same thing, but the distinction between the two was more and more sharply drawn as time went on.

Same—Legal authority of usage.

After the organisation of States, many of the customary rules of society still continued to be recognised, and acquired a further sanction. They had previously been enforced only by popular opinion, or by the licensed revenge of injured parties. They
*52 were now enforced by the political authority. *They became law; and were doubtless for the time the only laws known. They were the unwritten, but well known, opinions of the community as to social right and wrong.

[2] *Ἔστι δὲ τὸ ἔθος γνώμη μὲν τῶν χρωμένων κοινή, νόμος δὲ ἄγραφος ἔθνους ἢ πόλεως . . . εὕρημα δὲ ἀνθρώπων οὐδενός, ἀλλὰ βίου καὶ χρόνου.* Dio Chrys. Orat. 76, quoted by W. L. Newman, Arist. Pol. i. p. 75n.

Κυριώτεροι καὶ περὶ κυριωτέρων τῶν κατα γράμματα νόμων οἱ κατὰ τα ἔθη εἰσίν[3].

'Consuetudine ius est,' says Cicero, 'quod aut leviter a natura tractum aluit et magis fecit usus, ut religionem, aut si quid eorum quae ante diximus ab natura profectum, maius factum propter consuetudinem videmus, aut quod in morem vetustas vulgi approbatione perduxit; quod genus pactum, par, iudicatum[4].'

The laws of Draco were repealed, says Gellius, 'non decreto iussoque, sed tacito illiteratoque consensu[5].'

'Quid interest,' says Julian, 'suffragio populus voluntatem suam declaret an rebus ipsis et factis[6]?'

Justinian lays down in his Institutes that 'diuturni mores consensu utentium comprobati legem imitantur[7].' It would be more correct to say that written law was an imitation of custom.

And our own Bracton: 'consuetudo quandoque pro lege observatur in partibus ubi fuerit more utentium approbata, et vicem legis obtinet; longaevi enim temporis usus et consuetudinis non est vilis auctoritas[8].'

Custom exists as law in every country, though it everywhere tends to lose its importance relatively to other kinds of law. It was known at Rome as the 'ius moribus constitutum.' It is known in England as 'the common law,' or 'the custom of the realm,' the existence of which is now usually proved by showing that it has been affirmed by the Courts, or at least has been appealed
*53 to in the writings of great judicial *sages. At an earlier epoch it was doubtless known to all whom it concerned, much as are now the ordinary rules of morality[9]. Thus the law was declared in the English as in the Frankish hundredmoots, not by any judicial officer, but by the whole body of freemen present, who were represented in later times by the Rachimburgi, the

[3] Ar. Pol. iii. 16. 9.

[4] De Inv. ii. c. 54. Cf. 'consuetudinis autem ius esse putatur id quod voluntate omnium sine lege vetustas comprobavit,' ib. c. 22.

[5] Noct. Att. xi. c. 18.

[6] Dig. i. 3. 32.

[7] I. ii. § 9. Cf. Cod. viii. 53. 3.

[8] Bracton, lib. i. cap. 3, following Cod. viii. 53. 2, 'Consuetudinis ususque longaevi non vilis auctoritas est: verum non usque adeo sui valitura momento, ut aut rationem vincat aut legem;' cf. R. v. Essex, 4 T. R. p. 594.

[9] Cf. Savigny, System, i. p. 181.

Schöffen, and the Grand Jury. The increasing complexity of affairs, and the numerous other subjects opened up to human thought, have rendered the general consciousness of law-rules impossible, and have rendered necessary the more circuitous proof of their existence by means of Treatises and Reports.

It is certain that customs are not laws when they arise, but that they are largely adopted into the law by State recognition. How far does this recognition extend? Is it the case that all customary rules on proof of their existence as customs obtain State recognition as laws? In other words, does the determinate and organised will of the nation invariably adopt and confirm, for all matters within its cognisance, the rules which have been adopted for such matters by the indeterminate and unorganised will of the nation, or of portions of it?

This cannot be maintained. English Courts require not only that a custom shall be proved to exist, but also that it is 'reasonable[10].' And the legislature often abrogates customs, partially or wholesale.

Same—When a custom becomes law.

The State, through its delegates the judges, undoubtedly grants recognition as law to such customs as come up to a certain standard of general reception and usefulness. To these the Courts give operation, not merely prospectively from the date of such recognition, but also retrospectively; so far implying that the custom was law before it received the stamp of judicial authentication. The contrary view supported by Austin is at variance with fact.
*54 The element of *truth in his view, which he has done good service by bringing into prominence, is that usage, though it may make rules, cannot, without obtaining for them the recognition of the State, make laws. The element of mistake in his view is to date the State recognition from the moment that the usage has been called in question and allowed to be good in a court of justice.

If this is not the moment at which the State imprimatur is given to custom, what is that moment? We can only say that the rule

10 'Malus usus est abolendus.' Co. Litt. s. 212; cf. Cuthbert v. Cumming, 10 Ex. 809, 11 Ex. 405.

that a Court shall give binding force to certain kinds of custom is as well established as hundreds of other rules of law, and has been established in the same manner. The judges acting as delegates of the State, have long ago legislated upon this point as upon many others. Not having a code ready to their hand with rules for every emergency, they have invoked, as the ratio of their decisions, not only Equity, or the generally acknowledged view of what is fair, and previous decisions of the Courts, upon the faith of which it is to be presumed that people have been acting, but also customs, established among, and by, the people at large, as presumably embodying the rules which the people have found suitable to the circumstances of their lives. The Courts have therefore long ago established as a fundamental principle of law, subject of course in each case to many restrictions and qualifications, that, in the absence of a specific rule of written law, regard is to be had in looking for the rule which governs a given set of circumstances, not only to Equity and to previous decision, but also to custom[11].

Binding authority has thus been conceded to custom, provided it fulfils certain requirements, the nature of which has also long since been settled, and provided it is not superseded by law of a higher authority.

When, therefore, a given set of circumstances is brought into Court, and the Court decides upon them by bringing them
*55 within the operation of a custom, the Court appeals to *that
custom as it might to any other pre-existent law. It does not proprio motu then for the first time make that custom a law; it merely decides as a fact, that there exists a legal custom, about which there might up to that moment have been some question, as there might about the interpretation of an Act of Parliament. It then applies the custom to the circumstances just as it might have applied an Act of Parliament to them. A good custom or an intelligible Act of Parliament either exists or does not exist objectively, before the case comes into Court; although it is from the decision of the Court in the particular case that a subjective knowledge is first possible for the people of the existence or non-

[11] See a critique upon my view by Prof. Dewey, 9 Pol. Sci. Quarterly, p. 47.

existence of the alleged custom, or that this or that is the meaning of the Act of Parliament.

The legal character of reasonable ancient customs is to be ascribed, not to the mere fact of their being reasonable ancient customs, but to the existence of an express or tacit law of the State giving to such customs the effect of laws.

We have described the mode in which the State usually acts in giving to custom the force of law. It also may occasionally do so in express terms. It sometimes in express terms denies them any such force, and sometimes limits the force which has hitherto been ascribed to them. In some States greater force has been allowed than in others to custom as compared with express legislation. The theory of English law is that no statute can become obsolete by desuetude. The contrary view is maintained in Germany, and even in Scotland.

Same—Theories of the 'historical school.'

Such an account of the growth of custom and its transformation into law will not content a certain school of theorists, of whom Savigny and Puchta are the most illustrious. They tell us that the growth of Law (Recht) has no dependence upon individual arbitrary will or accident [12]. It is begotten in the People (Volk) by the Popular intelligence (Volksgeist)[13]. The People, however, has no actual existence *apart from its bodily form, the State[14]. Law has its existence (Daseyn) in the general-will (Gesammtwille); customary observance is not the cause of Law, but the evidence of its existence[15]. It does not make its first appearance in the form of logical rules[16]. Or, going still further afield, we are told by Hegel to see in the rise of Law the evolution of the Deity.

*56

We are in fact told that the principle is anterior to its applications. The true reply to which we conceive to be, that the principle is nothing else than a generalisation from the applications.

12 Savigny, System, i. p. 15.

13 Ib. i. pp. 175, 177.

14 Savigny, System, i. p. 22.

15 Ib. i. pp. 35, 168. Cf. Windscheid, Pand. i. p. 40.

16 Savigny, i. p. 16.

The only unity antecedent to the circumstances is the common constitution of mankind. The element of truth in the view of the so-called 'historical school' of Germany is that the adoption of customary rules of conduct is unconscious. It takes place in accordance with no deliberate plan, but comes into being piece-meal, as it is called for by the natural wants of mankind. We may remark as results of its mode of formation, first, that it is hence better adapted to national feeling than law which is otherwise manufactured. Secondly, that its importance declines with the growth in a nation of conscious critical power.

Religion.

II. Religion. The description of law as 'a discovery and gift of God' well expresses the view of the Greeks[17]. The influence of the priestly colleges can never be left out of account in studying the development of the law of Rome[18], nor has the Corpus Iuris Canonici failed to affect the secular systems of modern Europe. It has long been laid down, and has only recently been questioned, that 'Christianity is part of the law of England[19],' though few judges have gone so far as Chief Justice Prisot in declaring that
*57 'Scrip*ture est commun ley sur quel touts manieres de leis sont fondes[20].' But it is in the East that religion has been, to many nations besides the Jews, a direct and nearly exclusive source of law. The Pentateuch finds its parallel in the Koran and the Institutes of Manu. Hence arises the impossibility of any general legislation for British India. 'The Hindoo Law and the Mahomedan Law,' it has been authoritatively stated, 'derive their authority respectively from the Hindoo and the Mahomedan religion. It follows that, as a British legislature cannot make Mahomedan or Hindoo religion, so neither can it make Mahomedan or Hindoo law. A code of Mahomedan law, or a digest of any part of that law, if it were enacted as such by the Legislative Council of India,

17 Supra, p. *38.

18 For a perhaps exaggerated estimate of the influence of religion on Roman law, see Fustel de Coulanges, La Cité antique.

19 Cowan v. Milbourne, L. R. 2 Ex. 230, but see Lord Coleridge's charge in R. v. Foote, 48 L. T. N. S. 733.

20 Year Book, 34 Hen. VI. 40.

would not be entitled to be regarded by Mahomedans as the very law itself, but merely as an exposition of law, which possibly might be incorrect[21].'

Adjudication.

III. Adjudication: 'Res iudicatae,' 'Gerichtsgebrauch,' 'Jurisprudence des Tribunaux,' 'Usus fori.' As to the nature of this source of law there are two theories. According to the old English view, as stated by Blackstone, the judges are 'not delegated to pronounce a new law, but to maintain and expound the old one[22].' They
*58 are the depositaries of a body of *customary principles which have only to be applied to each new case as it arises. Most modern writers, on the other hand, agree with the criticisms of Austin, upon what he describes as: 'the childish fiction employed by our judges, that judiciary or common law is not made by them, but is a miraculous something made by nobody; existing from eternity, and merely declared, from time to time, by the judges[23].' In point of fact, the Courts in all countries have necessarily been entrusted with a certain power of making rules for cases not provided for previously; and even of modifying existing laws from

21 First Report of the Commissioners appointed to prepare a body of substantive law for India, p. 60. The Statute 21 Geo. III. c. 70, sect. 17, in declaring the powers of the Supreme Court at Calcutta, provides that 'inheritance and succession to lands, rents and goods, and all matters of contract and dealing between party and party, shall be determined in the case of Mahomedans by the laws and usages of Mahomedans, and in the case of Gentûs by the laws and usages of Gentûs, and when only one of the parties shall be a Mahomedan or Gentû, by the laws and usages of the defendant.' Similar provisions with reference to the Courts at Madras and Bombay are contained in 37 Geo. III. c. 142.

22 1 Comm. 69. For a recent defence of this theory by Professor Hammond of Iowa, see his edition of Lieber's Hermeneutics, p. 312. Lord Esher, M. R., goes so far as to say: 'There is in fact no such thing as judge-made law, for the judges do not make the law, though they frequently have to apply existing law to circumstances as to which it has not previously been authoritatively laid down that such law is applicable.' Willis v. Baddeley, '92, 2 Q. B. (C. A.) 324, 326.

23 Lectures, ii. p. 655. Cf. Bentham: 'a fiction of law may be defined as a wilful falsehood, having for its object the stealing legislative power by and for hands which could not, or durst not, openly claim it.' Works, vol. v. p. 13.

time to time in order to carry out the current ideas of what is equitable, or to adapt them to the changing needs of society[24]. So it was said in a recent English case: 'When merchants have disputed as to what the governing rule should be, the Courts have applied to the mercantile business brought before them what have been called legal principles, which have almost always been the fundamental rules of right and wrong[25];' and it has been judicially stated that 'justice, moral fitness, and public convenience, when applied to a new subject, make common law without a precedent[26].'

*59 *This power the Courts have rarely exercised avowedly[27], but rather under cover of exercising one or other of the functions with which they are more distinctly entrusted, viz. first, of deciding upon the existence or non-existence of such customs as they are authorised to recognise as binding; and, in the second place, of expounding, and applying to particular instances, laws which are necessarily expressed, or conceived of, in general terms[28].

24 It has indeed been suggested that law always begins as a generalisation from a series of judicial decisions. Cf. Maine, Ancient Law, p. 5. On the almost necessary connection between judicial decision and the production of law, see Dernburg, Lehrbuch des Preuss. Privatrechts, i. p. 43. Under art. 4 of the Code Civil, a judge cannot refuse to decide a case by reason of the silence, obscurity, or inadequacy of the law.

25 Robinson v. Mollett, L. R. 7 E. and I. App. 816.

26 Per Willes J., in Millar v. Taylor, 4 Burr. 2312. With reference to this dictum, Pollock C. B. in Jefferys v. Boosey, 4 H. L. 936, said: 'I entirely agree with the spirit of this passage, so far as it regards the repressing of what is a public evil . . . but I think the Common Law cannot create new rights and limit and define them, because, in the opinion of those who administer the law, such rights ought to exist according to their notions of what is just, right, and proper.' Cf. per Bowen L. J. in Dashwood v. Magniac, '91, 3 Ch. 367. Sir James Stephen thought it unlikely that any attempt would be made by the bench to create new offences at the present day. 3 Hist. Crim. Law, p. 359.

27 Lord Bacon mentions that when the French Parlements intended their decisions to make law they delivered them en robe rouge. Aug. Sci. viii. Aph. 7. These were the arrêts de règlements, which were thus solemnly delivered on the eves of the great festivals. Denisart, Collection de Jurisprudence, s. v. 'Arrest.'

28 On the vexed question of the value of judge-made law, see Hale, Pref. to Rolle's Abridgment; Bentham, Works, v. p. 477; Austin, Lectures, ii. p.

Same—The force of precedents.

In the weight which they attach to the decision of a court legal systems differ very widely. While in England and in the United States a reported case may be cited with almost as much confidence as an Act of Parliament, on the Continent a judgment, though useful as showing the view of the law held by a qualified body of men, seems powerless to constrain another court to take the same view in a similar case.

The Continental view is an inheritance from the law of Rome; for although Cicero enumerates 'res iudicatae' among the sources of law[29], and the Emperor Severus attributes binding force, in the interpretation of ambiguous laws, to the 'rerum perpetuo similiter iudicatarum auctoritas[30],' the contrary principle was finally established by a Constitution of Justin[31]. The Codes of Prussia [32] and Austria [33] expressly provide that judgments shall not
*60 have the force of law, and *although the Codes of France, Italy and Belgium are silent on the point, the rule in all these countries is substantially the same, viz. that previous decisions are instructive, but not authoritative; subject to certain special provisions of a strictly limited scope[34].

In England cases have been cited in court at least as early as the time of Edward I [35]. They are however stated by Lord Hale to

348; Prof. Hammond, in Lieber's Hermeneutics, Note N.; Sir F. Pollock, Essays, pp. 239, 273; Prof. Clark, Practical Jurisprudence, p. 255.

[29] Top. c. 5. Cf. Auct. ad Herenn. ii. 13.

[30] Dig. i. 3. 38.

[31] 'Nemo iudex vel arbiter existimet neque consultationes quas non rite iudicatas esse putaverit sequendum. et multo magis sententias eminentissimorum praefectorum, vel aliorum procerum; non enim si quid non bene dirimatur, hoc et in aliorum iudicum vitium extendi oportet, cum non exemplis sed legibus iudicandum sit.' Cod. vii. 45. 13.

[32] Landrecht, Einl. § 6.

[33] Bürgerl. Gesetzbuch, § 12.

[34] E. g. the French law of 27 Ventose, Ann. viii, art. 88; the Prussian Cabinet Orders of 1836, &c.; and similar Austrian ordinances. Cf. the Gerichtsverfassungsgesetz für das Deutsche Reich, art. 137. On the distinction between les considérants in a French decision and the judgment of an English court, see Proceedings in the Behring's Sea Arbitration, Pt. v. p. 1051.

[35] In Year Book 32 Ed. I, ed. Horwood, p. 32, the court is warned by counsel that its decision 'servira en chescun quare non admisit en Engleterre.'

be 'less than law,' though 'greater evidence thereof than the opinion of any private persons, as such, whatsoever [36];' and his contemporary, Arthur Duck, remarks, that the Common Law judges, in cases of difficulty, 'non recurrunt ad ius civile Romanorum, ut apud alias gentes Europeas, sed suo arbitrio et conscientiae relinquuntur [37].' But in Blackstone's time the view was established that 'the duty of the judge is to abide by former precedents [38];' and it has long been well understood that our courts are arranged in this respect in a regular hierarchy, those of each grade being bound by the decisions of those of the same or a higher grade, while the House of Lords is bound by its own decisions [39].

There have been of late some symptoms of an approximation between the two theories. While on the Continent judicial decisions are reported with more care, and cited with more
*61 *effect, than formerly, indications are not wanting that in England and in the United States they are beginning to be somewhat more freely criticised than has hitherto been usual [40].

If a decision is reversed by a higher court, a curious question arises as to the position of persons who have in the meantime acted in accordance with the original decision. Was that decision good law till it was reversed, or was it a mere mistake, upon which persons acted at their peril; their inability to predict the result of the appeal being 'ignorantia iuris' [41]?

[36] Hist. Comm. Law, ch. 4.

[37] He continues: 'Rerum per priorum saeculorum iudices iudicatorum exemplis non semper tenentur praesentis saeculi iudices, nisi coram se agitatis existimaverint convenire, neque enim par in parem imperium habet.' De Usu et Auct. ii. c. 8. 6, 8.

[38] 1 Comm. 69.

[39] On Decisions of the House of Lords, see Beamish v. Beamish, 9 H. L. Ca. 339; Caledonian Ry. Co. v. Walker's Trustees, L. R. 7 App. Ca. 275. For an ingenious parallel between the uniformity of judicial decision, which renders a science of case-law possible, and the uniformity of nature, see Sir F. Pollock's Essays, p. 239.

[40] The astounding growth of Reports in the United States must of itself tend to produce this result.

[41] It has been held in America that a 'subsequent decision is a legal adjudication that the prior one was not law at the time it was made,' Woodruff v. Woodruff, 52 N. Y. Ct. App. 53. In a case in the Q. B. Division, Henderson v. Folkestone Waterworks Co., apparently reported only in Times Law

Scientific discussion.

IV. Scientific discussion, 'Wissenschaft,' 'Jurisprudence,' has from time to time played a useful part in the development of rules which have often been adopted as laws. The 'responsa prudentium,' before they were clothed with an official character, received at Rome a deference similar to that which has been conceded in England to the 'practice of conveyancers[42],' and to the writings of such sages of the legal profession as Lord Coke and Sir Matthew Hale [43]. Of a similar character is the weight attributed to the 'obiter dicta' of English Judges, i. e. to such statements of law made by them as are not necessarily called for by the case before them [44].

Equity.

V. Equity. As old rules become too narrow, or are felt to
*62 *be out of harmony with advancing civilisation, a machinery is needed for their gradual enlargement and adaptation to new views of society. One mode of accomplishing this object on a large scale, without appearing to disregard existing law, is the introduction, by the prerogative of some high functionary, of a more perfect body of rules, discoverable in his judicial conscience, which is to stand side by side with the law of the land, overriding it in case of conflict, as on some title of inherent superiority, but not purporting to repeal it. Such a body of rules has been called 'Equity.' It consists in reality of such of the principles of received morality as are applicable to legal questions, and commend themselves to the functionary in question [45]. Of a resort to this expedient the two great historical instances are the action of the Praetor at Rome and of the Chancellor in England.

Rep. 1884–5, p. 329, a contrary view seems to have been taken. On the position of persons acting on a decision subsequently reversed, see Lieber, Hermeneutics, p. 326, and 1 Law Quarterly Review, p. 313.

[42] See Willoughby v. Willoughby, 1 T. R. 771.

[43] On the similar function of the Commentators upon Hindoo law, see Sir W. Markby. Elements of Law, § 83.

[44] Such, for instance, as the treatise upon Bailments imported by Holt C. J. into his judgment in the case of Coggs v. Bernard, 1 Sm. L. C. 176.

[45] Since the generality of a law is not the only hardship in its application which is redressed by Equity, Aristotle's definition of *τὸ ἐπιεικὲς* as *ἐπανόρθωμα νόμου ᾗ ἐλλείπει διὰ τὸ καθόλου*, Eth. v. c. 10, is hardly adequate. Elsewhere he de-

Same—The Praetor.

The Praetor, though technically without any authority to legislate, exerted, during his year of office, a power over all judicial process, which, at first confined within narrow bounds by the formality of the ancient system of pleading, became in later times almost unlimited. Each Praetor on entering upon his functions gave public notice in his edict of the modes in which he intended to give relief against the rigidity of the established system. The practical devices thus employed were developed by a long succession of Praetors into a body of 'ius honorarium' equal in bulk, and more than equal in importance, to the still unrepealed 'ius civile.' Thus it was that alongside of the proprietary rights open to Roman citizens alone, there was introduced a system of possession protected by interdicts and fictitious actions which had all the advantages of ownership. Effect was given to contracts
*63 *which could not be found in the limited list of those recognised by the law, and to wills which were neither sanctioned by the Comitia nor solemnised by a sale of the inheritance with copper and scales. While succession ab intestato still passed by law to the members of the artificial 'agnatic' family, its benefits were practically secured to the blood-relations. 'Naturali aequitate motus proconsul omnibus cognatis promittit bonorum possessionem, quos sanguinis ratio vocat ad hereditatem [46].'

Same—The Chancellor.

A very similar phenomenon of a double system of law, the newer practically overriding the older, while affecting to treat it with the utmost deference [47], occurred also in England, where however its introduction was less easily managed than at Rome. No great officer in England was invested with the attributes which enabled the Praetor to announce beforehand the principles upon which he intended so to administer the law as in effect to modify its opera-

scribes it as being *παρὰ τὸν γεγραμμένον νόμον*, and as looking *μὴ πρὸς τὸν νόμον ἀλλὰ πρὸς τὴν διάνοιαν τοῦ νομοθέτου, καὶ μὴ πρὸς τὴν τάξιν, ἀλλὰ πρὸς τὴν προαίρεσιν, καὶ μὴ πρὸς τὸ μέρος, ἀλλὰ πρὸς τὸ ὅλον.* Rhet. i. 13.

[46] Dig. xxxviii. 8. 2.

[47] 'Equity follows the law.' Cf. 'ius praetorium, quod ius civile subsequitur.' Dig. xxii. 5. 14.

tion. The Chancellor, with his clerks, could, it is true, frame new writs, but it was for the Common Law judges to decide upon their validity [48]. He therefore contented himself with what proved to be the very sufficient expedient of deciding each case that was brought before him, as nearly as he dared, in accordance with what seemed to him to be its merits. In his character of 'Keeper of the King's Conscience,' he was held justified in thus exerting the undefined residuary authority which in early times was attributed to an English king [49].

So it was sung of St. Thomas à Becket:

'Hic est qui regni leges cancellat iniquas,
Et mandata pii principis aequa facit [50].'

And Sir Christopher Hatton asserts: 'It is the holy con-
*64 *science of the Queen that is in some sort committed to the Chancellor [51].

On this foundation was built up that vast and complex theory of Trusts which is peculiar to the law of England, and that system of interference by means of 'Injunctions' by which the process of the Common-Law Courts was brought to a stand-still, when it seemed likely to work injustice.

The principles by which the Chancellors were guided in the exercise of their powers may best be gathered from their own mouths.

Lord Hardwicke said: 'When the Court finds the rules of law right, it will follow them, but then it will likewise go beyond them [52].'

Lord Cottenham: 'I think it is the duty of this Court to adapt its practice and course of proceeding to the existing state of society, and not, by too strict an adherence, to decline to administer justice, and to enforce rights for which there is no other remedy. This has always been the principle of this Court, though not at all times sufficiently attended to [53].'

48 Spence, Equitable Jurisdiction, i. p. 325.

49 Cf. Sir H. Maine, Ancient Law, c. iii, and Early Law and Custom, c. vii. p. 605.

50 Io. Sarisburiensis, Policraticus, Auctor ad opus suum.

51 Spence, i. p. 414. Cf. 'the general conscience of the realm, which is Chancery.' Fenner J., cited in Bacon's Reading on Uses, Works, vii. p. 401.

52 Paget v. Gee, Amb. App. p. 810.

53 Walworth v. Holt, 4 My. and Cr. 635.

It is not surprising that claims to a jurisdiction thus elastic should have given occasion to some criticism. 'Equity,' said Selden, 'is a roguish thing. For law we have a measure, we know what to trust to: equity is according to the conscience of him that is Chancellor, and as that is larger or narrower, so is equity. 'Tis all one as if they should make the standard for the measure, a Chancellor's foot. What an uncertain measure would this be! One Chancellor has a long foot, another a short foot, a third an indifferent foot; 'tis the same thing in the Chancellor's conscience [54].'

To this charge Lord Eldon replied in a judgment which traces the lines on which his own administration of equity
*65 *proceeded: 'The doctrines of this Court ought to be as well settled and made as uniform, almost, as those of the Common Law, laying down fixed principles, but taking care that they are to be applied according to the circumstances of each case I cannot agree that the doctrines of this Court are to be changed with every succeeding judge. Nothing would inflict on me greater pain, in quitting this place, than the recollection that I had done anything to justify the reproach that the equity of this Court varies like the Chancellor's foot [55].'

The latest authoritative exposition of the principles by which the court is guided approximates more nearly to the views of Lord Cottenham. Speaking of 'the modern rules of equity,' the Master of the Rolls (Jessel) said in a recent case: 'I intentionally say modern rules, because it must not be forgotten that the rules of Courts of Equity are not like the rules of the Common Law, supposed to be established from time immemorial. It is perfectly well known that they have been established from time to time—altered, improved, and refined from time to time. In many cases we know the names of the Chancellors who invented them. No doubt they were invented for the purpose of securing the better administration of justice, but still, they were invented. Take such things as these—the separate use of a married woman, the restraint on alienation, the modern rule against perpetuities, and the rules of equitable waste. We can name the Chancellors who first in-

[54] Table Talk, tit. 'Equity.'

[55] Gee v. Pritchard, 2 Swanst. 414; cf. Davis v. Duke of Marlborough ib. 152; Grierson v. Eyre, 9 Vesey, 347.

vented them, and state the date when they were first introduced into Equity jurisprudence; and, therefore, in cases of this kind the older precedents in Equity are of very little value. The doctrines are progressive, refined, and improved; and if we want to know what the rules of Equity are we must look, of course, rather to the more modern than the more ancient cases [56].'

As Sir Henry Maine points out, it was greatly owing to
*66 *Lord Eldon himself, during his long reign in the Court of Chancery, that equity became a body of rules scarcely more elastic than the Common Law. A similar stage was reached in the history of Roman equity when the edicts of the Praetors were consolidated by Salvius Iulianus in the time of the Emperor Hadrian[57]. The subsequent history of both systems is also not dissimilar. The work of the Praetors was finally adopted into the body of the law by the legislation of Justinian, as were the doctrines of the Chancellors into the law of England by the Judicature Act of 1873. In either case equity ceased to exist as an independent system, but bequeathed its principles to the system into which it was absorbed.

'Graecia capta ferum victorem cepit.'

Legislation.

VI. Legislation tends with advancing civilisation to become the nearly exclusive source of new law [58]. It may be the work not only of an autocrat or of a sovereign Parliament, but also of subordinate authorities permitted to exercise the function. The making of general orders by our Judges, or of bylaws by a railway company, is as true legislation as is carried on by the Crown and the estates of the realm in Parliament. Rules made by a subordinate legislative authority are, however, valid only in so far as that authority has acted within its delegated powers in making them, and it is the duty of the Courts of Law to declare, when occasion arises, whether the rules are in this respect well or ill made. This function of the Courts is every day exercised with reference to the by-

[56] Re Hallett's Estate, L. R. 13 Ch. Div. 710.

[57] Ancient Law, c. iii.

[58] On the relation of legislation to Nature, Custom, and Utility, see Cicero, de Inv. ii. c. 22.

laws of railway companies or municipal corporations. It is no less systematically, though not so frequently, exercised in testing the legality of laws made by the Governor-General of India in Council, by the Parliament of the Dominion of Canada, or by the Parliament of the Colony of New South Wales. When under a federal government the power of even the supreme legisla-
*67 ture *to make laws is strictly defined by a written constitution, this function of the courts is of the first importance. Hence the commanding position occupied in the United States by the federal Supreme Court. Congress, unlike the British Parliament, is not omnipotent. Its powers are circumscribed by a constitution which it cannot alter, and it is for the Supreme Court, in the last resort, to say whether a given act of Congress has the force of law, or, as being 'unconstitutional,' is mere waste paper [59].

'Written' and 'unwritten' law.

In legislation, both the contents of the rule are devised, and legal force is given to it, by simultaneous acts of the sovereign power which produce 'written law.' All the other law sources produce what is called 'unwritten law [60],' to which the sovereign authority gives its whole legal force, but not its contents, which are derived from popular tendency, professional discussion, judicial ingenuity, or otherwise, as the case may be. Rules thus developed obtain the force of law by complying with the standards which the State exacts from such rules before it gives them binding force. Having so complied, these rules are laws, even before the fact that they are so has been attested by a Tribunal.

The State has in general two, and only two, articulate organs for law-making purposes—the Legislature and the Tribunals. The first organ makes new law, the second attests and confirms old law, though under cover of so doing it introduces many new principles.

59 The relation of subordinate legislatures to the Law Courts is fully discussed in Professor Dicey's Law of the Constitution, ed. 3, c. 3, and Mr. Bryce's American Commonwealth, vol. i. c. 23.

60 Cf. Hale, Hist. C. L., p. 55; Blackstone, Comm. i. p. 63; Austin, Jurisprudence, i. p. 195; Lieber, Hermeneutics, by Hammond, p. 323. The Roman writers, on the other hand, give to these terms a merely accidental and literal meaning. Their 'ius scriptum' is that which is committed to writing, by whomsoever, at the time of its origin.

*68

*CHAPTER VI.

THE OBJECT OF LAW.

Law as restraining.

The most obvious characteristic of Law is that it is coercive. 'It was added because of transgressions':

'Iura inventa metu iniusti fateare necesse est [1].'

'Law was brought into the world,' says Hobbes, 'for nothing else, but to limit the naturall liberty of particular men, in such manner, as they might not hurt, but assist one another, and joyn together against a common enemy [2].' Even when it operates in favour of the legitimate action of individuals, it does so by restraining any interference with such action. It is accordingly defined by Kant as 'the totality of the conditions under which the free-will of one man can be united with the free-will of another, in accordance with a general law of freedom [3];' and by Savigny, as 'the rule which determines the invisible limit within which the existence and activity of each individual may obtain secure and free play [4].' Both of these high authorities make the function of Law to
*69 *be the preservation from interference of the freedom of the will. This conception is purely negative, and a wider and positive conception is needed to embrace the operation of Public as well as of Private Law.

The Kantian definition is wide enough to cover all rules which regulate the relations of individuals one to another, but it is too narrow to cover enactments providing, for instance, for the organisation of a ministry of education, or giving to certain great libraries a claim to a copy of every new book that is published.

1 Hor. Sat. i. 3. 111.

2 Leviathan, p. 138. Cf. 'Factae sunt autem leges ut earum metu humana coerceatur audacia, &c.' Decretum, Pars i, Dist. i, c. 1.

3 Rechtslehre, Werke, vii. p. 27.

4 System, i. p. 114.

Law as organising.

A school of writers, among whom Krause [5] and Ahrens [6] are representative men, demands that Law shall be conceived of as harmonising the conditions under which the human race accomplishes its destiny by realising the highest good of which it is capable. The pursuit of this highest good of the individual and of society needs a controlling power, which is Law, and an organisation for the application of its control, which is the State.

The truth which is contained in these somewhat obscure speculations is capable of much simpler expression; and to find a definition of the function of law which would leave these writers nothing to desire, we have only to turn to Lord Bacon, who says: 'Finis et scopus quem leges intueri, atque ad quem iussiones et sanctiones suas dirigere debent, non alius est quam ut cives feliciter degant [7].' The same idea is expressed by Locke, who asserts that 'Law, in its true notion, is not so much the limitation as the direction of a free and intelligent agent to his proper interest, and prescribes no further than is for the general good of those under the law. . so that, however it may be mistaken, the end of the law is, not to abolish or restrain, but to preserve or enlarge freedom [8].' So Ben-
*70 tham: 'Of the substantive branch of the law the only *defensible object or end in view is the maximisation of the happiness of the greatest number of the members of the community in question [9].' Still better perhaps is the statement of Leibnitz: 'humanae societatis custodiam non esse principium Iustitiae, sed tamen iustum esse quod societatem ratione utentium perficit [10].'

Law is something more than police. Its ultimate object is no doubt nothing less than the highest well-being of society: and the State, from which Law derives all its force, is something more than a 'Rechtsversicherungsanstalt,' or 'Institution for the protection of

[5] Abriss des Systemes der Philosophie des Rechtes, 1828.

[6] Cours de droit naturel, 1840.

[7] De Aug. lib. viii. aph. 5; cf. S. Thom. 1. 2. q. 90. art. 20 concl.

[8] Of Civil Government, i. § 57.

[9] Works, ii. p. 6.

[10] Obs. de princ. iuris, § ii, Opera, ed. Deutens, t. iv. p. 272. Cf. Portalis, Discours préliminaire sur le Code Civil.

rights,' as it has not inaptly been described. It is however no part of our undertaking to discuss the question how far Law may properly go in its endeavors to promote the well-being of those within its sphere. The merits of a paternal government, of centralisation, of factory acts, of State churches, are topics for the politician rather than the jurist [11].

Rights.

Jurisprudence is concerned not so much with the purposes which Law subserves, as with the means by which it subserves them. The purposes of Law are its remote objects. The means by which it effects those purposes are its immediate objects. The immediate objects of Law are the creation and protection of legal rights [12].

11 With the advance of civilisation the State naturally extends the sphere of its activity. It is represented by some writers as having been successively devoted to War, to Law, and to Culture and Well-being. The danger of a State which has attained this last stage is its tendency towards Communism. For an attack upon this tendency, amounting to an attack upon anything like a 'Kultur- oder Wohlfahrtstaat,' see Herbert Spencer, The Man versus the State, 1884.

12 The creation and enforcement of legal duties is of course the same thing from another point of view; and a point of view from which some writers prefer to regard the operation of Law. Cf. infra, p. *76.

*71

*CHAPTER VII.

RIGHTS.

A right generally.

What then is a 'legal right'? But first, what is a right generally?

It is one man's capacity of influencing the acts of another, by means, not of his own strength, but of the opinion or the force of society.

When a man is said to have a right to do anything, or over anything, or to be treated in a particular manner, what is meant is that public opinion would see him do the act, or make use of the thing, or be treated in that particular way, with approbation, or at least with acquiescence; but would reprobate the conduct of any one who should prevent him from doing the act, or making use of the thing, or should fail to treat him in that particular way.

A 'right' is thus the name given to the advantage a man has when he is so circumstanced that a general feeling of approval, or at least of acquiescence, results when he does or abstains from doing certain acts, and when other people act or forbear to act in accordance with his wishes; while a general feeling of disapproval results when any one prevents him from so doing or
*72 abstaining at his pleasure, or refuses to *act in accordance with his wishes. Further than this we need not go. It is for Psychology to inquire by what, if any, special faculty the mind is capable of affirming or denying the existence of rights. History may also to some extent unravel for us the growth of such conceptions as to rights as are now prevalent; and these are among the most vexed questions of Psychology and of the History of Civilisation respectively. Jurisprudence is absolved from such researches. The only conception of a Right which is essential to her arguments is that which we have already propounded, and about the truth of which, as far as it goes, there can be no question.

A legal right.

Jurisprudence is specifically concerned only with such rights as are recognised by law and enforced by the power of a State. We may therefore define a 'legal right,' in what we shall hereafter see is the strictest sense of that term, as a capacity residing in one man of controlling, with the assent and assistance of the State, the actions of others.

That which gives validity to a legal right is, in every case, the force which is lent to it by the State. Anything else may be the occasion, but is not the cause, of its obligatory character [1].

Sometimes it has reference to a tangible object. Sometimes it has no such reference. Thus, on the one hand, the ownership of land is a power residing in the landowner, as its subject, exercised over the land, as its object, and available against all other men. So a father has a certain power, residing in himself as its subject and exercised over his child as its object, available against all the world besides. On the other hand, a servant has a power residing in himself as its subject, over no tangible object, and available against his master to compel the payment of such wages as may be due to him.

Ambiguous uses of the term 'right.'

This simple meaning of the term 'a right' is for the purposes of the jurist entirely adequate. It has however been covered
*73 with endless confusion owing to its similarity to *'Right'; an abstract term formed from the adjective 'right,' in the same way that 'Justice' is formed from the adjective 'just.' Hence it is that Blackstone actually opposes 'rights' in the sense of capacities, to 'wrongs' in the sense of 'unrighteous acts [2].'

We in England are happily spared another ambiguity which in many languages besets the phrase expressing 'a right.' The Latin 'Ius,' the German 'Recht,' the Italian 'Diritto,' and the French 'Droit' express not only 'a right' but also 'Law' in the abstract. To express the distinction between 'Law' and 'a right' the Ger-

1 As Thomasius says of 'Pactum,' 'non est causa sed tantum occasio obligationis.'

2 The absurdity is carried a step further by people who write to the newspapers about 'copy-rights and copy-wrongs.'

mans are therefore obliged to resort to such phrases as 'objectives' and 'subjectives Recht,' meaning by the former, Law in the abstract, and by the latter, a concrete right. And Blackstone, paraphrasing the distinction drawn by Roman law between the 'ius quod ad res' and the 'ius quod ad personas pertinet,' devotes the first and second volumes of his Commentaries to the 'Rights of Persons' and the 'Rights of Things,' respectively.

Same—Resulting confusion.

If the expression of widely different ideas by one and the same term resulted only in the necessity for these clumsy periphrases, or obviously inaccurate paraphrases, no great harm would be done; but unfortunately the identity of terms seems irresistibly to suggest an identity between the ideas which are expressed by them. German writers have evidently the greatest difficulty in keeping apart Law and the rights which it is the business of Law to regulate. Jurisprudence is with them indifferently the 'science of rights' and the 'science of Law.' To this source of confusion they add that which has already been indicated as being a hindrance to ourselves. They have a vague impression of a more than merely etymological connection between 'a right' and the eulogistic adjective 'right.'

*74 **Definitions.*

The following are definitions of 'a right' by various authors:—

'Qualitas illa moralis qua recte vel personis imperamus vel res tenemus, aut cuius vi aliquid nobis debetur.'—Puffendorf [3].

'Quaedam potentia moralis.'—Leibnitz [4].

'Qualitas moralis activa ex concessione superioris personae competens ad aliquid ab altero homine cum quo in societate vivit iuste habendum vel agendum.'—Thomasius [5].

'Die Befugniss zu zwingen.'—Kant [6].

3 De I. Nat. et Gent. i. c. 1. 20.

4 Opera, i. p. 118.

5 Iurispr. Div. lib. iii. c. i. 1. 82.

6 'The right to compel.' Rechtslehre, Werke, vii. p. 29.

'Eine physische Macht, welche durch die Gebote der Autorität nicht allein sittlich verstärkt ist, sondern welche auch diese ihre Macht durch Anwendung von Zwang oder Uebel gegen den Verletzer schützen kann.'—Kirchmann [7].

'Eine Macht über einen Gegenstand, der vermöge dieses Rechts dem Willen des Berechtigten unterworfen ist.'—Puchta [8].

'Ein rechtlich geschütztes Interesse.'—Ihering [9].

Might, moral right and legal right.

It may be as well to re-state in a few words precisely what we mean by saying that any given individual has 'a right.'

If a man by his own force or persuasion can carry out his wishes, either by his own acts, or by influencing the acts of others, he has the 'might' so to carry out his wishes.

If, irrespectively of having or not having this might, public opinion would view with approval, or at least with acquiescence,
*75 his so carrying out his wishes, and with disapproval *any
resistance made to his so doing; then he has a 'moral right' so to carry out his wishes.

If, irrespectively of his having, or not having, either the might, or moral right on his side, the power of the State will protect him in so carrying out his wishes, and will compel such acts or forbearances on the part of other people as may be necessary in order that his wishes may be so carried out, then he has a 'legal right' so to carry out his wishes.

If it is a question of might, all depends upon a man's own powers of force or persuasion. If it is a question of moral right, all depends on the readiness of public opinion to express itself upon his side. If it is a question of legal right, all depends upon the

[7] 'A physical power, which through the precepts of the authority not only is morally strengthened, but also can protect this its power against a transgressor by the application of compulsion or evil.' Die Grundbegriffe des Rechts und der Moral, p. 111.

[8] 'A power over an object, which by means of this right is subjected to the will of the person enjoying the right.' Instit. ii. p. 393.

[9] 'A legally protected interest.' Geist des römischen Rechtes, iii. § 60.

readiness of the State to exert its force on his behalf. It is hence obvious that a moral and a legal right are so far from being identical that they may easily be opposed to one another. Moral rights have, in general, but a subjective support, legal rights have the objective support of the physical force of the State. The whole purpose of laws is to announce in what cases that objective support will be granted, and the manner in which it may be obtained. In other words, Law exists, as was stated previously, for the definition and protection of rights.

Every right, whether moral or legal, implies the active or passive furtherance by others of the wishes of the party having the right. Wherever any one is entitled to such furtherance on the part of others, such furtherance on their part is said to be their 'duty.'

Where such furtherance is merely expected by the public opinion of the society in which they live, it is their 'moral duty.'

Where it will be enforced by the power of the State to which they are amenable, it is their 'legal duty.'

The correlative of might is necessity, or susceptibility to force;
of moral right is moral duty; of legal right is legal duty.
*76 These pairs of correlative terms express, it will be *observed,
in each case, the same state of facts viewed from opposite
sides.

A state of facts in which a man has within himself the physical force to compel another to obey him, may be described either by saying that A has the might to control B, or that B is under a necessity of submitting to A. So when public opinion would approve of A commanding and of B obeying, the position may be described either by saying that A has a moral right to command, or that B is under a moral duty to obey. Similarly, when the State will compel B to carry out, either by act or forbearance, the wishes of A, we may indifferently say that A has a legal right, or that B is under a legal duty.

It is unimportant in theory whether a system of law starts with a consideration of rights or of duties. It is important only that whichever point of view be adopted should be consistently adhered to. We shall take Rights rather than Duties as the starting-point of our classification, although some authority may be adduced in favour of the opposite method [10].

The relation of law to rights.

Law has been for centuries described as a 'command,' but this description, though essentially true, is inadequate to the extent of being misleading. Austin, who very properly analyses a command into (1) a desire conceived by one rational being that another rational being should do or forbear, (2) an evil to proceed from the former and to be incurred by the latter in case of non-compliance with the wish, and (3) an expression of the wish by words or other signs, is unable to discover these characteristics in laws which are merely declaratory, or which repeal pre-existing law, or which, be-
*77 cause they can be disobeyed with *impunity, are said to be 'of imperfect obligation [11].' Similar difficulties have been raised by Austin's critics with reference to other classes of laws: by Mr. Frederic Harrison, for instance, with reference to enabling statutes, laws conferring franchises, and rules of interpretation or of procedure [12].

Such cases will however cease to be anomalous if we recognise that every law is a proposition announcing the will of the State, and implying, if not expressing, that the State will give effect only to acts which are in accordance with its will, so announced, while it will punish, or at least visit with nullity, any acts of a contrary character. The State thus makes known what advantages it will protect as being legal rights, what disadvantages it will enforce as being legal duties, and what methods it will pursue in so doing.

The announcement may be made in many different ways. A law may be imperative, as 'Honour thy father and thy mother'; but it may also be in the indicative mood, as 'No contract for the sale of any goods, wares and merchandises, for the price of £10 sterling or upwards, shall be allowed to be good, except the buyer shall accept part of the goods so sold, and actually receive the same, or give

[10] See Bentham, Works, iii. p. 181; Comte, Phil. pos. ed. 2, vi. p. 454; Am. Law Review, vii. p. 46. Prof. Terry of Tokio, Some Leading Principles of Anglo-American Law, combines the two methods.

[11] Jurisprudence, Lect. i.

[12] Fortnightly Review, 1878, p. 684.

something in earnest to bind the bargain, or in part of payment, or that some note or memorandum in writing of the said bargain be made and signed by the parties to be charged by such contract, or their agents thereunto lawfully authorised'; or 'From and after the commencement of this Act the several jurisdictions which by this Act are transferred to and vested in the said High Court of Justice and the said Court of Appeal respectively shall cease to be exercised, except by the said High Court of Justice and the said Court of Appeal respectively, as provided by this Act.'

The real meaning of all Law is that, unless acts conform to
*78 the course prescribed by it, the State will not only ignore *and render no aid to them, but will also, either of its own accord or if called upon, intervene to cancel their effects. This intervention of the State is what is called the 'sanction' of law [13]. It is true that the State intervenes not only with a view to punishment, and occasionally to prevent anticipated illegality, but also to effect restitution, and this is perhaps its principal function; but before the commission of the wrong the announcement of State intervention in case of its commission operates upon the general mind by way of threat of punishment. It is a punishment to a wrongdoer, or to one who neglects to comply with prescribed courses of procedure, if his wrong be merely undone, or his faulty procedure fails of its effect, so that he has, as the saying goes, 'his trouble for his pains.' Law is, in fact, formulated and armed public opinion, or the opinion of the ruling body. It announces not only that certain states of things and courses of action are viewed by it with favour, but also that, in case of the invasion of these states of things, or in case of contrary courses of action being pursued, it will not only look on with disfavour, but will also, in certain events, actively intervene to restore the disturbed balance.

Substantive and Adjective Law.

It defines the rights which it will aid, and specifies the way in which it will aid them. So far as it defines, thereby creating, it is 'Substantive Law.' So far as it provides a method of aiding and protecting, it is 'Adjective Law,' or Procedure.

[13] 'Legum eas partes quibus poenas constituimus adversus eos qui contra leges fecerint, sanctiones vocamus.' Iust. Inst. ii. 1. 10.

*79

*CHAPTER VIII.

ANALYSIS OF A RIGHT.

We have seen that a 'moral right' implies the existence of certain circumstances, with reference to which a certain course of action is viewed with general approbation, and the contrary course with disapprobation; that a 'legal right' exists where the one course of action is enforced, and the other prohibited, by that organised society which is called 'the State.'

The elements of a right.

We have next to consider more particularly what is the character of those elements from which a Right results.

They are

(1) A person 'in whom the right resides,' or who is 'clothed with the right,' or who is benefited by its existence.

(2) In many cases, an object over which the right is exercised.

(3) Acts or forbearances which the person in whom the right resides is entitled to exact.

(4) A person from whom these acts or forbearances can be exacted; in other words, against whom the right is available; in other words, whose duty it is to act or forbear for the benefit of the subject of the right.

*80 *The series of elements into which a Right may be resolved is therefore:

The Person entitled.	The Object.	The Act or Forbearance.	The Person obliged.

It will be observed that the first and the last terms of the series are a person. The second term is the object of the right (whether it be a physical thing, or what the law chooses to treat as such) if any (for there exist large classes of rights which have reference to no object, either physical or assimilated to such); and the third term is made up of the acts or forbearances to which the person in the fourth term is bound.

It will be convenient to call the person entitled 'the person of inherence'; and the person obliged, 'the person of incidence.' The intermediate terms may be shortly referred to as 'the object' and 'the act' respectively.

That this series is no technical abstraction but a simple formula for the representation of the indisputable elements of a right, may be more apparent from an example. A testator leaves to his daughter a silver tea-service. Here the daughter is the 'person of inherence,' i. e. in whom the right resides; the tea-service is the 'object' of the right; the delivery to her of the tea-service is the 'act' to which her right entitles her; and the executor is the 'person of incidence,' i. e. the person against whom her right is available. Or take an example of a right where, as we stated to be often the case, the second term of the series is wanting. A is B's servant. Here B is the 'person of inherence,' reasonable service is the 'act' to which he is entitled, and A is the 'person of incidence,' against whom the right is available. The nature of the right varies with a variation in any one of the four terms which are implied in it, and the variations in the nature of the right give rise to the main heads or departments of law.

*81 **Rights in motion—Facts.*

The preceding analysis of the nature of a right implies the ideas of 'Person,' 'Thing,' and 'Act.' These are the permanent phenomena of a right; its statical elements. A right, conceived of as at rest, postulates—a Person of inherence and a Person of incidence; Acts to which the former is entitled, and which the latter is obliged to perform; and often, though not always, an Object or Thing.

But if the right is put in motion, phenomena of a new kind intervene. They are shifting, dynamical, and may be expressed by the general term 'Facts'; under which are included, not only the 'Acts' of persons, but also the 'Events' which occur independently of volition.

It is, as we have seen, by 'Acts' that rights are enjoyed. And we shall see that it is through the agency of 'Acts' or of 'Events' that rights are created, transferred, transmuted, and extinguished. In order therefore to understand, not only the nature of a right and the mode of its enjoyment, but also the manner of its creation, transfer, and extinction, it is necessary to acquire clear ideas of the full meaning of the following terms:—

I. Person.
II. Thing.
III. Fact, under which term are included—
Event,
Act, of omission as well as of commission.

With reference to the important term 'Act' it is necessary to consider the relations of the will to its conscious exertion and its expression. It will also be necessary to classify acts.

I. PERSON.

A 'Person' is often defined as being the 'Subject, or Bearer, of a right [1];' but this is to narrow the significance of the term. Rights not only reside in, but also are available against, persons.
*82 In other words, there are persons of *incidence as well as of inherence. Persons are the subjects of Duties as well as of Rights. In persons rights inhere, and against them rights are available. For the benefit of persons duties are created, and it is on persons that duties are imposed.

Persons, i. e. subjects of Rights or of Duties, are in general individual human beings; but, in imitation of the personality of human beings, the law recognises certain groups, of men or of property, which it is convenient to treat as subjects of rights and duties; as Persons in an artificial sense.

Natural persons.

i. A 'natural,' as opposed to an 'artificial,' person is such a human being as is regarded by the law as capable of rights or duties: in the language of Roman law as having a 'status.' As having any such capacity recognised by the law, he is said to be a person, or, to approach more nearly to the phraseology of the Roman lawyers, to be clothed with, or to wear the mask (persona) of legal capacity [2].

Besides possessing this general legal capacity, or status, a man

[1] E. g. Savigny, System, ii. p. 1; Puchta, Inst. ii. p. 291.

[2] Cf. Cic. de Off. i. cc. 30, 32. The equivalent of 'persona' in the Institutes of Theophilus is πρόσωπον.

may also possess various special capacities, such as the 'tria capita' of liberty, citizenship, and family rights. A slave having, as such, neither rights nor liabilities, had in Roman law, strictly speaking, no 'status,' 'caput,' or 'persona.' On the day of his manumission, says Modestinus, 'incipit statum habere [3].' Before manumission, as we read in the Institutes 'nullum caput habuit [4].' So Theophilus: *οἱ οἰκέται ἀπρόσωποι ὄντες ἐκ τῶν προσώπων τῶν οἰκείων δεσποτῶν χαρακτηρίζονται*[5]. It must however be remembered that the terms 'persona' and 'caput' were also used in popular language as nearly equiva-
*83 lent to 'homo,' and in this sense were applied to *slaves as well as to freemen [6]. Many writers have supposed that Roman law recognised, besides the 'tria capita' which they distinguish as 'status civiles,' innumerable varieties of status, depending upon age, health and similar circumstances, which they describe as 'status naturales.' This view finds now little favour [7]; but the modern employment of the term 'status' in this flexible sense, apart from any supposed authority for it in the law of Rome, is both common and convenient. It is true to say that 'unus homo plures sustinet personas,' i. e. one individual may be clothed with different kinds of legal capacities [8]. A natural person is therefore well defined as 'homo cum statu suo consideratus [9].'

[3] Dig. iv. 5. 4.

[4] i. 16.

[5] iii. 17; cf. ii. 14. 'Servos quasi nec personam habentes.' Nov. Theod. tit. 44. 'Servos qui personam legibus non habebant.' Cassiodor. Var. vi. 8. *'Ο δοῦλος παρὰ τοῖς νόμοις ἀπρόσωπός ἐστι, τουτέστιν οὐδὲ δοκεῖ ζῆν ἢ ἀπεῖναι.* Theodor-Herm. vii. 6. 'Per fortunam in omnia obnoxii, tamen quasi secundum homi. num genus sunt.' Florus, Hist. iii. 20.

[6] Cf. Cic. de Off. i. 30–34; De Orat. ii. 24; Gai. Inst. i. 9; Dig. iv. 5. 3, 1. 17. 22.

[7] Cf. Savigny, System, ii. Append. p. 445; Baron, Pandekten, § 26.

[8] 'Tres personas unus sustineo.' Cic. de Orat. i. 40.

[9] 'Status' is defined by Heineccius as 'qualitas cuius ratione homines diverso iure utuntur,' Recit. i. tit. 3; and 'persona' by Mühlenbruch as 'potestas iuris, sive facultas, et iurium exercendorum et officiorum subeundorum, hominibus iure accommodata et quasi imposita.' Doct. Pand. ii. 1. Cf. Austin, Lect. xl, xli.

Same—Characteristics of a natural person.

A natural person must combine the following characteristics:—

(1) He must be a living human being: i. e. (a) he must be no monster[10]. (b) He must be born alive (vivus)[11], though not necessarily capable of continued existence (vitalis)[12]. But for certain purposes existence begins before birth. 'Qui in utero est perinde ac si in rebus humanis esset custoditur, quotiens de commodis ipsius partus quaeritur,' says Paulus[13]. So Blackstone: 'An infant in ventre sa mère is supposed to be born for many purposes. It is capable of having a legacy, or a surrender of a copyhold estate made to it. It may have an estate assigned to it; and
*84 it is enabled to have an *estate limited to its use, and to take afterwards by such limitation as if it were then actually born[14].' (c) On the other hand, he must not have ceased to live. He need not be rational.

(2) He must be recognised by the State as a person; so must not be a slave in the absolute control of his master, a 'caput lupinum,' or otherwise civilly dead, as was in English law a man who was banished, or abjured the realm, or who 'entered into religion' as a professed monk, when, says Blackstone, 'he might,

[10] Dig. i. 5. 14, l. 16. 38; Cod. vi. 29. 3; Co. Litt. 7 b, 29 b.

[11] Dig. l. 16. 129.

[12] Dig. xxv. 4. 1, l. 16. 129; but by the Code Civil, art. 725, 'l'enfant qui n'est pas né viable' is incapable of succession.

[13] Dig. i. 5. 7. A 'curator ventris' might be appointed to look after its interests. Dig. 37. 9.

[14] 1 Comm. 130. By the Code Civil, art. 906, 'pour être capable de recevoir entre-vifs, il suffit d'être conçu au moment de la donation; pour être capable de recevoir par testament, il suffit d'être conçu à l'époque du décès de testateur.' By the Prussian Landrecht, Pt. i, vol. i, § 10, 'the general rights of humanity' attach to a child from the moment of conception. Mr. Justice Holmes has kindly called my attention to a case in which an action was unsuccessfully brought by the administrator of a foetus for the injury to the mother which had caused its premature birth and almost simultaneous death. Dietrich v. Northampton, 138 Mass. 14, S. C. 52 Am. Rep. 243. Cf. Walker v. Gt. N. Ry. of Ireland, 28 L. R. Ir. 69, and an article on 'Unborn children and their rights,' in 26 Am. Law Review (1892), p. 50. It would seem that a child whose father at its conception was Belgian but before its birth had become an alien, may elect, on attaining majority, for Belgian nationality. Hall, Foreign Jurisdiction, p. 64 n.

like other dying men, make his testament and executors; or, if he made none, the ordinary might grant administration to his next of kin, as if he were actually dead intestate [15].

Any individual combining these two characteristics is a 'person,' i. e. is capable of rights and liable to duties. He may other-
*85 wise be said to sustain a personality; and the same *man may sustain different personalities, as an actor may play in several masks.

The various degrees in which individuals who are persons at all are capable of rights or liable to duties, are determined by circumstances to which different consequences have been attached by different systems of law. There are different grades of personality, and these depend upon the freedom, the maturity, the sex, the sanity, the citizenship, and so forth, of the individual [16]. As to freedom, for instance, a serf, not absolutely at the disposal of his master, might be said to have a personality, though a limited one. As to maturity, distinctions have been drawn depending sometimes on physical development, sometimes on the fulness of the reasoning powers.

Artificial persons.

ii. 'Artificial,' 'conventional,' or 'juristic' persons, are such groups of human beings or masses of property as are in the eye of the law capable of rights and liabilities, in other words to which the law gives a status [17].

[15] 1 Comm. 132. 'Cum semel quis se religioni contulerit renuntiat omnibus quae seculi sunt.' Bracton, 421 b; cf. Co. Litt. 132 a. Roman law declared certain persons, e. g. 'deportati,' to be 'mortuorum loco,' Dig. xxxvii. 4. 1. 8, but it did not include among them monks and nuns, Cod. i. 3. 56. 1, nor did it employ the technical term 'mors civilis.' The conception of 'mort civile,' as a result of conviction, was carried to great lengths in France, where it was e.g. applied to the émigrés in 1792, Merlin, Répertoire, s. v., but the articles of the Code Civil dealing with this subject, 22–33, have been superseded by the law of 31 May, 1854, by which 'la mort civile est abolie.' 'Der bürgerliche Tod' is little heard of in Germany.

[16] Cf. infra, c. xiv.

[17] 'Die juristische Person ist ein erlaubter, bleibender Zweck, welchem, kraft Rechtsfiction (zwar nicht die volle Rechtsfähigkeit, aber doch) die Vermögensfähigkeit zukommt.' Baron, Pandekten, § 30; v. infra, ch. xiv.

Such groups are treated as being persons, or as sustaining the mask of personality.

They are of two kinds—

(1) 'Universitates personarum'; such as, the State itself; departments or parishes; collegia; churches.

(2) 'Universitates bonorum'; such as, funds left to 'pious uses' without a trustee; a hereditas before 'aditio,' which 'personae vice fungitur, sicut mancipium et decuria et societas.' So the estate of an intestate before administration; the estate of a Bankrupt.

Same—Requisites of artificial persons.

Such juristic, or artificial, persons come into being when—

(1) There exists a group of persons, or mass of property, as the case may be, and

(2) The law gives to the group or mass in question the
*86 *character of a person. 'Neque societas neque collegium, neque huiusmodi corpus passim omnibus habere conceditur: nam et legibus et senatus consultis et principalibus rescriptis ea res coercetur [18].' This may occur by means of either—

(a) A general rule, applicable wherever its conditions are satisfied, e. g. 'the Companies Act, 1862.'

(b) A special act of sovereign power, e. g. an incorporating statute, or charter.

Same—Dissolution of artificial persons.

A 'universitas bonorum' comes to an end in ways too numerous to specify; a 'universitas personarum' comes to an end—

(1) By failure of its component parts. 'Sed si universitas ad unum redit, magis admittitur posse eum convenire et conveniri; cum ius omnium in unum reciderit, et stet nomen universitatis [19].' The number of individuals who must necessarily be members of a 'universitas personarum' is often defined by the instrument creating it.

[18] Dig. iii. 4. 1; cf. xlvii. 22. 3. There is much difference of opinion as to the scope of this rule of Roman law. Its stringency was undoubtedly much relaxed by the mediaeval civilians and canonists. V. infra, c. xiv.

[19] Dig. iii. 4. 7.

(2) In consequence of judicial proceedings, initiated by one of the corporators, or otherwise, as in the winding up of a Company.

(3) By forfeiture of privileges, as was alleged in the case of the revocation of the charter of the city of London by Charles II.

(4) By a surrender of its charter, such as took place in the case of the London College of Advocates in pursuance of 20 and 21 Vict. c. 77, s. 117.

II. THING.

A 'Thing' is the Object of a Right; i. e. is whatever is treated by the law as the object over which one person exercises a right, and with reference to which another person lies under a duty.[20]

*87 *_Physical and intellectual things._

Of 'Things,' in this sense, there are two kinds:—

(1) Material objects, i. e. physical things, 'res corporales,' such as a house, a tree, a stone, a horse, or a slave.

(2) Intellectual objects, artificial things, 'res incorporales,' 'Rechtsgesammtheiten,' such as a patent, a trademark, a copyright, an easement, a hereditas, a bankrupt's estate, a universitas; i. e. groups of advantages which for shortness are treated by the law as if they were material objects.

So that, just as we have seen that what the law means by a 'Person' is the Subject of a Right or Duty, irrespectively of the subject being, as is more frequently the case, or not being, a human individual; so a 'Thing' is what the law regards as the Object of Rights and Duties, irrespectively of that object being, as it usually is, a material object.

Same—Derivation of the distinction.

This artificial use of the term 'Thing' is not peculiar to legal science, but was in fact borrowed by it from speculative philosophy. Cicero, talking of 'res' in the sense of objects of thought,

[20] 'Sache,' in this its widest sense, is defined as 'dasjenige was in sich einheitlich ist, und einen bestimmten Vermögenswerth hat.' Baron, Pand. § 37; as 'alles was blos gegenständliche Bedeutung im Rechte hat.' Arndts, Pand. § 48.

says that they are divisible into 'eae quae sunt' and 'eae quae intelliguntur'; and he happens to mention, as instances of the latter, 'usucapio, gens, tutela [21].' In Jurisprudence the double use of the term is at least as old as Gaius. 'Quaedam praeterea res,' he says [22], 'corporales sunt, quaedam incorporales . . . quae tangi possunt . . . quae in iure consistunt'; and is carried by him, and by the Roman writers generally, to perhaps excessive lengths, when they extend this fictitious class so far as to embrace even 'obligations,' i. e. mere claims that one man has to control the acts of another.

It is no doubt convenient for the purposes of our science to include among 'Things,' not only physical objects, but also certain groups of rights, which, for purposes of transfer and otherwise, are occasionally treated as if they were physical objects.
*88 The fiction by which patents, bankrupts' estates, or *easements are regarded as 'Things,' is indeed not only harmless but almost indispensable.

The theory of this topic, as worked out by the Roman lawyers, and more fully developed in modern times, especially in Germany, is by no means free from difficulty, owing to considerable variations in the use of terms, but may be stated as follows:—

'Thing' (Res, Ding, Chose) is a term which, besides its proper meaning, has also an analogical application. In jurisprudence this analogical use is kept within due bounds. Legal science recognises 'Things' (Dinge) only so far as they are capable of standing in relation to the human Will ('Sachen,' in the widest sense of that term). Such things are either physical or artificial.

Same—Res corporales.

i. A Physical thing, 'res corporalis,' (Sache in the narrower, and proper, sense of the term [23]), is sometimes defined as 'a locally

[21] Top. c. 5. Cf. 'ius, quod sit incorporale, apprehendi manu non posse.' Quintil. v. 10.

[22] Inst. ii. 2.

[23] This term is said to be strictly applicable only to corporeal things, and accordingly is so defined in the draft Civil Code for Germany, § 778.

limited portion of volitionless Nature[24]:' perhaps better as 'a permanent external cause of sensations.'

The full meaning of any such definition is of course a question not of Jurisprudence but of Metaphysics. The jurist need not go further than to lay down that a physical thing is something which is perceptible by the external organs of sense, and is capable of being so perceived again and again. By the latter characteristic it is distinguished from an 'Event,' which, as a cause of sensation, is transient. As Austin says: 'The import of the expression "*permanent* sensible object" is, I think, this; it denotes an object which is perceptible *repeatedly*,
*89 *and which is considered, by those who repeatedly perceive it, as being (on those several occasions) one and the same object. Thus the horse or the house of to-day is the horse or house of yesterday; in spite of the intervening changes which its appearance may have undergone[25].'

This rough definition of a Thing, which indeed is little more than a somewhat precise statement of what is popularly meant by the term, is, as we have stated, generally sufficient for the purposes of Jurisprudence. It may however be remarked that even lawyers are occasionally called upon to consider more minutely in what the identity of a thing consists[26].

The Romans were content to describe 'res corporales' as 'quae tangi possunt,' giving as instances, a plot of ground, a slave, a coat[27].

Of such things there are three kinds[28], or rather such things occur under three conditions:

[24] 'Ein räumlich begrenztes Stück der willenlosen (oder als willenlos fingirten) Natur.' Baron, Pandekten, § 37. Cf. 'Ein Stück der nicht mit Vernunft begabten Aussenwelt.' Windscheid, Pand. i. § 40. 'Ein dem menschlichen Willen zugängliches, und seiner Herrschaft unterwerfbares, Stück der sinnlichen Aussenwelt, welches dergestalt räumlich begrenzt ist, dass es von seiner Umgebung dauernd unterschieden werden kann.' Kuntze, Cursus, i. § 357. Cf. Savigny, Obligationenrecht, i. p. 305. Austin, Jurisprudence, ii. p. 20.

[25] Austin, loc. cit., p. 21.

[26] See e.g. Buckley v. Gross, 3 B. and S. p. 566.

[27] Iust. Inst. ii. 2.

[28] Dig. xli. 3. 30.

(1) A simple thing 'quod continetur uno spiritu [29], et Graece ἡνωμένον, id est unitum, vocatur'; e. g. a slave, a beam, a stone[30].

(2) A compound thing, 'quod ex contingentibus, hoc est pluribus inter se cohaerentibus, constat, quod συνημμένον, id est connexum, vocatur'; as a house, a ship, a box [31]: later described as 'universitas rerum cohaerentium,' 'Sacheinheit.' The compound thing may be different from its parts, as is a house, or may be a mere aggregate of them, as is a bar of silver.

(3) An aggregate of distinct things conceived of as a whole, 'quod ex distantibus constat, ut corpora plura non soluta
*90 sed *uni nomini subiecta'; as a people, a regiment, a flock [32]; described by modern writers as a 'universitas facti,' 'universitas hominis' 'Sachgesammtheit [33].' Such a whole may continue to subsist though all its parts are changed.

Same—Res incorporales.

ii. Intellectual, or artificial, things, 'blos gedachte Dinge,' 'Res incorporales,' 'quae tangi non possunt,' 'quae in iure consistunt'; as a usufruct, a hereditas, a dos, a peculium, an obligation; where the 'ipsum ius' is incorporeal, though it often relates to corporeal objects [34]. This class might of course include all Rights [35], though

[29] Cf. 'tota statua uno spiritu continetur,' Dig. vi. 23. 5.

[30] The terms ἡνωμένον and συνημμένον are borrowed from the Stoic philosophy.

[31] Cf. Dig. vi. 1. 23. 5.

[32] Cf. Dig. ii. 20. 18. 1. 'Est enim gregis unum corpus ex distantibus capitibus.'

[33] It is disputed whether a whole of this sort is the object of a right. This Böcking, Inst. p. 31, denies. Windscheid, Pand. i. § 137, would allow it in the case of a natural aggregate, such as a flock, but not of an artificial aggregate, such as 'the tackle of a ship,' citing Dig. vi. i. 3. § 1; but mentions a case recently decided in which 'the properties of a theatre' were recognised as a whole, so that a mortgage of them included after-acquired properties. Seuffert, Archiv, xv. § 187.

[34] Iust. Inst. ii. 2. Cf. 'Rei appellatione et causae et iura continentur,' Dig. l. 16. 23; 'Hereditas etiam sine ullo corpore iuris intellectum habet,' Dig. v. 3. 50; 'Hereditas iuris nomen est,' Dig. l. 16. 178.

[35] So that a Right might be the object of a Right; in other words, might be one of the four terms into which, as we have shown, a Right may be analysed. This use of language, though convenient by way of a short description of certain groups of rights, such as a copyright, or of masses of mingled

as a matter of fact the Roman lawyers abstain from treating under it of 'dominium [36].' German writers express the idea by the term 'Rechtsgesammtheit.' It will be observed that some 'things' of this class are aggregates of duties as well as of rights; e. g. a hereditas which imposes on the heir liabilities as well as profit; and that modern civilisation has added to the class those groups of rights known as 'copy right,' 'patent right,' and the like, and collectively described as 'intellectual property'; of which more hereafter.

*91 *_Other classifications of things._

'Things' are further classified, in accordance with the different ways in which they are subservient to persons, under various heads, of which the following are the more important.

(1) Things divisible and indivisible.

When a simple thing is capable of physical division, its parts, from the moment when they are distributed (which does not imply actual severance), are held pro diviso, each thereupon becoming a new whole. 'Quod pro diviso nostrum est id non partem sed totum esse [37];' so each share of an estate 'non est pars fundi sed fundus [38].' As a general rule, a thing is juristically thus divisible which can be divided without destroying its essence or impairing its value [39]. Some things, though physically divisible, are juristically indivisible, because by division the character of their parts is entirely changed, e. g. a picture, an animal, a house. The thing may however also be divided into merely ideal parts of a whole, which is held pro indiviso, as in the case of joint owners of a slave, or the several joint tenants of an estate, each of whom is seised in it per my et per tout. Compound things are susceptible of division in this manner only [40]. 'Corpora ex distantibus corporibus,' as a flock of sheep, though only intellectual wholes, have physical parts. The

rights and duties, such as a 'hereditas,' seems less necessary in the case of simple obligations. This feeling finds expression in the rule, formerly prevalent in English law, that 'a *chose in action* is not assignable.'

[36] Cf. Baron, Pand 37; Wächter, Pand. § 59.

[37] Dig. l. 16. 25, § 1.

[38] Dig. viii. 4. 6, § 1.

[39] Dig. xxx. i. 26, § 2. Cf. Savigny, Obligationenrecht, i. p. 305.

[40] Opinions differ as to the nature of partes pro indiviso. E.g. Böcking, Inst. p. 30, holds that they are parts of the Right. Windscheid, Pand. i. §

parts of a 'res incorporalis,' such as a bankrupt's estate, which is itself a merely intellectual entity, are intellectual also.

(2) Res mobiles, immobiles. Moveable, as furniture or cattle, and immoveable, as land or houses. No distinction is more generally accepted or more far-reaching in its consequences. It is perhaps hardly necessary to remark that this distinction does not
*92 exactly correspond to that between 'real' and * 'personal' property, which is a result of feudal ideas, surviving only in the law of England [41].

(3) 'Res in commercio,' 'in patrimonio nostro,' 'in bonis,' and 'res extra commercium,' 'extra patrimonium,' 'nullius in bonis,' i. e. things which are, and which are not, capable of private ownership. Of the latter, some things, like the air, are incapable of appropriation; others are both owned, and exclusively used, by the State and its functionaries, and are then said to be 'in patrimonio populi'; as are, for instance, palaces and ships of war. Others, though owned by the State, are at the disposal of the community, as are parks and roads. Others again are set apart for religious purposes.

(4) Things principal, accessory.

(5) Res quae usu consumuntur, non consumuntur.

(6) Res fungibiles, non fungibiles. 'Fungible things,' 'quae mutua vice funguntur,' are those one specimen of which is as good as another, as is the case with half-crowns, or pounds of rice of the same quality. Horses, slaves, and so forth, are non-fungible things, because they differ individually in value and cannot be exchanged indifferently one for another [42].

142, and Baron, Pand. § 39, that they are parts, though only intellectual parts, of the Thing itself.

[41] On the derivation of this distinction from Bracton's division of actions into 'in rem' and 'in personam' (in a sense other than that of Roman law), see an article by Mr. T. C. Williams, 4 L. Q. R. 394. Still more arbitrary was the long obsolete distinction between 'res mancipi' and 'nec mancipi.' Sir H. Maine points out that the Roman distinction between moveable and immoveable things was relatively modern: an attempt to abandon the old historical classifications, and to classify objects of enjoyment according to their actual nature. Early Law and Custom, ch. x.

[42] On the application of this distinction in the contracts 'locatio-conductio' and 'depositum,' see Dig. xix. 2. 31.

III. FACTS.

'Facts' (Thatsachen, Faits), which have been inadequately defined as 'transient causes of sensation,' are either 'Events' or 'Acts.'

1. EVENTS.

'Events' (Ereignisse, zufällige Umstände, Zufall, Casus, Événements) may be either movements of external nature, such as
*93 a landslip, the increase of a flock of sheep, the death *of a relative, or an accidental fire; or may be acts of a human being other than the human being whose rights or duties are under consideration.

Lapse of time and change of place are among the events which are most productive of legal consequences [43].

2. ACTS.

'Acts' (Handlungen, Acts), in the widest sense of the term, are movements of the will. Mere determinations of the will are 'inward acts.' Determinations of the will which produce an effect upon the world of sense are 'outward acts.' 'The inner stage of an Act,' says a recent writer, 'ends with the determination (Entschluss), to which it is guided by a final cause (Zweck). The outer stage (die That) is the realisation of the former in the external world by the help of natural laws, such as gravity [44].' Jurisprudence is concerned only with outward acts [45]. An 'Act' may therefore be defined, for the purposes of the science, as 'a determination of will, producing an effect in the sensible world [46].' The effect may be negative, in which case the Act is properly described as a 'Forbearance.'

[43] Savigny, System, iii. p. 297; Windscheid, Pand. i. p. 291. Stat. 43 and 44 Vict. c. 9, was passed 'to remove doubts as to the meaning of expressions relative to Time in Acts of Parliament and other legal instruments.'

[44] Ihering, Der Zweck im Recht, i. p. 32.

[45] 'Nec consilium habuisse noceat, nisi et factum secutum fuerit. Dig. l. 16. 53.

[46] The 'Entschluss des Willens' plus the 'Aeusserung des Willens' is 'That,' which may be of omission or of commission. 'Die That ist überhaupt die hervorgebrachte Veränderung und Bestimmung des Daseyns. Zur Handlung aber gehört nur dasjenige was von der That im Entschlusse liegt, oder im Bewusstsein war, was somit der Wille als das seinige anerkennt.' Hegel, Propädeutik, Einl. § 9.

Essentials of an act.

The essential elements of such an Act are three, viz. an exercise of the will, an accompanying state of consciousness, a manifestation of the will.

1. *Will.*

Any discussion on the nature of the faculty of will and the mode of its exercise would here be out of place. We
*94 *may accept as sufficient for our purpose the definition of an act of will as, 'the psychical cause by which the motor nerves are immediately stimulated [47],' or as, 'that inward state which, as experience informs us, is always succeeded by motion while the body is in its normal condition,' e. g. is not paralysed [48].

Same—Vis.

If a movement is caused by physical compulsion, 'vis absoluta,' as when the hand of a person is forcibly guided in making a signature, there is no act, since will is absent.

Same—Metus.

But the will itself, being amenable to motives, may be coerced by threats, 'metus,' 'vis compulsiva,' 'duress per minas.' Here there is indeed an act, but one which produces none or few of the legal consequences which it would have produced had it been the result of free volition. 'If,' says Paulus, 'I have accepted an inheritance under the influence of fear, I am of opinion that I become heir, because, although if I had been free I should have refused, yet I did consent, though under compulsion (coactus volui). But the praetor will give me relief [49].' So in English law, a contract or will obtained by 'undue influence' will be set aside, and a wife who commits certain crimes in the presence of her husband, will be presumed to have acted under his coercion, and will therefore be excused from punishment.

A merely juristic person is obviously incapable of willing, unless by a representative, or by a majority of its members.

47 Zitelmann, Irrthum, p. 36.

48 Sir J. F. Stephen, General View of the Criminal Law, p. 76.

49 Dig. iv. 3. 21.

2. *Consciousness—Intention.*

The moral phenomena of an exertion of will are necessarily accompanied by intellectual phenomena. The only immediate result of a volition is a muscular movement on the part of the person willing, but certain further results are also always present to his mind, as likely to follow the muscular movement which alone he can directly control. Those among them to the attain-
*95 ment of which the act is *directed are said to be 'intended [50],' and wrongful acts done with intention, are in English law often said to be done 'maliciously [51].'

Same—Degrees of consciousness.

Such a state of consciousness may be possessed in very different degrees by different classes of persons, and at different times. It is wholly absent in a 'lunatic,' 'furiosi nulla voluntas est [52];' in an infant under years of discretion, 'sensus nullus infantis accipiendi possessionem [53].' It is imperfectly possessed by 'impuberes,' although 'infantia maiores'; by women, according to older systems of law; by decreed prodigals, and by minors. In some of these cases the defect of an understanding will is supplied by a provision of law, such as 'tutela.'

Same—Ignorance of fact or of law.

Intelligence may also be temporarily suspended by drunkenness or sleep; and it may be misled by 'error,' i. e. ignorance or mistake [54]. A distinction is usually drawn between ignorance of law and of fact. An act may be excusable or even rescissible when done in ignorance of a state of facts, while its consequences cannot be avoided by showing that it was done in ignorance of the

[50] On 'intention,' see James Mill, Analysis, ii. p. 399.

[51] 'Actual malice' is proved by evidence throwing light upon the state of mind with which an act is done, but malice is often presumed from the character of the act complained of, e.g. from the untruth of a defamatory statement, or from a prosecution without reasonable cause. In such cases the state of mind of the wrong-doer is immaterial to his guilt.

[52] Dig. xliv. 7. 1; l. 17. 5 et 40.

[53] Dig. xli. 2. 32.

[54] 'Der Irrthum ist unrichtige oder mangelnde Vorstellung.' Zitelmann, p. 327.

law. 'Regula est, iuris ignorantiam cuique nocere [55]:' so, says Paulus, 'If one knows that he is heir under a will, but does not know that the praetor will give "bonorum possessio" to an heir, time runs against him, because he is mistaken in his law [56].'
*96 And so it was held by Lord *Ellenborough, that a captain of a king's ship who had paid over to his admiral, according to a usage in the navy, one third of the freight received by him for bringing home treasure upon the public service, could not recover the payment upon discovering that there was no law compelling him to make it [57]. Persons have even been convicted of what became an offence only under an Act of Parliament passed subsequently to the fact; in accordance with the rule, since altered, that the operation of an Act of Parliament, in the absence of express provision, relates to the first day of the session in which it was passed [58]. The very artificial reason alleged in the Digest for the inexcusability of ignorance of law is that 'law both can and should be limited in extent [59];' and so Blackstone says, that 'every person of discretion, not only may, but is bound and presumed to know the law.' The true reason is no doubt, as Austin points out, that 'if ignorance of law were admitted as a ground of exemption, the courts would be involved in questions which it were scarcely possible to solve, and which would render the administration of justice next to impracticable.' It would be necessary for the Court to ascertain, first, whether the party was ignorant of the law at the time of the alleged wrong, and if so, secondly, was his ignorance of the law inevitable, or had he been previously placed in such a position that he might have known the law, if he had duly tried. Both of these questions are next to insoluble. 'Whether the party were really ignorant of the law, and was so ignorant of the law that he had no surmise of its provisions, could scarcely be deter-

55 Dig. xxii. 6. 9. Lord King C., in Lansdowne v. Lansdowne, Moseley, 364, is reported to have said that the maxim means that ignorance cannot be pleaded in excuse of crimes, but that it does not hold in Civil cases. But this is certainly not law.

59 Dig. xxii. 6. 2.

57 Brisbane v. Dacres, 5 Taunt. 143.

58 Attorney-General v. Panter, 6 Bro. P. C. 489; Latless v. Holmes, 4 T. R. 660; R. v. Thurston, 1 Lev. 91. Cf. R. v. Bailey, Russ. and Ry. Cr. Ca. 1.

59 Dig xxii. 6. 2.

mined by any evidence accessible to others, and for the purpose of discovering the cause of his ignorance (its reality being ascertained) it were incumbent upon the tribunal to unravel his previous history, and to search his whole life for the elements
*97 of a just *solution [60].' The stringency of the rule was in Roman law modified by exceptions in favour of certain classes of persons 'quibus permissum est ius ignorare.' Such were women, soldiers, and persons under the age of twenty-five, unless they had good legal advice within reach [61].

Same—Chance.

Results may also follow from acts without being intended. Such results, if the person acting had no means of foreseeing them, are ascribed to 'chance,' and no responsibility attaches to him in respect of them [62]. If they are such as he might have foreseen had he taken more pains to inform his mind before coming to a decision, they are attributed to his 'negligence.'

Same—Negligence.

This term, like its Latin equivalent 'culpa,' has been used to indicate a state of mind, the description of which has tasked the in-

[60] Jurisprudence, ii. p. 171. So Lord Ellenborough: 'There is no saying to what extent the excuse of ignorance might not be carried.' Bilbie v. Lumley, 2 East. 472. As against Austin's view, Mr. Justice Holmes maintains that 'every one must feel that ignorance of the law could never be admitted as an excuse, even if the fact could be proved by sight and hearing in every case,' and thinks the true explanation of the rule to be the same as that which accounts for the law's indifference to a man's particular temperament and faculties. The Common Law, p. 48. For an argument by Mr. Melville M. Bigelow in favour of extending the (in England) very rudimentary doctrine of equitable relief for mistake of law, see 1 Law Quarterly Review, p. 298.

[61] Dig. xxii. 6. 9.

[62] 'Impunitus est qui sine culpa et dolo malo casu quodam damnum committit.' Gaius, iii. 211. Sir F. Pollock, Torts, pp. 121–135, shews that while the English decisions for and against some liability for the accidental consequences of an act are almost evenly balanced, the view prevalent in the United States is in full accordance with that of the Roman lawyers. So it was held by the Supreme Court that 'no one is responsible for injuries resulting from unavoidable accident, whilst engaged in a lawful business.' The Nitro-glycerine Case, 15 Wallace, 524.

genuity of many generations of commentators. It covers all those shades of inadvertence, resulting in injury to others, which range between deliberate intention ('dolus'), on the one hand [63], and total absence of responsible consciousness, on the other [64]

*98 *Same—How negligence is measured.*

The state of mind of the doer of an act is often the subject of legal enquiry with a view to ascertaining whether it exhibits the phenomena of 'intention [65].' From the nature of the case, a similar enquiry can hardly be undertaken with a view to detecting the psychological phenomena of 'negligence.' Lawyers have therefore long been content, in enquiring into the alleged negligence of a given individual, to confine themselves to ascertaining whether or no his acts conform to an external standard of carefulness. Two such standards were employed by the Roman lawyers to measure that 'diligentia' the failure to attain which they called 'culpa.'

In some cases they measured due diligence by the amount of care which the person whose conduct was called in question was wont

[63] 'Culpa' in the widest sense included 'dolus'; and a high degree of 'culpa' is said to resemble, and even to be, 'dolus.' Cf. Dig. xi. 6. 1. 1; xvii. 1. 29; xlvii. 4. i; l. 16. 226.

[64] According to Austin, 'negligence' is the inadvertent omission to act as one ought, 'heedlessness' is the inadvertent acting as one ought not, while 'rashness,' 'temerity,' or 'foolhardiness' is the acting as one ought not, adverting to the consequences which may follow from the act, but assuming, upon insufficient reflection, that those consequences will not follow in the particular instance. Thus, I take up a rifle and shoot AB. This act may be accompanied by very different mental conditions. I may see AB, point the rifle at him and expect him to fall dead if I fire. Here I 'intend' his death. Or I may be firing at a target, and omit to make the signal which would have prevented AB from passing behind it and receiving my bullet. Here the death is due to my 'negligence.' Or I may fire without thinking of the likelihood of any one passing that way. The death is then due to my 'heedlessness.' Or, it may occur to me that some one may pass by, but I may think the chance so slight that it may be disregarded. The death of AB is here the result of my 'rashness.' These distinctions are interesting, but do not appear to be adopted in any system of positive law. See Austin's Lectures, ii. p. 103; Bentham, Pr. Morals and Legisl. c. ix.

[65] E.g. to establish the cancellation of a will, actual malice in libel, or the 'animus furandi.' But see Holmes, Common Law, p. 138.

to shew in the management of his own affairs, 'quantam in suis rebus adhibere solet.' Conduct falling short of this is described by modern civilians as 'culpa in concreto.' But a far more important measure of 'diligentia' is afforded by the care which would be exercised under the circumstances by the average good citizen, conduct falling short of which is the so-called 'culpa in abstracto.'
*99 This abstract, or ideal, *objective test is that which is applied in modern codes and is stated with growing clearness in the decisions of English and American Courts. So it was laid down by Tindal C. J., as early as 1837, that 'the care taken by a prudent man has always been the rule laid down: and as to the supposed difficulty of applying it, a jury has always been able to say whether, taking that rule as their guide, there has been negligence on the occasion in question. Instead of saying that the liability for negligence should be co-extensive with the judgment of each individual, which would be as variable as the length of the foot of each individual, we ought rather to adhere to the rule which requires in all cases a regard to caution such as a man of ordinary prudence would observe [66].' Actionable negligence has been well described as 'the omission to do something which a reasonable man would do, or the doing of something which a reasonable man would not do [67].' In a recent case in the Supreme Court of Massachusetts, Holmes J. explained that 'so far as civil liability is concerned at least, it is very clear that what we have called the external standard would be applied, and that if a man's conduct is such as would be reckless in a man of ordinary prudence, it is reckless in him. Unless he can bring himself within some broadly-defined exception to general rules, the law deliberately leaves his

[66] Vaughan v. Menlove, 3 Bingham, N. C., 468. In this case the question of the test of negligence was distinctly raised. The argument, unsuccessfully urged in favour of a new trial, having been that the jury should have been asked 'not whether the defendant had been guilty of gross negligence with reference to the standard of ordinary prudence, a standard too uncertain to afford any criterion, but whether he had acted bona fide to the best of his judgment; if he had, he ought not to be responsible for the misfortune of not possessing the highest order of intelligence.'

[67] Per Alderson B. in Blyth v. Birmingham Waterworks Co., 11 Ex. 781. Cf. Grill v. Gen. Iron Screw Collier Co., L. R. 1 C. P. 600; Brown v. Kendall, 6 Cush. 292.

personal equation or idiosyncrasies out of account, and per-
*100 emptorily assumes that he has as much capacity to *judge and to foresee consequences as a man of ordinary prudence would have in the same situation [68].'

Same—The degrees of negligence.

The care and skill which people are required to exhibit in their conduct ('diligentia') has two degrees [69]: that which is due from persons generally; and that which is due from persons occupying positions which mark them out as being exceptionally reliable with reference to the matter in question ('exacta diligentia'). A person of the former class is liable only for 'culpa lata,' i. e. 'nimia negligentia, id est, non intelligere quod omnes intelligunt [70],' for 'gross negligence [71].' A person of the latter class, of whom the Romans spoke as 'homo diligens et studiosus paterfamilias [72],' but who has been shortly described by some modern writers as a 'specialist [73],' is liable for even a slight deviation from the high standard to

[68] Commonwealth v. Pierce, 138 Mass. 165, S. C. 52 Am. Rep. 264.

[69] The view of the degrees of negligence given in the text is in the main that of Hasse, whose work, Die Culpa des Römischen Rechts, first published in 1815, is the foundation of the modern literature of the subject. An admirable résumé of Hasse's theories, with ample illustration from English and American decisions, will be found in Dr. Francis Wharton's Treatise on the Law of Negligence, of which much use has been made by the present writer.

[70] Dig. l. 16. 213, 223; cf. ix. 2. 31.

[71] Objections have been made of late years to the employment of this term. 'Gross' has been said to be a 'word of description and not of definition,' Willes J. in Grill v. Gen. Iron Screw Collier Co., L. R. 1 C. P. 600. But the Supreme Court of the U. S., while admitting 'that such expressions as "gross" and "ordinary" negligence are indicative rather of the degree of care and diligence which is due from a party, and which he fails to perform, than of the amount of inattention, carelessness, or stupidity, which he exhibits,' went on to say that 'if the modern authorities mean more than this, and seek to abolish the distinctions of degrees of care, skill, and diligence required in the performance of various duties, and the fulfilment of various contracts, we think they go too far.' New York Cent. R. Co. v. Lockwood, 17 Wallace, 357, cited by Wharton, u. s. § 49.

[72] E.g. Dig. xxii. 3. 25; xlv. 1. 137.

[73] Wharton, § 32. Cf. Hasse, § 24, on the 'diligentia diligentis.'

which he holds himself out as attaining, i. e. for 'culpa levis.'
*101 or 'ordinary negligence[74].' Although, as a *matter of fact, he may have done his work as well as he could, yet he is liable for his failure to do it better, 'spondet peritiam artis.' In his case, 'imperitia culpae adnumeratur[75].' His assumption of duties for which he is unqualified is in itself negligence.

The test of due diligence (or conversely of undue negligence) is in both cases, as has been already explained, an objective one. The ordinary person must exhibit what, in the opinion of the judge or jury, is the average care of a person of that class, and a specialist must similarly attain to the standard to which specialists are expected to conform[76].

Negligence may consist either 'in faciendo' or 'in non faciendo,' being indeed either non-performance, or inadequate performance of a legal duty.

An attempt has recently been made to generalise the law of actionable negligence, which, though not accepted, will doubtless influence judicial speculation upon the subject. According to the Master of the Rolls, 'When one person is by circumstances placed in such a position with regard to another that every one of ordinary sense who did think would at once recognise that, if he did not use ordinary care and skill in his own conduct with regard to those circumstances, he would cause danger of injury to the person or property of the other, a duty arises to use ordinary care and skill to avoid such danger[77].'

[74] Hasse is at much pains to disprove the existence of a third grade of culpa, viz. 'levissima.' In § 25 he ridicules the attempt of Salicetus to distinguish further a 'culpa levior.' There is however no doubt that the three grades of negligence, 'gross,' 'ordinary,' and 'slight,' favoured by Lord Holt and Sir W. Jones, are usually recognised in the English and American Courts. Cf. Wharton, § 59. Three grades are recognised in the Prussian Code, but two only in the, more modern, Codes of France, Italy, and Austria.

[75] Iust. Inst. iv. 3. 7. Cf. Dig. ix. 2. 8. § 1; l. 17. 132. On the skill and care expected from physicians or attorneys, see Hart v. Frame, 6 Cl. and F. 193; Lamphier v. Phipos, 8 C. and P. 475.

[76] On the ideal character of the standard, see Holmes, The Common Law, p. 108. Compare the maxim that 'every man is supposed to intend the necessary and reasonable consequences of his own acts.'

[77] Heaven v. Pender, L. R. 11 Q. B. Div. 506, per Brett M. R., diss. Cotton and Bowen L. JJ.

*102 *3. *Expression of the will—Agency—Imputation.*

The will must be manifested, or expressed; and in some cases may be expressed by some one other than the party willing, i. e. by an agent, whence the maxims 'qui facit per alium facit per se,' 'respondeat superior.'

For an act, in the sense of a manifestation of conscious volition, a man is said to be 'responsible.' The attributing of responsibility is 'imputation,' i. e. 'the judgment by which any one is regarded as originator (causa libera) of an act, which then is called "deed" (factum) and is regulated by laws [78].'

Same—Classification of acts.

Acts are divided by Jurisprudence into those which are 'lawful' and those which are 'unlawful.' The juristic result of the unlawful acts is never that aimed at by the doer. In the case of some lawful acts, their operation is independent of the intention of the doer, in the case of others his intention is directed to the juristic result.

Same—Juristic act.

In the last-mentioned case the act is technically described as 'negotium civile,' 'actus legitimus,' 'Acte juridique,' 'Rechtsgeschäft'; the nearest English equivalent for which terms is probably 'Juristic Act [79].' A recent writer has used for this purpose the phrase 'act in the law [80].'

It has been defined, by a high authority, as 'an act the intention of which is directed to the production of a legal result [81].'
*103 But this definition, as it stands, is wider than the *received use of the term would warrant. The judgment of a Court,

[78] Kant, Rechtslehre, Werke, vii. p. 24.

[79] It is not to be wondered at that no vernacular equivalent is available for the expression of an idea which, indispensable as it is, has hardly yet been naturalised in this country. On 'dispositiones iure efficaces,' see Leibnitz, Praef. ad Cod. Iur. Gentium, p. 16.

[80] Sir F. Pollock, Contract, c. i. This term would be convenient enough, could it be disentangled from its conveyancing associations, and were it not that 'act in law' has a special use as opposed to 'act of the party.' Hale, Analysis of the law, Sect. xxvii.

[81] 'Handlung, deren Absicht auf eine rechtliche Wirkung gerichtet ist.'

or an order of the Queen in Council might fairly be so described. A better definition is 'a manifestation of the will of a private individual directed to the origin, termination, or alteration of rights [82].' A 'Juristic Act' has also been well described as 'the form in which the Subjective Will developes its activity in creating rights, within the limits assigned to it by the law.' The same writer continues: 'only in so far as it keeps within these limits does it really operate, beyond them its act is either barren of result, is an empty nullity, or its operation is turned negatively against the will, as an obligation to undo what has been done, by suffering punishment or making reparation [83].'

Same—Requisites of.

Juristic Acts (Rechtsgeschäfte) must, of course, exhibit, in common with all Acts (Handlungen), an exertion of Will, accompanied by consciousness, and expressed; and any circumstances which prevent the free and intelligent exertion of the will may either prevent the occurrence of the Juristic Act, or may modify the consequences which result from it. What might appear to be a Juristic Act is thus 'null,' or 'void,' i. e. has, as such, no existence, if due to such actual violence as excludes an exertion of will, or if accompanied by states of consciousness, such as lunacy, drunkenness, and certain kinds of mistake, which are incompatible with an in-
*104 telligent exertion of will [84]. So also a Juristic *Act, which does come into existence, is 'voidable,' i. e. is liable to be at-

Puchta, Inst. ii. p. 342. 'Erlaubte Willensäusserung, durch welche ein Rechtsverhältniss, i. e. eine gewisse zufolge der Rechtsbestimmung geltende Beziehung der Willen der Rechtssubjecte, begründet, geändert, oder beendet wird.' Böcking, Inst. p. 44.

82 'Die auf die Entstehung, den Untergang, oder die Veränderung von Rechten gerichtete Privatwillenserklärung.' Windscheid, Pandekten, i. p. 174. 'Erlaubte Willenserklärung einer Partei, welche unmittelbar auf eine rechtliche Wirkung gerichtet ist.' Baron, Pand. i. p. 81. 'Eine Handlung, oder ein Complex von Handlungen, welche, oder welcher, nach den rechtlichen Auslegungsgrundsätzen betrachtet, die Absicht ausdrückt, einen vom objectiven Rechte zum Schutze der Wirksamkeit solcher Handlungen verheissenen Erfolg herbeizuführen.' Leonhard, Der Irrthum bei nichtigen Verträgen, i p. 250.

83 Ihering, Geist des R. R. iii. p. 132.

84 In Roman Law a similar effect might be produced by anger: 'Quidquid

tacked, and prevented from producing its ordinary results, if attended at its inception by 'duress per minas' (metus), by fraud (dolus) [85], and, in some exceptional cases, by mistaken motives.

Same—Mistake.

Of the circumstances which may thus affect the existence, or the operation, of a Juristic Act, that which has given rise to most discussion is 'mistake,' or 'error.' The language of the Roman lawyers upon this subject [86] is by no means clear, and has also been much misunderstood. It is obvious that such a proposition as 'nulla voluntas errantis est [87],' if taken literally, would sweep away a number of transactions which every one admits to be perfectly valid, and would, as has been pointed out, render superfluous the whole doctrine of fraud [88]. Savigny did good service in critically examining the passages in the Corpus Iuris which bear upon the point, and in carefully distinguishing between the error, whether 'in negotio,' 'in persona,' or 'in corpore [89],' which prevents a Juristic Act from coming into existence, and the error in motive, which may prevent such an act from producing its usual effects [90]. Error of the former kind he calls 'spurious' or 'negative,' as being merely the accompaniment of that absence of correspondence between the will and its expression which, as we shall see, is in his opinion fatal to the existence of a Juristic Act. Error of the latter kind he

in calore iracundiae vel fit vel dicitur non prius ratum est quam si perseverantia apparuit iudicium animi fuisse.' Dig. xxiv. 2. 3.

85 Dig. iv. 1 (De in integrum restitutionibus): 'Sub hoc titulo plurifariam praetor hominibus vel lapsis vel circumscriptis subvenit; sive metu, sive calliditate, sive aetate, sive absentia, inciderunt in captionem, sive per status mutationem, aut iustum errorem.' Cf. Dig. iv. 2 (Quod metus causa gestum erit); iv. 3 (De dolo malo); xliv. 4 (De doli mali et metus exceptione); Story, Equity Jur., §§ 184, 238. As to the effect of fraud upon wills, see Melhuish v. Milton, 3 Ch. D. 33; upon a judgment, ex parte Banner, 17 Ch. D. 480. As to the effect of duress and fraud on contracts, see infra, Chapter xii.

86 See especially, Dig. xxii. 6; Cod. i. 18.

87 Dig. xxix. 3. 20.

88 Savigny, System, iii. p. 342.

89 Cf. Dig. xviii. 1. 9.

90 System, iii. pp. 263, 441.

describes as 'genuine,' or 'positive,' because, though, as a
*105 *rule, it produces no effect upon such an act ('falsa causa non nocet') [91], yet in some exceptional cases, e.g. in testamentary matters [92], and in 'condictio indebiti,' it is in itself ground for an interference with the operation of the act.

Same—The correspondence of will and expression.

It was laid down by Savigny that, in order to the production of a Juristic Act, the will and its expression must be in correspondence [93]. This view is in accordance with the prima facie interpretation of most of the relevant passages in the Roman lawyers [94], and is still predominant in Germany [95], but certainly cannot be accepted as universally true. An investigation into the correspondence between the inner will and its outward manifestations is in most cases impossible [96], and where possible is in many cases undesirable. This was so clearly perceived as long ago as the sixteenth century, that Brissonius, in order to adapt the phraseology of Roman law to practical exigencies, boldly explains the term 'velle' as meaning 'expressis et disertis verbis testari et profiteri se velle [97].'

The cases in which the Will and its expression may differ have been distinguished as follows [98]:

i. The difference may be intentional, resulting from (1) a

[91] Cf. Dig. xii. 12. 65. 2: 'Id quoque quod ob causam datur, puta quod negotia mea adiuta ab eo putavi, licet non sit factum, quia donari volui, quamvis falso mihi persuaserim, repeti non posse.'

[92] Dig. v. 2. 28; xxviii. 5. 92; xxxv. 1. 72. 6; Inst. ii. 20. 4, 11, 31. Cf. Story, Equity Jur., § 179.

[93] System, iii. p. 368.

[94] E. g. Dig. xxxiv. 5. 3.

[95] See e.g. Windscheid, Pand. i. § 75, and his Essay on Wille und Willenserklärung, 1878; Zitelmann, Irrthum und Rechtsgeschäft, 1879.

[96] 'The intent of a man is uncertain, and a man should plead such matter as is or may be known to the jury.' Y. B., 4 Ed. IV. 8. 9.

'Warum kann der lebendige Geist dem Geist nicht erscheinen?
Spricht die Seele, so spricht ach! schon die *Seele* nicht mehr.'
Schiller (Votivtafeln), cited by Ihering, Geist des R. R. iii. p. 445.

[97] Brissonius, De Verborum Significatione, s. v. Cf. Glück, Pand. iv. p. 147.

[98] See e.g. Savigny, System, iii. p. 258; Windscheid, Pand. i. §§ 75–77.

mental reservation [99]: (2) a use of words which would usu-
*106 ally *amount to a Juristic Act, with an obvious absence of an intention that they should have this effect, e. g. when legal phrases are used in jest, or on the stage, or in the lecture-room; or when phrases appropriate to a Juristic Act of one kind are employed notoriously with a view to the production of a Juristic Act of another kind, e.g. in the sale of an inheritance by 'mancipatio,' or in the proceedings which took place in a 'common recovery'; or, lastly, when several persons are agreed to put a meaning upon their act other than that which it would naturally bear ('simulatio'), when the rule of Roman law was 'plus valere quod agitur quam quod simulate concipitur [100].'

ii. The difference may be unintentional, i.e. it may be the result of essential mistake.

The prevalent theory would seem to be that a want of correspondence between the will and its expression is in every case, except when the result of a mental reservation, a ground of nullity. It can, however, hardly be disputed that all the other cases of intentional non-correspondence must, to be ground for nullity, be known, or knowable, to others. There is in fact here no non-correspondence; if we remember that expression consists not in the literal, or surface, meaning of words and deeds, but in the meaning which, under all the circumstances, other persons are justified in putting on those words and deeds [101]. It would therefore seem that unintentional non-correspondence, i.e. such non-correspondence as arises from mistake, can alone be represented as preventing the production of a Juristic Act. Whether even this can be conceded is open to doubt. There is something to be said for the view, maintained by a recent school of writers, that, in enumerating the requisites

99 This case Savigny declines to consider, since it amounts to a lie, iii. p. 258, and Windscheid, Wille und Willenserklärung, p. 29, puts it aside as a case of fraud. The only authority for the nullity of a contract when there was a mental reservation seems to be a decision against a marriage so contracted, in Decretal iv. 1. 26.

100 Cod. iv. 22.

101 'In emptis et venditis potius id quod actum quam id quod dictum sit sequendum est.' Dig. xviii. 1. 1.

of a valid Juristic Act, we may leave out of account the
*107 *inscrutable will, and look solely to what purports to be its outward expression [102]. We shall hope later to establish that this is at all events the case with that species of Juristic Act which is called a 'Contract [103].'

Same—Form.

The mode in which the will ought to be expressed for the production of any given act is its 'form.' In some cases a special form is required by law, as in Roman law for a 'stipulatio,' and in English law for a contract not to be performed within a year, for a marriage, or for the probate of a will. The form may be such as to preclude certain classes of persons from doing the act, as 'peregrini' were incapable of pronouncing the solemn formula of the stipulation. In other cases the form of the act is immaterial, and the determination of will is sometimes expressed only by a course of conduct [104].

Same—Representation—Agency.

Most, but not all, juristic acts may in modern times be performed through a Representative. A representative whose authority extends only to the communication of the will of his principal is a

[102] This view has been maintained, with reference to all Juristic Acts, by Schall, Der Parteiwille im Rechtsgeschäft, 1877; to Juristic Acts inter vivos, by Röver, Ueber die Bedeutung des Willens bei Willenserklärungen, 1874; to Contracts, by Regelsberger, Civilr. Erörterungen, I. pp. 17–23, 1868, and Bähr, in Ihering's Jahrb. xiv. pp. 393–427, 1875; to obligatory Contracts, by Schlossmann, Der Vertrag, pp. 85–140, 1876. See Windscheid, Wille und Willenserklärung. It is temperately advocated, principally with reference to Contracts, by Leonhard, Der Irrthum bei nichtigen Verträgen, 1882–3. I am unable to agree with the learned author that Savigny is to be interpreted as agreeing with the newer theory, although Savigny confesses that a difference between Wille and Willenserklärung is important only when it can be known to others, System, iii. p. 258. So also Windscheid, u. s., has to define 'Willenserklärung' as 'Der Wille in seiner sinnenfälligen Erscheinung.'

[103] Infra, Chapter xii.

[104] So the acceptance of an executorship will be inferred from acting as an executor. In some cases the natural inference from a course of conduct may be rebutted by 'Protest,' or 'Reservation.' Cf. Dig. xxix. 2. 20; xx. 6. 4.

mere messenger, 'nuntius.' A representative whose instructions allow him to exercise an act of will on behalf of his principal,
*108 to act to some extent, *as it is said, 'at his own discretion,' is an 'Agent.' His authority may be express or implied, and he may, in his dealings with third parties, disclose, or he may not disclose, with different results, the fact that he is acting on behalf of another. The scanty and gradual admission of agency in Roman law is a well-known chapter in the history of that system [105]. The tendency of modern times is towards the fullest recognition of the principles proclaimed in the Canon law: 'potest quis per alium quod potest facere per seipsum'; 'qui facit per alium est perinde ac si faciat per seipsum [106].'

Same— One-sided and two-sided juristic acts.

Juristic Acts are distinguished into 'one-sided,' where the will of only one party is active, as in making a will, accepting an inheritance, or taking seisin; and 'two-sided,' where there is a concurrence of two or more wills to produce the effect of the act, which is then a 'contract,' in the widest sense of that term.

Same— Characteristics of juristic acts.

The characteristics of a juristic act of any given species are divided into those which are 'essentialia,' 'naturalia,' and 'accidentalia negotii.'

Same—Essentialia.

The 'essentialia' of the act are the facts without which it cannot exist, e. g. according to Roman law there could be no contract of sale without a price fixed.

Same—Naturalia.

The 'naturalia' are those facts which are always presumed to be part of the transaction in question, though the presumption may

105 Cf. the distinction drawn by Prof. Sohm between what he calls 'tutelary representation,' in cases where the principal is himself incapable of performing a juristic act, which was early recognised in Roman law, and what he calls 'procuratorial representation,' in the case of an agent appointed by a principal under no such disqualification, which was admitted by that system only for the purpose of acquiring possession. Institutionen, § 32. Transl. p. 145.

106 C. 68, de R. I. in Sext.; c. 72, eodem.

be contradicted, e. g. the presumption in Roman law that the property in goods sold did not pass till the price had been paid.

*109 *Same—Accidentalia.*

The 'accidentalia' are those facts which in the given cases are not presumed and must therefore be proved.

Same—Nullities.

A pretended act which is deficient in any one of the 'essentialia negotii' is a 'nullity,' 'void ab initio'; when, as a rule, the deficiency cannot be supplied by any subsequent change of circumstances, 'quod initio vitiosum est non potest tractu temporis convalescere [107].' In exceptional cases the deficiency can be waived, or is cured by lapse of time. In certain other cases the act, though not ipso facto void, is 'voidable' at the option of a party concerned.

Same—Conditions.

The 'naturalia' and 'accidentalia' can alone be varied by the will of the parties to the act. The variations which may thus be superadded to necessary portions of the act are its 'conditions.' Some of them, such as 'dies' (a future event which is certain to happen) and 'modus' (a direction for the application in a certain manner of property received), affect only its operation; others, which are conditions in the most accurate sense of the term, affect also its very existence. Such a 'condition' may be defined as 'the presupposition of a future uncertain circumstance, upon which the Will of the party makes the existence of his juristic act, or of its contents, wholly or partially to depend [108].'

A condition is 'suspensive' when the commencement, and 'resolutory' when the termination, of the operation of the act is made to depend upon its occurrence.

107 Dig. l. 17. 29.

108 Puchta, Inst. ii. p. 365; Sohm, Inst. § 30.

*110

*CHAPTER IX.

THE LEADING CLASSIFICATIONS OF RIGHTS.

The possible modes of classifying Rights are almost infinite, but four only are of first-rate importance. These depend respectively—

I. Upon the public or private character of the persons concerned.

II. Upon the normal or abnormal status of the persons concerned.

III. Upon the limited or unlimited extent of the person of incidence.

IV. Upon the act being due for its own sake, or being due merely in default of another act.

These various modes of dividing Rights have, be it observed, nothing to do with one another. They are what are called cross divisions, such as would be divisions of liquids into viscous and non-viscous, hot and cold, fermented and non-fermented; and consequently, though any given right can only exhibit one of the alternative characteristics of each mode of division, yet it may combine this with either of the characteristics of each of the other modes. Just as a liquid may be viscous, fermented, and cold, or viscous, fermented, and hot, or non-viscous, non-fermented,
*111 and hot, and so *forth, through all the possible combinations of viscosity, fermentation, heat, and their opposites.

Choice of a classification.

Since therefore every Right exhibits either the positive or the negative characteristic of each of the above-mentioned modes of division, i. e. since every Right may be classified in accordance with its relations to each and all of the above-mentioned distinctions, it becomes a question which of these is to be adopted by the Jurist as being the radical distinction, and in what order the others are to be subordinated to it; just as a writer on fluids might have to determine whether he would set out by classifying them into viscous and non-viscous, or into fermented and non-fermented. The question is to be decided upon grounds of convenience. Whichever division is most fertile in results should obviously be selected as the radical one, to which the rest should be subordinated in the order of their relative importance.

The relative importance of the four modes of division will perhaps be self-evident when the nature of each has been fully explained.

I. PUBLIC AND PRIVATE PERSONS.

A very radical division of Rights is based upon a broad distinction between the public or private character of the persons with whom the Right is connected. By a 'Public person' we mean either the State, or the sovereign part of it, or a body or individual holding delegated authority under it [1].

By a 'Private person' we mean an individual, or collection of individuals however large, who, or each one of whom, is of course a unit of the State, but in no sense represents it, even for a special purpose.

Resulting division of Rights and of Law.

When both of the persons with whom a right is connected
*112 *are private persons, the right also is private. When one of the persons is the Státe, while the other is a private person, the right is public.

From this division of rights there results a division of Law, as the definer and protector of Rights, which when they subsist—

(1) Between subject and subject, are regulated by 'Private' law.

(2) When between State and subject, by 'Public' law.

The radical division.

And this distribution of the whole field of law is of such capital importance that we have no hesitation in adopting the division of rights out of which it springs as the radical division of them.

[1] Cf. Wolff: 'Imperium publicum nihil aliud est quam ius universis in singulos competens, quatenus eorum actiones ad finem civitatis dirigendae.' Ius Naturae, Praef. ad Part. viii. All authority is of course exercised by permission of the State, e.g. of a father over his family, but it is better to see here only a relation of private life, sanctioned by the sovereign, not a delegation of the sovereign power.

We have now to explain the application of the distinction, and to justify our assertion that this is the radical distinction between Rights, and consequently between the departments of Law.

Value of this division.

By adopting this subdivision of municipal law, its whole field falls at once into two natural sections. On the one hand is the law which regulates rights where one of the persons concerned is 'public'; where the State is, directly or indirectly, one of the parties. Here the very power which defines and protects the right is itself a party interested in or affected by the right. That is to say, it is at the option of one of the persons who are concerned with the right to uphold or to extinguish it. If the State is the 'person of inherence' it will naturally, though of course not of compulsion, protect its own right. If the State is the 'person of incidence,' it may conceivably refuse to uphold the quasi-right of the person of inherence against itself. If the State executes laws which protect rights against itself, it is acting upon the maxim applied to their own conduct by the Roman Emperors: 'Legibus soluti legibus vivimus [2].' Opposed to this is the law which regulates rights where both of the persons concerned are 'private' persons.
*113 Here the parties *interested in or affected by the right have nothing to do with protecting it. This is done by the State, whenever the person of inherence invokes its aid.

Examples.

The punishment, for instance, of a traitor is a matter of public law. The right violated by him is a public right, because the person in whom it resides is the State. The State has a right not to be conspired against. The traitor violates this right, and the same State whose right has been violated intervenes to protect itself and to punish the offender. If, on the other hand, a carrier damages my goods, the question raised is one of private law. My right to have my goods safely carried is a private right, because both the carrier and myself are private individuals; though I am entitled to call for the intervention of the State to obtain compensation

[2] Inst. ii. 17. 8; cf. Dig. i. 3. 31, xxxii. 23; Cod. i. 14. 4.

from him for the injury I have sustained [3]. It is necessary, in order to obviate a frequent confusion upon the point, to mention that the same act may often infringe both a public and a private right. Thus an assault or a libel upon an individual is a violation of two distinct rights, i. e. of the private right of the individual to be unmolested, and of the public right of the State not to be disturbed by acts constituting, or tending towards, breaches of the public peace.

The distribution of Law which has been thus shown to be logically consistent possesses other advantages also. A moment's consideration will show the convenience of an arrangement in accordance with which constitutional, ecclesiastical, criminal, and administrative law, on the one hand, and the law of contracts, of real and personal property, of wills and successions and of torts, on the other hand, form two groups, to one or other of which every legal topic may be readily referred [4].

*114 *In recognising as the primary principle of the division of our science the distinction between public and private persons, resulting, through the severance of public and private rights, in the opposition of public and private law, we have the irrecusable authority of the Roman jurists. 'Publicum ius,' says Ulpian, and his words adopted by Justinian have influenced the legal speculation of the world, 'est quod ad statum rei Romanae spectat; privatum quod ad singulorum utilitatem pertinet [5].' Or as Paulus says: 'Alterum utilitas privatorum, alterum vigor publicae disciplinae postulat [6].'

But indeed the distinction is much older. It is beautifully worked out by Aristotle, who classifies offences according to those against whom they are committed. They are committed, he says, either against the State (τὸ κοινόν) or an individual (ἕνα τῶν κοινωνούντων).

[3] It is noteworthy that in the Articles of Union between England and Scotland (art. 18) a distinction is drawn between Scots laws 'concerning public right, policy, and civil government, and those which concern private right.'

[4] For Sohm's eccentric identification of Private Law with the Law of Property, see his Institutionen, § 19. Transl. p. 98.

[5] Dig. i. 1. 1; Inst. i. 1. 4.

[6] Dig. xxxix. iv. 9. 5; cf. Cod. i. 2. 23.

An assault is an injury to an individual, while avoiding military service is an injury to the State[7].

Although clearly grasped and stated by the Romans, and borrowed from them by most of the continental nations as the fundamental basis of legal division, the distinction has been relegated by writers of repute to a subordinate position, if not altogether rejected.

Austin's rejection of the distinction.

Thus Austin divides primarily the whole field of law into the law 'of Persons' and that 'of Things,' subordinating to the law of Persons the mighty cleavage between Public and Private law. 'Public law,' he says, 'is the law of political status [8].' Our reasons for disapproving of this arrangement will probably be suffi-
*115 ciently apparent when we have explained *the distinction which Austin thus treats as the primary one; we may however at once observe that when so secondary a function is assigned to the division of law into Public and Private, it is impossible to find a satisfactory position in the Corpus Iuris for the law of Crime [9].

Same—His absolute and relative duties.

Connected with the distinction which we have been discussing is the doctrine of 'absolute' and 'relative' duties [10], which Austin explains as follows: 'A relative duty is incumbent upon one party, and correlates with a right residing in another party. In other words, a relative duty answers to a right or implies and is implied by a right. . . . Where a duty is absolute, there is no right with which it correlates. There is no right to which it answers.

[7] Rhet. i. c. 13. So Demosthenes: *ἔστι δύο εἴδη περὶ ὧν εἰσὶν οἱ νόμοι, ὧν τὸ μέν ἐστι, δι' ὧν χρώμεθα ἀλλήλοις καὶ συναλλάττομεν καὶ περὶ τῶν ἰδίων ἃ χρὴ ποιεῖν διωρίσμεθα καὶ ζῶμεν ὅλως τὰ πρὸς ἡμᾶς αὐτούς, τὸ δ' ὃν τρόπον δεῖ τῷ κοινῷ τῆς πόλεως ἕνα ἕκαστον ἡμῶν χρῆσθαι.* In Timocrat. p. 760.

[8] Austin, ii. p. 71. He fortifies himself by the authority of Hale and Blackstone.

[9] See Austin, ii. p. 72. On the difference between civil and criminal law see Ed. Rev. vol. 54 (1831), pp. 220, 221.

[10] See Bentham, Traités de Législation, i. pp. 154, 247, 305; Princ. Morals and Leg. pp. 222, 289, 308.

It neither implies, nor is implied by, a right [11]. . . . A relative duty corresponds to a right, i. e. it is a duty to be fulfilled towards a *determinate person*, or *determinate persons*, other than the obliged, and other than the sovereign imposing the duty. . . . All absolute obligations are sanctioned criminally. They do not correspond with rights in the sovereign [12].'

He classifies absolute duties as being (1) towards self, (2) towards persons indefinitely, or towards the sovereign; (3) duties not regarding persons, but regarding God or the lower animals [13]. We are quite willing to concede not only that a man can have no relative duty towards himself, towards God, or towards the animals, but also that he can have no legal duty at all towards these beings, whatever may be his moral or religious obligations towards them. But we deny that there can be no relative duties to persons indefinitely, or, what seems to amount to the same thing, to the sovereign [14].

The State has rights and duties.

In other words, we assert that the sovereign may be clothed with a right. That this is so may be seen from the form
*116 *of indictment, which in England runs 'The Queen on the prosecution of A. B. against C. D.'; in America 'The People against E. F.' [15] The State is surely as capable of possessing a right as is the Corporation of London. The State has rights, and duties owed to it are as relative as any others.

Indeed it is not improper to talk of the State as having duties, namely such as it prescribes to itself, though it has the physical power to disregard, and the constitutional power to repudiate them [16]. Such duties we often see enforced, e. g. in England, principally but not exclusively, by a Petition of Right [17].

[11] Austin, ii. p. 67.

[12] Ib. ii. p. 73.

[13] Ib. ii. pp. 74–75.

[14] As laid down, ib. p. 59.

[15] So some Recognizances are in the nature of an acknowledgment of debt to the Crown, upon which, if it be broken, the Crown can take proceedings.

[16] This view is supported by Ihering, who says that the State may very well make laws applicable to itself as well as to its subjects. 'Recht, in diesem Sinne des Wortes, ist also die zweiseitig verbindende Kraft des Gesetzes,

[17] See note 17 on next page.

International Law.

The field of law, strictly so called, may be thus exhaustively divided between the law which regulates rights between subject and subject (civis and civis) and that which regulates rights between the State and its subjects (civitas and civis). But there is a
*117 third kind of law which it is for many reasons *convenient to co-ordinate with the two former kinds, although it can indeed be described as law only by courtesy, since the rights with which it is concerned cannot properly be described as legal. It is that body of rules, usually described as International law, which regulates the rights which prevail between State and State (civitas and civitas) [18].

The differences between these three kinds of Law, Private, Public, and International, depend upon the presence or absence of an arbiter of the rights of the parties.

die eigene Unterordnung der Staatsgewalt under die von ihr selber erlassenen Gesetze.' The motive of the State in submitting itself to law is self-interest, since it can prosper only through security. 'Das Recht ist die wohlverstandene Politik der Gewalt.' Der Zweck im Recht, i. pp. 344, 366.

17 It is a maxim of American law that 'the State, being a Sovereign, cannot be sued.' Claims against the United States, or the States individually, could therefore be arranged only by legislative action. The practical inconveniences hence resulting seem to have been considerable, and led to the institution in 1855 of a 'Court of Claims,' which has partially relieved the Congress of the United States from the decision of questions arising upon government contracts. As long ago as 1793, Judge Wilson, in the Supreme Court, said: 'On general principles of right, shall the State, when summoned to answer the fair demands of its creditors, be permitted, Proteus-like, to assume a new appearance, and to insult him and justice by declaring "I am a Sovereign State"? Surely not.' See an article on 'Suing the State,' by Mr. Davie, in the American Law Review. 1884, xviii. p. 814. An Act of 1887 has given concurrent jurisdiction with the Court of Claims to all District and Circuit Courts of the U. S. Ib., 1891, vol. xxv.

18 A statement remarkable for its date as to the nature of International law is to be found in Hooker's Ecclesiastical Polity, i. c. x. § 12: 'Besides that law which simply concerneth men as men [morality] and that which belongeth unto them as they are men linked to others in some political society [municipal law], there is a third kind of law which toucheth all such several bodies politic, so far as one of them hath public commerce with another, and this third is the law of Nations.' Montesquieu distinguishes 'droit civil,' 'droit politique,' 'droit des gens.' Esprit des Lois, i. c. 3.

In Private law, which in many respects is the only typically perfect law, it will be observed that both the parties concerned are private individuals, above and between whom stands the State as an impartial arbiter. In Public law also the State is present as arbiter, although it is at the same time one of the parties interested. But in International law there is no arbiter at all, but both parties are equally judges in their own cause. The law where a political arbiter is present, be he, or be he not, identical also with one of the parties, is often called 'Municipal,' to distinguish it from the so-called law which is described as 'International,' and which has no arbiter to which it can appeal other than the opinion of the civilised world.

Same—Nature of International Law.

It is plain that if Law be defined as we have defined it [19], a political arbiter by which it can be enforced is of its essence, and law without an arbiter is a contradiction in terms. Convenient therefore as is on many accounts the phrase 'International law,' to express those rules of conduct in accordance with which, either
*118 in consequence of their express *consent, or in pursuance of the usage of the civilised world, nations are expected to act, it is impossible to regard these rules as being in reality anything more than the moral code of nations.

Of the three departments therefore into which law may be divided, having regard to the political or non-political character of the persons whose rights it regulates, it must be borne in mind that what is not very happily described as 'Municipal law,' in its two departments 'Private' and 'Public,' is alone properly so called, while 'International law' is law only by analogy.

II. LAW OF PERSONS AND OF THINGS.

The status of the persons concerned is, as we before observed, another basis of the division of rights.

That is to say, there are some rights in which the status of the persons concerned has to be specially taken into consideration, while in others this is not the case.

This distinction has led to a division of Law into the 'law of

[19] Supra, p. *37.

persons' and the 'law of things'; but in order to trace the steps by which this result was obtained, we must go back to our analysis of a Right into its elements, and to the differences which exist between the first and last elements of a Right on the one hand, and its two intermediate elements on the other [20].

We see at once that, while the intermediate elements consist of an object and an act, each of the two extreme *elements
*119
is a person; and it becomes apparent that an important step will have been taken towards understanding the variations in Rights if we reduce the four terms upon which those variations depend to two only, by consolidating the two extreme elements into what has been called, distinctively enough, the 'law of persons,' and the two intermediate elements into what has been much more ambiguously called the 'law of things.'

The terminology.

Although the distinction, as now drawn, is of modern date, the phraseology in which it is expressed is as old as the time of Gaius, and probably much older [21]. There has been considerable discussion as to the precise meaning put by the Roman lawyers upon the

[20] Supra, p. *80.

[21] 'Omne autem ius quo utimur vel ad personas pertinet, vel ad res.' Inst. i. 8. He adds 'vel ad actiones,' i. e. to Procedure, which does not interfere with his division of the field of substantive law. The distinction was probably drawn in the edictum perpetuum. See the frag. of Hermogenianus, 'Primo de personarum statu, et post de ceteris, ordinem edicti perpetui secuti.' Dig. i. 5. 2. From the use by Gaius of 'vel' rather than 'aut,' it has been argued that the passage is an enumeration rather of points of view than of distinct classes. See Dr. Emerton's tract on 'The threefold division of Roman law,' 1888.

terms 'ius quod ad personas,' and 'ius quod ad res pertinet.' It is certain that this early attempt to map out the field of law was rather popularly than scientifically conceived. It was obvious enough to put on the one side the 'persons' for whose sake all law exists, and on the other, the 'things' about the enjoyment of which persons may dispute. When the analysis was pushed a little further, persons were divided into several classes, with reference mainly to their position in the Roman family, and it was observed that since things, in the literal sense, are not the only enjoyable objects, the term might receive an artificial extension, so as to cover 'incorporeal things,' and even obligations.

Each of the terms in question is open to objection on the ground of ambiguity.

Ius quod ad personas, pertinet.

The 'Ius quod ad personas pertinet' aptly enough expresses
*120 the law as to those variations in rights which arise *from varieties in the Persons who are connected with them. But it is unfortunately also used by the Roman jurists to express what the Germans call 'Familienrecht'; i. e. to express, not only the variation in rights which is caused by certain special variations in personality, but also the special rights which belong to certain personal relationships [22]. Not merely, for instance, the legal exemptions and disabilities of infants and femes covert, but also the rights of a father over his son, a husband over his wife, and a guardian over his ward.

Such questions, however, as how far a woman's capacity for contracting is affected by coverture, and what are the mutual rights of husband and wife, are radically different in character.

Ius quod ad res pertinet.

The 'Ius quod ad res pertinet' very ambiguously indicates the department of law which treats of such modifications of rights as result from varieties in the objects or in the acts with which they are concerned. That the Roman jurists meant to cover these mod-

22 The opinions as to what Gaius meant by 'Ius quod ad personas pertinet' are summed up by Savigny, System, i. p. 398, cf. ii. App. v, who asserts that the term is equivalent to 'Familienrecht.'

ifications by this phrase is quite clear from their own explanation of what they include under the term 'Things.' 'Res,' they tell us, are either 'corporeal,' things which can be touched, such as a farm, a slave; or 'incorporeal,' which cannot be touched, consisting in right only, such as a right of servitude, a right of action, a right arising out of contract [23]. Now 'corporeal' things are obviously what we have called the 'objects' of the right; 'incorporeal' things are the advantages which the person entitled can insist upon; in other words, 'the acts or forbearances' to which he is entitled.

We may identify, therefore, though only approximately,
*121 the two extreme members of our series with what the *Romans called the 'law of Persons' and the two intermediate members with what they called 'the law relating to Things.' The division turning upon the distinction between, on the one hand, the persons in whom a right resides or against whom it is available; and, on the other hand, the objects over which it is exercised and the acts by means of which it is enjoyed.

Equivalent phrases.

It will be observed that though the Roman writers shorten 'ius quod ad personas pertinet' into 'ius personarum [24],' they never abbreviate the 'ius quod ad res pertinet' into 'ius rerum.' Yet their later followers have talked of 'ius rerum,' as well as of 'ius personarum,' thereby causing not a little confusion; and Sir Matthew Hale, adopting these phrases, mistranslates them 'Rights of Persons and of Things,' and is followed by Blackstone [25].

The distinction, which probably made its first appearance in the Edict, which was adopted by Justinian, and is recognised more or less by almost all modern jurists [26], has also been expressed in other ways.

Bentham's distribution of the law into 'particular' and 'general' amounts to much the same thing [27].

23 Inst. ii. 2. pr.; cf. the phrases 'chose in possession' and 'chose in action.'

24 Inst. ii. 1. pr.

25 Comm. i. p. 122.

26 See Thibaut, Versuche, ii. über ius rer. et pers.; Savigny, System, i. p. 393; Austin, ii. pp. 383, 398.

27 Traités, i. pp. 150, 259, 294, 299; Austin, ii. p. 418; iii. p. 225.

M. Blondeau means to indicate the same distinction when he divides the law into that of 'capables' and of 'incapables [28].'

Mr. Westlake defines 'status' as 'that peculiar condition of a person whereby what is law for the average citizen is not law for him [29].'

Mr. Poste, guided perhaps by reminiscences of Aristotle, opposes the law of 'equals' to that of 'unequals [30].'

*122 **Normal and abnormal rights.*

It is not easy to find apt terms to express the true nature of the distinction. None of those already enumerated are satisfactory, and we would venture to suggest the adoption in their place of 'normal' and 'abnormal.' Why we prefer these terms to any others will appear from the closer examination of the subject upon which we are about to enter.

The distinction explained.

A Right varies with a variation in any one of the series of its constituent elements. The possible variations in the two extreme terms of the series are, however, far fewer than in the two intermediate terms. This is the case, first, because both of the extreme terms are Persons, so that they are subject to the same sets of variations; and, secondly, because as a matter of fact the possible varieties in juristic personality are far fewer than those in the juristic character of objects or acts.

The order of study.

The Law of Persons, as a source of variety in rights, is therefore distinct from and much smaller than the residue of the Law, which is generally called the Law of Things. The jurist may make either one or the other species of characteristics his starting-point in considering the aggregate of rights which make up the whole field of Law. He may consider seriatim the possible varieties in the persons with whom rights may be connected; treating under each personality of the various objects and acts with which it may be combined: or, he may start from the variations in objects and acts; considering by way of supplement the modifications which the

[28] Cited by Austin, ii. pp. 411, 417. [29] Private International Law, § 89.
[30] Gaius, i. § 8.

rights connected with these undergo in each case from varieties in personality. Thus the aggregate of rights may be likened to a figure of two dimensions: the shorter of these dimensions representing the Law of Persons; the longer the Law of Things. And the figure may be supposed to be marked off into squares, like a chessboard, by the intersection of a few horizontal lines expressing the possible varieties of personality, and of a multitude of vertical lines expressing the possible varieties of object or act.

*123

*Law of Things.

Law of Persons.	Shipping.	Banking.	Torts.	Family.	Succession.	&c.
Normal.						
Lunatic.						
Alien.						
Covert.						
Infant.						
&c.						

It is a mere choice of the more convenient course, whether the jurist makes the 'personal' dimension of the right or its 'real' dimension the basis of his classification. Now as a matter of fact the personal dimension is one which in the majority of cases needs no consideration at all. When the Persons both of inherence and of incidence are human beings who are citizens of full age and sound mind, not under coverture, or convicted of crime, in other words when their personality is 'normal,' the personal dimension of the right in question is wholly disregarded. It is only when one or both of the Persons concerned are 'abnormal,' i. e. are 'artificial' persons, or infants, or under coverture, or convict, or lunatic, and so forth, that the special effect upon the right in question of this abnormal Personality has to be considered. Since therefore in most cases Personality is not considered at all; and since when it is considered, because abnormal, its aberrations are confined within very narrow limits of possibility; it would form a most inconvenient basis for the classification of rights, compared with

those characteristics which depend upon the object or act with which the right is concerned. The variations of these characteristics are incalculably numerous, and to an account of the
*124 right in *question, founded upon these, it is easy to add by way of supplement any modification which it may receive on account of abnormal personality.

What has been said may be made clearer by an instance. The right of an infant to build on his land so as to obstruct the windows of the house of his neighbour who is a person of unsound mind, is capable of being considered from at least four points of view, viz. as a branch of the law (1) of Infancy, (2) of Ownership, (3) of Servitudes, (4) of Lunacy. But it is clear that the first and the last points of view, (1) and (4), belong to one and the same department of law, viz. the way in which rights are varied by variations in the conditions of Persons; and a little reflection will show that these variations are not very numerous; infancy, lunacy, coverture, alienage and a few more, nearly exhaust the list of varieties in personality; while, on the contrary, the intermediate points of view, (2) and (3), raise classes of questions which are of almost unlimited extent, because they are bounded only by the varieties of physical objects and the modes in which they may be treated.

By abstracting the law of Persons from the rest of the law the description of a right is thus much simplified. Two terms only, instead of four, have primarily to be considered, viz. the physical object and the act. Only when there is any peculiarity in the condition of the person of inherence or of incidence need the first or fourth terms of the series, now consolidated into the 'Law of Persons,' be considered at all.

The inquiry into the law of Persons is thus supplementary and secondary to that into the residue of the law, commonly called the law of Things. The order of exposition, either of the science of Jurisprudence, or of a body of law, should, therefore, be: first, the law generally, without regard to peculiarities of personality; secondly, the law of Persons. Austin is doubtless right in pointing out that Blackstone made a mistake in discussing what he
*125 calls 'the *Rights of Persons' before the 'Rights of Things'; herein following the Roman institutional writers, but depart-

ing from the better arrangement of his great forerunner Sir Matthew Hale.

The line between the law of Things and that of Persons.

Assuming it to be convenient to draw a line between the law of Things and that of Persons, where is the line to be drawn? The tests which have been proposed of the characteristics of the law that ought to be treated of under the latter head are various and unsatisfactory. The marks of a status or condition are, according to Austin, three. 'First, it resides in a person as member of a class. Secondly, the rights and duties, capacities and incapacities, composing the status or condition, regard or interest specially the persons of that class. Thirdly, these rights and duties, capacities and incapacities, are so considerable in number that they give a conspicuous character to the individual, or extensively influence his relations with other members of society.' This last quality he thinks is not essential, and would not be regarded in a body of law rationally constructed [31].

These marks are however not sufficiently distinctive, as they will be found not only in infants or lunatics, to whom a special status is generally attributed, but also in landlords or stockholders, to whom as members of a class nothing of the sort is conceded. It has been ingeniously suggested that 'the essential feature of a status is that the rights and liabilities affecting the class which constitutes each particular status are such as no member of the class can vary by contract [32].' But something more is necessary. The true test is surely this. Does the peculiarity of the Per-
*126 sonality arise from anything unconnected with the nature *of the act itself which the person of inherence can enforce against the person of incidence?

In order to determine, for instance, whether the rights of land-

[31] Jurisprudence, Lect. xl. p. 712, Ed. 3. Cf. Bentham, Princ. Morals and Legislation, c. 16.

[32] Sir W. R. Anson, Principles of Contract, Ed. 1, p. 328. Mr. Hunter's proposed use of 'status' as covering 'those cases where a permanent relationship is created by the law: when duties imposed upon a person are imposed upon him as a member of a class' (Roman Law, p. 475), is still more vague than those above mentioned.

lords should be considered under the law of persons, we must ask whether landlords as a class have any juristic peculiarities unconnected with the acts which they are entitled to demand from their tenants; such as the payment of rent, the observance of covenants, &c. They clearly have not. A landlord merely means a person who is entitled to these acts. On the other hand, suppose the landlord to be an infant; here at once a whole set of characteristics are present, modifying the right to rent, &c., and quite unconnected with it. Nor is it only because the same person sustains the two characters of infant and landlord that this is the case; a man may be a pawnbroker and landlord, but the rights as landlord will not be affected by his occupation as pawnbroker. The personality recognised in the law of persons is such as modifies indefinitely the legal relations into which the individual clothed with the personality may enter.

Classes of Personality.

Of such affections of Personality there are two classes:—

(1) The person may be 'artificial,' i. e. may be not a human being.

(2) The person may be under disability, or may enjoy exemption, on account of age, sex, mental incapacity, crime, alienage, or public station.

All of these are abnormal deviations from the ordinary case of both parties concerned in a right being human beings, under no special and far-reaching disability or exemption. When the disability or exemption is not of a far-reaching character, it will not be treated in practice as founding a special status, although, upon the principles above stated, otherwise capable of being so treated. Thus, as a rule, soldiers, or blind, or illegitimate, persons are not held to occupy a status, although in several respects, and in particular with reference to testamentary powers and rights of succeeding ab intestato, they may respectively exhibit peculiar-
*127 ities *which are not involved in the statement that they are in military service, blind, or illegitimate [33].

[33] The modern civilians recognise status founded upon physical characteristics as 'naturales,' opposing them to the 'status civiles' (libertatis, civitatis, and familiae) recognised in the older Roman law. Savigny objects to this,

We have already pointed out what we conceive to be Austin's mistake in subordinating to the distinction now under discussion, what is in our opinion the still more radical one between 'Public,' 'Private' and 'International' Law; a mistake to which we attribute much of the imperfection which mars the result of the labours of this great jurist.

The distinction is traceable both in Private and in Public law.

The contrast between the law of persons and of things, or between 'normal' and 'abnormal' law, i. e. the law 'of normal' and 'of abnormal persons,' is sharply defined only in one of the departments into which the whole subject may be divided in accordance with this threefold distinction, though something analogous to it may be detected in the others.

In Private law, where all the characteristics of law are fully present, the law of Persons is, as we have already described it, a statement of the ways in which the general law is modified by varieties of status; while the law of Things is a description of the various kinds of rights enjoyed in private capacities by persons as being within the jurisdiction of a State, but not as being in any way representative of the sovereign power in the State.

*128 In Public law, which, as we have seen, possesses the characteristics of law in a lower degree of development, the *distinction is but faintly traceable. What is analogous to the law of Persons here consists in a description of the State as a whole, of its ruling body, of bodies or persons enjoying delegated ruling power, and of its constituent members as such; in short, in what is usually known as 'Constitutional' law. On the other hand,

and to the vague definition of status as 'a quality by means of which a man has certain rights,' that the list of status would be interminable, and the law of status would become identical with the whole body of the law. System, ii. p. 445, Appendix. His objection would not apply to such a definition as is now proposed. Prof. A. V. Dicey, in a most able review of the first edition of this book, points out that status as here defined would be one of the 'real kinds' of J. S. Mill, 'which have, besides the patent qualities which have led us so to class them, an indefinite number of common characteristics which we have not before our minds, and may not even have within our knowledge.' Law Magazine, 1880, p. 400.

the residue of Public law has its analogies to the law of Things. It consists in—

(1) A description of the way in which the different delegacies of the governing body are set in motion. This may be called 'Administrative' law.

(2) A description of those rights of the community at large which are violated by injuries done to it as a whole, or to any member of it, and of the punishments with which infractions of such rights are visited. This is commonly called 'Criminal' or 'Penal' law; because the usual mode of stating and circumscribing such rights is by defining violations of them, and by prescribing the punishment due to such violations.

In International law.

The nearest approach to a law of Persons in International law is contained in that portion of the science which describes the characteristics of a fully Sovereign State, and the modes in which the rights of a State are affected by the absence of such characteristics.

III. RIGHTS IN REM AND IN PERSONAM.

Another grand division of rights turns upon the limited or unlimited extent of the person of incidence, by which phrase, as may be remembered, we mean the person against whom the right is available. A right is available either against a definite person or persons, or against all persons indefinitely. A servant, for instance, has a right to his wages for the work he has done available against a definite individual, his master; while the owner of a garden has a right to its exclusive enjoyment available against no one individual more than another, but against everybody.

This distinction between rights has been expressed by calling
*129 ing a right of the definite kind a right in personam, of *the indefinite kind a right in rem. And these terms, though not perfectly satisfactory, have obtained a currency which is of itself a recommendation, and moreover are perhaps as good as any substitutes which could be suggested for them. The former term indicates with tolerable perspicuity a right available 'in personam (certam)' against a definite individual, while the latter implies that the right is capable of exercise over its object, 'in rem,' without reference to any one person more than another.

History of the terms.

The use of these terms to distinguish between two classes of rights is of comparatively recent date, but is quite in harmony with their use by the classical Roman jurists, in distinguishing between different classes of stipulations, pacts, actions, exceptions and edicts. Any of these are said to be 'in personam' if referring to the duties of a given individual, 'in rem' if operating generally. Thus we are told: 'Praetor in hoc edicto, i. e. quod metus causa, generaliter et in rem loquitur, nec adicit a quo gestum.' 'Pactorum quaedam in rem sunt, quaedam in personam. In rem sunt, quotiens generaliter paciscor ne petam; in personam quotiens ne a persona petam, id est ne a Lucio Titio petam [34].' This use is also analogous to the description of judgments as being in rem or in personam, and to the mediaeval distinction between 'statuta realia' and 'personalia [35].'

Equivalent terms.

The same opposition has also been denoted by the less descriptive terms 'ius in re' and 'ius ad rem,' which first occur in the canon law [36]; and by the terms 'absolute' and 'relative,' which by employment with many other meanings are too void of precision for the purpose.

*130 *Longer, but more complete, expressions are 'rights against individuals,' and 'rights against the world,' and these, originally suggested by Hugo [37], are perfectly unobjectionable.

If the terms 'in rem' and 'in personam' were to be discarded, we should prefer to speak of 'rights of determinate,' and 'rights of indeterminate incidence.'

[34] Dig. iv. 2. 9; ii. 14. 7. 8. Cf. ii. 14, 57; vii. 9. 5; xxxix. 1. 10; xxxix. 2. 19; xliv. 4. 2. 2; xliv. 4. 4. 33; Gai. Inst. iv. 1–4.

[35] See Chapter xviii, infra.

[36] C. 40 de conc. praeb. in Sext.; c. 8 de praeb. eod. 'Ius in re' is classical, e. g. Dig. xxxix. 2. 19. The distinction is thus explained by Huber: 'Ius in re est facultas homini ad rem competens, sine respectu ad certam personam. Ius ad rem est facultas competens in aliam personam ut nobis aliquid det vel faciat.' Praelect. ii. 1. 12. Cf. Glück, Pandekten, ii. § 175; Thibaut, Versuche, ii. p. 26.

[37] Lehrbuch eines civilistischen Cursus, v. p. 72.

IV. RIGHTS ANTECEDENT AND REMEDIAL.

The last of the great divisions of rights distinguishes those where the act is due for its own sake, from those where it is made due merely on default of another act. The former kind have been by various writers styled rights 'primary,' 'sanctioned,' 'of enjoyment'; the latter kind have been described as rights 'sanctioning,' 'secondary,' 'restitutory,' 'of redress.' We prefer to distinguish them as rights 'antecedent' and rights 'remedial.'

The nature of the distinction is sufficiently simple. The rights of the owner of a garden not to have it trespassed upon, of a servant to have his wages paid, of a purchaser to have his goods delivered to him, are all of the former kind, viz. rights 'antecedent,' which exist before any wrongful act or omission. They are rights which are given for their own sake. The right of the owner of a garden to get damages from a party of men who have broken into his grounds, of a servant to sue his master for unpaid wages, of a purchaser to get damages from a vendor who refuses to deliver the goods sold, are, on the other hand, of the latter kind, or rights 'remedial'; they are given merely in substitution or compensation for rights antecedent, the exercise of which has been impeded, or which have turned out not to be available.

If all went smoothly, antecedent, or primary, rights would alone exist. Remedial, or sanctioning, rights are merely part of the machinery provided by the State for the redress of injury done to antecedent rights. This whole department of law is, in an especial sense, 'added because of transgressions.'

*131 *SUMMARY—RESULTING DIVISIONS OF LAW.

Out of each of the four grand divisions of rights there arises also a grand division of law. Including therefore the distinction between 'substantive' and 'adjective' law, explained in a former chapter[38], we have five main principles upon which the field of law may be divided, viz. into—

Substantive and Adjective law;
Private, Public, and International law;
Normal and Abnormal law;

[38] P *78.

The law of rights 'in rem,' and of rights 'in personam';
The law of rights antecedent, and of rights remedial.

One or other of these principles must be selected as determining the fundamental division. Each limb of the subject may be then subdivided in accordance with the other principles one after another.

The primary division.

Adopting as the primary division of rights that which turns upon the distinction between the political or non-political quality of the persons with whom they are connected, we shall divide law, in the first instance, into—

Private,
Public, and
International;

and shall deal with each of these great topics in the order in which we have enumerated them. But before doing so, we propose to call attention to certain characteristics of rights generally, which may be now most conveniently explained, once for all.

*132

*CHAPTER X.

RIGHTS AT REST AND IN MOTION.

Rights may be regarded under two aspects, either as at rest or as in motion. In other words, the jurist has to consider not only the nature, or scope, of any given right, but also the causes which originate or terminate its connection with the person in whom it resides [1]. He must include, for instance, in a survey of the law of real property, not only an account of the various rights of the owner of land, but also a description of the various kinds of 'titles.' He has therefore to determine whether to divide his work into two halves, one of which shall deal with rights, and the other with the causes by which rights are connected or disconnected with persons; or whether to make rights his sole topic, bringing in under each kind of right all needful information as to the causes by which it is set in motion.

We propose to adopt the latter alternative, as presenting, upon the whole, the fewer difficulties. We shall, at any rate, be spared the awkwardness of discussing possessory rights apart from the acts of possession out of which they arise, or contractual rights apart from the agreements to which they owe their existence.
*133 Some repetition is no doubt inseparable *from the proposed method, but it is hoped that the amount of this may be considerably lessened by the general statements respecting both the nature and the movement of rights which will be comprised in the present chapter.

I. RIGHTS AT REST.

Orbit—Infringement.

A right which is at rest requires to be studied with reference to its 'orbit' and its 'infringement.' By its 'orbit,' we mean the sum, or extent, of the advantages which are conferred by its enjoyment. By its 'infringement,' we mean an act, in the strict sense of the term [2], which interferes with the enjoyment of those advantages. A knowledge of the former necessarily implies a knowledge of the

[1] Supra, p. *81. [2] Supra, p. *93.

latter, and vice versa, since the one is always precisely correlative with the other. It is obvious that to know the whole extent of the advantage conferred by the enjoyment of a right is the same thing as to know what acts are infringements of it. Thus the right may be such as to exact from the world an abstention only from any deliberate interference with it, or it may be such as to exact an abstention even from such an infraction of it as may result from want of care. Again, the person of inherence may be entitled absolutely to abstention on the part of others from certain acts, although they may 'cost him nothing, no not so much as a little diachylon [3],' or only to abstention from those acts when they occasion him actual loss, not only iniuria but also damnum [4]. If it be established that a solicitor has an absolute right that no one shall falsely impute to him professional misconduct, irrespectively of any pecuniary loss resulting or not resulting from the
*134 *charge, and that a street passenger has a right not to be run over by negligent driving, it follows that slander of a solicitor, though unaccompanied by loss, and negligent driving causing injury to a street passenger, are alike wrongful acts.

On the other hand the orbit of a right may be, and very generally is, ascertained by an enumeration of the acts which are violations of it; as a right of property is consecrated by the commandment 'Thou shalt not steal.'

It is necessary to observe that what might appear to be an infringement of a right often turns out upon investigation not to be one. This may be the case, because the apparent act is no act at all, or because it is not the true cause of the damage complained of, or because the right which seems to have been infringed has been waived, or because the right has been forfeited, or is disallowed on grounds of public policy.

3 See Lord Holt's remarks in Ashby v. White, Lord Raymond, 938.

4 Cf. the liability which arises upon subsidence of land, caused by the otherwise innocent excavations of the owner of the subsoil, Bonomi v. Backhouse, 9 H. L. C. 503; and upon damage done by the bursting of a reservoir, the storage of water in which gives of itself no right of action, Fletcher v. Rylands, L. R. 3 H. L. 330, or by the escape from custody of an animal of known dangerous propensities, May v. Burdett, 9 Q. B. 101. Damage so done is actionable without proof of negligence. The excavation is made, and the dangerous substance, or animal, is kept 'at one's peril.'

Act.

1. When the apparent act is really the result of circumstances over which the apparent agent had no control; as, for instance, if the horse which he is driving is frightened by the sudden noise of a cart driven furiously along the street, and becoming unmanageable does injury to persons and property, he is not responsible. The result here is a mere accident, since a true act must be accompanied either by intention, or at least by negligence [5].

Cause.

2. No one circumstance in this world can be called with perfect accuracy the cause of any other. Even if I fire a pistol at a man and kill him, many other causes are at work besides the agency of my will upon my finger, and so upon the trigger of the pistol. There must be, for instance, the explosive power of the powder, the law of gravitation permitting the passage of the bullet, the manufacture and sale of the pistol, and so forth. In many cases the share of the person whom we wish to make answerable is mixed up in a far more complex manner with the other events and
*135 acts *which have led to the result. In a case in which a squib was thrown by A at B, and B, to get rid of it, threw it at C, and it was thus passed on, till it ultimately hit and injured Z, it was held that A was liable. 'He who does the first wrong,' said the Court, 'is answerable for all the consequential damages. All that was done subsequently to the original throwing was a continuation of the first force and first act, which will continue till the squib was spent by bursting, and I think that any innocent person removing the danger from himself to another is justifiable [6].' It is conceivable that the decision in this case might have been otherwise, and it must be remembered that the law will refuse to consider an act to be the cause of a result which is either, in the language of English law, 'too remote,' or to which the injured party has 'contributed' by his own negligence.

[5] Supra, pp. *95, *97. Cf. Holmes v. Mather, L. R. 10 Ex. 261.

[6] Scott v. Shepherd, 1 Sm. L. C. 399; cf. the opinion of Labeo; 'Si, cum vi ventorum navis impulsa esset in funes anchorarum alterius, et nautae funes praecidissent, si nullo alio modo nisi praecisis funibus explicare se potuit, nullam actionem dandam.' Dig. ix. 2. 29. 3. Ib. 49. 1.

Same—Remoteness.

As to remoteness, it was said by Lord Bacon: 'It were infinite for the law to consider the causes of causes, and their impulsions one of another; therefore it contenteth itself with the immediate cause, and judgeth the acts by that, without looking at any further degree [7].' The wrong and the damage must be, it has been said, 'concatenated as cause and effect [8].' The difficulty is, of course, to decide when this can fairly be said to be the case. Lord Ellenborough held that where special damage must be shewn, it must be the legal, as well as the natural, consequence of the act complained of, and accordingly that A had no action against B for the utterance of slanders which had caused A to be wrongfully dismissed from his situation [9]. Much doubt has however been thrown upon the correctness of this view [10].

*136 **Same—Contributory negligence.*

A person is said to contribute to his own injury, when he so acts as to become a 'co-operative cause' of it. For instance, the owner of cattle which have been injured by a railway train cannot recover from the Company if they have strayed on to the line through his own negligence in not shutting gates [11]. But the negligence of the sufferer is not held to be contributory, when the result complained of might have been avoided by the exercise of ordinary care on the part of the wrong-doer.

Same—Contributory negligence of third party.

The contributory negligence of a third party is no excuse for the negligence of the defendant [12]. To this rule two exceptions have been recognised. First, when the cause of action is derived from a negligent third party, which is the case where a parent or guardian sues for injury to a child, caused by its own careless-

[7] Maxims, Reg. 1.

[8] Gerhard v. Bates, 2 Ell. and B. 490.

[9] Vicars v. Wilcox, 8 East. 3; cf. Ward v. Weeks, 7 Bing. 211.

[10] Knight v. Gibbs, 1 Ad. and E. 46; Lynch v. Knight, 9 H. L. C. 577; Pollock, Torts, p. 221. The cases on remoteness of cause were elaborately considered by Cockburn, C. J. in Clark v. Chambers, L. R. 3 Q. B. 327.

[11] Ellis v. London and S. W. Ry., 2 H. and N. 424.

[12] Burrows v. March Gas Co., L. R. 5 Ex. 67.

ness[13]; and secondly, where the plaintiff has 'identified himself' with the negligent third party, as where the plaintiff was a passenger in a vehicle the driver of which contributed by his negligence to the injury caused by the driver of another vehicle, who was the defendant in the action[14]. This latter doctrine, which is disapproved of in Scotland[15] and generally in the United States[16], has at length, after a currency of forty years, been repudiated by the House of Lords[17].

Same—Apportionment of negligence.

The Admiralty practice in cases of contributory negligence was to apportion the liability between the plaintiff and defendant (the rusticorum iudicium), and this rule is now extended by the
*137 Judicature Act of 1873 to all cases of *collision between two ships[18]. In all other cases, according to the law of England, a plea of the contributory negligence of the plaintiff is, if supported, fatal to his right of action[19].

Roman law seems to have arrived at the same result in practice, though on somewhat different theoretical grounds. The question is treated in the Digest not as one of causation but as one of set-off, in which the negligence of the plaintiff balances that of the de-

13 Mangau v. Atherton, L. R. 1 Ex. 239, but cf. Lynch v. Nurdin, 1 Q. B. 29.

14 Thoroughgood v. Bryan, 8 C. B. 115; cf. Armstrong v. Lanc. and Yorks. Ry. Co., L. R. 10 Ex. 47.

15 Hobbs v. Glasgow Ry., 3 Ct. of Session Cases, Ser. 4. 215.

16 Webster v. Hudson Ry., 19 N. Y. Rep. 341.

17 The Bernina, 12 Prob. Div. 58, confirmed in H. L., as Mills v. Armstrong, 13 App. Ca. 1.

18 For a review of the cases on the Admiralty practice, see 2 L. Q. R. p. 357. The principle of the rusticorum iudicium has recently been extended by the Supreme Court of the U. S. to all cases of maritime tort. The Max Morris, 137 U. S. Rep. 1.

19 See an able article by Mr. E. H. Crosby in the American Law Review for 1880, p. 770, and the notes to Ashby v. White, 1 Sm. L. C. In Illinois, and some other states, it seems that the courts weigh the question of 'comparative negligence,' allowing a plaintiff whose negligence is 'slight' to recover against a defendant whose negligence is 'gross.' It has lately been held that the plaintiff is bound not only to prove the negligence of the defendant, but also to disprove any contributory negligence of his own; Davey v. L. and S. W. Ry., 12 Q. B. Div. 70; Wakelin v. L. and S. W. Ry., 12 App. Ca. 41; but see Dublin, &c. Ry. v. Slattery, L. R. 3 App. Cases, 1155.

fendant[20]. 'Quod quis ex culpa sua sentit, non intelligitur sentire,' says Pomponius[21].

Waiver.

3. 'Volenti non fit iniuria.' If a right is waived, an act which would otherwise be an infringement of it becomes permissible[22]. Thus consent on the part of the husband was a good plea in bar of the old action for criminal conversation. So 'leave and licence' is an answer to an action for trespass, and a similar defence may be pleaded for what might appear to be a breach of covenant. The waiver must of course be given freely and with knowledge of the circumstances.

Forfeiture.

4. If a right is forfeited, or suspended, by misconduct, an
*138 *act which would previously have been a violation of it ceases to be unlawful. An assault may be justified on the ground that it was committed upon a person who had forced his way into one's house and refused to leave it, or an arrest by the production of the warrant of a competent authority.

Public policy.

5. A right may also be suspended on grounds of public policy. So a trespass on land adjoining a highway may be justified if the highway is impassable.

Responsibility.

The responsibility for an infringement does not always attach exclusively to the visible wrong-doer. In accordance with the maxims 'respondeat superior' and 'qui facit per alium facit per se,'

20 This is sometimes described as 'Culpa-compensation.' See Pernice, Zur Lehre von den Sachbeschädigungen, p. 58.

21 Dig. l. 17, 203. So Ulpian: 'Si in loco periculoso sellam habenti tonsori se quis commiserit, ipse de se queri debere,' Dig. ix. 2. 11. pr.; and Paulus: 'Multa huiusmodi deprehenduntur quibus summovetur petitor si evitare periculum poterit.' Ib. 28, cf. S. R. i. 15. 3. The culpa of the plaintiff is immaterial when the defendant is in dolo. Dig. ix. 2. 9. 4.

22 On the difference between 'voluntas' and 'scientia,' see Smith v. Baker, '91 App. Ca. 325.

a person is liable for those acts of his agents or servants which either were expressly authorised by him, or which were done by them in the course of their employment [23].

Common employment.

By way of exception to this principle, it was for many years settled English law that 'one fellow servant could not recover for injuries sustained in their common employment from the negligence of a fellow servant, unless such fellow servant is shown to be either an unfit or improper person to have been employed for the purpose [24]'; the reason given being that an implied contract is entered into by servants to accept the consequences of the negligence of a properly selected fellow servant, as an ordinary
*139 risk of their employment. The *exception was, however, much restricted in its operation by a statute passed in 1880 [25].

II. RIGHTS IN MOTION.

Dispositive facts.

The origination, transfer, and extinction of rights, or, as the Germans would say, the connection and disconnection of 'Rechtsverhältnisse' with their Subjects [26], are due to Facts, but may be the result of either of the two species of Facts, i. e. either of an Event or an Act [27]. A fact giving rise to a right has long been described as a 'title'; but no such well-worn equivalent can be

[23] Mr. Justice Holmes brings forward a mass of curious evidence, beginning with Exodus xxi. 28, to show that the remedy was in early times against the immediate cause of damage, even inanimate, the owner of which was therefore bound to surrender it ('noxae deditio'), though in later times he was allowed to redeem the offending property by a money payment. This is reversing the order of ideas which looks upon the surrender as having been a substitute for payment. The Common Law, pp. 7–35. On the connected institution of the 'Deodand,' see 1 Bl. Comm., 300.

[24] Feltham v. England, L. R. 2 Q. B. 36. This view, first held in the case of Priestly v. Fowler, 3 M. & W. 1 (1837), seems to be unknown on the Continent; see Parliamentary Papers, 1886, [c. 4784]. It is settled law in the U. S. See Murray v. S. C. Rail. Co., 1 McMullan (South Carol.), 385 (1841), and Farwell v. Boston and Worc. Rail. Co., 4 Metcalf (Massachusetts), 49.

[25] 43 and 44 Vict. c. 42. Cf. Sir F. Pollock, Torts, ed. 2, p. 87.

[26] Cf. Savigny, System, ii. p. 374; ii. p. 1; Windscheid, Pand. i. p. 170.

[27] Supra, pp. *81, *92.

found for a fact through which a right is transferred, or for one by which a right is extinguished. A new nomenclature was accordingly invented by Bentham, which is convenient for scientific use, although it has not found its way into ordinary language. He describes this whole class of facts as 'Dispositive,' distinguishing as 'Investitive' those by means of which a right comes into existence, as 'Divestitive' those through which it terminates, and as 'Translative' those through which it passes from one person to another [28].

1. *Investitive facts.*

An 'investitive fact' finds its nearest equivalents in classical Latin in the terms 'iusta causa,' 'iustum initium,' and 'titulus.' In some, but not in all, cases, it is possible to detect two stages in the acquisition of a right, a more remote and a nearer, and it has been proposed to distinguish them by describing the 'causa remota' as 'titulus,' the 'causa proxima' as 'modus acquirendi.' 'Cavendum est ante omnia,' says Heineccius, 'ne confundamus titulum et modum adquirendi, quippe qui toto coelo differunt'; and he goes on to assert that 'dominium' can never be gained without the
*140 *combination of a 'titulus,' giving a 'ius in personam,' and a 'modus adquirendi,' which superadds the 'ius in rem.' These two stages are undoubtedly traceable in such a transaction as a Roman contract of sale followed by delivery, but they are by no means universally present in the acquisition even of real rights, and it is now admitted that the importance of the distinction has been much overrated [29].

A right may be conferred either by a direct act of the sovereign power, or by some fact which brings a particular instance within the operation of a general law. In the former case the investitive fact would be properly described as a 'privilegium,' in the latter case as a 'title.' The grant of a monopoly would be a fact of the former kind, the death of an ancestor, bringing into operation the

[28] His further distinction of 'Investitive' facts into 'collative' as conferring rights, and 'impositive' as imposing duties, and of 'Divestitive' facts into 'destitutive' or 'ablative' as extinguishing rights, and 'exonerative' as extinguishing duties, seems to be of less value. Cf. Works, iii. p. 189.

[29] Hein. Recit. ii. tit. 2. 339. 'Der vergebliche Versuch, jede Rechtserwerbung auf einen iustus titulus und s. g. modus adquirendi zurückzuführen, ist nun allgemein aufgegeben.' Böcking, Inst. p. 44.

law of inheritance, would be a fact of the latter kind, and would be an instance of what is described by some writers as 'Qualification,' i. e. the substitution by the course of events of a definite individual instead of an 'incerta persona' as the person entitled to a right [30].

2. *Divestitive facts.*

A 'divestitive fact' puts an end to a right altogether; so the right of a tenant terminates with the expiration of his lease, and the right of a creditor is at an end when his debt has been paid.

3. *Translative facts.*

Rights are more commonly transferred than altogether extinguished, so that a divestitive fact is very often capable of being regarded, from another point of view, as investitive also. A conveyance of land not only terminates the rights of the vendor, but also originates those of the purchaser. A fact which fulfils this double function is called by Bentham 'translative,' and the right which results from such a fact is said to be acquired 'derivatively [31].

*141 *Translative facts may be regarded from several points of view, and may be classified with reference to their voluntary or involuntary character, to the persons between whom the right passes, and to the extent of the right passed.

Same—Voluntary and involuntary.

The fact may be involuntary, i. e. as far as the parties to the right are concerned, it may be a mere external event, such as a bankruptcy, the death of an intestate, accession, adjudication, escheat; or it may be a voluntary act on the part of the person from whom the right passes, such as a contract of sale, or a testament. In the latter case it is called 'Alienation [32]:' which again may be gratuitous, when the resulting acquisition is said to be 'ex lucrativa causa,' or for an equivalent. The distinction between

[30] Austin, iii. pp. 93–98.

[31] Puchta, Inst. ii. p. 325, points out that in all derivative acquisitions there is a legal relation between the auctor and the person acquiring; not merely a loss by one and gain to another, as in usucapio.

[32] On Alienation, cf. infra, p. *189.

involuntary and voluntary investitive facts is expressed by the English law-terms 'act of law' and 'act of party.'

Same—The persons.

A translative fact may operate wholly 'inter vivos,' or it may pass a right from a deceased to a living person, or from a natural to an artificial person, or from one artificial person to another. The artificial person may in some cases be the State itself.

Same—The extent—Succession.

The right passed by the translative fact cannot, as a rule, be of greater extent than the right whence it is derived. 'Non debeo melioris conditionis esse quam auctor meus a quo ius in me transit [33].' It may however either be of less extent, as when a leasehold interest, or an easement, is granted by an owner of land; or it may be the very right itself, in which latter case the translative fact is called a 'Succession.'

Same—Singular succession.

When, as is usually the case, the succession passes one or more separate rights, as the ownership of an estate, or a leasehold
*142 interest in a house, it is called 'singular,' and was *described in Roman law by the phrases 'succedere in rem,' 'in rei dominium.'

Same—Universal succession.

But there is a more complex kind of succession, known as 'universal,' which the Romans described by the phrases 'succedere per universitatem,' 'in universum ius,' 'in universa bona [34],' 'adquirere per universitatem [35].' What here passes is what German jurists call the 'Gesammtheit des Vermögens,' the whole mass of a man's property, whether consisting of rights 'in rem' or of rights 'in personam,' or of both combined; and with the property, or assets,

[33] Dig. l. 17. 175. 1. But Casaregis would substitute in mercantile transfers the principle 'possession vaut titre.' This theory seems to have been carried very far, in the interests of commerce, by recent German decisions. Vierteljahresschrift für Rechtswissenschaft, &c., N. F. vii. p. 204.

[34] Dig. xii. 2. 8; xxi. 3. 3. 1; xxxix. 2. 24. 1; xliii. 3. 1. 13.

[35] Gai. ii. 97.

'bona activa,' the liabilities, 'bona passiva,' pass also. Such a 'universal succession' takes place when an executor, or administrator, or trustee in bankruptcy succeeds to a whole group of the rights and liabilities of a testator, or an intestate, or a bankrupt respectively.

Many forms of universal succession have now only an antiquarian interest. This is the case, for instance, with the 'addictio bonorum libertatium conservandarum causa [36],' with the Senatusconsultum Claudianum [37], with the 'bonorum venditio.' Other forms, such as confiscation to the State, bankruptcy and heirship, can never be out of date.

The passage of the rights of a deceased person to his heirs, the 'successio in universum ius quod defunctus habuit [38],' which is the most important of all universal successions, is brought about either by an involuntary fact, the man's death intestate, or by a voluntary act, the making of his will.

Same—Intestate succession.

Intestate is chronologically anterior to testamentary succession. Recent investigators, and especially Sir Henry Maine, have abundantly shown that there is in early times but little trace of individual ownership. Even grown-up children had only the most
*143 precarious interest during their lives in the *property which they were allowed to handle, and on their deaths their father took possession of it as a matter of course. When the father himself died, his property passed of right to his surviving children, or if he left no children, then to certain precisely designated collateral members of his family, or in default, to that wider family which is known as a 'gens' or clan. The idea that property really belongs to a family group, and that the right of an individual is merely to administer his share of it during his lifetime, may be said still to survive in those provisions against the total disinheriting of relations which modern systems have borrowed from Roman law [39], and less obviously in the rights given to next of kin under statutes of distribution. The feudal doctrine as to the suc-

[36] Inst. iii. 11. [37] Inst. ii. 12. [38] Gaius, Dig. l. 16. 24.

[39] E. g. Code Civil, liv. iii. tit. 2. chap. 3, 'de la Portion de Biens disponible et de la Réduction.'

cession of the heir-at-law to real property, and of escheat, in default of an heir, to the lord of the fee, is widely different in character. It is as a consequence of this latter doctrine, that no one individual is recognised by English law as succeeding to all the rights of an intestate who dies leaving both real and personal property, and that the heir and the administrator divide between them what under the Roman system devolved wholly on the 'heres.'

Same—Testamentary succession.

The principle that a man may voluntarily select the person on whom his property is to devolve after his death [40] is of later origin than the principle of intestate succession. Such a selection had at first to be ratified by legislative authority, in order to oust the rights of the relatives. The gradual growth of the power of making a will, from the days when it could only be made in the
*144 'comitia calata,' or in the face of the *people drawn up in battle array, 'in procinctu,' through the twelve tables, and the praetorian relaxations, down to the wide liberty enjoyed under the later Empire, is one of the most interesting topics of the history of Roman law. The points to which attention must be directed in studying the subject of testamentary disposition in its fully developed form, and with reference to each of which very various provisions are contained in actual systems of law, are the following:

(1) The capacity of the testator, as to age, freedom from 'patria potestas,' 'coverture,' or the like.

(2) The effect, if any, to be given to proof that the testator acted under mistake or undue influence [41].

(3) The formalities necessary for the execution of a will, such as

[40] 'Le testament est un acte par lequel le testateur dispose pour le temps où il n'existera plus, de tout ou partie de ses biens.' Code Civil, art. 895. 'Neque enim aliud videtur soda tium mortis quam voluntas ultra mortem.' Quint. Declam. 308. A curious a priori justification of Wills is given by Leibnitz: 'Testamenta mero iure nullius essent momenti, nisi anima esset immortalis. Sed quia mortui revera adhuc vivunt, ideo manent domini rerum, quod vero heredes reliquerant, concipiendi sunt procuratores in rem suam.' Nova Methodus Iurisprudentiae, P. II. § 20.

[41] On the differences between Roman and modern English law on this point, see Lord Hardwicke's judgment in Milner v. Milner. 1 Vesey, 106, and Story, Equity Jurispr. § 179.

signing, sealing, attestation, or enrolment in a public office; and the special cases in which fewer or more formalities than ordinary are insisted upon [42].

(4) The contents of the will. Whether any relatives must be expressly, or may be only tacitly, disinherited; whether the heir must be instituted before other matters are mentioned; and so forth.

(5) The capacity of the heir, or other person who is to take beneficially under the will. The incapacities, under various systems, of 'incertae personae,' corporations, priests, witnesses, charities and churches.

(6) The modes in which a will, when once well made, may subsequently become invalid; as in Roman law by the agnation of a new 'suus heres,' and in English law by marriage; or in which it may be set aside, e. g. by the 'querela inofficiosi.'

(7) Whether the inheritance devolves immediately through the
operation of the will, or whether any act is necessary on the
*145 part of the heir or executor, such as the 'cretio' or 'aditio' *of
heirs other than the 'necessarii' in Roman law [43], or the procuring of probate from a judicial authority, which is demanded from an English executor [44].

(8) Whether the heir can refuse to accept, and how far he can claim to be relieved from liabilities in excess of assets.

It may be well to observe that although an English executor does not take the whole property of a person who dies leaving real as well as personal property, yet he may well be regarded as a universal successor, so far as relates to the personal property and the claims upon it [45].

[42] The formalities will, for instance, be more elaborate in the case of a blind man, less so in the case of a soldier on active service.

[43] Before which the hereditas was described as 'iacens,' and was treated as a juristic person.

[44] He may also render himself liable by intermeddling with the estate, when he is said to become 'executor de son tort.'

[45] The early history of the English executor is discussed with great learning by Mr. Justice Holmes, The Common Law, p. 344.

Same—Legacies.

One form of singular succession is so closely connected with universal succession under a testament as to be unintelligible apart from it [46]. A Legacy, 'donatio quaedam a defuncto relicta [47],' is a deduction from an inheritance for the benefit of some one. It is the creation of a claim upon the universal successor [48], and a distinction is drawn between the 'vesting' of the legacy, 'dies cedit,' and its becoming payable, 'dies venit.' It may be revoked by the testator, or it may 'lapse.' It will be void if inconsistent with any rule of law as to the amount of legacies, or as to the proportion which they may bear to the property which is to remain with the heir, or as to the persons who may receive them.

Same—Donationes mortis causa.

A Legacy must be distinguished from a 'donatio mortis
*146 *causa [49]' which, though it takes effect on the death of the donor, does not do so by way of deduction from the inheritance.

The further examination of subject.

Having now considered the general characteristics of law and of rights, we are in a position to enter upon a more detailed examination of our subject, under the three great heads of 'private,' 'public,' and 'international' law.

46 'Quae pars iuris extra propositam quidem materiam videtur: nam loquimur de his iuris figuris quibus per universitatem res nobis adquiruntur: sed cum omnimodo de testamentis . . . locuti sumus, non sine causa sequenti loco poterat haec iuris materia tractari.' Gai. ii. 191.

47 Inst. ii. 20. 1.

48 Although, according to Neratius, 'ea quae legantur recta via ab eo qui legavit ad eum cui legata sunt transeunt.' Dig. xlvii. 2. 64.

49 'Cum magis se quis velit habere quam eum cui donatur, magisque eum cui donat quam heredem suum.' Inst. ii. 20. 1. On the evils of the wide applicability to securities of 'donatio mortis causa' at the present day, see 2 L. Q. R. 444.

*147

*CHAPTER XI.

PRIVATE LAW: RIGHTS 'IN REM.'

The great department of law, upon a detailed examination of which we are about to enter, may be most conveniently studied if we distinguish at the outset the main topics which are contained in it. These are to be ascertained by a successive application of the principles of division which were explained in a preceding chapter, in the order which seems best suited to the subject.

Substantive and adjective law.

Private law, as thus treated, is either 'substantive' or 'adjective,' that is to say, it either defines the rights of individuals, or indicates the procedure by which they are to be enforced.

Normal and abnormal rights.

The rights dealt with by substantive law may be either 'normal' or 'abnormal,' as the persons with whom they are connected are of the ordinary type, or deviate from it.

Antecedent and remedial rights.

Both classes of rights are either 'antecedent' or 'remedial.' A right of the former kind, it will be remembered, is one which exists irrespectively of any wrong having been committed. It is an exceptional advantage granted to the person who is clothed with it. The devisee of a house in Middlesex, or the merchant
*148 who has bought a cargo of rice, *is, by virtue of being thus devisee or purchaser, in enjoyment of powers which are not possessed by the rest of the population. A right of the latter kind is one which is given by way of compensation when an 'antecedent' right has been violated.

Rights in rem and in personam.

Antecedent rights are either 'in rem' or 'in personam'; that is to say, they are available either against the whole world or only against a definite individual. Thus the proprietary right of the owner of a house is good against all the world, while the right of a landlord to his rent is good only against his tenant. Remedial rights are most usually available only 'in personam,' though proceedings against a ship in the Court of Admiralty, or to obtain a divorce, are undoubtedly 'in rem,' as was the 'actio quod metus causa' in Roman law [1]. Ulpian pointed out that all interdicts, 'licet in rem videantur concepta, vi tamen ipsa personalia sunt [2].' The distribution of the subject may be more shortly expressed as follows:

Private law is either
- Substantive, defining rights, which are
  - Normal
    - Antecedent
      - in rem.
      - in personam.
    - Remedial.
  - Abnormal.
- Adjective, providing for the protection of rights.

We shall begin with the consideration of the substantive law of the various species of normal rights. We shall then treat of the law of abnormal rights, and conclude with the topic of adjective law or Procedure.

Order of study.

Normal rights may be, as has been already explained, either Antecedent or Remedial, and rights of the former kind may be either 'in rem' or 'in personam.' The study of Private law will nat-
*149 urally commence with an examination of *normal antecedent
rights 'in rem,' i. e. of rights which, irrespectively of any wrong having been committed, are available for the benefit of the person of inherence against a person of incidence so unlimited as to comprise the whole world [3]. Rights of this kind are both numerous and important, and must be examined in due order.

A distinction is very generally drawn by German writers be-

[1] 'Cum autem haec actio in rem sit scripta, nec personam vim facientis coerceat, sed adversus omnes restitui velit quod metus causa factum est.' Dig. iv. 2. 9. 8.

[2] Dig. xliii. 1. 1.

[3] The draft Civil Code for Germany, by an inversion of the order of treatment hitherto accustomed, deals with 'Sachenrecht' after the 'Recht der Schuldverhältnisse.'

tween what they call 'Urrechte' and 'erworbene Rechte [4].' Rights of the former kind, which are also said to be 'inborn,' 'fundamental,' 'inalienable,' 'natural,' 'immediate,' 'universal,' 'essential,' 'unconditional,' or 'absolute,' are such as every human being possesses independently of any act of his own; while rights of the latter kind, described also as 'derivative,' 'mediate,' 'alienable,' 'accidental,' or 'hypothetical,' are the result of some free act of the person entitled to them. The line between the two classes of rights is however so variously drawn, and must always be drawn subject to so many qualifications and reservations, that the distinction is of little value. We have called attention to it only as illustrating that graduated intimacy of relation between the right and its subject which we shall take as our guide in determining the order of the investigation upon which we are about to enter.

We shall begin with the right which is most closely connected with the personality of the individual entitled to it, and shall proceed to consider, one after another, those rights which are progressively less connected with his proper personality, and are more connected with the control which he is allowed to exercise over the actions of others, and with the advantages which he is allowed to derive from the world in which he lives [5].

*150 **Classification of antecedent rights in rem.*

Taken in this order, the rights of the class now under consideration may be ranked as follows:

I. To personal safety and freedom.

II. To the society and control of one's family and dependents.

III. To reputation.

IV. To advantages open to the community generally; such as the free exercise of one's calling.

V. To possession and ownership.

VI. To immunity from damage by fraud.

[4] 'Officia et iura connata ... acquisita.' Wolfius, Ius Naturae, Pars. i. c. i; Röder, Naturrecht, i. p. 174; but see Savigny, System, i. p. 335.

[5] On the essential difference between the right to personal safety and the right to property, see Brunsden v. Humphrey, 14 Q. B. D. 141. Cf. 'Dominus membrorum suorum nemo videtur.' Dig. ix. 2. 13. pr.

In each case we shall have to consider not only the nature of the right in question, but also the character of the act by which it is violated, and the modes of its origination, transfer and extinction. Our illustrations will here, as elsewhere, be drawn chiefly from the law of England.

I. PERSONAL SAFETY.

Rights to personal safety and freedom are the most widely enjoyed of any. They are possessed by every one who has not waived or forfeited them. They are acquired at the moment of birth, and are therefore said to be 'innate,' though they are limited, during the earlier years of life, by the right of parents and guardians to chastise and keep in their custody persons of tender age. Similar rights of custody, and even of chastisement, have been at various periods recognised also with reference to women. These rights are of course, from their nature, incapable of transfer. They may be partially waived. A person who engages in a lawful contest of strength waives, by so doing, as against his antagonist, his right not to be assaulted and battered [6], and any complaint made by him in such a case would be well answered by the defence of 'volenti non fit iniuria,' or 'leave and licence.' So a sailor who enters on *board ship waives for the voyage his right to di-
*151
rect his own movements. An unlimited waiver of rights of this kind, such as a self-sale into slavery, or a self-dedication to monkish seclusion, though recognised in early systems of law, is discountenanced by modern civilisation [7]. They may be temporarily forfeited. In other words complaints founded upon a violation of them may be met by a plea of 'justification'; as in English law a complaint of assault is well answered by a plea of son assault demesne, provided always that the violence complained of is not out of all proportion to the violence first used by the complainant. They terminate with death. They are, in many cases, violated by acts exhibiting only that degree of will which is called negligence.

In enumerating the rights of this kind which are recognised in

[6] Similarly by submission to a surgical operation. See Pollock, Torts, ed. 2, p. 145.

[7] For limitations on the rule 'liberos privatis pactis non posse servos fieri,' see Dig. xl. 13. 3, Inst. i. 3. 4.

advanced states of society, it will be convenient to begin with those which have the widest extent, i. e. where the injury is an act of the slightest kind, and to proceed in order to rights more and more restricted in scope, i. e. where there is no injury unless the act is of a distinctly violent character, or is accompanied by actual damage.

1. *Menace and assault.*

A man has a right not to be even menaced by gestures, as by the shaking of a fist, the brandishing of a stick, or the presenting of a pistol. Such acts may however be deprived of any wrongful character, if the parties be so distant that no contact is possible [8], or if words are used showing that no harm is intended, as where a man laid his hand on his sword in a threatening manner, but said, 'If it were not Assize time I would not take such language from you [9].'

2. *Assault and battery.*

A man has a right not to be touched, pushed, or struck in a rude or hostile manner, thus sustaining a 'battery' in English law. This right is not interfered with by one who is pushing his
*152 way gently in a crowd, or who touches his *neighbour to attract his attention, or gives him a jocular and friendly blow, or is duly executing legal process [10].

3. *Wounding.*

A man has a right not to be wounded or disabled, whether by deliberate assault, or by negligence [11], such as that of a reckless cab-driver, or of a railway company, which sends a train over a level crossing at an improper speed.

4. *Imprisonment.*

A man has a right to go where he pleases, so long as he does not interfere with the rights of others, and any one who prevents him from so doing, whether by constraint actually applied, or by such show of authority or force as has an effect on the will equiva-

[8] Cobbett v. Grey, 4 Ex. 744.

[9] Tuberville v. Savage, 1 Mod. 3.

[10] Williams v. Jones, Hard. 301.

[11] Supra, p. *97.

lent to actual constraint, is said in English law to be guilty of 'false imprisonment.'

An act which appears to infringe a right of one of the three last mentioned kinds often does not really do so. It may be justified on the ground of self-defence, of defence of a friend or of property, of preservation of the peace, or of the execution of legal process [12]. The right is in fact to be taken subject to qualification on various grounds.

The heads of right hitherto mentioned may be violated without causing actual damage. This is not the case with those which we are about to describe.

5. *Dangerous things.*

A man has a right not to receive injury from any dangerous substance or animal kept by another. Any one who stores up a great bulk of water in a reservoir, or keeps a caravan of wild beasts, is said, by English law, to do so 'at his own peril,' and will be liable, should damage be done by the bursting of the reservoir, or the escape of a tiger, although he may have taken the greatest possible care to prevent the mischief. The same liability would attach to the keeping of animals mansuetae naturae, if known to be vicious.

6. *Dangerous places.*

A man has a right that his personal safety shall not be infringed by the negligent exercise on the part of others of
*153 *their own rights, or rather of what might appear to be their own rights; as when a person allows his house to be in such bad repair that it falls on a passer-by, or allows the existence of latent dangerous places in his house or land, whereby damage is sustained by persons having lawful business there, or exercises a statutory power without due care.

7. *Right not to be killed.*

It might perhaps be supposed that since a man has a right not to sustain personal injury, he has a fortiori a right not to be killed.

[12] 'Is qui iure publico utitur non videtur iniuriae faciendae causa hoc facere, iuris enim executio nemini facit injuriam.' Dig. xlvii. 10, 13.

This is however hardly the case, since no 'antecedent' right can be said to exist, unless its infringement gives rise to a 'remedial' right; but the right, if any, to redress for the infringement of the right in question dies with the injured man at the very moment when it vests in him [13].

It would seem that a man has no right of immunity from needless mental suffering, uncombined with physical damage [14].

II. FAMILY RIGHTS.

Rights to the society and control of one's family. These family-rights 'in rem' must be carefully distinguished from those rights 'in personam' which a member of a family may have against its other members, and with which we have at present no concern. They all result, directly or indirectly, from the institution of marriage, which, as Bentham well said, 'has drawn woman from the severest and most humiliating servitude, has distributed the
*154 mass of *the community into distinct families, has created a
domestic magistracy, has formed citizens, has extended the views of men to the future through affection for the rising generation, has multiplied social sympathies [15].' They may be distinguished as 'marital,' 'parental,' 'tutelary,' and 'dominical.'

1. *Marital Rights.*

The marital right of a husband, as against the world, is that no other man shall, by force or persuasion, deprive him of his wife's

[13] In this, as in most other cases of delict, 'actio personalis moritur cum persona,' i. e. the remedy ceases to be enforceable upon the death of either the party injured or the wrong-doer. Lord Campbell's Act, 9 & 10 Vict. c. 93, does not keep alive the right for the benefit of executors, but creates a new right, on the analogy of what was already common law in Scotland, for the benefit of the 'wife, husband, parent and child,' and no other person, to compensation for the shortened life and labours of the deceased. It is, however, held that if the deceased has accepted compensation for his injuries, his representatives have no further right of action. Read v. Gt. E. Ry. Co., L. R. 3 Q. B. 555.

[14] So held in the Supreme Court of Maine (1880), in Wyman v. Leavitt, 36 Am. Rep. 303; where see the learned note, citing dicta in Lynch v. Knight, 9 H. L. 598. A different view has prevailed in certain later cases in Texas.

[15] Bentham, Principes du Code Civil, par Dumont, iii. c. 5.

society [16], still less be criminally intimate with her. An analogous right might of course be conceivably recognised as vested in the wife, and has been recognised in recent American cases [17].

Same—Marriage.

The right is acquired by Marriage, the nature of which has varied with varying civilisation. In primitive races it seems to have consisted in the forcible capture of the woman by the man. Later the capture becomes a symbolical ceremony, following on a voluntary sale or gift of the woman by her relatives to the man. The still more modern form of marriage, possible only when the individuality of the woman has received recognition, is that of a mutual and voluntary conveyance, or dedication, of the one to the other [18]. This mutual conveyance has been very generally associated with some religious observance, and in modern times is, as a rule,
*155 *valid only when performed in the manner prescribed, and in the presence of officials recognised, by the State. It is generally only permissible between persons who have attained a certain age, and who are outside of certain degrees of relationship, amongst which 'fosterage' is sometimes reckoned. The consent of parents or other guardians is often also necessary [19].

16 Cf. the interdict 'de uxore exhibenda ac ducenda,' which could be obtained even by a filiusfamilias against his father. Dig. xliii. 30. 2.

17 See Westlake v. Westlake, 34 Ohio St. R. 621, Kneesy v. Exner, Brooklyn Superior Court, N. Y., Mehrhoff v. Mehrhoff, U. S. Circuit Court, 26 Federal Reporter, 13 (with a reference to which the author was kindly furnished by Mr. Roger Foster, of New York); Foot v. Card, 58 Conn.; and an article on 'The Husband-seducer,' in 26 Am. Law Review (1892). The proposed Civil Code for the State of New York expressly forbids, Pt. ii. § 32, 'the abduction of a husband from his wife, or of a parent from his child.' Cf. Lords Campbell and Brougham, in Lynch v. Knight, 9 H. L. 577.

18 This 'marriage contract' is, for obvious reasons, governed by rules varying in some respects from the rules governing contracts generally; see, e. g. the discussion as to the effect on marriage of mistake, in Decr. Grat. Causa. xxix. q. 1. Cf. as to fraud, Swift v. Kelly, 3 Knapp 256, and, as to duress, Scott v. Sebright, 12 Prob. Div. 21. As to the effect of conditions 'contra substantiam coniugii,' see Decr. Greg. iv. 5. 7.

19 But the Council of Trent, Sess. xxiv, Decretum de Reform. Matr., c. 1. anathematizes 'qui falso affirmant matrimonia a filiis familias sine consensu parentum contracta irrita esse.' See A. Rivier, Droit de Famille Romain,' p. 142.

Marriage is defined by Modestinus as 'Coniunctio maris et feminae et consortium omnis vitae, divini et humani iuris communicatio [20];' by Kant as 'die Verbindung zweier Personen verschiedenen Geschlechts zum lebenswierigen wechselseitigen Besitz ihrer Geschlechtseigenschaften [21].' Polygamy, i. e. polygynaiky or polyandry, has been and is recognised as marriage in many parts of the world, but the tendency of the higher races of mankind is doubtless towards a recognition of monogamy as alone legitimate [22]. Of marriage for a definite period but slight traces occur in legal systems [23].

Under the marriage law of ancient Egypt, which was strictly monogamous, the woman seems regularly to have been taken on probation for a year, after which she was 'established as a wife [24].'

The marital right is of course inalienable, and incapable of waiver [25]. It terminates on the death of one of the parties,
*156 *or their divorce. As to the permissibility of divorce, and the grounds on which it ought to be granted, the widest difference has prevailed in different systems. At Rome either party might repudiate the relationship at pleasure [26], while according to the canon law it is a sacrament, indissoluble under any circumstances [27].

[20] Dig. xxiii. 2. 1.

[21] Werke, vii. p. 76.

[22] So the English Courts have refused recognition in Hyde v. Hyde, L. R. 1 P. and M. 130, to a Mormon, and in Bethell v. Hilliard, 38 Ch. D. 220, to a Baralong marriage. On the other hand, a Japanese (monogamous) marriage was declared valid in Brinkley v. Atty. Gen., 15 P. D. 76.

[23] Such marriages are regulated with the utmost precision by the Shiah system of Muhammadan law. Tagore Lectures, 1874, p. 373. But it is expressly enacted by art. 13 of the Egyptian 'Statut personnel du droit Musulman,' that 'le mariage temporaire, celui dont la durée est limitée à un temps déterminé, ne se contracte pas valablement.'

[24] Revillout, Chrestomathie Démotique, 1880, p. cxxxii.

[25] No damages will however be granted if collusion is shown.

[26] 'Libera matrimonia esse antiquitus placuit, ideoque pacta, ne liceret divertere, non valere.' Cod. viii. 39. 2. In the older Roman law, a paterfamilias could divorce a son or daughter in his power; but see Dig. lxiii. 30. 1. 5.

[27] Divorce is still unknown in Italy, as was the case in France (except during the interval 1792–1816) till the year 1884, and in England (except by Act of Parliament) till the institution of the Court for Divorce and Matrimonial causes, in 1857. In Germany divorce has long been generally and

The right is infringed by abduction or harbouring of, or by criminal intimacy with, another man's wife; also by so injuring the wife as to deprive the husband of her services. The 'co-respondent,' as the adulterer is now called in English law, is not liable for his act if he was unaware that the woman was married [28].

2. *Parental Rights.*

The parental right extends to the custody and control of children, and to the produce of their labour, till they arrive at years of discretion. In case of disagreement between the parents it becomes necessary to determine to which of them the right shall belong, or to apportion it between them.

It is acquired on the birth, and also, under some systems, on the adoption of a child. It is, under some systems, alienable by emancipation of the child to another person who adopts him, or by the father giving himself, together with his children, in adoption to another. It may be delegated; for instance, to a school-
*157 master, or to the master of an apprentice. *It terminates with the death of the parent or child, with the emancipation of the child, or by his attaining full age, by marriage, also by judicial sentence.

It is infringed by an act which interferes with the control of a parent over his children, or with the advantage which he derives from their services. The much-abused English action for seduction is quite in harmony with legal principles. The person wronged is not the girl herself, who ex hypothesi has consented to the act, but her parent, or other person entitled to her services, who is damnified by its results [29]. It is true that English law has, on grounds of policy, allowed damages to be recovered in this action far in excess of the value of the lost service [30].

readily permitted, as it is in most of the States of the American Union. See the interesting work of Dr. Theodore D. Woolsey, Divorce and Divorce Legislation, 1882.

28 This infringement of the right, besides giving rise to a right of redress, may, according to English law, also affect indirectly the matrimonial status itself; as will appear hereafter.

29 But by Scots law a woman seduced, with professions of honourable intentions, has herself an action. Gray v. Brown (1878), 5 Rettie's Rep. 971.

30 See Dicey, Parties, p. 329, n.

3. *Tutelary Rights.*

The right of a 'tutor,' or guardian, defined by Servius as 'ius ac potestas in capite libero ad tuendum eum qui propter aetatem se defendere nequit[31],' is of course given to him not for his own benefit, but for that of his 'pupillus,' or ward[32], whose want of understanding he supplements, and whose affairs he manages. It is an artificial extension of the parental power, and may be conferred by the last will of the parent, or by a deed executed by him[33], or by a judicial act, or by devolution on certain defined classes of relatives, or may vest in a tribunal, such as the Court of Chancery. According to some systems, the guardian cannot refuse to accept the office, which is regarded as being of a public character. In French law a 'subrogé tuteur' is appointed by the family council as a check on the 'tuteur[34].' The right terminates on the death of tutor or ward, on the resignation or removal of the former, and on the marriage of the latter or his attainment of a certain
*158 age. By the older Roman law, a woman was under *perpetual guardianship. Under those systems which release the ward at an early age, generally at fourteen in the case of a boy and twelve in the case of a girl, from the superintendence of his guardian, he may be placed for a further period under the lighter control of a 'curator,' whose duties cease when the ward attains the age of full majority. Such curators, and the curators, or committees, of lunatics or persons interdicted as prodigals, are generally appointed by a court of justice.

The right is infringed by any interference with the control of the tutor or curator over the person or property of the ward, lunatic, or prodigal[35].

[31] Dig. xxvi. 1. 1.

[32] The lord's wardship in chivalry, without account of profits, was, on the contrary, for his own benefit.

[33] See Stat. 12 Car. II. c. 24. s. 8, as varied, in favour of the mother, by 49 & 50 Vict. c. 27.

[34] Code Civil, art. 420.

[35] On the writ of 'ravishment of gard,' see 2 Inst. 440. When the tutelary right has been vested in a Court, any infringement of it becomes a matter of public law. Thus interference with a ward of Chancery is treated as 'contempt of Court.'

4. *Dominical Rights.*

The right of a master over his slave was, in early law, of precisely the same extent and character as that which he had over his cattle. It was also acquired, lost and transferred in the same way, except that the slave was capable of being manumitted; and the peculiarities of the subject all had reference to the modes of manumission, and the legal position of those who had ceased to be slaves. The disabilities of 'libertini,' and their duty towards their 'patroni,' fill a large chapter in Roman law. The right is infringed by killing the slave, by injuring him so that he becomes less valuable [36], or by enticing him away [37].

Same—Contractual Rights.

Certain rights arising out of contract strikingly resemble the two classes of family rights last considered. They must be mentioned in this place in so far as they are available against all the world, and are therefore capable of being violated by third parties; although the mode in which such rights are acquired and lost,
*159 and their effect as between the *contractors themselves, can be explained only at a later stage of our inquiry.

A master has a right, as against the world, to the services of his servant, and can sue not only any one by whose act he is rendered less capable of [38], or is hindered from [39], performing his duties, but also any one who entices him away from the performance of them [40]: and this principle has been declared to apply not only to domestic service, but also to any kind of employment. In a modern English case, when a celebrated singer had agreed with the manager of

36 Acts for which remedies were provided by chapters 1 and 3 of the Lex Aquilia.

37 In which case the owner had in Roman law an action 'servi corrupti.'

38 It was held in Osborne v. Gillett, L. R. 8 Ex. 88, diss. Bramwell B., that a master has no redress for an act which causes the immediate death of his servant.

39 Cf. the writ (14 Ed. IV. pl. 13) 'quare tenentes suos verberavit per quod a tenura sua recesserunt,' and others cited by Sir F. Pollock, Torts, p. 216, and his remark that 'picketing' may be a trespass at common law against the employer.

40 The seduction of a maid-servant may give a right of action to her master. Fores v. Wilson Peake, 55.

an opera to sing for him during a definite period, and for no one else, but had been persuaded by the manager of another opera to break her contract, it was held that the first manager had a right of action against the second. The claim was resisted on the ground that the employment was not of such a nature as to warrant the application of the exceptional remedy given against any one who wrongfully and maliciously entices a servant away from his master, indeed that this remedy was itself an anomalous relic of the times of serfdom. But the majority of the Court adopted the view expressed by Mr. Justice Crompton, who said:—'The nature of the injury and of the damage being the same, and the supposed right of action being in strict analogy to the ordinary case of master and servant, I see no reason for confining the case to services or engagements under contracts for services of any particular description [41].'

III. RIGHT TO REPUTATION.

A man has a right, as against the world, to his
*160 *good name; that is to say, he has a right that the respect, so far as it is well-founded, which others feel for him shall not be diminished [42]. The right is however subject to two limitations. First, there are certain trivial imputations which do not infringe it. Secondly, there are certain circumstances under which an imputation which would otherwise be wrongful is held to be justifiable. Since the right is only to respect so far as it is well-founded, it is obviously not infringed by a truthful imputation [43]. It is innate, or common to all men, and lasts till death.

The infringement may consist not only in words, spoken or written, but also in gestures or pictures. It may be direct or indirect, i. e. it may disparage the man himself, or his family and belong-

[41] Lumley v. Gye, 2 E. and B. 216, diss. Coleridge J.; Walker v. Cronin, 107 Mass. 555. The principle was affirmed by the Court of Appeals in Bowen v. Hall, L. R. 6 Q. B. Div. 333, diss. Lord Coleridge, C. J.

[42] The Twelve Tables recognized it to be a grave offence: 'si quis occentavisset, sive carmen condidisset quod infamiam faceret flagitiumve alteri.' Cic. de Rep. iv. 10.

[43] Niemand ein Recht auf einen Scheinwerth und auf Lügen haben kann.' Dresch, Naturrecht, p. 158. Cf. Dig. xlvii. 10. 18. pr.

ings. So, according to Roman law, the heirs of a deceased person would have an action for any insult to his dead body, or to his funeral procession; and a son could sue for damage done to a statue of his father set up upon his tomb [44]. 'Publication' is essential to an infringement of this right, which is therefore not violated by abuse of a man in a letter addressed to himself, or uttered by word of mouth when no one else is near. There is no infringement without a wrong intention, though it need not necessarily have been directed against the complainant [45]. 'Iniuriam potest facere nemo, nisi qui scit se iniuriam facere, etiam si nesciat cui faciat [46];' and no more than this is meant by the English doctrine of 'malice' being essential to defamation, since malice will be 'presumed' where there exists no legal justification. 'If
*161 I traduce a man,' said Mr. Justice Bayley, *'whether I know him or not, and whether I intend to do him an injury or not, the law considers it as done of malice, because it is wrongful and intentional [47].'

Degrees of Defamation.

Roman law classified acts of insult according to the rank of the person insulted, the place where, and the mode in which, the insult was given [48], but did not clearly distinguish defamation from insult given by blows. The grades of defamatory statement recognised by English law may be probably summed up as follows:—

1. Some statements are wrongful irrespectively either of the mode in which they are published, or of their consequences, e. g. the imputation of an indictable offence, or of ignorance of one's profession, or of insolvency in trade. There is an absolute right that such statements shall not be made.

2. Others, short of these in importance and tending to make a man ridiculous rather than odious, are wrongful only if put into a

[44] Dig. xlvii. 1. 4; ib. 27. Cf. an art. in 23 Am. Law Review, 578.

[45] But the repetition of a rumour may be actionable, Watkin v. Hall. L. R. 3 Q. B. 396.

[46] Dig. xlvii. 5. 2; cf. ib. 10. 18. 3.

[47] Bromage v. Prosser, 4 B. and C. 255.

[48] Compare in English law the statutes against 'scandalum magnatum.'

permanent form, i. e. only if they are written, printed, or suggested by pictures [49], when they are said to be a 'libel.'

3. Others are wrongful only if special and 'temporal' loss can be shown to have resulted from their being made. It has been for instance laid down that, without proof of special damage, it is not actionable to say of a man that 'he is a scoundrel, a blackguard, a swindler,' 'he is a disgrace to the town and unfit for decent society,' 'he has cheated his brother-in-law of £2000 [50].' Only by a recent statute [51] has it been made actionable merely to impute unchastity to a woman.

Justification.

The most important of the modes in which a defamatory
*162 *statement may be justified is by showing that it is 'privileged.' This can be done by showing either that the defendant was acting in a certain capacity, e. g. as a Judge, an advocate, or a witness; or that the circumstances are of a certain class, e. g. that a character was given to a servant, the presumption of malice is then rebutted, and the onus of proving actual malice is thrown upon the plaintiff. If, however, this can be proved [52], or if the statement was carelessly so made as to reach others than those to whom it might properly be addressed [53], the plea of 'privilege' is unavailing. Statements made in the course of judicial proceedings or to a person having an interest in their being made, fair reports of trials, legislative debates, or public meetings, fair comments on

[49] Or by exhibiting a man's waxwork effigy in propinquity to effigies of infamous characters. Mason v Toussauds, '94, 1 Q. B. 671.

[50] See Savile v. Jardine, 2 H. Bl. 532; Lumley v. Allday, 1 Cr. and Jer. 301; Hopwood v. Thorn, 8 C. B. 316. 'Defamation was also a common subject for spiritual censures, and the fact that it was so explains the rule of the common law that no action lies for words spoken unless they impute a crime, or relate to a man's profession or trade, or cause special damage.' Stephen, History of the Criminal Law in England, ii. p. 409.

[51] 54 & 55 Vict. c. 51.

[52] See Taylor v. Hawkins, 16 Q. B. 321.

[53] Williamson v. Freer, L. R. 9 C. P. 393; although it has been held that where a privileged communication, by being carelessly placed in a wrong envelope, was published in a quarter to which the privilege did not extend, the presumption of malice was rebutted. Thompson v. Dashwood, 11 Q. B. Div. 43.

public men, and fair criticisms of literary and artistic productions are privileged [54].

IV. EXERCISE OF ORDINARY RIGHTS.

The next class of rights is of a vaguer character and a wider range than those which have already been considered. Every one is entitled without molestation to perform all lawful acts and to enjoy all the privileges which attach to him as an inhabitant of the country in which he lives.

1. *Livelihood.*

The most specific right of this kind is to the unmolested pursuit of the occupation by which a man gains his livelihood. The English law upon this subject is thus explained by Lord Holt:—'He that hinders another in his trade or livelihood is liable to an action for so hindering him. . . . There are two sorts of acts for doing damage to a man's employment, for which an action lies; the one is in respect of a man's privilege, the other in respect of his property. In that of a man's franchise or privilege, where-
*163 by he hath a fair, *market or ferry; if another should use the like liberty, though out of his limits, he shall be liable to an action though by grant from the king. But therein is the difference to be taken between a liberty in which the public hath a benefit, and that wherein the public is not concerned. The other is where a violent or malicious act is done to a man's occupation, or profession, or way of getting a livelihood. There an action lies in all cases. But if a man doth him damage by using the same employment, no action will lie [55].' Not dissimilar also are statements in disparagement of title to property, giving rise to the action for 'slander to title [56].'

54 See 3 & 4 Vict. c. 9; 51 & 52 Vict. c. 64.

55 Keeble v. Hickeringill, 11 East, 575, n. The innocence of commercial competition, causing, even intentionally, loss to others, was conclusively established in the Mogul Steamship Co. v. McGregor, '92 A. C. 25. For the confused state of the law on this point in America, see 7 Harvard Law Review, p. 338.

56 See Pollock, Torts, c. viii, citing American cases in which this remedy has been applied to the protection of inchoate interests under an agreement.

2. *Highways.*

Every one has a right to the free and unobstructed use of the public highways and of navigable rivers. Not only is any interference with the use of them a public wrong, which may be redressed criminally, but each one of the community has also a private-law right not to be inconvenienced by such interference. This right has been held to be violated where a traveller found his accustomed road blocked up, and was forced to go by a longer way to his destination; where an omnibus was wilfully so driven as to hinder the progress of another omnibus; where damage was caused by a house which was so built as to intrude upon the highway, and where a vessel was injured by piles which had been driven into the bed of a river during the doing of some work and had been left there after its completion.

3. *Abuse of legal process.*

Every one has a right that the machinery of the law, which is established for his protection, shall not be maliciously set
*164 in motion to his detriment. This right is infringed by the *act known in English law as 'malicious prosecution,' the essence of which is that it is done both maliciously, i. e. from some motive other than that of bringing an offender to justice, and without reasonable and probable cause [57]. A prosecution, though it originated bona fide, may subsequently become malicious, 'if the prosecutor, having acquired positive knowledge of the innocence of the accused, perseveres malo animo in the prosecution, with the intention of procuring per nefas a conviction [58].' A malicious arrest, malicious proceedings to cause a bankruptcy, and abuse of a writ of execution, are acts of the same character [59]; as is the statutory wrong called 'maintenance,' i. e. assistance rendered in a suit by a stranger to it, without lawful cause [60]. The vexatious institution of a civil action was redressed in the earlier Roman law by the 'calumniae iudicium,' which the successful de-

[57] See Abrath v. N. E. Ry. Co., 11 App. Ca. 247.

[58] Fitz-John v. Mackinder, 9 C. B. N. S. 531.

[59] Cf. Quartz Hill Gold Mining Co. v. Eyre, 11 Q. B. Div. 674.

[60] But charity is such cause: Harris v. Brisco, 17 Q. B. D. 504. See Pollock, Torts, c. viii.

fendant might in his turn bring against the dishonest plaintiff. But by the time of Justinian almost the only restraint upon malicious or frivolous suits was the infliction of costs upon the losing party [61], and this is also the policy of the law of England [62]. Sometimes the plaintiff is compelled to give security for the costs for which he may become liable in case he should lose his action [63].

V. PROPRIETARY RIGHTS.

Many of the rights which have hitherto engaged our attention, although of the highest importance, relate to no tangible ex-
*165 ternal object. One's good name, for instance, *though invaluable, may be regarded from this point of view as an 'airy nothing [64].' The same remark will not apply to the group of rights which we are now about to consider. Proprietary rights are extensions of the power of a person over portions of the physical world. These rights, like all others, are made available by means of the acts or forbearances of the person of incidence; but such acts or forbearances are, in this case, due with especial reference to an object, or thing, from which the person of inherence derives some advantage [65].

It is not every portion of the material world which is capable of being thus appropriated. The air, the sea, and the water of rivers are for the common use of all men, but belong to none. Most things, on the other hand, are capable of subjection to the

61 Cf. Cod. iii. 1. 13.

62 It seems that there may be cases in which a combination of malice, groundlessness, and special damage will entitle a defendant to an action; see Williams J., in Cotterell v. Jones, 11 C. B. 730. According to the older law the plaintiff found pledges, who were amerced if his claim was not sustained.

63 Such security, under the name 'cautio iudicatum solvi,' is commonly exacted on the Continent from a foreign plaintiff.

64 Still less tangible would be the 'right to privacy,' or 'right to be let alone,' which, it has been suggested, ought to be so far recognised as to shield a man from the publication, without his consent, of his portrait, or of the details of his private life. See 4 Harvard Law Review, p. 195; cf. 7 ibid., p. 182. A French law of 1868 provides that 'toute publication dans un écrit périodique, relative à un fait de la vie privée, constitue une contravention punie d'une amende de 150 francs.'

65 Supra, p. *80.

human will, and in them proprietary rights may be acquired which vary in extent from absolute ownership to a narrowly limited power of user. The essence of all such rights lies not so much in the enjoyment of the thing, as in the legal power of excluding others from interfering with such enjoyment. 'If a man were alone in the world,' says Kant, 'he could properly hold or acquire nothing as his own; because between himself, as Person, and all other outward objects, as Things, there is no relation [66].' The relation is between him and other people whom he excludes from the thing. The whole class of rights may be said to be an extension of the advantage which a man has when a physical object is ac-
*166 tually within his grasp. As was well *observed by Bentham:—'The savage who has hidden the game that he has killed may hope to keep it for himself, so long as his cave is undiscovered; so long as he watches to defend it, or is stronger than his rivals; but that is all. How wretched and precarious is such a possession [67]!' In an advanced state of society a man is secured in the exclusive enjoyment of an object to an extent far beyond what he can assert for himself by his own force. His personality, as some writers would say, is extended over a wide circle of matter.

Degrees of the proprietary right.

What had up to this time been a mere fact now begins, by the aid of the law, to assume the character of a right. In its lowest form it is a right of Possession, in its highest form a right of Ownership. The former is indeed included in the latter, but may also exist apart from it; in which case its nature is so peculiar that some deny it to be a right at all. The owner of an object has, as we shall see presently, the right, unless he has expressly parted with it, to the possession of that object. But a person who is in possession, merely as a matter of fact, has also a right to continue in possession, and to be restored to possession, should he

[66] Rechtslehre, Werke, vii. p. 60. 'Mein—Dasjenige womit ich so verbunden bin, dass der Gebrauch, den ein Anderer ohne meine Einwilligung von ihm machen möchte, mich lädiren würde.' Ib. p. 44.

[67] Bentham, Principes du Code Civil, par Dumont, c. ix.

have been deprived of it; and this sometimes even as against the owner.

1. POSSESSION.

The right of the owner to possess is technically called the 'ius possidendi.' The right of the possessor to continue to possess is call the 'ius possessionis.' In order to ascertain what the right is, if any, which results from possession, it is necessary to enquire what that possession is which is recognised as having legal consequences. This, as Bentham says, 'is no vain speculation of metaphysics. Everything which is most precious to a man may depend upon this question: his property, his liberty, his honour, and even his life. Indeed in defence of my possession I may lawfully strike, wound and even kill, if necessary [68].' The ascertainment of the nature of legal possession is, in fact, indispen-
*167 sable in every depart*ment of law. It is as essential to the determination of international controversies arising out of the settlement of new countries, or to the conviction of a prisoner for larceny, as it is to the selection of the plaintiff in an action of trover or trespass. It is therefore not surprising that the literature of the topic is a very large one, and its intricacies not a few. We shall endeavour to present it in as simple a form as possible.

Its elements.

A moment's reflection must show that 'possession,' in any sense of the term, must imply, first, some actual power over the object possessed, and, secondly, some amount of will to avail oneself of that power. Neither the mere wish to catch a bird which is out of my reach, nor the mere power which I have, without the least notion of exercising it, to seize a horse which I find standing at a shop door, will suffice to put me in possession of the bird or the horse. The Romans, by whom this topic was treated with great fulness and subtlety, describe these essential elements of possession by the terms 'corpus' and 'animus' respectively.

68 Bentham, Works, v. p. 188.

i. *Corpus.*

The corporeal element presents the fewer difficulties. He who is popularly said to be in possession of an object, though he need not be in actual contact with it [69], must doubtless have it so far under his control as to be able, unless overpowered by violence, to exclude others from its enjoyment. But this requirement has long been, for legal purposes, very liberally construed. It was admitted by the Roman lawyers that possession acquired in the first instance by exclusive physical appropriation might be continued by something falling far short of this, as the possession of a mountain pasture may continue uninterrupted, although it remains unvisited during the months of winter [70]; and a possession is in many
*168 *cases recognised by them which, even at its inception, never amounted to full physical control over its object: so the purchaser of a quantity of wheat is put into possession of it by being given the keys of the warehouse in which it is stored [71], and the donee of an estate may take possession of the whole by entering upon any one portion of it, or even by having the land shown to him from some neighbouring point of view [72]. A long succession of writers has maintained that the acquisition of possession in these cases is symbolical, or fictitious; that the 'claves horrei,' for instance, are a mere symbol of the contents of the warehouse. The error of attributing this view to the Roman jurists was conclusively shown by Savigny [73], and the reason why in English law delivery of the key of bulky goods has been allowed as delivery of the possession is stated by Lord Hardwicke to be 'because it is the way of coming at the possession or to make use of the thing [74].'

[69] No one would deny that a soldier lying on the ground with his rifle within easy reach of him, is in possession of the rifle. Cf. 'Non enim corpore et actu [tactu?] necesse est apprehendere possessionem, sed etiam oculis et affectu.' Dig. xli. 2. 1. 21.

[70] Saltus hibernos aestivosque animo possidemus, quamvis certis temporibus eos relinquamus.' Dig. xli. 2. 3. 11.

[71] Dig. xviii. 1. 74; xli. 2. 1. 21.

[72] Dig. vi. 1. 77; xli. 2. 3. 1, and 18. 2.

[73] Recht des Besitzes, § 17.

[74] He adds: 'and therefore the key is not a symbol, which would not do.' Ward v. Turner, 2 Ves. Sen. 431, cited in Pollock and Wright on Possession,

On the same principle it was said that a man who has purchased goods acquires possession of them by their delivery at the house where he is residing, though no one has touched them on his behalf [75] He does not acquire possession of a treasure or other object which is buried in his land, since this is not within his exclusive control in the same way that a house is, unless he actually digs it up [76], nor of a wild animal which he has wounded, till he actually catches it [77] The distinction between the cases has been said to turn upon the greater or less probability of the power to exclude others from the object being interfered with.
*169 'Every one will acknowledge that a wounded *hare may easily get away from him, or that he may search in vain for hidden treasure so long that some one else may forestall him, but that the sanctity of his house should be interfered with by force, or that in the short space of time necessary to enter an adjoining field, a new possessor should spring up, who was not previously to be seen, are circumstances so improbable that no one would take their probability into consideration [78]' The distinction must obviously be a fine one. On the one hand, it has been held that when fish were nearly surrounded by a seine with an opening of seven fathoms between the two ends, at which point boats were stationed to frighten them from escaping, they were not reduced to possession as against a stranger who rowed in and helped himself. On the other hand, it has been decided that the custom of the American whalemen in the Arctic ocean is a good one, which gives a whale to the vessel whose iron first remains in it, provided claim be made before cutting in [79] If an object be under the control of a servant, exercised on behalf of his master, it is under the control of the master.

p. 63. On the other hand, when a locked box was delivered, the owner retaining the key, it was held that the contents of the box had not been delivered. Reddel v Dobree, 10 Sim. 244, cited ibid. p. 68.

75 Dig. xli. 2. 18; xxiii. 3. 9. 3.

76 Dig. xli. 2. 3. 3.

77 Ib. xli. 1. 5.

78 Savigny, § 19.

79 Young v Hichens, 6 Q. B. 606; Swift v Gifford, 2 Lowell, 110; cited in a very valuable article upon Possession contributed by Mr. Justice Holmes to the American Law Review, vol. xii. See also his 'Common Law,' p. 206.

ii. *Animus.*

Mere juxtaposition is not possession. 'Furiosus, et pupillus sine tutoris auctoritate, non potest incipere possidere, quia affectionem tenendi non habent, licet maxime corpore suo rem contingant, sicuti si quis dormienti aliquid in manu ponat [80].' To some possibility of physical control there must, at any rate for the commencement of possession, be superadded a will to exercise such control.

Same—Degrees of mental element.

This mental element in possession may conceivably be manifested in three degrees.

In its lowest degree of manifestation, the intent of the
*170 *holder of an object goes merely to the length of meaning to protect it against violence, without asserting any right over it on his own behalf. Such is the intent of a servant who is entrusted with the property of his master. Such possession as he may seem to have is fitly described as 'representative.'

A higher degree of intention is exhibited by those persons, other than servants, to whom objects are delivered for various purposes. A usufructuary, a borrower, the lessee of land, a carrier, all intend to dispose of the object over which they are given a control otherwise than as they may be from time to time directed, although none of them deny the title of the 'dominus proprietatis,' or of the person who has delivered the objects to them, as the case may be, to be still outstanding.

The highest degree of intention is a denial of the right of any other than the possessor himself; inasmuch as the possessor means to pay no regard to any other right than his own. This is the intention manifested, on the one hand, by a person who thinks himself, rightly or wrongly, to be the owner of the object in question, and on the other hand by a thief who well knows that he has stolen it.

[80] Dig. xli. 2. 1. 3. Such a relation between a person and an object was described by the Glossators as 'possessio asinina,' i. e. the possession which a donkey could be said to have of its saddle.

So far there is little room for varieties of opinion. The controversies begin when we proceed to enquire what, if any, differences of legal result flow from a difference between these several degrees of intention. We have to consider, in the first place, the view of the question taken by the Roman lawyers and modern civilians by whom the enquiry has till quite lately been almost exclusively conducted; and, secondly, how far similar ideas have influenced other legal systems, and more especially the common law.

Same—The theory of Roman law.

(1) There is no doubt that the classical Roman jurists recognised two degrees of control over an object, the lower of which they described by such phrases as, 'in possessione esse,' 'naturaliter
*171 possidere,' 'corporaliter tenere,' 'alieno nomine *possidere [81].'
The higher degree was alone recognised by them as 'possessio,' properly so called [82], and such possession alone was protected by the Interdicts, irrespectively of the justice or injustice of its origin [83], against any one from whom it had not been acquired 'vi clam aut precario [84].' The lower degree of possession is called by modern civilians 'Detentio' (Inhabung), while they distinguish the higher as 'Possessio,' properly so called (Besitz).

Same—Savigny.

According to what may perhaps still be called the accepted view, these two degrees were differentiated by the intention of the pos-

81 'Nec idem est possidere et alieno nomine possidere: nam possidet cuius nomine possidetur, procurator alienae possessioni praestat ministerium.' Dig. xli. 2. 18. Cf. 'Generaliter quisquis omnino nostro nomine sit in possessione, veluti procurator, hospes, amicus, nos possidere videmur.' Ib. xli. 2. 9.

82 Improperly described by the earlier commentators as 'possessio civilis,' a term which, as Savigny has shown, § 7, is used in the sources to describe possession exhibiting those additional characteristics which enable it by means of 'usucapio' to ripen into ownership.

83 'Iusta enim an iniusta adversus ceteros in hoc edicto [sc. uti possidetis] nihil refert, qualiscunque enim possessor, hoc ipso, quod possessor est, plus iuris habet quam ille qui non possidet.' Dig. xliii. 17. 2; cf. ib. xli. 2. 3. 5.

84 The remedies, such as 'actio furti,' enjoyed by persons having only 'possessio naturalis,' were conferred upon them in respect of some interest beyond that of bare possession. See Savigny, § 42.

sessor. Mere detention, or 'naturalis possessio,' exists when the intention to dispose of the object is limited by a distinct recognition of the outstanding right of another; and this equally whether the holder be a slave, a usufructuary or a bailee. 'Possessio' exists, when the holder believes himself to be the rightful owner of the object, or, having merely found it, means to keep it subject to the possibility of the owner making his appearance [85], or, having stolen it, means to keep it against all comers [86]. The intention of such a possessor has been described by modern civil-
*172 ians as *the 'animus domini [87],' but more recently as 'animus possidendi,' a term for which there is classical authority [88]. This view of the grounds of the distinction drawn by the Roman lawyers between the possession which would be and that which would not be protected by the Interdicts, is associated with the great name of Savigny, by whom it was for the first time luminously set forth. It is in general accordance with the language of the classical jurists, and is supported by the fact that the classes of persons to whom possessory remedies were denied, such as the fructuary, the lessee, the borrower and the carrier, were just those whose intent to dispose of the object possessed is limited by a distinct recognition of the outstanding right of another. Savigny's theory is, however, open to the objection that it does not account for the fact that the Interdicts were also accorded to the 'emphyteuta,' the pledge holder, the 'precario tenens' and the 'sequester,' to none of whom can the 'animus domini' be attributed. Savigny was only able to reply by saying that for practical reasons what he calls a 'derivative' ('abgeleiteter') possession was admitted in these cases [89]. This and other difficulties in the current view have recently led a writer of great vigour and

[85] Dig. xliii. 17. 2.

[86] 'Pro possessore vero possidet praedo, qui interrogatus cur possideat responsurus sit, quia possideo, . . . nec ullam causam possessionis possit dicere.' Dig. v. 3. 11–13.

[87] Apparently coined by Cuiacius, Obs. ix. 33. It was doubtless suggested by the phraseology of Theophilus, *διαφορὰ γὰρ τοῦ κρατεῖν καὶ τοῦ νέμεσθαι αὕτη· ὅτι κρατεῖν μέν ἐστι τὸ φυσικῶς κατέχειν, νέμεσθαι δὲ τὸ ψυχῇ δεσπόζοντος κατέχειν*, iii. 29. 2; cf. ii. 9. 4.

[88] Dig. xiii. 7. 37; xli. 2. 1. 20.

[89] § 9.

originality to attack Savigny's account of the Roman theory of possession as a whole.

Same—Ihering.

In a work published nearly thirty years ago [90], Professor von Ihering showed that Savigny's requirement of actual control can only be discovered in the writings of the Roman jurists by doing considerable violence to their language; and that the amount of control demanded by Roman law varied, as it reasonably should vary, according to the nature of the object in question, so that cut timber in a wood might well be held to remain in the possession of a purchaser who had left it lying where he cut it, al-
*173 though his watch, if found in *the same place, might be
treated as lost property [91]. In going on to assert that possession was protected merely as the 'actuality of ownership [92],' or as being to ownership what an outwork is to a fortress [93], Ihering appears to us to come into conflict with clear statements in the sources, to maintain an anachronism, and to be inconsistent with his own maturer views upon this point as incidentally stated in his latest work, 'Ueber den Besitzwillen [94].' It is in this work that Ihering has delivered a long-prepared attack upon the key to Savigny's position, the 'animus domini.' Shortly stated, von Ihering's thesis [95] is that the difference between Detention and Interdict-Possession has nothing to do with the will; that whoever so far exerts his will over an object as to obtain Detention of it, possesses it for all purposes, except in so far as possession is denied to him by some special rule of law. For just as Savigny was obliged to allow a fictitious 'derivative' possession in the case of the pledge-holders and others who on principle would not be possessors, so does Ihering pray in aid a variety of special rules

[90] Grund des Besitzesschutzes, 1867.

[91] Cf. 'by possession is meant possession of that character of which the thing is capable.' Ld. Advoc. v. Young, 12 App. Ca. 556.

[92] p. 45.

[93] p. 64. May it not rather be compared to an earthwork, worth defending, whether or no the fortress of ownership lies behind it?

[94] Jena, 1889, v. p. 327.

[95] Which he describes as the 'Objectivitätstheorie,' as opposed to the 'Subjectivitätstheorie' of Savigny and his predecessors.

of law to explain the denial to borrowers, lessees, and the like, of the possessory remedies to which in accordance with his theory they are prima facie entitled. The arguments of von Ihering will have to be reckoned with by any future writer upon the subject, but it would as yet be premature to proclaim the victory of his views over those of Savigny as to the true meaning of the classical jurists. It is also important to remember that a theory more nearly approaching that of Savigny than that of his critic has derived new interest from its long acceptance in the countries ruled
*174 by *modernized Roman law [96], and especially from the ineffaceable imprint which it has left upon modern codes [97].

Same—Teutonic theory.

(2) The jurists of the Teutonic races seem never to have recognised the two grades of possession which have given so much trouble to the civilians. They granted possessory remedies without scruple to persons who in Roman law could never have profited by the Interdicts. Under the Salic law the person from whose custody cattle were stolen, irrespectively of his having any further interest in them, seems to have been the only person entitled to have them restored to him; and Bracton says that, in suing for

[96] Cf. Ihering, Besitzwille, pp. 429, 457.

[97] E. g. The Prussian Landrecht, I. 7. § 1, 'Wer das physische Vermögen hat, über eine Sache mit Ausschliessung Anderer zu verfügen, der hat sie in seinem Gewahrsam und wird Inhaber derselben genannt.' § 3, 'Wer aber eine Sache, in der Absicht darüber für sich selbst zu verfügen, unmittelbar oder durch Andere, in seinen Gewahrsam nimmt, der wird Besitzer der Sache.' §§ 6, 7, distinguish between the 'imperfect' and the 'perfect' Besitzer, the latter being defined as 'welcher eine Sache, oder ein Recht, als sein eigen besitzt.'

The Austrian Civil Code, § 309, 'Wer eine Sache in seiner Macht oder Gewahrsam hat, heisst ihr Inhaber. Hat der Inhaber einer Sache den Willen, sie als die seinige zu behalten, so ist er ihr Besitzer.'

The Draft Civil Code for Germany, § 797, 'Der Besitz einer Sache wird erworben durch die Erlangung der thatsächlichen Gewalt über die Sache (Inhabung) in Verbindung mit dem Willen des Inhabers, die Sache als die seinige zu haben (Besitzwille).' The French and Italian Codes are less explicit. Code Civil, §§ 2228, 2234; Codice Civile, §§ 685, 2115. The tendency of the Codes, while retaining in terms the distinction between Detention and Possession, is to assimilate their legal results.

stolen goods, it makes no difference whether the goods belonged to the plaintiff or not, provided only they had been in his custody [98].

Same—Theory of English law.

The theory of English law at the present day is not dissimilar. Possessory rights are, it is true, denied to servants [99];
*175 *but, with this exception, the common law ignores the distinction between Detention and Possession, granting possessory remedies to all persons in occupation of land or having the custody of goods. Previously to the invention in the thirteenth century of the writ 'de eiectione firmae,' the tenant of a farm was regarded as a mere bailiff for the landlord, but by means of the writ he acquired what in the phraseology of that day could be described as a 'seisin' of his term [100], and he alone can now bring trespass for interference with his possession [101]. A similar right

[98] 'Dum tamen de custodia sua.' Bract. fol. 151. Cited by Mr. Justice Holmes, Am. Law Rev. u. s.

[99] See Dicey, Parties, pp. 335, 358; Pollock and Wright, Possession, p. 59. Mr. Justice Holmes, Common Law, p. 227, thinks the rule explicable only as a survival from the times when a servant was a slave, since 'the servant has as much the intent to exclude the world at large as the borrower.' But see Pollock and Wright, u. s. The non-attribution of possession to servants is well established in criminal law, e. g. if goods are stolen from a servant to whom they have been entrusted by his master they are alleged in the indictment to be 'the property,' i. e. in the possession, of his master, though some doubts upon this point led to the Statute 21 Hen. VIII. c. 7. (A new offence of embezzlement was created by 39 G. III. c. 85, to meet the case of misappropriation by a servant of goods delivered to him for his master, but of which the latter had not yet taken possession); but there are cases in private law which can with difficulty be reconciled with the rule as now stated, and suggest the distinction, said now to be obsolete, once drawn between servants at home and servants sent on distant errands. See Y. B., 21 H. VII. 14, pl. 21, cited in Holmes, u. s., p. 226. Thus the master of a fly-boat hired at weekly wages by a canal company was allowed to bring trespass for the cutting of a tow-rope, the property of the company. Moore v. Robinson, 2 B. and Ad. 817. Persons, such as guests at an Inn, who have there the use of plate and other objects, as bare licencees without bailment, have no possession. Holmes, u. s., p. 226.

[100] Bracton, fol. 220. See Digby, History of the Law of Real Property, p. 175; Maitland, on the seisin of chattels, 1 L. Q. R. p. 333.

[101] Dicey, Parties, p. 334.

in the case of bailees of goods seems to have a much older pedigree.[102] 'In all these instances,' says Blackstone, 'there is a special qualified property transferred from the bailor to the bailee, together with the possession. And on account of this qualified property of the bailee, he may, . . . maintain an action against such as injure or take away these chattels. The tailor, the carrier, the innkeeper, the agisting farmer, the pawnbroker, the distreinor,
*176 and the general bailee, *may all of them vindicate in their own right this their possessory interest[103].'

Same— Wrongful possession.

Alike in Roman and in the common law, a mere finder, or even a wrongful taker, has a possession which will be protected against a stranger; nor will such stranger be allowed to allege a superior ius tertii, unless he can show that he was acting under the authority of the person having such a right[104].

Same—Possessio plurium.

After being a topic of controversy between the Proculian and Sabinian schools, it was finally determined in Roman law that only one person can possess the same object at the same time, 'non magis enim eadem possessio apud duos esse potest, quam ut tu stare videaris in eo loco in quo ego sto, vel in quo loco ego sedeo tu sedere videaris[105].'

[102] Holmes, Common Law, p. 166, citing Laband, Vermögensrechtliche Klagen, § 16, and Heusler, Gewere, 487, 492.

[103] 2 Comm. 453. He continues, 'For being responsible to the bailor, or if the goods are lost or damaged by his wilful default or gross negligence, or if he do not deliver up the chattels on lawful demand, it is therefore reasonable that he should have a right of action against all other persons who may have purloined or injured them; that he may always be ready to answer the call of the bailor.' This reasoning, though found also in Beaumanoir, xxx. 1, and in Y. B. 11 H. IV., seems to be erroneous. See Holmes, Common Law, pp. 167, 170. It is probably derived from a misunderstanding of the remedies given in Roman law to certain bailees for the protection of interests other than those resulting from bare possession. Cf. Inst. iv. 1. 14 and 17; Dig. xlvii. 2. 46.

[104] Dig. xliii. 17. 2. Armory v. Delamirie, 1 Sm. L. C. 301; Buckley v. Gross, 32 L. J. Q. B. 131; Dicey, Parties, pp. 334, 354, 356; Pollock and Wright, pp. 49, 148.

[105] Dig. xli. 2. 3. 5; cf. xliii. 26. 15. 4. The possession by several of dif-

The strictness of this rule seems not to have been followed in the indigenous law of Germany [106], and was departed from at an early date in the law of England. When the tenant farmer acquired the writ of ejectment, his lord none the less retained his possessory remedy by Assize of novel disseisin [107]; and in the time of
*177 *Edward III, we find that bailors had gained the right to bring trespass concurrently with their bailees against a third party [108]. In modern times, at any rate, this right is restricted, as would seem more in accordance with principle, to the case of simple bailments, i. e. those in which the bailor is at liberty to resume possession at any moment [109]. When during the bailment the right of the bailee is good even against the bailor, the former can alone sue for any interference with his possession [110].

Reasons for protecting possession.

More than one motive may have induced the law to give protection to possession. The predominant motive was probably a regard for the preservation of the peace. 'The ground of this protection,' says Savigny, 'and of this condition similar to a right, has to be ascertained. Now this ground lies in the connection between the above condition of fact and the party possessing, the inviolability of whose person extends to those sorts of disturbance by which the person

ferent parts or shares of a thing is a different question. Savigny, Besitz, § 11; Puchta, Inst. ii. p. 564.

106 See authorities cited by Prof. Maitland, 1 L. Q. R. p. 344.

107 Poterit enim quilibet illorum sine praeiudicio alterius in seisina esse eiusdem tenementi, unus ut de termino, et alius ut de feudo vel libero tenemento.' Bracton, fol. 220. See Maitland, 1 L. Q. R. p. 341. But note that the landlord cannot bring trespass or ejectment during the continuance of the term. Dicey, Parties, pp. 337, 489.

108 Y. B. 48 Ed. III. 20, pl. 8, 22 Ed. IV. 5, pl. 16, cited in Holmes, Common Law, p. 170. He thinks this an anomaly, p. 175. The reason usually given for it is that 'a right of immediate possession without possession is sufficient.' Cf. Smith v. Milles, 1 T. R. 480. So the purchaser of goods may bring trespass before delivery, Dicey, p. 348; aliter as to a purchaser of land before entry, Pollock and Wright, p. 28.

109 Nicholls v. Bastard, 2 C. M. and R., 659; Dicey, Parties, p. 345.

110 Gordon v. Harper, 7 T. R. 9; 'It cannot be that two men can be entitled at the same time to maintain an action of trover for the same goods.' Lord v. Price, L. R. 9 Ex. 54.

might at the same time be interfered with. The case occurs when the violence offered to the person disturbs or puts an end to possession. An independent right is not, in this case, violated, but some change is effected in the condition of the person to his prejudice; and if the injury, which consists in the violence against the person, is to be wholly effaced in all its consequences, this can only be effected by the restoration or protection of the status quo, to
*178 which the violence extended *itself [111].' The same view is also to be found, where anything so abstract would scarcely be expected, in a volume of Meeson and Welsby's Reports. 'These rights of action,' said the Court of Exchequer Chamber, 'are given in respect of the immediate and present violation of possession, independently of rights of property. They are an extension of that protection which the law throws around the person [112].'

The suggestion that possession was protected because possessors are in most cases rightful owners [113], is hardly in accordance with legal history.

Place of possession in the corpus iuris.

As to the place which the doctrine of possession should occupy in a body of law, Savigny is of opinion that, since it only comes in question as a condition to the granting of Interdicts, it belongs to the department of 'obligationes ex delicto.' By what has preceded, it will have sufficiently appeared that we agree rather with those who, like Alciatus, Halm, and Gans, class possession among the 'iura in re.'

Orbit.

The orbit of the right may be inferred from a list of the acts which are recognised as infringing it. Among the acts so recognised in English law are those long known as 'trespass' and 'conversion.' A 'trespass to goods' would consist in their removal or injury, but might be justified, as done in the exercise of a rightful 'distress,' or in self-

111 Savigny, § 6, Perry's Translation (1843).

112 Rogers v. Spence, 13 M. & W. 581 (1844).

113 Ihering, Ueber den Grund des Besitzesschutzes. ed. 2, p. 45. At p. 4, he gives an exhaustive classification of the theories on this point. According to his own opinion, Possession is 'eine dem Eigenthümer zugedachte Beweiserleichterung, die aber nothwendigerweise auch dem Nichteigenthümer zu Gute kommt,' p. 45.

defence; while goods would be said to be 'converted' by any one who wrongfully assumed to act as their owner.

Commencement.

The 'ius possessionis' comes into existence on the occurrence of such a combination of control and intention as is demanded by a given system of law.

*179 *The corporeal and mental elements of the act of acquisition may be separated, as where the former is exercised by an agent and the latter by his principal; or both may be exercised by an agent, who has general authority from, or whose acts are subsequently ratified by, his principal [114].

Termination.

The right of possession may be of course extinguished by an express abandonment of the object, but the same effect may be produced by tacit relaxation of corporeal control or of intention. The cases in which this occurs are defined by different rules in different systems of law [115].

Quasi-possession.

The doctrine of possession has been extended, under the name of 'quasi-possession,' or of 'possessio iuris,' to the control which may be exercised over advantages, short of ownership, which may be derived from objects. A right of way, an advowson or perpetual right of appointment to a benefice, and similar rights, the nature of which will shortly have to be explained, are susceptible of a quasi-possession, the rules for which are analogous to those which govern possession properly so called.

2. OWNERSHIP.

It is a great advance in civilization when law throws around the mere fact of possession that protection which the possessor could

[114] Savigny, § 26.

[115] Thus Roman law, on grounds of policy, declined to treat the possession of the absentee owner of a farm as ousted by wrongful occupation by an intruder. It was a legal fiction that the possessor in such a case, though dispossessed in point of fact, was not to be regarded as dispossessed till he had received notice of what had occurred. Dig. xli. 2. 46; ib. 3. 7 and 8; Savigny, Besitz, § 33.

previously have won for it only by his own right hand. It is a still further advance when law gives to a man that far ampler measure of right over an object, quite irrespectively of his having any actual, or even constructive, control over it, which is known as 'Ownership [116].'

Definitions.

The higher is no doubt a development of the lower right.
*180 *'Dominium rerum ex naturali possessione coepisse Nerva filius ait [117].' It is usually defined as a plenary control over an object. 'Das Eigenthum ist eine totale Herrschaft über eine Sache [118].' 'La propriété est le pouvoir juridique plein et entier d'une personne sur une chose corporelle'; 'Le pouvoir de droit d'une personne sur une chose d'après tous les buts rationnels d'utilité possible, inhérents à sa nature [119].'

How limited.

The right of ownership is, however, unlimited only in comparison with other rights over objects. In accordance with the maxim 'sic utere tuo ut alienum non laedas,' it must always be enjoyed in such a way as not to interfere with the rights of others, and is therefore defined in the French Code as 'le droit de jouir et disposer des choses de la manière la plus absolue, pourvu qu'on n'en fasse pas un usage prohibé par les lois ou par les règlements [120].' It may also, as we shall see hereafter, continue to subsist although stripped of almost every attribute which makes it valuable, in which condition it is described in Roman law as 'nuda proprietas.' A really satisfactory definition of a right thus wide, yet necessarily limited in several re-

[116] So that Ulpian goes so far as to say: 'Nihil commune habet possessio cum proprietate.' Dig. xli. 2. 12. 1.

[117] Dig. 41. 2. 1. 1. Cf. Cic. De Off. i. 7.

[118] Puchta, Inst. ii. p. 581.

[119] Ahrens, Droit Naturel, ii. p. 143; cf. 'Dominus incipit plenam habere in re potestatem.' Inst. ii. 4. 4.

[120] Art. 544. According to the draft civil code for Germany, § 848, 'Der Eigenthümer einer Sache hat das Recht, mit Ausschliessung Anderer, nach Willkür mit der Sache zu verfahren und über dieselbe zu verfügen, soweit nicht Beschränkungen dieses Rechtes durch Gesetz oder durch Rechte Dritter begründet sind.'

spects and conceivably limited in many more, has perhaps never been suggested. It is difficult to do more than to describe it, with Austin, as a right 'over a determinate thing, indefinite in point of user, unrestricted in point of disposition, and unlimited in point of duration [121].'

Component rights.

Various attempts have been made to enumerate the attributes or powers of an owner. He is said to have rights, 'utendi,' 'fruendi,' 'abutendi,' 'fructus percipiendi,' 'possidendi,' 'alienandi,' and
*181 'vindicandi.' But what has to be said with *reference to the orbit, or contents, of the right of ownership may be conveniently arranged under the three heads of possession, enjoyment, and disposition.

Same—Possession.

1. Of the right to possess, little more need be said than that it includes the 'ius vindicandi,' and that it is inherent in ownership unless expressly severed from it, as is the case when the owner has let, lent, or mortgaged his property.

Same—Enjoyment.

2. The right of enjoyment implies rights of user, and of acquiring the fruits or increase of the thing, as timber, the young of cattle, or soil added to an estate by alluvion. The right is limited only by the rights of the State or of other individuals [122].

The State may of course, as is sometimes said by virtue of its 'dominium eminens,' take such portions of the produce of property, or even of property itself, as it may think fit; or it may authorize undertakings in the neighbourhood, whereby the value of the property may be diminished without compensation [123]. The State can

[121] Jurisprudence, ii. p. 477; cf. iii. p. 2.

[122] The right of freely using one's own land although to the detriment of one's neighbours, is very amply recognised by English law (see Chasemore v. Richards, 7 H. L. C. 349); but by Roman law, apparently, only 'si non animo vicino nocendi, sed suum agrum meliorem faciendi' (D. xxxix. 3. 1), cf. Pollock, Torts, p. 143; and so Scotch law prohibits what is done in aemulationem vicini. Ersk. Inst. ii. 1. 2.

[123] E. g. by vibration caused by trains passing over a railway made in pur-

also prohibit any particular use of the property, e. g. the growth of tobacco upon land in England and Ireland [124], or the carrying on of noxious trades in towns. The rights of the owner may also be limited by those of his co-owners, if the property is held jointly, or by those of strangers. The owner of land, for instance, may be restrained in the interest of neighbouring owners from dealing with it entirely at his pleasure; and this either in consequence
*182 *of some exceptional advantage, such as a right of way, which may have been conferred upon another; or in consequence of the ordinary, or, as it is sometimes called, 'natural' right of his neighbours not to have their land deprived of its accustomed support from the land adjacent, to receive the water of a stream, or the like.

Same—Disposition.

3. The right of disposition carries with it the right of alteration or destruction, and also the right of alienation. Some objects are of course practically indestructible. The alienation may either be total, when the right itself, or partial, when a fraction of it only, is transferred. Alienation for certain purposes is sometimes forbidden, e. g. in fraud of creditors, or in mortmain.

Objects of ownership.

Ownership is exercised, in its primary and fullest sense, over physical objects only. It is also exercised, in a secondary and conventional sense, over certain collections of rights which it is convenient to treat upon the analogy of physical objects. In the primary sense of the term, a man may be owner of a house, in the secondary sense he may be owner of a patent for an invention. The object owned is in either case described as 'property,' which is defined by Mirabeau as signifying 'un avantage conféré par les conventions sociales [125].' The terms 'ownership' and 'property' are sometimes also used in a third, and still looser sense. The sum-total

suance of an Act of Parliament, Hammersmith Railway Company v. Brand, L. R. 4 H. L. 171.

124 By 12 Car. II. c. 34. On the principle that when private property is affected with a public interest it ceases to be iuris privati, see Lord Holt, De portibus maris, 1 Harg. Law Tracts; and on the recent application of this principle in the grain 'elevator' cases, see Munn v. Illinois, 4 Otto, 113.

125 Hist. Parlementaire de la Révolution Française, t. ix. p. 290.

of a man's fortune, including not only the objects of which he is owner, but also the value of any claims which he may have against other persons, after deducting the amount of any claims which might be made good against himself, is described as his 'property,' and he is said to 'own' it [126].

*183 *It will be desirable to discuss each of these kinds of 'property' separately.

1. *Tangible objects.*

It is not every physical object that will answer the description of property, as being 'un bien matériel sujet au pouvoir immédiat d'une personne [127].' Some things are in their nature incapable of appropriation. Air and, in most cases, water [128] are for the free use of all mankind. Objects which are capable of becoming property are divisible upon various principles, as has been already explained [129].

Same—Orbit.

The right of the owner of a physical object is of course modified by the character of the object. His right is in general that the object shall neither be taken away from him, nor impaired in value, nor shall his title to it be weakened. Among the acts by which his right is infringed are those known to English law as conversion, detinue, trespass, slander of title, and nuisance.

126 The Roman use of the term 'res' was equally ambiguous. Sometimes it is the thing itself (res corporalis), sometimes a right over a thing, or even to the performance of an act (res incorporalis). Cf. supra, p. *90. With the use of the term, as covering a mere right to performance, cf. the Code Civil (Art. 529); 'sont meubles par la détermination de la loi, les obligations et actions qui ont pour objet des sommes exigibles,' &c.; and the definition of 'Property' in 44 & 45 Vict. c. 41, § 1, and in 45 & 46 Vict. c. 39, § 2 (the Conveyancing Acts, 1881, 1882), as including 'any debt, and any thing in action, and any other right or interest.' Cf. also the Bankruptcy Act, 1883, 46 & 47 Vict. c. 52. § 168 (1). On the question whether shares in a Company are 'things in action,' under the Bankruptcy Act, see Colonial Bank v. Whinney, 11 App. Ca. 426. A power of appointment is not property, ex parte Gilchrist, 17 Q. B. D. 167 and 521.

127 Ahrens, Cours, ii. p. 117.

128 But see Ormerod v. Todmorden Mill Co., 11 Q. B. Div. 155.

129 Supra, p. *91.

2. *Intangible property.*

We have already mentioned that the idea of ownership has been so far extended as to make it applicable to certain closely coherent masses of rights; which are thus, by a legal fiction, treated, for certain purposes, as if they were tangible objects [130].

*184 **Same—Patents, Copy-right, and Trade-marks.*

In modern times the inventor of a new process obtains from the State, by way of recompense for the benefit he has conferred upon society, and in order to encourage others to follow his example, not only an exclusive privilege of using the new process for a fixed term of years, but also the right of letting or selling his privilege to another. Such an indulgence is called a patent-right, and a very similar favour, known as copy-right, is granted to the authors of books. and to painters, engravers, and sculptors, in the productions of their genius [131]. It has been a somewhat vexed question whether a 'trade-mark' is to be added to the list of intangible objects of ownership. It was at any rate so treated in a series of judgments by Lord Westbury, which, it seems, are still good law. He says, for instance, 'Imposition on the public is indeed necessary for the plaintiff's title, but in this way only, that it is the test of the invasion by the defendant of the plaintiff's right of property [132].' It was also so described in the 'Trade Marks Registration Act,' 1875 [133], as it was in the French law of 1857 relating to 'Marques de fabrique et de

[130] 'The notion that nothing is property which cannot be ear-marked and recovered in detinue or trover, may be true in an early stage of society, when property is in its simple form, and the remedies for violation of it are also simple, but it is not true in a more civilised state, when the relations of life and the interests arising therefrom are complicated.' Erle J., in Jefferys v. Boosey, 4 H. L. Ca. 815. But see contra Pollock C. B. in the same case, and Windscheid, Pand. § 168.

[131] On the copyright retained in a letter by the writer of it, see Pope v. Curll, 2 Atk. 342; Oliver v. Oliver, 11 C. B. N. S. 139. A painter's copyright in his pictures, under 25 & 26 Vict. c. 68, is not infringed by the exhibition of tableaux vivants reproducing their effect, Hanfstaengl v. Empire Co., '94, 2 Ch. 1; nor by the publication of sketches of such tableaux, Hanfstaengl v. Newnes, '94, 3 Ch. 109.

[132] Hall v. Barrows, 33 L. J. Ch. 204. Cf. Oakley v. Dalton, 35 Ch. D.

[133] ss. 3, 4, 5.

commerce[134].' The extension of the idea of ownership to these three rights is of comparatively recent date. Patent-right in England is older than the Statute of Monopolies, 21 Iac. I. c. 3, and copy-
*185 right is obscurely trace*able previously to the Act of 8 Anne, c. 19[135], but trade-marks were first protected in the present century. Violations of this sort of property are described in English law as 'infringements.'

Same—Franchises.

With such intangible property should probably also be classified those royal privileges subsisting in the hands of a subject which are known in English law as 'franchises,' such as the right to have a fair or market, a forest, free-warren or free-fishery.

The once well-known privileges described in German law as 'Bannrechte,' e. g. of having all the corn of the neighbourhood brought to one's mill to be ground, 'Mühlenzwang,' all the bread brought to one's oven to be baked, 'Backofenzwang,' and the like, belong to the same category.

134 This view is further countenanced by § 2 of the Trade Marks Registration Act, 1875, which provides that a Mark can be assigned only together with the goodwill of the business concerned. The 'Patents, Designs and Trademarks Act, 1883,' 46 & 47 Vict. § 57, which has superseded the earlier Statutes upon these subjects, speaks of the 'copy-right' in a trade-mark (§ 76), and of the 'proprietor of the patent, copy-right in the design, or trade-mark' (§ 87). It may be noted that, under this Act, a patent right will be good as against the crown (§ 26). On such right as a trader may have to an exclusive use of his name, see Burgess v. Burgess, 3 D. M. G. 896.

135 On the curious question of a copyright at common law, see the case of Jefferys v. Boosey, u. s., which decides, overruling Donaldson v. Beckett, 2 Bro. P. C. 129, against a considerable weight of judicial opinion, unfavourably to the existence of any such right, at any rate since the Statute of Anne. Cf. the Report of the Royal Commission on Copyright of 1878, embodying a draft Digest of the existing law upon the subject, by Sir J. F. Stephen. On the question of a common law copyright in an orally delivered lecture, see Abernethy v. Hutchinson, 1 Hall & Tw. 28; Nichols v. Pitman, 26 Ch. D. 374; and Sime v. Caird, 12 App. Ca. 326, in which the House of Lords, on appeal from the Court of Session, held that the delivery of a University lecture does not divest the author of his copyright in it. Cf. Dalloz, t. xl. P. 2. p. 187.

Same—Bonorum universitates.

3. A still bolder fiction than those just considered was familiar to the Romans. All that a given individual can be said to be worth, reckoning together not only all his rights of ownership, but also the value of any claims which he may have against others ('bona activa'), but deducting the amount of any claims which others may have against him ('bona passiva'), is sometimes said to be his 'property,' and he is said to be the 'owner' of the whole complex mass of rights 'in rem' and 'in personam,' less deductions [136].

*186 *Such a totality of property has been described by the phrases 'bona,' 'patrimonie,' 'avoir,' 'estate,' 'assets,' 'Vermögen.' The last-mentioned term has been defined as 'alles was uns zusteht oder gehört [137];' also as 'der Inbegriff der Rechte einer Person, die einen Sachwerth haben, oder deren Werth sich in Geld anschlagen lässt [138].' Such a mass of property, should its subject die, becomes a 'hereditas.'

Commencement of the right.

Although some few modes of acquisition, or 'titles,' are applicable to all three classes of property, each class has also a set of modes of acquisition appropriate to itself. It may be convenient to mention the special modes first, those, namely, which are respectively applicable to the acquisition of physical objects, of groups of rights treated as if they were physical objects, and of complex masses of rights and duties.

[136] 'La notion de la propriété est alors identifiée avec celle de l'avoir, quoiqu'il faille toujours distinguer les biens matériels qui sont immédiatement dans notre pouvoir de ceux par rapport auxquels nous avons des droits à faire valoir.' Ahrens, ii. 121. 'Bona intelliguntur cuiusque quae deducto aere alieno supersunt.' Dig. l. 39. 1. 'Bonorum appellatio, sicut hereditatis, universitatem quandam ac ius successionis et non singulas res demonstrat.' Dig. l. 16. 208. 'Bona autem hic, ut plerumque solemus dicere, itâ accipienda sunt, universitatis cuiusque successionem, qua succeditur in ius demortui, suscipiturque eius rei commodum et incommodum: nam sive solvendo sunt bona, sive non sunt, sive damnum habent, sive lucrum, sive in corporibus sunt sive in actionibus, in hoc loco proprie bona appellabuntur.' Dig. xxxvii. 1. 3 pr.; cf. l. 16. 49.

[137] Röder, ii. p. 239.

[138] Puchta, ii. p. 302; cf. 578.

Same—Over physical objects.

Physical objects, 'res corporales,' 'res quae tangi possunt,' are capable of being acquired in a variety of ways, which are either 'original' or 'derivative.'

Same—Original acquisition.

1. Original acquisition takes place either with or without an act of possession.

Same—With possession.

1. With such an act, the right is gained by:

(a) 'Occupatio'; the taking of what previously belonged to no one: 'quod enim nullius est, id ratione naturali occupanti conceditur [139].' Among 'res nullius' are wild animals; derelicts, which on abandonment cease to belong to their former owners; the property of enemies; and a 'thesaurus,' i. e. 'vetus quaedam depositio pe-
*187 cuniae, cuius non exstat *memoria, ut iam dominum non habeat [140].' It must be remembered that the right of the finder of such objects is by no means recognised as unqualified. Most systems of law hold that property taken from an enemy vests primarily in the nation, 'bello parta cedunt reipublicae,' a rule which is the foundation of the law of booty and prize; and the right to capture animals 'ferae naturae,' or to appropriate a treasure-trove, is usually qualified by the rights of landowners and of the State itself.

(b) 'Specificatio'; i. e. the working up of materials belonging to another into a new product. There is room for much difference of opinion as to the cases in which ownership may thus be acquired by manufacture, and a long controversy was carried on between the jurists of the Proculian and Sabinian schools upon the subject.

(c) 'Fructuum perceptio,' i. e. the rightful taking of the produce of property by a person who is not owner of the property.

(d) Lawful possession, continued for such periods as may be recognised by law as sufficient for the purpose. So, in the older Roman law, the possession of an object which had been acquired bona fide and 'ex iusta causa' gave in one or two years, according as the object was a moveable or an immoveable, full ownership of it, by the title

139 Dig. li. 1. 3. pr.

140 Dig. li. 31. 1.

called 'usucapio.' And so English law, which does not favour this title, practically transmutes long possession of real property into ownership, by bringing to an end the right of the owner; for by the Statute 3 & 4 W. IV. c. 27. s. 34, it is enacted that, 'at the determination of the period limited by this Act, to any person for making an entry or distress, or bringing any writ of quare impedit or other action or suit [141], the right and title of such person to the land, rent or advowson, for the recovery whereof such entry, distress,
*188 action or suit re*spectively might have been made or brought within such period, shall be extinguished.'

This mode of acquisition, sometimes called 'acquisitive Prescription,' must be carefully distinguished from 'extinctive Prescription,' or the 'Limitation of actions,' which, as will presently appear, causes not a transfer of a right, but merely the loss of a remedy.

Same— Without possession.

2. The right is obtained without an act of possession by:

(a) 'Accession,' when the owner of the principal object becomes also owner of its accessory [142].

Immoveables may accede, or adhere, to immoveables, as is the case when soil is carried from one bank of a river to another, 'alluvio,' 'avulsio'; or an island is formed, 'insula nata,' and is divided between the riparian proprietors, or assigned to him to whose land it is nearest; or a river leaves its bed, 'alveus derelictus,' which is then shared by the owners of the banks.

Moveables may accede to immoveables. So beams and other objects fastened into a house become part of it by 'inaedificatio,' except so far as they come within the indulgence granted by the law of 'fixtures'; and trees and crops become inseparable from the soil in which they are planted by 'satio' or 'plantatio'; in pursuance of the maxim 'quidquid plantatur solo cedit.'

Moveables may accede to moveables, as an embroidery to a garment. On the other hand, 'proprietas totius navis carinae causam sequitur [143].' The rule and the exceptions to it were dis-

[141] I. e. as a rule twenty years, which period has been reduced by 37 & 38 Vict. c. 57 to twelve years.

[142] It may be worth while to observe that 'accessio' in Latin is not the name of a title, but signifies the accessory thing. Cf. Dig. xxxiv. 2. 19. 13.

[143] Dig. vi. 1. 61.

cussed by the Romans under the heads of 'scriptura,' 'pictura,' 'partus ancillae,' 'adiunctio.'

(b) 'Confusio' and 'commixtio,' which usually produce joint-ownership.

Same—Derivative acquisition.

2. Derivative acquisition may take place inter vivos or
*189 *upon death. In the former case, it is often described as 'alienation,' or 'conveyance,' and implies in Roman law the concurrence both of the alienor and the alienee. 'In omnibus rebus quae dominium transferunt, concurrat oportet affectus ex utraque parte contrahentium [144].' Such concurrence is a 'contract,' in the wider sense of that term, in which it has been defined as 'the union of several persons in a coincident expression of will by which their legal relations are determined [145].' Derivative acquisition of single objects upon death takes place by legacy or by 'donatio mortis causa [146].'

Alienation inter vivos required, according to Roman law, not only the agreement of the parties, but also a delivery of possession, 'traditio.' 'Traditionibus et usucapionibus dominia rerum, non nudis pactis transferuntur.' On the other hand, a mere delivery, without a valid accompanying agreement, was not enough. 'Nunquam nuda traditio transfert dominium, sed ita si venditio, aut aliqua iusta causa, praecesserit, propter quam traditio sequeretur [147].' So in English law, the gift of a chattel, unless it be by deed, must be accompanied by delivery of possession, and 'livery of seisin' was essential to pass a freehold estate in land: and in the older French law, 'pour qu'une obligation transmît la propriété, elle devait être suivie de la tradition. Celui qui achetait une maison, par exemple, n'en devenait propriétaire que du moment où la maison lui était livrée; si elle était livrée à une autre personne c'était cette personne qui l'acquérait. L'obligation

144 Dig. xliv. 7. 55. As to English law, v. infra, chapter xii.

145 Savigny, Obligationenrecht, ii. p. 7. Kant defines contract, in the sense of conveyance, as 'Der Act der vereinigten Willkühr zweier Personem, wodurch überhaupt das Seine des Einen auf den Anderen übergeht.' Rechtslehre, Werke, vii. p. 71.

146 Cod. 2. 3. 30.

147 Dig. xli. 1. 41.

n'était alors qu'un titre pour se faire donner la propriété; le moyen d'acquérir cette propriété était la tradition [148].'

As a general rule, however, in English, and, it seems, also
*190 *in modern French law [149], the alienation of specific property is effected as soon as the alienatory contract is complete. A purchaser who chooses an article in a shop becomes the owner of it from the moment that he has agreed with the shopkeeper upon the price [150]. Special formalities are, however, superadded to the consent of the parties in particular cases. Thus, according to the law of England, a grant of land must be under seal, and the assignment of a ship must be by bill of sale. On the continent the presence of a notary public is often needed to give validity to the act, or it has to be registered in a public office.

Ulpian gives a list of the modes of acquiring physical objects, some of which are peculiar to Roman law. 'Singularum rerum dominia,' he says, 'nobis adquiruntur mancipatione, traditione, usucapione, in iure cessione, adiudicatione, lege [151].'

Same—Intangible property.

Such property as may be had in inventions and in works of art is recognised by law only after compliance with certain formalities, which are intended both to bring to a test the merit of the inventor or artist, and at the same time to define the right for which protection is claimed. The inventor has in England to present a petition to the Crown and lodge a description of the alleged invention at a public office. After a certain time has elapsed and opportunity has been given for objections to be made, letters patent are issued, granting to the petitioner the exclusive right of using his invention for fourteen years, a term which is sometimes extended. The patentee may by a registered deed assign his right, or may grant licences for the manufacture of the article to which it relates.

148 Code Civil, expliqué par Rogron, art. 711.

149 Code Civil, 1583, Codice Civile, 1448. Scots Law was modified in the same direction by 19 & 20 Vict. c. 60, and is now assimilated to English law by the Sale of Goods Act, 1893, ss. 17, 18.

150 Gilmour v. Supple, 11 Moo. P. C. 566.

151 Reg. xix. 2; cf. Varro, de R. R. ii. 10.

What is described as 'literary and artistic property' is in
*191 *general acquired by producing and making public a work of literature or art, although till a copy of the work has been deposited or registered in a public office, the law in most cases gives it no protection. A copy-right is allowed not only in books, paintings, and sculpture, but also for casts, engravings, drawings, photographs, and designs for articles, whether of ornament or utility. And the right may be assigned.

A trade-mark is acquired by use followed by registration, and is capable of assignment. The law of many countries will recognise foreign patents, copy-rights and trade-marks, and treaties are made to arrange the conditions under which this favour will be granted [152]. A franchise can be acquired only by royal grant, actual or presumed, and may be assigned by deed.

Same—Complex masses of rights and duties.

Those complex masses of rights and duties which are sometimes treated as property, grow up gradually round a man as a result of the various circumstances of his life. They are transferred from him, so far as they are capable of transfer, by some form of universal succession [153].

Dispositive facts of general application.

Besides the 'dispositive facts' which are thus proper to each species of property, there are others of quite general application. These are either 'voluntary,' or 'involuntary,' i. e. they are the result of the act of at least one of the parties concerned, such as purchase, or gift, or testament, or are the result of causes external to the parties, such as the decision of a Court, or the operation of a rule of law upon a given set of circumstances, such as bankruptcy, marriage, or proximity of relationship. It is hard-
*192 ly necessary to observe *how large a space is occupied in every system of law by the definition of the right to succeed

[152] A Convention for an 'International Union for the protection of Industrial Property' was signed at Paris, on behalf of a number of Powers, 20 March, 1883. Great Britain acceded to it 17 March 1884, and is also a party to a Convention for an 'International Union for the protection of Literary and Artistic Works,' signed at Berne, 6 September, 1886.

[153] Supra, p. *142.

to property enjoyed by the various classes of heirs and next of kin, and how comparatively modern is the right to defeat the expectations of such persons by leaving the property away from them by will.

Same—Divestitive facts.

As something has been said in a former chapter of 'divestitive facts' generally [154], it may be sufficient to add here that property of all kinds is lost not only by the death of its owner, but also by his ceasing to enjoy legal recognition as a person, a consequence which, under some systems, follows from 'entering into religion,' from conviction of serious crime, from outlawry, and generally from causes which produce forfeiture [155]. It may also be lost not only by the various forms of alienation, but also by abandonment. It is of course lost by the destruction of the object owned.

The modes of acquiring and losing ownership vary, it need not be said, with the progress of civilisation, the tendency of which is generally towards their simplification. The attention of the student of Jurisprudence should be mainly directed to those modes which he finds to be more 'constant' than the rest, most of which were recognised by the Romans as being institutes of the 'ius gentium [156].'

Modes of ownership.

Ownership may be exclusive, or enjoyed in common with others, 'condominium.' In the latter case, either each of
*193 *the co-owners may have a quantitative share in the property, as is the case with English tenants-in-common, or no

[154] Cf. supra, p. *140.

[155] Cf. supra, p. *84 n.

[156] It may perhaps be worth while to compare with what has been said in the text the classification of the titles to property (*things*) which was proposed by Bentham. He reduces them to the following heads:—1. Actual possession; 2. Ancient possession in good faith; 3. Possession of the contents and produce of land; 4. Possession of what land supports and of what it receives; 5 Possession of adjacent lands; 6. Amelioration of one's own property; 7. Possession in good faith with amelioration of another's property; 8. Exploration of mines in the land of another; 9. Liberty of fishing in great waters, 10. Liberty of hunting upon unappropriated grounds; 11. Consent; 12. Succession; 13. Testament. Traités, par Dumont, t. i. p. 276.

quantitative shares may be recognised, as in the Indian village communities.

In some systems a distinction is drawn between the strictly legal, and the beneficial, ownership of one and the same object, a distinction expressed in English law by the terms 'legal' and 'equitable,' and in Roman law by 'Quiritarian' and 'Bonitarian' property.

Same—Iura in re aliena.

One or more of the subordinate elements of ownership, such as a right of possession, or user, may be granted out while the residuary right of ownership, called by the Romans 'nuda proprietas,' remains unimpaired. The elements of the right which may thus be disposed of without interference with the right itself, in other words, which may be granted to one person over an object of which another continues to be the owner, are known as 'iura in re aliena.'

Same—Classification.

The permanently important species of such rights are 'Servitude' and 'Pledge.' Two others, 'Emphyteusis' and 'Superficies,' were peculiar to Roman law, and may therefore be dismissed in a few words.

Same—Emphyteusis and superficies.

'Emphyteusis' was the right of a person who was not the owner of a piece of land to use it as his own in perpetuity, subject to forfeiture on non-payment of a fixed rent ('canon') and on certain other contingencies. The position of the 'emphyteuta' presents obvious analogies to that of a feudal tenant or an Indian ryot. 'Superficies' was the right which one person might have, in perpetuity or for a very long term of years [157], over a building which, having been erected on the land of another person, became, upon the principle 'quidquid inaedeficatur solo cedit,' the property of the owner of the land.

[157] In the latter case, paying a 'solarium.'

Same—Servitudes.

We have seen that the rights of the owner of a given
*194 *piece of property sometimes involve a restriction on the rights of others to do what they will with their own. Thus the owner of land unburdened by buildings is said to have a 'natural right' that no excavation shall be carried on either under it or so near to it as to cause it to fall away. He has also a 'natural right' that a stream which reaches his land shall not be intercepted in its course through the land of his neighbour [158].

The earliest 'servitudes' seem to have been artificial extensions of such natural rights. They derive their name from imposing a sort of subjection upon the landowner whose rights they restrict in favour of his neighbour; or rather upon the plot of land itself in favour of the neighbouring plot, for it is said, 'non personae sed praedia debent [159].' The land which benefits by a servitude is called the 'praedium dominans,' 'dominant tenement': the land which is burdened with it is the 'praedium serviens,' 'servient tenement.' These Servitudes, since they exist not for the benefit of any individual as such, but as giving increased value to a given piece of land, are called 'real,' 'praedial,' or 'appurtenant.' A later recognition seems to have been given to the class of servitudes which are described, by way of contrast, as being 'personal,' or 'in gross,' and which may be enjoyed by an individual, as such, irrespectively of the ownership of land. A right analogous to servitude, though not reducible to either of these classes, is that which, in English law, the inhabitants of a given place may have, by custom, to go upon a neighbouring piece of land at certain times for a given purpose, e. g. to hold horse-races or to dance on the green [160].

*195 *A Servitude has been defined as 'a real right, constituted for the exclusive advantage of a definite person or

[158] The French Code, art. 639, includes these rights under 'Servitudes,' or 'Services fonciers'; enumerating, among the ways in which servitudes may arise, 'de la situation naturelle des lieux'

[159] Dig. viii. 3. 34; cf. ib. 1. 15.

[160] Cf. Mounsey v. Ismay, 3 H. and C. 486. According to recent views, such customs are a survival of the old common use of the lands of a township, rather than an intrusion on the rights of the lord. Cf. Pollock, Land Laws, p. 39; Warwick v. Queen's College, Oxford, L. R. 10 Eq. 105.

definite piece of land, by means of which single discretionary rights of user in the property of another belong to the person entitled [161].'

Certain characteristics applicable chiefly to real servitudes, and for the most part easily deducible from what precedes, are summed up in the following passages from the Roman law:—

'Servitutum non ea natura est, ut aliquid faciat quis, sed ut aliquid patiatur aut non faciat [162].'

'Nulli res sua servit [163].'

'Servitus servitutis esse non potest [164].'

Same—Classification of Servitudes.

Servitudes may be classified in various ways. They may be 'positive,' consisting 'in patiendo,' or 'negative,' consisting 'in non faciendo'; 'continuous' or 'discontinuous'; 'rural' or 'urban'; 'apparent' or 'non-apparent.' Their most important division is, however, into 'real' and 'personal [165].'

Same—Real Servitudes.

A real servitude is defined in the French Code as 'une charge imposée sur un héritage pour l'usage et l'utilité d'un héritage appartenant à une autre personne [166].' Such servitudes may be divided, although the distinction is unknown to Roman law or French, into what are technically described, in the language of English law, as 'profits à prendre' and 'easements.'

Same—Profits.

A right of the former kind implies that the owner of the dominant tenement is entitled to remove certain tangible
*196 *objects from the servient tenement. Of this kind are the English rights of 'common of pasture,' 'of piscary,' 'of tur-

[161] Von Vangerow, Pandekten, iii. § 338.

[162] Dig. viii. 1. 15. As to the one exception to this rule, see Dig. viii. 5. 6 and 8; viii. 2. 33.

[163] Dig. viii. 1. 26.

[164] Ib. viii. 3. 33. 1.

[165] 'Servitutes aut personarum sunt, ut usus et ususfructus; aut rerum, ut servitutes rusticorum praediorum et urbanorum.' Dig. viii. 1. 1.

[166] Code Civil, Liv. ii. tit. 4, 'Des Servitudes et Services Fonciers.

bary,' i. e. of digging turves, 'of estovers,' i. e. of cutting wood [167]. These, like the Roman 'iura pascendi,' 'calcis coquendae,' 'harenae fodiendae [168],' are all for the benefit of agriculture. Of a somewhat different character are rights of 'common in the soil,' e. g. of quarrying, or digging for coal or minerals.

Same—Easements.

That species of real servitude for which Roman law has no distinguishing name, but which English law calls an Easement, is defined in an ancient work of authority as 'a privilege that one neighbour hath of another, by writing or prescription, without profit, as a way or sink through his land, or the like [169].'

The more important easements are rights of way, to the use of water, to the free reception of light and air, to the support of buildings [170]. The Roman distinction between 'rural' and 'urban' servitudes, as to the precise meaning of which more has perhaps been written than was necessary, turned upon the general suitability of the right for the enjoyment of land or of buildings respectively.

English law will not allow of the creation of an easement of a kind hitherto unknown [171]. The list of analogous servitudes in Roman law was more elastic, and the French Code lays down that 'il est permis aux propriétaires d'établir sur leurs propriétés, ou en faveur de leurs propriétés, telles servitudes que bon leur semble, pourvu néanmoins que les services établis ne soient im-
*197 posés ni à la personne, ni en faveur de la *personne, mais
seulement à un fonds et pour un fonds, et pourvu que ces services n'aient d'ailleurs rien de contraire à l'ordre public [172].'

[167] A right to go on another's land to draw water is not a profit.

[168] Inst. ii. 3. 2; Dig. viii. 3. 1–6, 24.

[169] Termes de la ley, p. 284. This definition would however be misleading without explanation. See Goddard on Easements, p. 2.

[170] The doubt which was entertained as to the possibility of gaining a right by prescription to lateral support from land for land as burdened by buildings has been set at rest by Angus v. Dalton, L. R. 6 App. Ca. 740. A similar right to lateral support from buildings was allowed in Lemaistre v. Davis, L. R. 19 Ch. D. 281.

[171] Keppel v. Bailey, 2 My. and K. 535.

[172] Code Civil, art. 686.

Some things are too trivial to be the object of a servitude. So in English law there can be no easement of a fine view. 'For prospect,' it is decided, 'which is a matter of delight and not of necessity, no action lies for stopping thereof [173].' Roman law was more indulgent to the pleasures of the eye [174]; although it refused to reckon among servitudes a right to gather apples, or to take a stroll, or to pic-nic, in the grounds of one's neighbour [175].

Real servitudes are usually acquired by grant, testament, or prescription. They may terminate in consequence of express release, of abandonment, or of a union of the ownership of the dominant and servient tenements.

Same—Personal Servitudes.

Rights of enjoyment exercisable by a given individual, as such, over the property of another, are 'personal servitudes [176].' They may be imposed upon movable as well as immoveable property; not only upon lands, but also upon cattle, furniture, and slaves.

'Profits-à-prendre' may similarly, according to English law, be enjoyed by an individual, apart from his ownership of land; but an easement, according to the modern definition of the right which identifies it with a real servitude, can never be thus 'in gross [177].'

*198 **Same—Use and Usufruct.*

The Romans distinguished two grades of such rights. The lower, 'usus,' implied in strictness a user of the object itself, without any advantage from the products of the object. They defined the higher, 'ususfructus,' as 'ius alienis rebus utendi fruendi salva

173 Aldred's Case, 9 Rep. 576.

174 Dig. viii. 3. 15, 16.

175 Ib. viii. 1. 8.

176 'Servitudes aut personarum sunt . . . aut rerum.' Dig. viii. 1. 1. Such servitudes, as being imposed upon a thing in favour of a person, were called by the mediaeval jurists 'mixed,' to distinguish them alike from 'real servitudes,' which are imposed upon a thing in favour of another thing, and from 'personal servitudes,' which, according to this terminology, are imposed upon a person, a slave, for the benefit of another person, his master.

177 See per Lord Cairns C., in Rangeley v. Midland Railway Co., L. R. 3 Ch. Ap. 306.

rerum substantia'; and allowed to the 'fructuarius' rights of enjoyment of the object and its products, which, as long as they lasted, excluded that of the owner. In several modern systems of law, the grant of a usufruct answers the purpose which is attained in English law by the creation of a life interest. When an English testator gives to A a life estate with remainder to B, a Frenchman would leave the property to B subject to a 'usufruit' to A for life [178]. The Scotch 'life-rent' in heritable objects or money, of which 'terce' and 'curtesy' are species, is of the same nature [179].

The servitudes recognised by Roman law under the names 'Habitatio' and 'Operae servorum et animalium' were somewhat abnormal species of 'usus.'

Same—Quasi-usufruct.

A personal servitude, as originally conceived of, could be enjoyed only over things which 'usu non consumuntur,' and which would therefore be capable, on the termination of the right, of being handed over to their proprietor in as good condition as they were in when received. A flock was, for this purpose, regarded as an ideal whole, capable of being restored as such, although the usufructuary had replaced some of the individual sheep by new ones; but wine, corn, dresses, and even money, since no use could be made of such objects without destroying them, were not allowed to be susceptible of usufruct. A 'quasi-usufruct' of such things was, however, authorised by a Senatus-consultum under the early Empire; 'not that this enactment created a usufruct,
*199 properly so *called,' says Gaius, 'for the Senate is powerless to vary natural reason, but a quasi-usufruct was introduced when an action was given for its protection [180].'

The usufructuary of perishable things has to give security that the proper quantity, or amount, of them shall be forth-coming at the proper time; and with this safeguard the principle of the

[178] The French Code is so careful to prevent any revival of praerevolutionary ideas, that it avoids recognising usufruct or any other rights as 'personal servitudes.' The same feeling dictated art 638, 'La servitude n'établit aucune pré-éminence d'un héritage sur l'autre'; and art. 686, against the imposition of servitudes 'ni à la personne ni en faveur de la personne.

[179] Ersk. Inst. ii. 9. § 40.

[180] Dig. vii. 5. 2; cf. Inst. ii. 4. 2.

later Roman law is adopted in the French Code. By art. 581, 'l'usufruit peut être établi sur toute espèce de biens, meubles ou immeubles.'

The rights of a usufructuary, or other person enjoying analogous advantages over property which after his lifetime, or at some otherwise determined epoch, will pass to another person, whether such other person be called the 'propriétaire,' or the 'remainder-man,' follow from the nature of the case. They may vary in detail under different systems of law, but the object of all systems is to give to the person who has the immediate interest in the property such advantages from it as are not inconsistent with the interests of the persons who will be entitled to it ultimately. Acts which are detrimental to such expectant interests are sometimes described in English law as 'injury to the reversion.'

A usufruct in Roman law was a life-interest. In modern law it may be granted for a less period. Roman law did not allow it to be granted to a corporation for more than a hundred years, a period which is reduced in the French Code to thirty [181].

Same—Fruits.

The usufructuary is entitled to the 'fruits' of the property; whether 'natural,' as brushwood and the young of animals, 'industrial,' as crops and vintages, or 'civil,' as rent of land and interest of money. He has, in general, to exercise the right 'en bon père de famille †.' The right may be left by will or granted inter vivos. It is sometimes implied by law. So in France
*200 parents have the usufruct of the property of *their children
till they attain the age of eighteen [182]. It may be let or alienated. It comes to an end with the death of the usufructuary, or other termination of the period for which it was granted, with the destruction of the property over which it is enjoyable, with a 'consolidatio' of the title of the proprietor with that of the usufructuary. It may also be forfeited by wrongful user, or by non-user.

[181] Code Civil, art. 619.

† As to the right of the usufructuary, and a life-tenant, to cut great timber, see per Bowen L. J. in Dashwood v. Magniac, '91, 3 Ch. 307.

[182] Code Civil, art. 384.

Same—Reallasten.

Certain rights known to German law as 'Reallasten' resemble servitudes, because they impose a duty upon a given piece of land. They are not servitudes, because the duty consists 'in faciendo.' A 'Reallast' is defined as 'a duty attached to a piece of land of periodically performing positive acts.' The owner of the land for the time being is bound to perform these acts, 'homo dat, sed fundus debet.' Of such a nature are the payment of ground-rent, the maintenance of dykes and sluices, 'Deich- und Sielrecht,' and many feudal incidents.

Same—Licences.

Another class of rights which somewhat resemble servitudes are those which are enjoyed by licencees. But a 'licence,' as has been authoritatively stated, 'passeth no interest, nor alters, or transfers property in anything, but only makes an action lawful which without it had been unlawful[183].' A canal company granted to one Hill the exclusive right of putting pleasure-boats on their canal. Another person having put boats there was sued by Hill, on the ground that, as the owner of an estate may grant a right to cut turves, or to fish or hunt, there was no reason why he should not grant such a right as that in question. The Court however held that no such right could be given. 'A new species of incorporeal hereditament cannot,' it was laid down, 'be created at the will and pleasure of the owner of property, but he must be content to accept the estate and the right to dispose of
*201 it subject to the law. *A grantor may bind himself by covenant to allow any right he pleases over his property, but he cannot annex to it a new incident so as to enable the grantee to sue in his own name for an infringement of such a limited right as that now claimed[184].'

Same—Pledge.

The 'iura in re aliena' which have hitherto been considered are given with a single purpose. Their object is to extend the advantages enjoyed by a person beyond the bounds of his own property.

183 Thomas v. Sorrell, Vaughan, 351.

184 Hill v. Tupper, 2 H. and C. 121.

But there is also a right of the same class which is given, not with this object, but for the merely subsidiary purpose of enabling the person to whom it is granted to make sure of receiving a certain value to which he is entitled, if not otherwise, then at all events by means of the right in question. The other rights 'in re aliena' enable the person entitled to them to enjoy the physical qualities of a thing. This right, which is known as Pledge, merely enables a person who is entitled to receive a definite value from another, in default of so receiving it, to realise it by eventual sale of the thing which is given to him in pledge.

The right of sale is one of the component rights of ownership, and may be parted with separately in order thus to add security to a personal obligation. When so parted with it is a right of pledge, which may be defined as 'a right in rem, realisable by sale, given to a creditor by way of accessory security to a right in personam.' It follows from this definition that the pledge-right subsists only as long as the right 'in personam' to which it is accessory[185]; that the right extends no further than is necessary for the sale of the thing pledged, not to its use or possession; and that the realisation of the value of the thing by sale puts an end to the title of the original owner. The thing pledged need not be the property of the person who is liable personally. Although it is usually a physical object, it may also be a 'ius
*202 in re aliena,' including *even a right of pledge, or a right
'in personam,' in which last case the realisation of its value may take place rather by receipt of payment than by sale[186].

Same—Purposes of Pledge.

The objects aimed at by a law of pledge are obviously, on the one hand, to give the creditor a security on the value of which he can rely, which he can readily turn into money, and which he can follow even in the hands of third parties; on the other hand, to

[185] This right need not arise out of contract, and it may consist in what is called a 'natural' obligation, a term which will be explained hereafter.

[186] In order to cover these possible varieties of objects, Pledge has been defined as 'das Recht an fremden Rechtsobjecten, sich ihren Werth in Geld (durch Verkauf oder auf andere Weise) zur Befriedigung einer forderung zu verschaffen.' Holtzendorff, Encyclopädie, ii. p 111.

leave the enjoyment of the thing in the mean time to its owner, and to give him every facility for disencumbering it when the debt for which it is security shall have been paid.

S me—Mortgage.

The methods by which these objects can best be attained, and the degree in which they are attainable, must vary to some extent with the nature of the thing pledged. Probably the rudest method is that which involves an actual transfer of ownership in the thing from the debtor to the creditor, accompanied by a condition for its re-transfer upon due payment of the debt. Such was the 'fiducia' of the older Roman law, such is the Scotch wadset, and such is the English mortgage, of lands or goods, at the present day, except in so far as its theory has been modified by the determination of the Court of Chancery and of the Legislature to continue, as long as possible, to regard the mortgagor as the owner of the property [187]. Lord Mansfield was unsuccessful in attempting to induce the Courts of Common Law to take the same view [188].

*203 **Same—Pawn.*

Another method, which must always have been practised, is that in which the ownership of the object remains with the debtor, but its possession is transferred to the creditor [189]. This was called by the Romans 'pignus [190].' As a rule the creditor cannot make use of the thing which is thus in his custody. If he is to take its profits by way of interest, the arrangement is called 'antichresis.' He had originally no power of sale without express agreement, but this became customary, and was at last presumed.

[187] In vivum vadium, or Welsh mortgage, the creditor repays himself out of the profits of the property, which then reverts to the debtor. Bl. 2 Comm. 157, but see Fisher, Mortg. § 13. In mortuum vadium if the debt be not paid by the time fixed, the property becomes absolute in the mortgagee, except that, by the intervention of the Court of Chancery, the mortgagor is still allowed during a further period an 'equity of redemption.'

[188] See Eaton v. Jacques, Doug. 455.

[189] Though he may sometimes receive it back again to hold 'precario.'

[190] Ital. 'pegno,' Fr. 'gage,' Germ. "Faustpfand,' Engl. 'pawn.'

A 'pignus' may result from the execution of a judicial sentence, 'ob causam iudicati . . . . pignoris iure teneri ac distrahi posse saepe rescriptum est [191];' but more frequently arises from a contract, which under some systems must be in writing [192]. The trade of lending money upon pledge is frequently placed under legislative restrictions, such as the Pawnbrokers' Acts in England, and the laws regulating 'Monts de Piété' in some countries of the Continent.

Same—Lien.

Another right which, like pawn, depends upon the possession of an object, is not dissimilar to it. Vendors of property, persons who have expended work and labour on goods, and others, are said to have a 'lien' on the property so long as they are still in possession of it; that is to say, they have a right of retaining it in their possession till their claims in respect of it have been satisfied.

Lien must be allowed to be a real right, in so far as redress may be had against any one interfering with it [193]; but, as has been said by Lord Chief Justice Cockburn, 'a lien is a mere right to retain possession of a chattel, and which right is immediately lost on the possession being parted with. In the contract of pledge the pawnor invests the pawnee with much more than this. He
*204 is invested with a right to deal with the *thing pledged as his own if the debt be not paid and the thing redeemed at the appointed time [194].'

Same—Hypothec.

Yet another mode of creating a security is possible, by which not merely the ownership of the thing but its possession also remains with the debtor. This is called by the Roman lawyers and their modern followers 'hypotheca.' Hypothecs may arise by the direct application of a rule of law, by judicial decision, or by agreement.

191 Cod. viii. 23. 2.

192 Code Civil, art. 2074; Codice Civile, art. 1878.

193 The person enjoying it could maintain Trover.

194 Donald v. Suckling, L. R. 1 Q. B. 612.

Same—Tacit.

Those implied by law, generally described as 'tacit hypothecs,' are probably the earliest. They are first heard of in Roman law in connection with that right of a landlord over the goods of his tenant, which is still well known on the Continent and in Scotland under its old name, and which in England takes the form of a right of Distress [195]. Similar rights were subsequently granted to wives [196], pupils, minors [197], and legatees [198], over the property of husbands, tutors, curators, and heirs respectively [199].

Same—Conventional.

The action by which the praetor Servius first enabled a landlord to claim the goods of his defaulting tenant in order to realise his rent, even if they had passed into the hands of third parties, was soon extended so as to give similar rights to any creditor over property which its owner had agreed should be held liable for a debt. A real right was thus created by the mere consent of the parties, without any transfer of possession, which, although opposed to the theory of Roman law, became firmly established as applicable both to immoveable and moveable property [200]. Of the modern States which have adopted the law of hypothec, Spain perhaps stands alone in adopting it to the fullest extent. The rest have, as a rule, recognised it only in relation to immoveables. Thus the Dutch law holds to the maxim 'mobilia non habent
*205 *sequelam,' and the French Code, following the coutumes of Paris and Normandy, lays down that 'les meubles n'ont pas de suite par hypothèque [201].' But by the 'Code de Commerce,' ships, though moveables, are capable of hypothecation [202]; and in England what is called a mortgage, but is essentially a hypo-

[195] Which however implied no power of sale till 2 W. and M. sess. i. c. 5.

[196] Cod. v. 14. 11.

[197] Dig. xxvii. 9. 3.

[198] Cod. vi. 43. 1.

[199] As to similar rights for recovery of funeral expenses, wages of the servants of a deceased person, &c., see Code Civil, arts. 2101, 2107.

[200] On the difference between 'pignus' and 'hypotheca,' see Dig. xiii. 7. 9. § 2; l. 16. 238.

[201] Code Civil, art. 2119; cf. Codice Civile, art. 1967.

[202] Art. 190.

thec, of ships is recognised and regulated by the 'Merchant Shipping Acts,' under which the mortgage must be recorded by the registrar of the port at which the ship itself is registered [203]. So also in the old contract of 'bottomry,' the ship is made security for money lent to enable it to proceed upon its voyage.

Same—Judicial.

Property may sometimes become subject to a hypothec by a judicial sentence. So under the older French law [204]: but under the Code, the judgment must be entered upon the register of 'hypothèques [205].' An English judgment has analogous effects, but must be registered. According to Roman law, no real right was gained over the property till judgment had been followed by execution, i. e. till possession of it had been gained by the creditor [206].

A hypothec presents this great convenience, that it effects no change of ownership and leaves the debtor in possession. It labours under the disadvantage of easily lending itself to a fraudulent preference of one creditor over another, since it may be effected by an agreement of the parties concerned without the knowledge of any one else. It is also difficult for the creditor to whom the property is offered as security to make certain that it has not been already encumbered.

Same—Registration.

The system of 'Registration,' 'Inscriptions,' or 'Hypothekenbücher,' now general upon the Continent, has obviated these evils [207]. Every hypothec, in order to have any effect, must be entered by the proper officer, and remains valid till it is
*206 *removed from the register. Should a sale become necessary, this can no longer be effected by the creditor, but must be authorised by the Court.

Mortgages share with hypothec the disadvantages which result from secrecy; and, so far as relates to land, it is notorious that

203 17 and 18 Vict. c. 104.

204 Pothier, Hypoth. c. 1. art. 2.

205 Art. 2134.

206 Cod. viii. 23. 1.

207 They were ineffectually attacked by a constitution of the Emperor Leo, Cod. viii. 18. 11.

all attempts to establish in this country a 'register of encumbrances' have hitherto failed [208]. Mortgages of chattels, effected by an instrument called a Bill of Sale, which is in effect an assignment subject to a conditional right to call for a re-assignment, although not accompanied by a delivery of possession, were, till recently, good as against other creditors, unless fraudulent [209]. A hotel-keeper might, for instance, mortgage the furniture of the hotel, arranging that it should remain in the house, so that he might continue to carry on the business. Since the year 1854 it has, however, been necessary that the Bill of Sale should be duly registered [210].

Same—Privileges.

Since one object may be successively pledged to several creditors, it becomes necessary to fix the order in which they may resort to the security.

The obvious rule would be expressed by the maxim 'qui prior est tempore potior est iure'; and it seems to have been adopted in Roman law, to the extent of disregarding all considerations other than chronological order, even as between a creditor who had actual possession of a 'pignus' and one who enjoyed merely
*207 a 'hypotheca [211].' To this rule a number of *exceptions were made, called in later law 'privileges,' which took precedence irrespectively of date [212]. According to modern systems a pledge-holder with possession has a 'privilege [213];' but the distinction be-

[208] E. g. 25 and 26 Vict. c. 53.

[209] In which case they are void by 13 Eliz. c. 5, and under the Bankruptcy laws.

[210] By 17 and 18 Vict. c. 36, which recites that 'frauds are frequently committed upon creditors by secret bills of sale of personal chattels, the holders of which have the power of taking possession of the property to the exclusion of the rest of their creditors'; and defines 'Bill of Sale' so as to include 'assignments, transfers, declarations of trust without transfer, or other assurances of personal chattels, and also powers of attorney, authorities or licences to take possession of personal chattels as security for any debt.' These provisions were repeated and extended in the 'Bills of Sale Act,' 1878, amended by subsequent Acts.

[211] Dig. xx. 1. 10.

[212] See Code Civil, Liv. iii. tit. 18, 'Des Privilèges et Hypothèques.' A Privilège is defined in art. 2095.

[213] Ib. art. 2073; Codice Civile, art. 1958. 4.

tween 'privileges' and other securities has almost disappeared with the introduction of the system of registration, according to which each charge takes rank only in accordance with the order in which it is entered. The English equitable doctrine of 'tacking' introduces another exception to the chronological ranking of securities, by uniting securities given at different times, so as to prevent any intermediate purchaser from claiming a title to redeem or otherwise to discharge, one lien, which is prior, without redeeming or discharging the other liens also, which are subsequent to his own title [214].

Same—Transfer and termination.

A security is usually transferable only together with the claim to which it is accessory. The right terminates by discharge of the claim to which it is accessory; by being released; by destruction of the thing pledged; by the creditor becoming owner of the thing; or, if the right was limited in duration, by efflux of time [215].

Under a system of registration, it is further necessary that the charge be removed from the books.

VI. IMMUNITY FROM FRAUD.

But one more antecedent right 'in rem' remains for consideration. It differs essentially from those already described, in that while they are infringed only by acts done against the will of the person of inherence, this is infringed while the person of inherence is a consenting party to his own loss. It is the right not to be induced by fraud to assent to a transaction which causes one damage. Its nature will be best understood from an examination of the nature of the *act by which it is violated.
*208
Fraud may be said to be the intentional determination of the will of another to a decision harmful to his interests by means of a representation which is neither true or believed to be true by the person making it [216].

214 Story, Equity Jurisprudence, § 412.

215 Cf. Code Civil, art. 2180.

216 'Dolus malus' is defined by Servius, 'machinatio quaedam alterius decipiendi causa, cum aliud simulatur et aliud agitur'; by Labeo, 'omnis calliditas, fallacia, machinatio ad circumveniendum, fallendum, decipiendum, alterum adhibita.' Dig. iv. 3. 1.

Fraudulent representations.

The essentials of a fraudulent representation, according to English law, are that it is (1) untrue in fact, (2) made with knowledge of its untruth, or without belief in its truth, or with recklessness as to its truth or falsehood, (3) made for the purpose of inducing another to act upon it [217]. It seems not to be material that the maker of the statement should know it to be untrue, or should have an interest in its being acted on, or have any wicked wish to injure. Nor need the statement be addressed specifically to the person who suffers in consequence. So the directors of a company who, for the purpose of selling shares, publish fraudulent representations, may be sued by any one who, having been induced thereby to take shares from the company, has lost money [218].

On the question of knowledge, it has been laid down that 'if a man, having no knowledge whatever upon the subject, takes upon himself to represent a certain state of facts to exist, he does so at his peril, and if it be done either with a view to secure some benefit to himself, or to deceive a third person, he is in law guilty of a fraud: for he takes upon himself to warrant his own belief of the truth of that which he asserts. Although the person making the representation may have no knowledge of its falsehood, the representation may, nevertheless, have been fraudulently made [219].'

A recent attempt to carry still further the responsibility
*209 for *false statements has so far not been successful. The question raised was whether absence of reasonable ground for making a false statement which causes damage is in itself 'legal fraud,' or is only evidence from which an absence of belief in the truth of the statement on the part of the person making it may be inferred. In other words, whether the actual state of mind of the defendant is material, or whether it is enough if the statement be such as an ordinarily careful man in the defendant's position would not have believed to be true.

[217] Such a representation, apart from contractual relations, was first recognised as actionable in Pasley v. Freeman (1789), 2 Sm. L. C. 74.

[218] Aliter if the shares are bought in the market. Peek v. Gurney, L. R. 6, H. L. 377.

[219] Evans v. Edmonds, 13 C. B. 777. Cf. Arkwright v. Newbold. 17 Ch. D. 320.

The latter view was taken by the Court of Appeal in the case of Peek v. Derry [220], but the decision was reversed by the House of Lords [221], which has thus reestablished the rule that no liability for deceit can arise upon a statement made with an honest belief in its truth [222].

It will be worth while to indicate some of the more usual forms of fraudulent representation.

1. When a man fraudulently represents that he is the agent of another, whereby a third party suffers loss. For instance, a person pretends that he has authority to order goods for another, and the goods having been supplied accordingly, and the alleged principal having repudiated the transaction, the tradesman has an action against the pretended agent [223]. And this is so even if the allegation of agency be bona fide, for it is equitable that the loss, which must fall on some one, should fall on him who has brought it about by an untrue statement, believed and acted on as he
*210 *intended it should be, as to which he gave the other party no opportunity of judging for himself.

2. When false statements are made in the prospectus of a Company, to the detriment of persons who are thereby induced to become shareholders.

3. When false statements are made as to the credit or honesty of third persons, such as customers or servants, whereby loss is occasioned to tradesmen or employers [224].

4. When a man who has a wife living, pretending that he is single, induces another woman to marry him [225].

220 17 Ch. Div. 54, and in the subsequent American case, Chatham Furnace Co. v. Moffatt, 147 Mass. 403.

221 14 App. Ca. 337.

222 The view of the Court of Appeal is strenuously supported by Sir F. Pollock, 5 L. Q. R. 410, that of the House of Lords by Sir W. Anson, 6 Ibid. 72. The decision of the House of Lords gave rise to the Directors Liability Act, 1890.

223 Randall v. Trimen, 18 C. B. 786. The more usual remedy in such a case is now upon the implied warranty of authority, Collen v. Wright, 7 E. & B. 301, 8 E. & B. 647. Cf. Dig. iv. 3. 8.

224 Pasley v. Freeman, u. s. Such statements must by 9 Geo. IV. c. 14 be in writing.

225 Anon. Skin. 119.

5. When a master, by show of authority, gets his servant to do an illegal act [226].

6. When dangerous articles are knowingly bailed, without due notice to the bailee of their quality [227].

Warranty.

7. When an untrue warranty is knowingly superadded to a contract of sale; and that apart from the important consequences of fraud upon the contract itself, with which we are not here concerned [228]. It was at one time held that an untrue warranty is actionable, whether or no the vendor is aware of its untruth [229]; but it is now well settled that no one is liable for a statement which he believes, and has reason to believe, to be true [230].

Same— When warranty is implied.

A warranty is of course often implied. The seller of goods distinguished by a trade-mark implies that it has been rightfully affixed to them, and a purchaser who is induced to give a higher price for the goods than they would be worth without the trade-mark has an action for deceit [231]. The action given to the proprietor of the trade-mark is also sometimes said to be found-
*211 ed on the deceit, but it will probably be sufficient *to refer to what we have already said upon this subject in order to show that this right is not a right to immunity from a perversion of one's will by means of a fraudulent representation [232].

226 Adamson v. Jarvis, 4 Bing. 72.

227 Williams v. E. I. Co., 3 East, 192; cf. Longmeid v. Holliday, 6 Ex. 766.

228 Cf. Dig. iv. 3. 37.

229 Williamson v. Allison (1802), 2 East, 446.

230 Collins v. Evans (1844), in Ex. Ch., 5 Q. B. 820; Weir v. Bell, 3 Ex. D. 243.

231 This is so even independently of the Trade-marks Acts. Cro. Jac. 471.

232 Supra, p. *184. It is submitted that not only are trade-mark cases, so far as the proprietor of the mark is concerned, mistakenly said to turn upon fraud, but that a similar error has been made in such cases as Collins v. Evans, u. s., and Butterly v. Vyse, 2 H. & C. 42. In the former of these, a person who misinformed a sheriff's officer as to the ownership of goods, whereby they were wrongfully taken in distress, was held liable 'for the deceit' to their owner. In the latter, a builder was allowed to get damages 'for the deceit' against a person who had fraudulently prevented an architect from granting a certificate, which was necessary to enable the plaintiff to be paid for his work.

*212

*CHAPTER XII.

PRIVATE LAW: RIGHTS 'IN PERSONAM.'

The method adopted.

We have now arrived at a point where our method parts company with that of the Roman jurists and their followers. Adopting as the radical distinction of rights that which depends upon the restricted or unrestricted character of the person of incidence, they oppose to rights 'in rem' the topic of 'Obligations,' under which one term are included all rights 'in personam,' whether prior to wrong-doing or arising out of it.

We have ventured to pursue a different course. Our radical distinction of rights turns upon their existing or not existing antecedently to wrong-doing. Reserving all rights of the latter kind for separate treatment, we are now engaged in the examination of antecedent rights only, and having dealt with such of those rights as avail 'in rem' against the whole world, have next to describe such of them as avail 'in personam' against ascertained individuals [1].

It will be readily understood that our 'antecedent rights in personam' will correspond to the 'obligationes ex contractu'
*213 *and 'quasi ex contractu' of Roman law, while the Roman law of 'obligationes ex delicto' and 'quasi ex delicto,' and of obligations arising from breach of contract, for which last there exists no technical Latin name, will correspond to the rights which we call 'remedial [2].'

The Conception of Obligation.

Although we propose to distinguish thus broadly between topics which are more usually grouped together under the head of 'Obligations,' we are none the less able to make full use of the ad-

1 Supra, pp. *128, *148.

2 Mr. Bishop has recently published a work entitled 'Commentaries on the non-contract law,' Chicago, 1889, which term is explained to be equivalent to 'Obligationes ex delicto.'

mirable analysis of the ideas conveyed by that term, which has been so potent a factor in the history of legal speculation. 'Obligationum substantia,' says Paulus in a well-known passage, 'non in eo consistit ut aliquod corpus nostrum faciat, sed ut alium nobis obstringat ad dandum aliquid vel faciendum vel praestandum [3].' Still more familiar is the definition of 'obligatio' as 'iuris vinculum, quo necessitate adstringimur alicuius solvendae rei, secundum nostrae civitatis iura [4].' In the fuller language of Savigny, an obligation is 'the control over another person, yet not over this person in all respects (in which case his personality would be destroyed), but over single acts of his, which must be conceived of as subtracted from his free-will, and subjected to our will [5];' or, according to Kant, 'the possession of the will of another, as a means of determining it, through my own, in accordance with the law of freedom, to a definite act [6].' An obligation, as its etymology denotes, is a tie; whereby one person is bound to perform some act for the benefit of another. In some cases the two parties agree thus to be bound together, in other cases they are
*214 bound without *their consent. In every case it is the Law
which ties the knot, and its untying, 'solutio,' is competent only to the same authority. There are cases in which a merely moral duty, giving rise to what is called a 'natural,' as opposed to a 'civil,' obligation will incidentally receive legal recognition. So if a person who owes a debt pays it in ignorance that it is barred by the statutes of limitation, he will not be allowed to recover it back.

Iura in personam.

The right which, looked at from the point of view of the Law which imposes it, is described as an obligation, is described, from the point of view of the person of inherence, as a 'ius in personam.'

[3] Dig. xliv. 7. 3. pr. On obligations as measureable in money, see Dig. xl. 7. 9. 2. For a list of the sources of obligation, see Dig. xliv. 7. 52.

[4] Inst. iii. 13. Cf. ἐνοχή ἐστι δέσμος δικαίου δι' οὗ τις ἀναγκάζεται κατὰ τὸ ἐποφειλόμενον. Theoph. iii. 13.

[5] Obligationenrecht, i. p. 4. Obligations are considered by Bentham under the title 'Rights to Services.'

[6] Rechtslehre, Werke, vii. p. 70.

The difference between a right of this kind and of the kind discussed in the preceding chapter is obvious enough.

When a man owns an estate, a general duty is laid upon all the world to refrain from trespassing on his land. If he contracts with a landscape gardener to keep his grounds in order for so much a year, then the gardener owes to the landowner a special duty, over and above the duty owed to him by all the world besides. If a surgeon is practising in a town, while there is a duty incumbent on all not to intimidate patients from resorting to him, or otherwise molest him in the exercise of his profession, there is no general duty not to compete for his practice. Any one may legally establish a rival surgery next door. Suppose, however, that the surgeon has bought his business from a predecessor, who, in consideration of being well paid, has covenanted not to practice within twenty miles of the town in question. Here the predecessor, beyond and above the duties owed by others to his successor, owes him the special duty of not competing with him by the exercise of his profession in the neighbourhood. In the cases supposed, the landowner and the practising surgeon have respectively rights 'in personam,' against the gardener and the retired surgeon, over and above the rights 'in rem' which they enjoy as against every one else.

How rights in personam arise.

Most frequently antecedent rights 'in personam' arise, as
*215 *in the above cases, out of the agreement of the parties. They are however often due to some cause with which the parties have nothing to do. In these cases, although the person of incidence has not undertaken a special duty to the person of inherence, yet the Law casts that duty upon him, as if he had so undertaken it. There is a ligeance between two individuals, although the chain that binds them was not linked by their own hands. Every one has, for instance, a right that public ministerial officers, such as sheriffs, registrars, or postmen, shall exercise their functions for his benefit when occasions arise entitling him to their services. Similar rights 'in personam' are enjoyed against persons filling certain private fiduciary positions, such as trustees, executors, administrators, and trustees of bankrupts. So also

against persons who happen to enter into certain transitory relations with others, such as persons to whom money has been paid by mistake, or whose affairs have been managed by a 'negotiorum gestor.' Finally, against persons who occupy certain family relationships to others, e. g. against wives and children, and vice versa against husbands and parents.

Classification of Rights in Personam.

Antecedent rights 'in personam' are divisible, according to the investitive fact to which they owe their origin, into two great classes. Such rights either arise or do not arise out of a contract. In the former case they are described as rights 'ex contractu.' In the latter case, since they arise from facts of various kinds to which it pleases the Law to affix similar results, we shall describe them as rights 'ex lege'; and it will be convenient to consider the rights which arise thus variously before treating of those which arise solely from contract [7].

I. RIGHTS ARISING EX LEGE.

The rights which we describe as arising 'ex lege' were described by the Roman lawyers as arising 'quasi ex con-
*216 *tractu,' and more simply, 'ex variis causarum figuris [8].' We propose to subdivide them into four classes, which we shall distinguish as i. the Domestic; ii. the Fiduciary; iii. the Meritorious; and iv. the Official, respectively.

[7] A distinction, which does not quite square with the above, is sometimes drawn between obligations which arise from certain positions, 'obligations d'états,' 'Zustandsobligationen,' and those which arise from certain acts. 'obligations d'affaires,' 'Geschäftsobligationen.'

[8] Gaius, Dig. xliv. 7. 1. pr. Windscheid, Pandekten, endeavours to approximate them to contractual rights. They are sometimes, but improperly, described as 'Quasi-contracts.' See Ramm, Der Quasicontract, Leipzig, 1882. See also 'A selection of cases on the law of Quasi-contract,' by Prof. Keener, Cambridge, U. S., 1889. The author defines 'a quasi-contract right, or right of restoration,' as 'a right to obtain the restoration of a benefit, or the equivalent thereof, conferred by the claimant, but unjustly retained by the defendant'; stating that it may arise from 'mis-reliance,' 'compulsion' or 'circumvention.' It is, however, obvious that the right of a cestui qui trust against his trustee arises in none of these ways. Chapter v of the Indian Contract Act deals with 'Certain relations resembling those created by Contract.'

Domestic rights in personam.

i. We have already discussed those rights 'in rem,' i. e. against the outside world, which arise from the family relations, and have stated how such relations commence and terminate [9]; but from the same relations there arise also rights 'in personam,' i. e. of one member of a family against another. Rights of this sort are of a somewhat undefined character, and their corresponding duties consist often in lifelong courses of conduct rather than in lists of acts capable of accurate enumeration; nor are they reducible to a money value [10]. In advanced systems such rights are only to a limited extent enforced by law, and that rather by permitted self-help than by judicial process.

Same—Husband and wife.

It may appear questionable whether the rights of husband and wife can be reckoned among those which arise by operation of law rather than out of contract. It is however submitted that this is the true view. The matrimonial status is indeed entered upon, in modern times, in pursuance of an agreement between the parties, accompanied by certain religious or civil formalities; but its personal incidents are wholly attached to it by uniform rules
*217 of law, in *no sense depending on the agreement of the parties, either at the time of the marriage or subsequently. The effect of the contract, coupled with the other acts required by law, in producing a status, to which rights of definite kinds are incident, closely resembles that of a sale of property. In the one case, as in the other, the contractual act is complete, so far as its direct effects are concerned, when the status has been produced or the ownership changed. The necessarily resulting rights of the person newly invested with the status, or newly become owner of the property respectively, are the creatures not of the will of the parties but of fixed rules of law [11]. The rights of husband and wife are summed up in the French code as follows: 'les époux se

[9] Supra, p. *153.

[10] Cf. Sohm, Institutionen, (Transl.) p. 278.

[11] See the remarks of Hegel, Phil. des Rechts, § 75, on the treatment by Kant, Rechtslehre, Werke, vii. p. 76, of marriage as an obligatory contract. The nature of marriage was discussed in Niboyet v. Niboyet, L. R. 4 P. D. 9.

doivent mutuellement, fidélité, secours, assistance. Le mari doit protection à la femme, la femme obéissance à son mari. La femme est obligée d'habiter avec le mari, et de le suivre partout où il le juge à propos de résider; le mari est obligé de la reçevoir et de lui fournir tout ce qui est nécessaire pour les besoins de la vie, selon ses facultés et son état [12].' The rights of a husband according to English law, as against his wife, seem to be that she shall associate with him, in default of which he can petition for 'restitution of conjugal rights,' and that she shall not commit adultery, in which case he may, by obtaining a divorce, deprive her of any claim to his society or support. He might formerly have chastised her for levity of conduct, and in quite recent times was allowed to restrain her personal liberty, but his right so to do has been negatived by a recent decision of the Court of Appeal [13]. A wife also may petition against her husband for 'restitution of
*218 conjugal rights [14],' or for a divorce. *A decree for 'restitution of conjugal rights' is no longer enforceable by attachment [15].

Same—Parent and child.

A parent acquires on the birth of a child a right, which he may enforce by moderate chastisement or restraint, of controlling his actions while of tender years. Under some systems a child has a right to be supported by his parents, and a parent to be supported by his children. Under the French Code, a necessitous son-in-law may insist on being maintained by his father-in-law [16]; but a judgment in accordance with this provision having recently been obtained from the French Courts, the American Courts refused to

[12] Code Civil, arts. 212–214.

[13] R. v. Jackson, '91, 1 Q. B. 671.

[14] On which see Orme v. Orme, 2 Addams, 382. There seems to have existed in the old French law a proceeding by which a wife might petition 'pour être embesoignée '

[15] In Weldon v. Weldon, L. R. 9 P. D. 52, the cases upon this subject were reviewed, and an attachment was reluctantly granted by Sir J. Hannen. By 47 & 48 Vict. c. 68 disobedience to an order for restitution of conjugal rights is no longer punishable by attachment, but is a ground for judicial separation.

[16] Code Civil, art. 206.

give effect to it in the United States, as being contrary to the policy of the laws of that country [17].

Same—Guardian and ward.

The relation of guardian and ward is an artificial imitation of that of parent and child, and is entirely regulated by law. Another artificial relationship, that of 'patronus' and 'libertus,' is now obsolete; as is, for most purposes, that of feudal lord and vassal.

Fiduciary rights in personam.

ii. Express trusts were in Roman law created only by an act of a testamentary character. They were requests to the heir, or to a legatee, to hand over the inheritance, or portions of the property included in it, to the person intended to be benefited, and were resorted to in order to evade certain stringent rules which beset the institution of a legal heir and the bequest of legacies properly so called.

Same—Trusts.

According to the law of England, trusts may be created inter vivos as well as by testament, and their history is a curious one, beginning, like that of the Roman fideicommissa, with an attempt to evade the law. The Statutes of Mortmain, passed to pre-
*219 vent the alienation of lands to religious *houses, led to the introduction of 'uses,' by which the grantor alienated his land to a friend to hold 'to the use' of a monastery, the clerical chancellors giving legal validity to the wish thus expressed. Although this particular device was put a stop to by 15 Ric. II. c. 5, 'uses' continued to be employed for other purposes, having been found more malleable than what was called, by way of contrast, 'the legal estate.' They offered indeed so many modes of escaping the rigour of the law, that, after several other statutes had been passed with a view of curtailing their advantages, the 27 Hen. VIII. c. 10 enacted that, where any one was seised to a use, the legal estate should be deemed to be in him to whose use he was seised. The statute did not apply to trusts of personal property, nor to trusts of land where any active duty was cast upon the

[17] Journal du Droit Int. Privé, t. vi. p. 22.

trustee, nor where a use was limited 'upon a use,' i. e. where the person in whose favour a use was created was himself to hold the estate to the use of some one else. There continued therefore to be a number of cases in which, in spite of the 'Statute of Uses,' the Court of Chancery was able to carry out its policy of enforcing what had otherwise been merely moral duties. The system thus arising has grown to enormous dimensions, and trusts, which, according to the definition of Lord Hardwicke, are 'such a confidence between parties that no action at law will lie, but there is merely a case for the consideration of courts of equity [18],' are inserted not only in wills, but also in marriage settlements, arrangements with creditors, and numberless other instruments necessary for the comfort of families and the development of commerce [19].

Under a system of trusts, the person of inherence, 'fideicommissarius,' 'cestui-qui-trust,' enjoys a right 'in personam' against the person of incidence, 'fiduciarius,' 'trustee.'

*220 *Very similar rights are enjoyed against executors, administrators, 'heredes,' trustees of bankrupts, and co-proprietors. Thus a legatee and a creditor of the estate of a testator have rights to be paid the amount of the legacy and the debt respectively by the executor. The creditor of a bankrupt has a right against the trustee in bankruptcy to be paid out of the assets. Co-heirs, or other joint owners, irrespectively of partnership, have rights against one another for the due management of the property; and similar rights result from the relation of proprietor and usufructuary, and from 'Bannrechte [20].'

Same—Implied trusts.

In many cases a fiduciary relation is implied by law. Thus, according to the law of England, where land is conveyed on trusts not yet declared, the alienee is a trustee for the alienor. So also the intending vendor of land, after executing an agreement for a sale of it, holds it in trust for the intending purchaser, and a per-

[18] 2 Atk. 612.

[19] By 29 Car. II. c. 3. § 9, an express trust relating to land must be in writing. In Scots law a trust is said to be 'of the nature of depositation.' Ersk. Inst. iii. tit. 1. § 32.

[20] Supra, p. *185; cf. Savigny, System, iii. p. 338.

son in whose name property is bought with the money of another is trustee for that other. It is a principle of English law that a trust shall never fail for want of a trustee.

Some of the above fiduciary relations are an obvious result of the acceptance of the view expressed in the maxim, 'Iure Naturae aequum est neminem cum alterius detrimento et iniuria fieri locupletiorem [21].' Hence also the right of one who has paid money under a mistake to recover it back again, a right which in English law is expressed by saying that the causeless receiver is a 'trustee' for the mistaken payer. In this and in a multitude of similar cases the money might be recovered as having been 'received to the use' of the person claiming it [22].

Meritorious rights in personam.

iii. According to Roman law, a 'negotiorum gestor,' or person who volunteered to render some necessary service to
*221 *property, or to a business, in the absence of its owner, had a claim to be compensated by the owner for the trouble he had taken, and the owner had also a claim for any loss which had resulted from the interference of the 'negotiorum gestor [23].' Of a similar character are the rights given by English law to the salvors of ships in distress, and recaptors of ships which have been made prize by the enemy; and to those who have supplied necessaries to persons who, being lunatics or in a state of drunkenness, were incapable of entering into an agreement. 'A contract,' it has been said, 'may be implied by law in many cases even where the other party protested against any contract. The law says he did contract because he ought to have done so. On that ground the creditor might recover against him when sober for necessaries supplied to him when drunk . . . the law makes a contract for the parties [24].' In a recent case, the Court, while justly complaining of

[21] Dig. l. 17. 206; cf. Savigny, Obligationenrecht, i. p. 26.

[22] See the long note upon the common count for 'money had and received' in Bullen and Leake's 'Precedents of Pleadings.'

[23] So in Scots law.

[24] Per Pollock, C. B. in Gore v. Gibson, 13 M. & W. 623. As to lunatics, see Baxter v. Portsmouth, 5 B. & C. 170. Cf. the liability of a husband for necessaries for a wife who is wrongfully obliged to live separate from him. Wilson v. Glossop, 20 Q. B. D. 354. Cf. infra, ch. xiv.

the ambiguous use in these cases of the term 'implied contract,' employed the perhaps more objectionable term 'implied obligation [25].' The obligation attaches by express judicial declaration, whatever may be the ground for it. 'This title to indemnity,' says Bentham, 'is founded upon the best reasons. Grant it, and he by whom it is furnished will still be a gainer; refuse it, and you leave him who has done the service in a condition of loss. Such a regulation is less for the benefit of him who receives the compensation than for the benefit of those who need the service. It is a promise of indemnity made beforehand to every man who may have the power of rendering a burdensome service, in order that a prudent regard to his own personal interest may not come into opposition with his benevolence. Three precautions must be observed
*222 in arranging *the interests of the two parties. First, to prevent a hypocritical generosity from converting itself into tyranny, and exacting the price of a service which would not have been accepted had it not been supposed disinterested. Secondly, not to authorise a mercenary zeal to snatch rewards for services which the person obliged might have rendered to himself, or have obtained elsewhere at a less cost. Thirdly, not to suffer a man to be overwhelmed by a crowd of helpers, who cannot be fully indemnified without counterbalancing by an equivalent loss the whole advantage of the service [26].'

Official rights in personam.

iv. Any member of the community who becomes entitled by circumstances to call upon a public official to exercise his functions on his behalf, acquires thereupon a right 'in personam' against such official to that effect. This right, in so far as it is enforceable by action against the official, is a private law right. Such rights are enforced in English law against all ministerial officers, as collectors of customs, registrars of births, bishops, lords of manors, sheriffs, or postmen [27]; but high officials, such as the Postmaster-General, are not responsible for the negligence of their subordinates.

25 Re Rhodes, 44 Ch. Div. 94.

26 Dumont's Theory of Legislation, Hildreth's translation, p. 191.

27 See Ashby v. White, 1 Smith, L. C.

In Roman law, a suitor had a right, enforceable by action, that a judge should decide his cause properly. The judge was liable 'si litem suam fecerit,' and this was the case when he gave a wrong decision, either corruptly, 'si evidens arguatur eius vel gratia vel inimicitia, vel etiam sordes [28],' or from ignorance, 'licet per imprudentiam [29].' According to the law of England, however, no person holding a judicial office, be he judge, juryman, coroner, or arbitrator, unless he exceeds the bounds of his authority, is liable for his judicial acts.

Special duties are sometimes imposed on particular classes of persons, in which case any individual who has a right to
*223 *call for the performance of those duties possesses a right 'in personam' against the person upon whom such performance is made incumbent. Thus, according to English law, an innkeeper, having room in his inn, is bound to receive every well-conducted traveller who is ready to pay for his entertainment, and a 'common carrier' is bound to convey all suitable goods for which he has room and the carriage of which is duly paid. Duties of this sort are often created by statute. So, it having been enacted that shipowners must keep medicines on board for the crew, it was held that any sailor who suffers from a neglect of this duty may sue for the damage he has sustained [30]. Under the Lands' Clauses Consolidation Act, 1845, and similar statutes, a relationship of vendor and purchaser may be constituted without the concurrence of the owner of the land, by the exercise of the compulsory powers conferred by these acts upon railway and other companies [31]. The desirability has been suggested of recognising a right, which, if recognised, would belong to the class now under consideration, but is probably unknown to any system of law. 'When a person is in danger, why,' asks Bentham, 'should it not be the duty of every man to save another from mischief, when it can be done without prejudicing himself, as well as to abstain from bringing it on him [32]?'

28 Dig. v. 1. 15.

29 Dig. xliv. 7. 5.

30 Couch v. Steel, 3 E. & B. 415; sed vide Atkinson v. Newcastle Waterworks Co., L. R. 2 Ex. Div. 441.

31 Cf. Lord Justice Fry's Specific Performance of Contracts, 3rd edit. p. 57.

32 Works, i. p. 148.

Torts founded on contract.

Under the head of rights available against a definite person, which person is specifically ascertained before any infringement of the right, one might be tempted to place those rights the violations of which have sometimes been called in English law 'torts founded on contract.' Actions against surgeons for want of skill, against carriers for want of care, and the like, have sometimes been treated as if brought in pursuance of a right existing
*224 against persons pursuing *such vocations, independently of any contract. It has been said, for instance, that 'the right which a passenger by railway has to be carried safely does not depend on his having made a contract, but that the fact of his being a passenger casts a duty on the Company to carry him safely [33].' The simpler, and it is submitted, the truer view, would be to treat all such rights as contractual. What is called, with reference to carriers, the 'custom of the realm,' is really a term implied by law in the contract of carriage. Any one taking a railway ticket knows, or is presumed to know, what interpretation is put by the law upon the agreement with the Company into which he enters by the simple act of taking a ticket. He knows that, in return for his money, the Company not only undertakes to put him into a train and to start it for its destination, but also undertakes by all reasonable precautions to ensure his safety during the journey. If, through the negligence of the Company, what is called an accident occurs on the road, and the passenger's leg is broken, he may fairly say that the Company is just as much guilty of a breach of their contract with him as if they had stopped their train half way, and had told him that he must accomplish the rest of the distance as best he could.

II. RIGHTS ARISING EX CONTRACTU.

By far the most important class of rights 'in personam' are those which arise from that particular species of act which is called a 'Contract.' We have already explained that acts which are directed to the production of a legal result, 'Rechtsgeschäfte,'

[33] Per Blackburn, J., in Austin v. Great Western Railway Co., L. R. 2 Q. B. 447. So in Taylor v. Manchester, Sheffield and Lincolnshire Railway Co., Q. B., 9 Nov., 1894.

may be either one-sided, when the will of one party only is active, or two-sided, when there is a concurrence of two or more wills in producing a modification of the rights of the parties concerned. Such a two-sided act, having for its function the creation of a right, is a 'Contract,' in the widest sense of that term, in
*225 which it *would include not only the creation of rights 'in personam' but also assignments of property, marriage, and other transfers or creations of rights 'in rem [34].'

Two senses of contract.

Thus if a man goes into a shop and buys a watch for ready money, a contract has taken place. The watchmaker and his customer have united in a concordant expression of will, and the result has affected once for all their legal rights. The customer has, according to English law [35], become owner of the watch, and the watchmaker of its price, and the transaction is at an end. But suppose that, instead of the instantaneous sale of the watch, the agreement had been merely for its purchase at a future day, in this case also there is a contract, but the right to which it gives rise is not a vested right of ownership in the watch, but an out-

[34] Supra, pp. *108, *189. So in English law 'contract of sale' is used to describe both a sale out and out, or, as it is sometimes described, 'a bargain and sale,' and a contract to sell. A similar ambiguity lurks in the term 'marriage contract,' which may denote either the marriage itself, or a contract to marry hereafter. The term is sometimes employed in a very misleading manner. Thus, by 'The Married Women's Property Act, 1882,' it is provided that 'the word "contract" in this Act shall include the acceptance of a trust, or of the office of executrix or administratrix.' So it has been held that the incorporation of a College is a 'contract,' and therefore, under the Constitution of the United States, cannot be interfered with. Dartmouth College v. Woodward, 4 Wheat. 518. There is no contract to pay for the compulsory attendance of a child at school. London School Board v. Wright, 12 Q. B. D. 578.

On the necessity of acceptance for complete alienation in Roman law, see supra, p. *189. In English law acceptance is not necessary. See Butler and Baker's Case, 3 Rep. 25; Thompson v. Leach, 3 Mod. 296; Siggers v. Evans, 5 E. & B. 367; Standing v. Bowring, 31 Ch. D. 283.

[35] On the causes which led to the adoption of this rule, which seems not to have been fully established even in Elizabeth's reign, see Cochrane v. Moore, 25 Q. B. D. (C. A.) 65.

standing, or continuing, right in the customer to buy it at the time and for the price agreed upon, with a correlative right in the shopkeeper to receive the price in due course. In the former case, the contract has given rise to rights 'in rem,' and in so doing its force is instantaneously spent. In the latter case, the results of the contract are deferred. It produces merely claims, or
*226 *rights 'in personam,' which continue to be operative till the thing agreed upon is performed.

Obligatory contract.

We are concerned in the present chapter only with that narrower, and more usual, sense of the term contract, which restricts it to signify such a two-sided act as gives rise to rights 'in personam [36].'

In this sense it is defined by Savigny as 'the union of several in an accordant expression of will, with the object of creating an obligation between them [37];' by an old English authority as 'a speech between two parties whereby something is to be done [38];' by Pothier as 'l'espèce de convention qui a pour objet de former quelque engagement [39];' by M. Ahrens as 'le consentement exprimé de plusieurs personnes à l'effet de créer entre elles un rapport obligatoire sur un objet de droit [40].' 'When,' said Vice-Chancellor Kindersley, 'both parties will the same thing, and each communicates his will to the other, with a mutual engagement to carry it into effect, then an agreement or contract between the two is constituted [41].' It is an expression of agreement entered into by several, by which rights 'in personam' are created available against one or more of them.

[36] This is by some writers maintained to be the only proper sense of the term, e. g. Vangerow, Pand. i. § 121. An 'Obligatorischer Vertrag' is sometimes also described as a 'Schuldvertrag.'

[37] Obligationenrecht, ii. p. 8; cf. Puchta, Inst. iii. p. 89.

[38] The Mirrour.

[39] Oblig. art. 1.

[40] Cours, ii. p. 226.

[41] Haynes v. Haynes, 1 Dr. & Sm. 433.

Cause and effect.

It is necessary carefully to distinguish between the two-sided act itself and the results to which it gives rise. The act alone is the contract, the resulting contractual relation is quite a different thing; although, from the want of an appropriate terminology, the two things are sometimes confused with one another in English law. Thus we talk of 'assigning a contract,' while what is really meant is the assignment of the rights and liabilities which arise out of the contract. In the language of Roman law, the two
*227 ideas are distinguished *with the utmost precision. The 'contractus' is one thing, the 'obligatio ex contractu' is another.

Enforcement.

It has been paradoxically maintained by more than one writer of eminence that no assistance should be given by law to the enforcement of agreements, on the ground that they should be entered into only with those whose honour can be trusted; and the laws of Charondas and of the ancient Indians are stated to have proceeded upon this principle [42]. The contrary view, embodied in the maxim, 'pacta sunt servanda,' *Κύρια εἶναι ὅ τι ἂν ἕτερος ἑτέρῳ ὁμολογήσῃ* [43], even apart from such solemnities as we shall have occasion shortly to mention, has, it is hardly necessary to say, long ago received the adhesion of the civilised world [44].

Mr. Justice Holmes' theory.

The State lends its force to assure the performance of those promises of which it thinks fit to take cognisance. This it endeavours to do by putting some sort of pressure upon the will of the promisor, which it therefore indubitably so far subjected to the will of the promisee. The fact that the pressure thus applied

[42] *Οὗτοι γὰρ παραχρῆμα κελεύουσι διδόναι καὶ λαμβάνειν, ἐὰν δέ τις πιστεύῃ, μὴ εἶναι δίκην, αὐτὸν γὰρ αἰτίαν εἶναι τῆς ἀδικίας.* Stob. Flor., tit. 44. 21; Strabo, xv. p. 709; cf. Arist. Eth. Nic. viii. 15. 6, ix. 1. 9.

[43] Demosth. in Euerg. p. 1162. 'Quid enim tam congruum fidei humanae quam ea quae inter eos placuerunt servare?' Dig. ii. 14. 1. Cf. Puffendorf, De Off. Hominis et Civis, i. c. 9. § 3.

[44] By the Constitution of the United States, 'no State shall pass . . . any law impairing the obligation of contracts.' Art. 1. § 10.

may often fail of its effect has given rise to an ingenious inversion of the theory of contract. According to Mr. Justice Holmes, a contract may be regarded as 'the taking of a risk.' 'The only universal consequence of a legally binding promise is, that the law makes the promisor pay damages if the promised event does not come to pass. In every case it leaves him free from interference until the time for fulfilment has gone by, and therefore free to break his contract if he chooses [45].' But, as the able advocate of this view is compelled to admit, 'when people make contracts they usu-
*228 ally contemplate the performance rather than the *breach'; nor can it be seriously maintained that the performance of a contract is more optional than that of any other legal duty. Libel or assault, equally with breach of contract, are possible to any one who is prepared to be answerable in damages for the indulgence of a taste for defamation or violence.

An obligatory contract is, as we have seen, a species of agreement. But many agreements produce no legal effect upon the relations of the parties one to another. It will therefore be necessary to enquire more minutely into the characteristics of those consensual acts which are recognised by law as giving rise to obligations.

Savigny's analysis of a contract.

Savigny's analysis of contract, substantially accepted by the majority of the more recent German authorities, is to the following effect. Its constitutent elements are, he says: (i) several parties, (ii) an agreement of their wills (sie müssen irgend Etwas, und zwar Beide dasselbe, bestimmt gewollt haben), (iii) a mutual communication of this agreement (sie müssen sich dieser Uebereinstimmung bewusst geworden seyn, das heisst der Wille muss gegenseitig erklärt worden seyn), (iv) an intention to create a legal relation between the parties [46].

Is consensus necessary?

In one point only does this analysis seem open to criticism, Is it the case that a contract is not entered into unless the wills of the parties are really at one? Must there be, as Savigny puts it, 'a

[45] The Common Law, p. 301.

[46] System, iii. p. 308.

union of several wills to a single, whole and undivided will[47]'? Or should we not rather say that here, more even than elsewhere, the law looks, not at the will itself, but at the will as voluntarily manifested[48]? When the law enforces contracts, it does so to prevent disappointment of well-founded expectations, which, though they usually arise from expressions truly representing intention, yet may occasionally arise otherwise.

If, for instance, one of the parties to a contract enters into it, and induces the other party to enter into it, resolved all
*229 *the while not to perform his part under it, the contract will
surely be good nevertheless. Not only will the dishonest contractor be unable to set up his original dishonest intent as an excuse for non-performance, but should he, from any change of circumstances, become desirous of enforcing the agreement against the other party, the latter will never be heard to establish, even were he in a position to do so by irrefragable proof, that at the time when the agreement was made the parties to it were not really of one mind.

The older theory.

This view, opposed as it is to the current of authority from Javolenus[49] to Sir F. Pollock[50] and Sir W. Anson[51], was origi-

[47] Ibid. p. 309.

[48] Cf. supra. p. *105.

[49] 'In omnibus rebus quae dominium transferunt, concurrat oportet affectus ex utraque parte contrahentium.' Dig. xliv. 7. 55; cf. xiv. 1. 3.

[50] 'There must be the meeting of two minds in one and the same intention.' This he admits may be a mere inference of fact which must be proved, and in some cases may not be disproved. 'Under certain circumstances the law of evidence does not allow a party to show that his intention was not in truth as he made it appear.' Contract, p. 3. But in his sixth edition, p. 2, Sir F. Pollock uses a phrase which, though hardly to be reconciled with the above, leaves, in the view of the present writer, little to be desired. 'Men can justly rely on one another's intentions, and courts of justice hold them bound to their fulfilment, only when they have been expressed in a manner that would convey to an indifferent person, reasonable and reasonably competent in the matter in hand, the sense in which the expression is relied on by the party claiming satisfaction.'

[51] For a criticism of the views of the present writer upon this question, see pp. 10–13 of the second edition of Sir W. Anson's work.

nally put forward with some diffidence. It is now restated with more confidence, since English friends who were at first decidedly opposed to it are converts to its truth, while a similar view, after having been, as it seems, for some years academically debated in Germany, has definitely come to the surface in the impor-
*230 tant work of Professor Leonhard [52]. *Indeed when the question is once raised it is hard to see how it can be supposed that the true consensus of the parties is within the province of law, which must needs regard not the will itself but the will as expressed by one party to the other, taking care only that the expression of will exhibits all those characteristics of a true act which have already been enumerated [53].

An adequate discussion of the question whether a contract can be said to demand for its validity a true union of wills, would be out of place in the present work, which can attempt only to indicate the nature of the problem and the general character of the arguments by which one or other solution of it may be supported. The language of systems of positive law upon the point is generally ambiguous, nor is this to be wondered at. The question is practically a new one. The process of giving effect to the free acts of the parties to a contract, rather than to the fact that certain rigidly defined formalities have been complied with, has lasted so long that legal speculation has only recently begun to analyse the free act itself into its two factors of an inner will and an outward expression, and to assign to one or to the other a dominant place in the theory of contract.

[52] Der Irrthum bei nichtigen Verträgen, Berlin, 1882–83. See also O'Donnell v. Clinton, 145 Mass. 461, where Holmes, J., says that 'assent, in the sense of the law, is a matter of overt acts, not of inward unanimity in motives, design, or the interpretation of words'; and two articles by Hartmann, in the Archiv für civilistische Praxis, Bd. 72, p. 161, and Bd 77, p. 161, citing Fichte, System der Sittenlehre, p. 383. Cf. the following remarkable passage from Dr. Adam Ferguson's Institutes of Moral Philosophy, ed 1800, p. 155: 'An action of any kind performed with a view to raise expectation, or by which it is known that expectations are naturally raised, is sufficient to constitute a contract.'

[53] Supra, p. *93.

Roman law.

Just as the Romans used, without analysing them, the terms 'velle,' 'consensus,' 'sententia [54],' so the modern Codes, though some appear to look rather to the inner will [55], others rather to
*231 its outward expression [56], as a rule employ *language which is capable of being interpreted in either direction.

English cases.

The same may be said of the English cases. In these one constantly meets with such phrases as 'between him and them there was no consensus of mind,' 'with him they never intended to deal [57];' but one also meets with much that supports the view of the question which we venture to hope may ultimately commend itself to the Courts as being at once the most logical and the most favourable to the interests of commerce. The class of cases in which this view may be traced may be said to commence with that of Pickard v. Sears, decided in 1838 [58], and the principle which they involve was thus stated by Chief Baron Pollock in 1859: 'If any person, by a course of conduct or by actual expressions, so conducts himself that another may reasonably infer the existence of an agreement or licence, whether the party intends that he should do so or not, it has the effect that the party using that language, or who has so conducted himself, cannot afterwards gainsay the reasonable inference to be drawn from his words or conduct [59].' Still clearer was the language held in 1871 in the case of Smith v. Hughes [60], when Mr. Justice Blackburn said: 'If, whatever a

[54] See Leonhard, i. p. 11; but on the other hand Windscheid and Zitelmann, as cited, supra, p. *105.

[55] E. g. the Code Civil, art. 1109; the Codice Civile, arts. 1098, 1114; the Codes of Prussia, §§ 4, 52–56, 75–79; of Saxony, §§ 91, 95, 843, 844; and of Zürich, § 926.

[56] E. g. the Austrian Code, art 871; the Swiss Code fédéral des obligations, art. 1. Cf. the draft Civil Code for Germany, §§ 77, 95–100.

[57] In Cundy v. Lindsay, L. R. 3 App. Ca. 459. Cf. per Bowen, L. J. in Carlill v. Carbolic Smoke-ball Co., '93, 1 Q. B. 269.

[58] 6 A. and E. 475; cf. Freeman v. Cooke, 2 Ex. 654.

[59] Cornish v. Abington, 4 H. and N. 549.

[60] L. R. 6 Q. B. 607. Cf. Carr v. London and N. W. Co., L. R. 10 C. P. 317. In Scott v. Littledale, 8 E. and B. 815, the contract was held good, al-

man's real intention may be, he so conducts himself that a reasonable man would believe he was assenting to the terms proposed by the other party, and that the other party on that belief enters into the contract with him, the man thus conducting himself would be equally bound as if he had intended to agree to the other party's terms [61].'

*232 *The newer theory.*

In other words: the legal meaning of such acts on the part of one man as induce another to enter into a contract with him, is not what the former really intended, nor what the latter really supposed the former to intend, but what a 'reasonable man,' i. e. a judge or jury, would put upon such acts [62]. This luminous principle at once sweeps away the ingenious speculations of several generations of moralists [63], while it renders needless long lists of subtle distinctions which have been drawn from decided cases [64].

The truth and practical importance of what may be called the objective theory of contract are confirmed by the generally received rules as to contracts made by post; where the question, whether or no the contract is made, turns, as we shall see [65], not

though the vendor had by mistake shown a wrong sample. See also Leake, Contract, p. 12.

[61] Mr. Schuster in a very able article 'Der Vertragsschluss nach Englischem Rechte,' in the Archiv für Handels- u. Wechselrecht, xlv. p. 324, seems to think that according to these cases it is necessary that the expression of will should be accompanied with an intention that it should induce the other party to act, and that the other party should, with a knowledge of this intention, undertake so to act.

[62] 'It may well be in contracts that a man may be bound to a meaning which demonstrably was not his.' Leonhard, i. p. 119. Cf. Lord Selborne's statement that 'the doctrine of reputed ownership does not require any investigation into the actual state of knowledge or belief' of creditors, or of the outside world, 'as to the position of particular goods. It is enough for the doctrine if those goods are in such a situation as to convey to the minds of those who know their situation the reputation of ownership.' Ex parte Watkins, L. R. 8 Ch. Ap. 528.

[63] E. g. Grotius, De I. B. et P. iii. 23. 4; Paley, Moral Phil. vol. i. c. 5; Austin, ii. p. 123.

[64] E. g. the rules set forth by Sir W. Anson, Contract, ed. vi. p. 135.

[65] Infra, p. *237.

on the coincidence of the wills of the parties, but on the fact of their having exchanged expressions of intention: and by the law of Agency; since the liability of a principal continues not merely so long as he continues mentally to empower his agent to act for him, but also so long as he has not, to the knowledge of third parties, revoked the agent's authority [66].

Nor is there any inconsistency between this view and the well-established effect of what is known as 'essential error' in pre-
*233 venting a contract from coming into existence. When *such error is present, it is no doubt true to say 'non videntur qui errant consentire [67].' All liability under the apparent agreement may be repudiated, and any payments made in pursuance of it may be recovered back. But we shall find that even here the failure of the contract is due not to the psychological fact of mistaken belief, which, as has been well observed, is a mere 'dramatic circumstance [68],' but to other causes, which may be reduced to two. (1) The language employed is such as under the circumstances is meaningless, either from referring to an object not in existence, as in the case of the sale of a cargo of corn, supposed to be on its homeward voyage, while in reality it had become so heated that it had been unloaded and sold [69]; or from ambiguity, as in the case of the sale of a cargo of cotton 'to arrive ex Peerless from Bombay,' whereas there were two ships, either of which would have answered the description [70]. (2) The true meaning of the mistaken party is, or might be, known to the other party. This will cover the cases of 'error in persona,' 'in corpore,' 'in negotio,' &c., as, for instance, the case where a customer sent an order for goods to a tradesman with whom he had been accustomed to deal, but who

[66] See Drew v. Nunn, 4 Q. B. D. 668, and cf. infra, p. *241.

[67] Dig. l. 16. 116; xliv. 55, 57. Cf. supra, p. *104.

[68] Holmes, Common Law, p. 308.

[69] Couturier v. Hastie, 5 H. L. 673. 'Domum emi cum eam et ego et venditor combustam ignoremus. Nerva, Sabinus, Cassius, nihil venisse, quamvis area maneat, pecuniamque solutam condici posse aiunt.' Dig. xviii. 1. 57. Cf. 'Nec emptio nec venditio sine re quæ veneat potest intelligi.' Ib. 8 pr.

[70] Raffles v. Wichelhaus, 2 H. & C. 906. The judgment in this case merely supports the plea, which sets out the facts and avers a difference of intention between the parties. Cf. 'si Stichum stipulatus de alio sentiam, tu de alio, nihil actum erit.' Dig. xlv. 1. 83. 1.

had disposed of his business to a successor, who, having supplied the goods without any notification of the change, was not
*234 allowed to recover their price [71]. The *question in these cases should always be: was the expression of one party such as should fairly have induced the other to act upon it? If so, but not otherwise, it is in the interest of society that the loss should fall upon the former.

Elements of a contract.

We shall therefore treat of the constituent elements of a contract as being: i. several parties; ii. a two-sided act by which they express their agreement; iii. a matter agreed upon which is both possible and legal; iv. is of a nature to produce a legally binding result; v. and such a result as affects the relations of the parties one to another; also, vi. very generally, either a solemn form, or some fact which affords a motive for the agreement.

i. *Parties.*

The very idea of a contract demands for its formation at least two parties, a 'promisor' and a 'promisee,' who in Roman law are described as 'debitor' and 'creditor'; which terms have however a more general application. So it has been held that where one and the same company had two departments, one for insurance and one for annuities, an insurance effected by the latter department with the former was a nullity [72]. The promisee must not be an 'incerta persona,' e. g. 'the secretary for the time being,' but the offer may be, in the first instance, made to an unascertained member of a class, e. g. to the finder of a lost purse, whoever he may be [73].

[71] Boulton v. Jones, 2 H. & N. 564; Boston Ice Co. v. Potter, 123 Mass. 28. In such cases, as Leonhard says, 'the essentiality of error depends entirely on the question whether the absence of error is made a cognisable condition of the transaction.' Irrthum, ii. p. 586.

[72] Grey v. Ellison, 1 Giff. 438.

[73] Such a proposal is called in German 'Auslobung.' The same principle applies to the offer of a prize, to announcements in railway time-tables, and to sales by auction.

Same—Joint contractors.

There may be more parties than one to either side of a contract, 'plures rei,' 'joint contractors'; and these are, according to the position which they occupy, either 'correi credendi,' 'joint creditors,' or 'correi debendi,' 'joint debtors [74].'

ii. *Offer and acceptance.*

The two-sided act, expressive of agreement. This con-
*235 sists *of an offer, 'pollicitatio [75],' on one side, and an acceptance on the other [76]. One party expresses his readiness to be bound to a performance, and the other side expresses his acceptance of this readiness. An unaccepted offer creates no liabilities [77]. The rules upon this subject are as follows:—

1. The acceptance must unconditionally correspond to the offer. An expression of readiness to buy a horse for fifty pounds is no acceptance of an offer to sell the horse for sixty pounds [78].

2. The acceptance must be contemporaneous with the offer, which may therefore be withdrawn at any time before it has been accepted. So it has been held that a bidder at an auction is not bound till the hammer has fallen. 'An auction is not inaptly called a locus poenitentiae. Every bidding is nothing more than an offer on one side, which is not binding on the other side till it is assented to [79].'

[74] On the vexed question of the true nature of a correal obligation, see Savigny, Obligationenrecht, § 23; Moyle, Institutes of Justinian, excursus vii; Sohm, Institutionen (Transl.), § 61; Hunter's Roman Law, p. 590.

[75] 'Pollicitatio est solius offerentis promissum.' Dig. 2. 12. 3 pr.

[76] An offer, 'Antrag,' may sometimes be confused with an inquiry about an offer, 'Aufforderung zu einem Antrage.' Vang. Pand. § 603. So an 'offer to be bound' with an 'offer to negotiate'; see Bowen, L. J. in the Smoke-ball case, u. s.

[77] 'Ex nuda pollicitatione nulla actio nascitur.' Paul R. S. v. 12. 9. But some curious exceptions to this rule were recognised in Roman law. Dig. l. 12. As to the effect of an unaccepted offer by deed in English law, see infra, p. *245n.

[78] A reply to this effect would amount to a rejection of the offer and the making of a counter-offer. Hyde v. Wrench, 3 Beav. 334. So the draft Civil Code for Germany, § 88.

[79] Payne v. Cave, 3 T. R. 148.

Several subordinate questions arise with reference to this rule, some of them giving rise to very fine distinctions.

(a) How long does an offer which has not been expressly revoked remain open? It is in accordance with common sense, and has been so held, that an offer is intended to remain open only for a reasonable time [80]. The German Commercial Code keeps an offer made to a party at a distance open only till an answer to it could have been received in due course [81].

*236 *(b) Is an offer revoked by the death before it has been accepted of the person who makes it? There is some difference of view as to this result following from the mere fact of death, uncommunicated to the acceptor [82].

(c) Must acceptance be notified in every case to the offeror; or does the nature of the offer sometimes imply that acting on the proposal will be enough without notification [83]?

(d) When the parties are at a distance, is the expression of intention by either party, or the communication of such an expression to the other party, to be regarded? This difficulty, which continues to the present day to exercise the ingenuity of the Courts and divide the opinions of jurists, was perceived and discussed by the earliest commentators on the civil law [84]. It arises chiefly with reference to acceptance of an offer, but also with reference to revocation either of an offer or of an acceptance. The views upon the subject are classified by German writers under three heads.

[80] Meynell v. Surtees, 1 Jur. N. S. 737; cf. Ramsgate Hotel Co. v. Montefiore, L. R. 1 Ex. 109.

[81] Handelsgesetzbuch, art. 319. For a decision under this article, see Seuffert, Archiv, xxix. No. 60. So the draft Civil Code, § 84. A promise by the offeror to keep his offer open for a reasonable, or any, time, would be void in English law from want of consideration.

[82] The Indian Contract Act requires communication. In English law the mere fact seems to be sufficient. See Dickenson v. Dodds, L. R. 2 Ch. D. 475. Some authorities would deny the existence of a contract, but would indemnify an ignorant acceptor. Windscheid, Pand. § 307.

[83] As e. g. in Carlill v. Carbolic Smoke-ball Co., '93, 1 Q. B. 256.

[84] On l. 1 of the title 'De Contr. Empt.' (Dig. xviii. 1), Accursius writes: 'Item quid si antequam literae vel nuntius ad eum perveniant venditor renuntiat? Quidam dicunt non valere contractum. Sed Ald. dicit tenere, quod puto verum.'

According to the 'Aeusserungstheorie' ('Declarationstheorie'), it is enough if an acceptance is posted; according to the 'Empfangstheorie,' the acceptance must reach the offeror; while according to the 'Vernehmungstheorie' ('Rescissions- Agnitions- Recognitionstheorie') it must actually come to his knowledge [85]. The
*237 French authorities are similarly at variance, Merlin for *instance holding that the contract is complete on acceptance, Pothier that the acceptance must become known to the other party [86]. The English Courts, after a period of uncertainty, seem now to have arrived at conclusions which may be shortly stated as follows: An offer is irrevocable after it has been accepted. Acceptance must be no merely mental act, but a communication to the proposer, which may however be sufficiently made by posting a letter containing it [87], although this letter be delayed [88], or even fail altogether to reach its destination [89]. A revocation of an offer, despatched before, but reaching the acceptor after, the posting of the acceptance comes too late [90]. A revocation of an acceptance, posted after, but reaching the proposer simultaneously with, the acceptance, probably prevents the formation of the contract [91].

Our judges, it will be observed, refuse to give effect to an expression of intention by one party unless actually communicated to the other, except that, in the case of an acceptance only, they hold the posting of an acceptance to be equivalent to such com-

[85] Windscheid, Pandekten, § 306; cf. Vangerow, Pand. § 603; Baron, Pand. § 212. For a full and interesting discussion on the several theories of 'dichiarazione', 'spedizione', and 'recezione,' see the Report upon the draft Code of Commerce, presented in 1878 to the Italian Senate by the Minister of Justice, Mancini, pp. 115–143.

[86] Cf. Dalloz, 'Obligations,' No. 98.

[87] Brogden v. Metropolitan Ry. Co. 2 App. Ca. 691. The despatch of a telegram has the same effect, Cowan v. O'Connor, 20 Q. B. D. 640.

[88] Adams v. Lindsell, 1 B. and Ald. 681.

[89] Dunlop v. Higgins, 1 H. L. Ca. 381; Household Fire and Carriage Co. v. Grant, L. R. 4 Ex. D. 216, where see the dissenting judgment of Bramwell, L. J. Cf. Tayloe v. Merchants Fire Insurance Co., 9 Howard S. Ct. Rep. 390.

[90] Byrne v. Van Tienhoven, 5 C. P. D. 344; Henthorne v. Fraser, '92, 2 Ch. (C. A.) 27.

[91] Dunmore v. Alexander, 9 Shaw and Dunlop, 190. Cf. Handelsgesetzbuch, art. 320.

munication. They do not attribute a similar effect to the posting of a revocation.

Those foreign jurists who, insisting upon a truly continuing consensus of the parties, think that a proposer may revoke at any moment before the acceptance reaches him, grant to the acceptor of a contract which may thus fail to come into being an in-
*238 demnity for any loss which *he may have sustained by the proposer's 'culpa in contrahendo [92].'

The topic is dealt with in several of the modern codes [93].

Reality of consent.

3. There are circumstances which, while they do not, like those already mentioned, by negativing the presence of what is often described as a consensus ad idem, but would be more accurately described as a concordant expression of will, render the apparent contract void ab initio, yet operate as flaws in its formation, rendering the resulting obligation voidable at the option of the party who is disadvantaged by it [94].

Same—Fraud.

Where one party has been guilty of fraudulent misrepresentation or concealment, he is not permitted to hold the other party to his bargain [95]. The rhetorical phrases of a vendor are not necessarily fraudulent, 'simplex commendatio non obligat,' nor is the contract voidable unless it has been materially induced by the misrepresentation. The fraud of an agent will be imputed to his principal, although the latter may have acted with bona fides. In

[92] Pothier, Contr. de Vente, § 32; Windscheid, Pandekten, § 307.

[93] Indian Contract Act, § 4; Handelsgesetzbuch, art. 318–321; the new Italian Codice di Commercio, art. 35; the new Swiss Code fédéral des Obligations, arts. 5–8.

[94] On the distinction between void and voidable acts, cf. supra, p. *103. The French and Italian Codes seem to give to 'essential error' no higher effect upon a contract than they attribute to fraud and duress. Plato mentions duress, fraud and haste, as grounds for avoiding a contract. Crito, 52 E.

[95] An 'exceptio doli mali' was first permitted to actions upon the formal contracts in the time of Cicero. On fraud as an infringement of a right 'in rem,' v. supra, p. *207.

recent English cases it has been held that innocent misrepresentations are ground for setting aside a contract which they have induced, or for refusal of specific performance of it [96].

Same—Undue influence.

What is known in English law as 'undue influence' is also held to make a contract voidable. This consists in acts which, though not fraudulent, amount to an abuse of the power which circumstances have given to the will of one individual over that of
*239 *another. In some relations, such as that of solicitor and client, or parent and child, the existence of this exceptional power is often presumed, but its existence is capable of being proved in other cases also [97].

Same—Duress.

Duress, which is another ground on which a contract is voidable, consists either in violence to the person, or in threatened violence of the same character, 'duress per minas.' It will not be enough if the safety of a man's house or goods only be threatened [98], and the fear caused must be, as has been said, 'not a vain fear, but such as may befall a constant man'; 'vani timoris iusta excusatio non est [99].'

According to English law the fraud or duress of a third party has no effect upon a contract; and this is the generally accepted rule as to fraud [100], though not as to duress [101].

Mode of expression.

4. The expression of agreement may be in writing, or by words, or by signs, or merely by a course of conduct, in which last case it is called an 'implied contract [102].' In an old case, it was said, with

[96] Redgrave v. Hurd, 20 Ch. D. 1; Newbigging v. Adam, 34 Ch. D. 582.

[97] On the doctrine of 'laesio enormis,' as applied in the contract of sale, v. infra, p. *253.

[98] Aliter Code Civil, art. 1111; Codice Civile, art. 1112.

[99] Dig. l. 17. 184. Cf. supra, p. *94.

[100] Though it is criticised by some commentators on the French Code: see Dalloz, Répertoire, s. v. 'Obligation.'

[101] Dig. iv. 2. 9. 1, ib. 14. 3; Code Civil, art. 1111; Codice Civile, art. 1111.

[102] It is necessary carefully to distinguish from this appropriate use of

reference to an unexpressed acceptance, 'you having it in your own mind is nothing, for it is trite law that the thought of man is not triable, for even the devil himself does not know what the thought of man is [103].'

Same—By agent.

It must be expressed by the parties to one another; but in developed systems of law it is not necessary that the parties
*240 *shall be face to face at the time. They may communicate, for the purpose of contracting, as well as for the purpose of otherwise affecting their legal relations, by letter, or by telegraph, or by means of a messenger or other go-between. This go-between, when entrusted with a certain amount of discretion, is called an agent, or mandatory, and he acts by virtue of the authority, or 'mandate,' confided to him by his principal [104]. The giving of this authority on the one hand, and its acceptance on the other, constitute a special contract, resulting in mutual rights and duties between the principal and the agent, which will have to be discussed hereafter. We are now only concerned with agents as being, for the purposes of all contracts alike [105], capable of giving binding expression to the will of their principals. Each party to a contract may be represented by an agent. It is a universally received maxim, that a person who at the time had no authority to act for another, may be retrospectively made his agent by subsequent ratification. 'Omnis ratihabitio retrotrahitur et mandato priori aequiparatur [106].'

the term its use as descriptive of terms imported into a contract by the law (supra, p. *224, infra, p. *250), and of a transaction to which the law chooses to attach the consequences of a contract, although it is nothing of the kind (supra, p. *215).

103 Per Brian, C. J., 17 Ed. IV, quoted by Lord Blackburn in Brogden v. Metropolitan Railway Co., L. R. 2 App. 692.

104 Supra, pp. *102, *107.

105 The ratification of the promise of an infant could not however, under Lord Tenterden's Act, be made by an agent.

106 Cf. Bird v. Brown, 4 Ex. 798; Fleckner v. U. S. Bank, 8 Wheaton, 363; and it seems that an unauthorized acceptance may be ratified even after the withdrawal of the offer. Bolton v. Lambert, 41 Ch. D. 295.

Same—Authority of agent.

An agent may in general be appointed without any formality, though in English law an agent to execute a deed must be appointed by deed, and for the purpose of binding his principal under the Statute of Frauds, sections 1 and 2, must be appointed in writing. Agency may also be implied from the acts of the principal, on the ground that if one person by his acts represents another person to be his agent, he ought to be liable upon the contracts into which third parties may enter on the faith of such a representation. A servant, for instance, who is in the habit of ordering goods for his master on credit, may continue to bind his master after his authority has been withdrawn, with reference to third parties
*241
*who have had no notice of such withdrawal. So the master of a ship is, in emergency, an agent to pledge the credit of his employer for the good of the ship. It has however been held that mere necessity does not, in general, create agency; so a railway company is not liable for the fees of a surgeon who has been called in by one of their station-masters to attend to the sufferers from an accident [107]. A wife, as such, has no implied authority to bind her husband's credit; and it has been held accordingly that a prohibition to her to order goods, though uncommunicated to her tradesmen, is sufficient to relieve the husband, as such, from liability for her purchases [108].

The authority of an agent is terminated, in English law, by the death, or bankruptcy, and perhaps by the lunacy, of his principal. Before 1883 also by the marriage of a principal who was a woman.

Same—Agents, special and general.

Agents are said to be 'general' when their authority is defined by their character or business, as in the case of factors, brokers, or partners; or 'special' when their authority is limited by the terms of their appointment. No private instructions, contrary to the

[107] Cox v. Midland Railway Co., 3 Ex. 268.

[108] Jolly v. Rees, 19 C. B., N. S. 628. The principle of this case has been affirmed by the House of Lords in Debenham v. Mellon, L. R. 6 App. Ca. 24. But a husband is liable (quasi ex contractu) for necessaries supplied to a wife whom he has wrongfully deserted, as being his 'agent of necessity.' Eastland v. Burchell, 3 Q. B. D. 436. Cf. supra, p. *221.

usages of a general agent's business, will limit the liability of his principal. It follows from the nature of agency, that a contract made by an agent is regarded as the contract of his principal, who alone therefore can as a rule sue or be sued upon it. The agent, having done his part by acting as the intermediary, drops out of the transaction [109]. The fraud of an agent will render voidable the contract of his principal. In marine insurance the insured may be responsible for non-disclosure of facts unknown to him-
*242 self, *if, but for the fraud or negligence of the agent through whom he has effected the insurance, they ought to have been known to him [110]. If a man contracts avowedly as the agent of another, though without authority, neither can be charged upon the contract, but the pretended agent is liable for the deceit [111].

iii. *Possibility and legality.*

The matter agreed upon must be at the time of the agreement both possible and legally permissible [112]. A thing is said to be impossible, not only 'quod natura fieri non concedit,' but also if it be practically out of the question, because it can only be accomplished at an unreasonable cost, e. g. the recovery of a ring which is known to be lying at the bottom of the sea; or if it imports to have a legal effect unknown to the law. A contract to do an act illegal because prohibited by law is equally void. So a sale of pork or wine is void according to Mohammedan law [113]; and the law of England will not enforce a contract of 'marriage brokage [114],' or for assigning the salary of a public officer.

Public policy.

Such contracts are sometimes said to be 'against public policy.' But this doctrine has been called 'a very unruly horse'; and in a recent case Sir G. Jessel observed: 'You are not to extend arbi-

109 For a list of the exceptions, real or apparent, to this rule recognised in English law, and a discussion of the difference between 'disclosed' and 'undisclosed' principals, see Dicey's Parties to an Action, pp. 134–143.

110 Blackburn v. Vigors, 12 App. Ca. 531.

111 Cf. supra, p. *209.

112 Inst. iii. 19. 1; Dig. xliv. 7. 31, xlv. 1. 35.

113 Hidâyah, ii. p. 429.

114 Cf. Cod. v. 1. 6; Dig. xlv. 1. 134.

trarily those rules which say that a given contract is void as being against public policy; because, if there is one thing which more than another public policy requires, it is that men shall have the utmost liberty of contracting, and that their contracts, when entered into freely and voluntarily, shall be held sacred, and shall be enforced by courts of justice. Therefore you have this paramount public policy to consider, that you are not lightly to interfere with freedom of contract [115].'

*243 iv. **Producing legal effects.*

The agreement must purport to produce a legally binding result. Thus the acceptance of an invitation to dinner, or an engagement to take a walking tour with a friend in Switzerland, are no contracts [116].

v. *On the relations of the parties.*

It must be of a nature to produce a binding result upon the mutual relations of the parties; therein differing from the agreement of a bench of judges, or of a board of directors, which has no reference to the relations of the judges, or directors, one to another.

vi. *Form or 'causa.'*

No system of law will enforce as a contract any transaction which does not exhibit all of the five characteristics already described. Even when these are all present, the transaction will generally be treated as a 'nudum pactum,' unless it is either effected in compliance with certain prescribed formalities, or is the result of some underlying fact, which the Roman jurists called 'causa.' First as to superadded formalities [117].

Form.

1. It is a topic of controversy whether 'formal' or 'informal' contracts are historically the earlier. Roman legal speculation

[115] Printing Company v. Sampson, L. R. 19 Eq. 465.

[116] 'Verborum quoque obligatio constat si inter contrahentes id agatur: nec enim si per iocum puta, vel demonstrandi intellectus causa ego tibi dixero "Spondes?" et tu responderis "Spondeo," nascetur obligatio.' Dig. xiv. 7. 3. Cf. Carlill v. Carbolic Smoke-Ball Co., '93, 1 Q. B. 256.

[117] Cf. supra, p. *107.

seems to have derived the informal contracts, which were attributed to the 'ius gentium,' from a primitive state of nature, formal contracts being regarded as later in date, because resulting from the idiosyncrasy of the Roman people.

Recent investigators, after examination of a far wider range of facts than was formerly accessible, are led to the conclusion that complexity, rather than simplicity, is the characteristic of primitive customs, and that the consensual kernel of contract has only gradually dispensed with the husk of ceremonial with which during long ages it was almost identified. The evidence in support
*244 of this view is very *strong, though it may be questioned whether its adherents have sufficiently noticed the fact that such bailments of every-day use as pledging and letting seem to have been made in very early times with no more formality than the mere transfer of the possession of an object, the ownership of which was probably notorious.

Same—Advantages of form.

A solemn form, be it observed, has two distinct advantages. In the first place, it prevents the bargain from being rashly struck; and in the second place, it facilitates the proof of what has occurred. The formal contract of the best ages of Roman law was the 'stipulatio,' or solemn question and answer, imitations of which may be found in the Marriage and Baptismal Services of the English Church. This, according to many writers, must have been a relic of a still more formal ceremony in which the solemn words were accompanied by the symbolic weighing of pieces of copper in the presence of a balance-holder and five witnesses; but Mr. W. A. Hunter has recently given some reason for thinking that the 'stipulatio' was independent of, and as old as, the 'mancipatio' itself [118]. It became usual to draw up a written memorandum, 'cautio,' of the stipulation, and this was held to be presumptive evidence that the contract had been entered into. The restriction which originally prevented a stipulation from being entered into by means of an agent was done away with in the later legislation.

118 Roman Law, p. 352.

Same—Varieties of form.

Among the Teutonic conquerors of the Roman empire, it seems that such contracts only were recognised as were either accompanied by a bailment, 're praestita,' or entered into by means of a formality, 'fides facta,' 'Wette,' 'Treugelobniss,' consisting in the delivery of a wand, 'festuca,' or similar object [119]. This was represented in later times by a shake of the hand, 'Hand-
*245 schlag,' 'Handsale.' Part payment *was represented by the 'Denier à Dieu,' 'Paumée,' or 'Weinkauf [120].'

Same—Seal.

Besides these methods the old French customary law recognised also obligation by a writing under seal [121]. So also the most solemn form known to the law of England is a deed, or document sealed and delivered. An agreement if thus entered into is called a 'specialty contract,' while if made in any other way, even in writing, it is a 'simple' or 'parol contract.' As Roman law enforced a 'stipulatio [122],' so English law enforces a 'specialty contract,' without looking behind it to enquire into its equitableness, or into the motives which caused it to be made; although both stipulations and deeds may be impeached on the ground of fraud, mistake, or duress [123]. The parties are also, as it is said,

119 See the references to Sohm's 'Eheschliessung' and 'Lex Salica,' contained in two articles by M. Esmein, 'sur les contrats dans le très-ancien droit français,' Nouv. Rev. Historique, t. iv. p. 656, t. v. p. 21, whence are derived several of the statements in the text. See also Essays in Anglo-Saxon Law, p. 189.

120 'Statuimus quod omnis emptio et venditio rata sit er firma perpetuo, si facta fuerit cum denario Dei iuridico et recepto.' Stat. municip. de la ville de Salon (1293). 'Emptio vel venditio non valet palmata, vel sine solutione pretii peculiari vel universali, vel sine rei traditione.' Cout. de Montpellier, cited by M. Esmein.

121 Beaumanoir, xxxv. 1.

122 The novel doctrine, that a stipulation needs a 'causa,' is combated by Savigny, Obligationenrecht, ii. pp. 249–266.

123 'For a time, a man was bound by his seal, although it was affixed against his will.' Holmes, Common Law, p. 272, citing Glanville, Britton, and other early authorities. In many States of the United States it is held that a mere flourish of the pen is a sufficient seal, and in some of them

'estopped' from denying the truth of the statements to which they have set their seals, and there is some authority for saying that an offer by deed is irrevocable, although it has not been accepted by the other party [124]. Certain agreements cannot be made otherwise than by deed [125].

*246 *The view that a merely consensual contract, which, says Bracton [126], was not enforced in the king's court, 'nisi aliquando de gratia,' ought to be recognised as legally binding, seems to be due to the canon law [127]. The customary civil law followed suit, enforcing at first promises under oath, and then promises generally, till Beaumanoir could assert, towards the end of the thirteenth century, 'Toutes convenences font à tenir et por ce dit on "convenence loi vaint [128]," exceptées les convenences qui sont fetes por malveses causes [129].'

Same—Writing.

A less solemn formality consists in the reduction of a bargain to writing.

the distinction between sealed and unsealed instruments has been expressly abolished. Ib. p. 273.

124 Xenos v. Wickham, L. R. 2 H. L. 296, in which some earlier cases are cited. It may however be hoped that this case may some day be explained away. The doctrine to which it gives countenance has, not unnaturally, been stigmatised as 'ein juristisches Monstrum,' Schlossman, Der Vertrag, p. 150, cited by Schuster, Archiv für Handelsrecht. xlv. p. 21.

125 It has been given as the reason of the sufficient character of a deed that it 'imports consideration.' The statement is artificial on the face of it, and becomes doubly so when we remember that deeds were binding before the doctrine of consideration had been worked out. See Sir W. R. Anson, Contract, ed. vii. p. 44.

126 Fol. 100 a. Cf. Glanville, liv. x. c. 18.

127 See c. 1. X. 35; c. 3. X. 1. 35; c. 13. X. 2. 1. On the early jurisdiction of the Court of Chancery in matters of contract, see an article by Mr. Justice Holmes in L. Q. R. i. p. 171.

128 Beaumanoir, says M. Esmein, knowingly puts a new meaning on this phrase, which in the Assize of Jerusalem merely approves of assignment inter vivos of property to which the assignor's heirs would be entitled on his death. Nouv. Rev. Hist. t. iv. p. 683.

129 Coutume de Beauvoisis, xxxiv. 2.

Same—Bills of exchange.

The 'chirographa' and 'syngraphae' of Roman law, and the bills of exchange and promissory notes of modern Europe, must be made in this way, or they could not be made at all; but many agreements which might very well be entered into by word of mouth have been rendered by positive enactment void unless embodied in a written document. This has of course been done with a view to guard against deception and disputes.

Same—The statute of frauds.

Increased freedom of contracting leads naturally to increasing difficulty in deciding whether a contract has been made or not. Hence in France the Ordonnance de Moulins, 1566, 'pour obvier à la multiplication des faits que l'on a vu ci-devant être mis en evant en jugement, sujets à preuve de témoins et reproches d'iceux, dont adviennent plusieurs inconvénients et involutions de procès,'
*247 prohibits proof by *witnesses when the matter in dispute exceeds 100 francs. Hence also the English 'Statute of Frauds,' passed 'for the prevention of many fraudulent practices, which are commonly endeavoured to be upheld by perjury and subornation of perjury,' provided that no contract for the sale of goods for the price of ten pounds and upwards, should 'be allowed to be good' unless there should be part delivery of the goods, or part payment of the price, or some note or memorandum in writing of the bargain made and signed by the parties, or their agents [130]. By the same Statute, 'no action shall be brought' on a contract which makes an executor personally liable, or guarantees the debt or default of another, or creates a liability in consideration of marriage, or relates to an interest in land, or is not to be performed within a year, unless it, 'or some memorandum or

[130] 29 Car. II. c. 3. s. 17. This section has been repealed by the Sale of Goods Act, 1893, but is reproduced, with slight variations, in s. 4 of that Act, as follows: 'A contract for the sale of any goods of *the value* of ten pounds or upwards shall not be *enforceable by action* unless the buyer shall accept part of the goods so sold, and actually receive the same, or give something in earnest to bind the contract, or in part payment, or unless some note or memorandum in writing of the contract be made and signed by the party to be charged or his agent in that behalf.'

note thereof, shall be in writing, and signed by the party to be charged therewith,' or by his agent [131]. An acknowledgment of a debt barred by the statutes of limitation must also be written and signed [132].

Cause.

2. Apart from those cases for which particular formalities are required, every legally permitted agreement is, according to French law, legally binding. This view has long prevailed, and is expressed in the old saying 'on lie les bœufs par les cornes et les hommes par les paroles [133].' It is qualified only by the
*248 rule that the agreement must have 'a cause,' *the precise meaning of which seems to be far from clear to the French commentators themselves [134].

Roman law only approximated, and that very gradually, to this point. It recognised but eight informal contracts, four of which, loan for consumption, loan for use, deposit and pledge, were accompanied by a bailment; while the other four—sale, letting, agency, and partnership—related to indispensable transactions of every-day occurrence. Other agreements, though never dignified by the name of contracts, were in later times enforced as 'pacta vestita.' All of these were accompanied by a 'causa,' which, though often consisting in part performance, was in effect only the mark by which an arbitrarily defined class of agreements were distinguishable; and agreements where there was no 'causa' continued to be treated as 'nuda pacta,' on which, though they might be ground for a plea, no action could be founded [135].

[131] 29 Car. II. c. 3. s. 4.

[132] 9 Geo. IV. c. 14. s. 1; 19 & 20 Vict. c. 97. s. 13. Cf. Code Civil, art. 134; Allg. Landrecht, i. tit. v. § 131.

[133] Loisel, Inst. Cout. liv. 3. tit. 1 règle 2. He continues· 'autant vaut une simple promesse ou convenance que les stipulations du droit romain.'

[134] Code Civil, arts. 1108, 1131; Pothier, Oblig. art 42. But see Dalloz, s. v. 'Obligation,' No. 498, where we are warned against taking 'cause' to be equivalent to 'motif,' to 'pourquoi,' or to 'objet.'

[135] 'Sed cum nulla subest causa, propter [praeter?] conventionem, hic constat non posse constitui obligationem.' Dig. ii. 14. 7. 4.

Consideration.

The binding force of a mere agreement is limited in another way by the law of England; which recognises no promise, unless it be under seal, for which there is no 'consideration[136].' It has been laid down by the highest authority, that, although 'it is undoubtedly true that every man is, by the law of nature, bound to fulfil his engagements, it is equally true that the law of this country supplies no means nor affords any remedy to compel the performance of an agreement made without sufficient consideration. All contracts are by the laws of England distinguished into agreements by specialty and agreements by parol; nor is there
*249 *any such third class as contracts in writing. If they be merely written and not specialties, they are parol, and a consideration must be proved[137].' A 'consideration' has been explained to be 'any act of the plaintiff from which the defendant, or a stranger, derives a benefit or advantage, or any labour, detriment, or inconvenience sustained by the plaintiff, however small the detriment or inconvenience may be, if such act is performed, or inconvenience suffered by the plaintiff with the assent, express or implied, of the defendant, or, in the language of pleading, at the special instance and request of the defendant[138].' The topic of consideration is one which is dealt with by the English and American Courts in great detail; most of the rules upon the subject may, however, be reduced to two principles. On the one hand, it is not necessary that the consideration be adequate: so where a person had undertaken gratuitously to carry for another, and deposit in a cellar, certain hogsheads of brandy, and he, or his serv-

[136] 'In one sense,' it has been said, 'everything is form which the law requires in order to make a promise binding, over and above the mere expression of the promisor's will. Consideration is a form as much as a seal.' Holmes, Common Law, p. 273. Cf. the dictum of Lord Mansfield, 'I take it that the ancient notion about the want of consideration was for the sake of evidence only,' in Pillans v. Van Mierop, 3 Burr. 1663.

[137] Rann v. Hughes, 8 T. R. 550. After this decision it was impossible to admit of exceptions to the rule, as had been suggested by Lord Mansfield, u. supra, in favour of written mercantile contracts. As to negotiable instruments, however, see Anson, Contract, ed. vii. p. 240.

[138] Per Tindal, C. J., Laythoarp v. Bryant, 3 Scott, 238. Cf. Currie v. Misa, L. R. 10 Ex. 162.

ants, so carelessly performed his promise that some of the brandy was lost, it was held that the owner trusting him with the goods was a sufficient consideration to oblige him to a careful management[139]; and when, in consideration of receiving permission to weigh two boilers, a promise was given that they should be returned in good condition, the permission was held to be a sufficient consideration[140]. On the other hand, the consideration must have some value. A promise therefore, to perform an already existing legal duty is no consideration; and a past fact, although it may be an influencing motive, can never be a good consideration,
*250 *which must always be either present ('executed') or future ('executory')[141]. It has indeed been truly observed that a consideration must always be present, since a future, or 'executory,' consideration consists in a present promise of the one party to do something in return for the present promise of the other party.

Modes of strengthening a contract.

In addition to the requisites insisted on by law as essential to the validity of a contract, other modes of strengthening its obligation have been resorted to by the contractors themselves. Some of these are of a supernatural character, consisting in oaths, by which the Deity is as it were made a party to the bargain, and which are sometimes taken in consecrated buildings or in the presence of sacred objects. The desired effect is however now more ordinarily produced by getting third parties to guarantee the contract, or by giving property by way of security for its due performance[142].

139 Coggs v. Bernard, 1 Smith, L. C. On this case see Holmes, Common Law, pp. 196, 292. The principle upon which it proceeds has been acutely criticised by Dr. Grueber in the Law Quarterly Review, ii. p. 33.

140 Bainbridge v. Firmstone, 8 A. & E. 743.

141 On the alleged exception to this rule, supported by the case of Lampleigh v. Braithwait, (1616)) Hob. 105, the principle of which is adopted by the Indian Contract Act, § 25, see Sir W. Anson, Contract, ed. vii. p. 95, and the remarks of Bowen, L. J. in Stewart v. Casey, '92, 1 Ch. 104.

142 Vid. supra, p. *201.

Rights resulting from a contract.

Supposing a contract to have been duly formed, what is its result? An obligation has been created between the contracting parties, by which rights are conferred upon the one and duties are imposed upon the other, partly stipulated for in the agreement, but partly also implied by law, which, as Bentham observes, 'has thus in every country supplied the shortsightedness of individuals, by doing for them what they would have done for themselves, if their imagination had anticipated the course of nature [143].' The character of those rights and liabilities depends of course in each case upon the special character of the contract.

Possible principles of classification of contracts.

Contracts have been classified upon many different principles. With reference, for instance, to—

(1) The number of parties on either side, they are 'joint' or 'several';

*251 *(2) Both parties, or only one, being bound to a performance, they are 'unilateral' or 'bilateral' ('synallagmatic [144]');

(3) Special solemnities being or not being required for their formation, they are 'formal' or 'formless';

(4) Their being entered into on their own account, or necessarily presupposing some other contract, they are 'principal' or 'accessory';

(5) Their object being liberality or gain, they are 'gratuitous' or 'onerous';

(6) Their being accompanied or not being accompanied by the delivery of an object, they are 'real' ('bailments [145]') or 'consensual';

(7) Their depending or not depending upon an uncertain event, they are 'aleatory' or not;

(8) Their being conditional or unconditional.

(9) They may also be classified with reference to the particular kind of benefit promised, e. g. exchange, rendering of services, &c.

143 Works, iii. p. 190. Cf. Hoadley v. Macleane, 10 Bing. 487.

144 'Ex uno latere constat contractus.' Dig. xix. 1. 13. 29.

145 Cf. infra, p. *262. Can there be a bailment without contract? See the cases cited in Pollock and Wright, Possession, p. 41 n.

Neglect of classification.

Most Codes go through the heads of contract seriatim, without attempting to arrange them upon any principle. The order of the French code, for instance, is the following: marriage, sale, letting, partnership, loan for use, loan for consumption, deposit, wagering contracts, mandate, suretyship, compromise, pledge, antichrèse, hypothèque [146]. This is hardly an advance upon the list of contracts incidentally given by Aristotle, viz. sale, loan of money, security, loan for use, deposit, letting for hire [147].

It is however not only possible, but instructive, to group the various contracts according to their natural affinities, which we shall now endeavour to do [148].

*252 * *Classification adopted.*

Contracts may be divided, in the first place, into those which are 'principal,' that is to say, which are entered into without an ulterior object, and those which are 'accessory,' i. e. which are entered into only for the better carrying out of a principal contract.

I. *Principal.*

Principal contracts may be subdivided into six classes, according as their object is, i. alienation; ii. permissive use; iii. marriage; iv. service; v. negative service; vi. aleatory gain.

For alienation.

i. An alienatory contract may be a mere act of liberality on one side, or each party may intend by means of it to secure some advantage for himself. In the former case it is a contract to give; in the latter, a contract to exchange.

146 Code Civil, arts. 1387–2203.

147 Eth. Nic. v. 2. 13. Other divisions will be found in Paley, Mor. Phil. i. p. 161; Hegel, Phil. des Rechts, p. 119; Trendelenburg, Naturrecht, Th. ii. § 105; Ihering, Der Zweck im Recht, i. p. 32.

148 The need of some reasonable grouping may be inferred from the fact that Mr. Story, jun., in his well-known work on Contracts, vol. i. p. 75, divides them into 1. bailments, 2. sale and warranty, 3. guarantee, 4. between landlord and tenant, 5. between master and servant.

Same—Liberalities.

A contract to give is usually enforceable only in certain rigidly defined cases. Thus in England it must be entered into by deed, in France before a notary [149]; in Roman law, though it may be made by word of mouth, it must be registered if dealing with a value exceeding five hundred solidi [150]. In Roman law and the derived systems ungrateful conduct on the part of the beneficiary would be ground for a rescission of the gift. Liberality is also often restrained by the claims of the family, or the creditors, of the giver. Thus, according to the French Code, the father of one child cannot give more than half of his fortune to a stranger [151], and a 'voluntary' alienation is not allowed by the law of England to defeat the claims of creditors [152].

Gifts in contemplation of marriage, which is, in the language of English law, a 'valuable' consideration, are not considered to be mere liberalities. The rules therefore which regulate the
*253 presents made to the husband by means of the *Roman 'dos,' and the presents made to the wife by means of an English jointure, or marriage settlement, are not those which would regulate merely 'voluntary' agreements.

Same—Exchange—Barter—Sale.

The earliest form of Exchange, or commutative alienation, is Barter, in which one commodity is given for another. So the Greeks before Troy are represented as bartering brass, iron, hides, oxen, and slaves for wine [153]. The exchange of commodities for a price in money, which superseded this ruder form of dealing, 'quia non semper nec facile concurrebat, ut cum tu haberes quod ego desiderarem, invicem haberem quod tu accipere velles [154],' is Sale. After a long controversy between opposing schools of the Roman jurists, it was finally settled that an agreement for barter, 'permutatio,' was a different contract from an agreement for sale, 'emptio venditio [155].' The latter is an agreement for the future transfer of property, 'merx,' in consideration of the payment, or an undertaking for the future payment, of a price in money, 'pret-

149 Code Civil, art. 931.

150 Inst. ii. 7. 2.

151 Code Civil, art. 913.

152 13 Eliz. c. 5.

153 Il. vii. 472.

154 Dig. xviii. 1. 1.

155 Inst. iii. 23.

ium.' When the price falls utterly short of the true value of the thing sold, the contract is, under some systems, rescissible on the ground of 'laesio enormis[156].'

Special formalities have been imposed upon contracts for the sale of certain kinds of property, such as 'res mancipi' by Roman law, and 'real property,' and goods of the value of ten pounds and upwards[157] by the law of England. The Anglo-Saxon laws directed every sale to be contracted before credible witnesses, and prohibited the sale of anything above the value of 20d. except in market overt. Subject to the observance of such formalities, where required, the contract is complete when the price is agreed
*254 upon[158]; and the vendor is bound to *place the property at the disposal of the vendee, who is then immediately bound to pay the price, unless the sale was on credit. The vendor is usually protected by being given a 'lien' upon moveable property sold, i. e. right to retain possession of it till the price is paid[159]. The law of England gives this further protection, known as the right of 'stoppage in transitu,' to the unpaid vendor, that he is allowed, even after he has parted with the possession of the goods, while they are still in transit and not delivered to the vendee, on hearing of the insolvency of the latter, to reclaim them and determine the contract.

Same—Warranties.

There is much divergence of view between different systems of law as to the extent to which a vendor impliedly warrants his title to the property sold or its quality. 'The guarantee,' says the French Code, 'which the vendor owes to the vendee is twofold. It regards, in the first place, the peaceable possession of the thing sold, in the second place, the latent faults of the thing, or its red-

[156] This doctrine originated in 285 A. D., when a Rescript of Diocletian and Maximian ordered that a sale of land for less than half its value should be rescissible, unless the purchaser should elect to pay a fair price. Cod. iv. 44. 2. For the application of the principle in modern codes, see Holzendorff, Rechtslexicon, ii. p. 623, and Pollock, Contract, Note L.

[157] V. supra, p. *247n.

[158] On the actual transfer of ownership, vid. supra, p. *189.

[159] This was unnecessary in Roman law, where, unless credit was given, no property passed before payment.

hibitory vices[160].' This is in general correspondence with the rules of Roman law, according to which the vendor, though he did not undertake to make the purchaser owner of the property, did guarantee him against being evicted from it[161], and also against all latent defects in the thing sold, on discovery of which the purchaser might proceed against him by the actions 'redhibitoria,' for rescission of the contract, or 'quanti minoris,' for proportional reduction of the price. The law of England is more lenient to the vendor, its general principle being 'caveat emptor.' With reference to quality, the exceptions to this principle are very few. A warranty of title was at one time held to be implied by a feoffment, and the use of the words 'grant' or 'give' in a conveyance was treated as equivalent to a covenant for quiet enjoyment, but this construction has been negatived by a
*255 modern *Act of Parliament[162]. The rules as to implied warranties of title or quality on a sale of goods have been recently codified[163].

For use.

ii. Contracts for permissive use are: 1. Loan for consumption, 'mutuum'; 2. Loan for use, 'commodatum'; 3. Letting for hire, 'locatio conductio.'

Same—Mutuum.

1. A Loan for consumption takes place when money or things 'quae pondere, numero, mensurave constant,' sometimes called 'res fungibiles[164],' are given to a man on the understanding that he shall on a future day return to the giver, not necessarily the things themselves, but their equivalent in kind. Since the object given becomes the property of the borrower, the contract might be regarded as one of alienation. It is however practically one for use only, since either the identical object, or a similar object, has to be returned to the lender. The contract takes of course many

160 Art. 1625. 161 Dig. xxi. 2. 1. 162 8 & 9 Vict. c. 106. s. 4.

163 See the Sale of Goods Act, 1893, 56 & 57 Vict. c. 71. ss. 12–15.

164 Supra, p. *92. The various theories as to the true meaning of these distinctions are exhaustively discussed in 'Les choses fongibles et les choses de consommation,' par E. Roguin, Lausanne, 1892.

forms. Thus money at a banker's is a loan for consumption to the banker, to be returned when, and as, it is called for by cheques. The loan is, as a rule, gratuitous, interest not being usually due upon it, in the absence of special agreement. The highest amount of interest which may be agreed upon has very generally been fixed by law; but the inefficacy of thus attempting to protect borrowers against extortion was conclusively established by Bentham, and the English usury laws were repealed by a Statute of the present reign [165].

The sole duty of the borrower, in the absence of any liability for interest, is to return objects of the same quantity and quality as those which he has received, and no excuse will avail him for the non-performance of this duty.

Same—Commodatum.

2. In a Loan for use, which is essentially gratuitous, the
*256 *duty of the borrower is to return the identical thing lent, and to use it in the meantime in accordance with the terms of the contract. He is not generally responsible for ordinary wear and tear, nor for loss by theft, but, since the contract is wholly for his benefit, he will be generally expected to bestow great care upon the thing.

Same—Letting.

3. Letting differs from Loan for use in being for the advantage of both parties, since the hirer pays a rent, 'merces,' to the latter [166]. A hirer therefore is not bound, in the absence of express stipulation, to exercise the same care as is expected from a borrower.

A lease of lands is usually accompanied by greater formalities than a letting of moveables. If for more than three years,

[165] 17 & 18 Vict. c. 90.

[166] Under 'locatio conductio' Roman law included not only the hiring of the use of a thing, 'rei,' but the hiring of services, 'operarum' (which we shall treat separately), and agreement for the doing of a given piece of work, 'operis.' With reference to this last-mentioned application of the contract, the usual terminology is inverted. The person for whom the work is to be done is the 'locator,' the person who undertakes to do it is the 'conductor.' Cf. Code Civil, art. 1708.

it must, according to English law, be by deed. Different views are taken of the right of the hirer to sub-let; of the effect of the accidental destruction during the term of the thing let; of the extent to which the lessor guarantees that the thing shall prove suitable for the purpose for which it is hired; of the respective rights of landlord and tenant in the case of improvements effected by the latter, especially as to those additions to a building which English law calls 'fixtures,' and with regard to 'emblements,' or crops annually produced by the labour of the cultivator ('fructus industriales,' as opposed to 'fructus naturales'), which may be growing on the land at the expiration of the tenancy.

To marry.

iii. Engagements to marry, 'sponsalia [167],' are easily distinguishable from marriage itself. Just as an agreement for sale
*257 gives rise only to personal claims, while an actual *conveyance creates new real rights, so an engagement is a contract 'per verba de futuro,' creating a right 'in personam' to its fulfilment at the appointed time, while marriage is entered into 'per verba de praesenti,' and creates a 'status.' The former is a true obligatory contract such as those which we are now considering. The latter is a contract only in that wide sense of the term in which it may be applied to any agreement affecting the legal rights of the parties, but leaving no outstanding claims between them [168].

Same—Betrothal and marriage.

This theory, developed by the canonists from the doctrines of Roman law, has at length superseded the theory of the Teutonic races which attached more importance to the betrothal than to the subsequent wedding. Betrothal, 'Verlobung,' seems to have been a sale of the woman by her guardian for a 'pretium puellae,' 'Mundschatz,' or 'Witthum.' This came to be represented by a handsel, and was not paid over till the wedding, 'Trauung,' actually took

[167] 'Sponsalia sunt mentio et repromissio nuptiarum futurarum.' Dig. xxiii. 1. 1.

[168] Supra, pp. *189, *216. The canonists distinguish 'sponsalia de futuro' (betrothal) from 'sponsalia de praesenti' (marriage).

place. In later times the betrothal was the woman's own act, and the handsel was payable to herself [169].

Same—Clandestine and regular marriages.

The distinction between 'sponsalia' and 'matrimonium' has been to some extent obscured by another which divides actual marriages into 'clandestine' and 'regular.' A clandestine marriage is one which rests merely on the agreement of the parties. The Christian Church, adopting from Roman law the maxim that 'consensus facit matrimonium,' though it stigmatised such marriages as irregular, because not made 'in facie ecclesiae,' nevertheless upheld them as valid, till the Council of Trent declared all marriages to be void unless made in the presence of a priest and witnesses. Before the time of the Council, and after it in countries, such as France and England, where the decree in question was not received, either of the parties to a clandestine marriage 'per
*258 verba de *praesenti' could compel the other, by a suit in the
ecclesiastical court, to solemnise it in due form. It has been judicially stated that the English common law never recognised a contract 'per verba de praesenti' as a valid marriage till it had been duly solemnised [170], although it recognised it, under the name of a 'pre-contract of marriage,' a term which covered also promises 'per verba de futuro,' down to the middle of the last century, as giving either of the parties a right to sue for celebration, and as impeding his or her marriage with a stranger to the contract [171].

Same—The action for breach of promise.

It has been much discussed whether an engagement to marry 'per verba de futuro,' as distinguished from an actual marriage, whether 'clandestine' or 'regular,' ought to be enforced by law. It seems to have been the old practice in Latium, and probably also at Rome, for the father of a girl to enter into a stipulation with her lover on which he could bring an action [172]. According to

169 See Baring-Gould, Germany, Present and Past, p. 98, citing Friedberg, Verlobung und Trauung, 1876.

170 R. v. Millis, 10 Cl. & Fin., 655.

171 These consequences were removed by 26 Geo. II. c. 33.

172 Gell. iv. 4; Dig. xxiii. 1. 2.

later Roman law 'sponsalia' were entered into without any formalities, and could be repudiated at will by either party, though if 'arrhae' had been given, the party which broke off the match would lose twice the amount [173]. It must however be remembered that marriage itself could be dissolved with equal ease. Actions for breach of promise of marriage seem to have first gained a footing in England in the reign of Charles I, when it was held that the promise is a 'good' and not merely a 'spiritual' consideration, and that whether it be made to a man or to a woman [174]. Modern continental law admits very sparingly of such an action. It
*259 is recognised by the Prussian Landrecht [175], *but expressly denied by the code of Italy [176]. In the silence of the French code, the courts have expressed contradictory views upon the subject, but, according to the better opinion, interference with the freedom of matrimonial choice being contrary to public policy, no action will lie unless the plaintiff has sustained a 'préjudice réel [177],' and the Austrian code contains an express provision to this effect [178].

For services.

iv. The more important contracts for services are: 1. for caretaking; 2. for doing work on materials; 3. for carriage; 4. for professional or domestic services; 5. for agency; 6. for partnership. Service of any kind may be to be rendered either gratuitously or for reward, the responsibility of undertaking to render it being considerably greater in the latter case than in the former.

173 'Alii desponsatae renuntiare conditioni et nubere alii non prohibentur.' Cod. v. 1. 1. Cf. Frag. Vat. 262; Cod. Theod. iii. 5; Dig. xxiii. 1, xxiv. 2. 2. 2. According to Paulus, 'inhonestum visum est vinculo paenae matrimonia obstringi, sive futura, sive iam contracta.' Dig. xlv. 1. 134 pr.

174 Rolle Abr. 22; 2 Bulstr. 48.

175 Th. ii. tit. 1. ss. 75, 82.

176 Art. 53.

177 i. e. it is held that the remedy, if any, is under art. 1382 of the Code, and not under art. 1142.

178 Arts. 45, 46. Cf. the draft Civil Code for Germany, § 1228, which goes on to provide that one betrothed party whose misconduct obliges the other to rescind the contract is liable to compensate the latter for expenses incurred.

Thus the gratuitous contractor is, in English law, not liable for an omission to perform, and liable only for gross negligence in performing.

Same—Deposit.

1. Gratuitous care-taking of an object, commonly called 'deposit,' is well defined as 'a naked bailment of goods to be kept by the bailee without reward.' Of this contract, 'sequestratio' and the 'depositum miserabile,' or 'necessarium,' are recognised as species by the civilians [179]. The former occurs when an object, the right to which is disputed, is placed in the custody of a third party, pending the decision of the dispute; the latter, when the deposit is made under circumstances, such as fire or shipwreck, which leave the depositor no choice. Care-taking for reward is exercised, for instance, by warehousemen, wharfingers, the 'cloak rooms' of railway companies, livery-stable keepers, and inn-
*260 keepers. The very *extensive liabilities attaching to the last-mentioned class of depositaries by the English common law have been much reduced by a modern Act of Parliament [180].

Same—Work on materials.

2. A gratuitous contractor to do work upon materials belonging to the other contractor is usually liable only for gross negligence in the doing of it. If the contract be for reward, each of the parties is responsible to the other for the exercise of a high degree of care [181]. English law gives to the person who does the work a 'lien' upon the article upon which he has done it till he has been paid for his trouble [182]. A gratuitous agreement to do work upon materials belonging to the contractor, for the benefit of another, would amount to a promise to give an article as yet unfinished. If the work is to be done for reward, as when a builder undertakes to construct a house or a tailor to make a coat, it may be ques-

179 Dig. xvi. 3. 1; xxiv. 3. 22; Code Civil, arts. 1947–1963.

180 26 & 27 Vict. c. 41.

181 This contract is narrower than 'locatio conductio operis,' which covers not only agreements for working upon materials, but also for doing any definite piece of work, such as navigating a ship from one port to another.

182 Supra, p. *203.

tioned whether the contract is one of sale, or for the performance of services [183].

Same—Carriage.

3. A contract of carriage may relate to conveyance by land or by sea, and to goods or to passengers. Carriers of goods, besides their duty to carry, share many of the responsibilities of depositaries, and especially of inn-keepers, in respect of the property confided to them. According to English law, a 'common carrier' is bound to take all goods of the kind which he usually carries, unless his conveyance is full, or the goods be specially dangerous; but may charge different rates to different customers. He is supposed to warrant 'safely and securely to carry,' and so is said to be 'an insurer against all loss not immediately caused by
*261 "the act of God [184]" *or the king's enemies.' He is thus responsible, even though he is robbed, or the goods are accidentally burnt. By recent legislation his right of limiting his liability by public notice has been much curtailed, while, on the other hand, he is no longer to be liable for the loss of very valuable articles, unless the sender has declared their value and paid a higher rate for their carriage accordingly [185]. An ordinary common carrier may still limit his liability by a special contract, but such a contract, if made by a railway or canal company, must not only be signed by the sender, but must also be such as the Courts will hold to be just and reasonable. And a railway is not allowed to charge different rates to different customers [186].

The carriage of goods by sea is usually regulated by a special contract between the ship-owner and the freighter called a 'charter

[183] Inst. iii. 24. 4; Dig. xviii. 1. 65, xix. 2. 22. 2. Cf. Lee v. Griffin, 1 B. & S. 272.

[184] See the remarks of Sir F. Pollock, Contract, ed. vi., p. 396, on 'Act of God,' which he is unable to define more precisely than as 'an event which, as *between the parties*, and *for the purpose of the matter in hand*, cannot be definitely foreseen or controlled.' Cf. Bailey v. De Crespigny, L. R. 4 Q. B. 185. 'Vis maior,' says Gaius, 'quam Graeci θεοῦ βίαν appellant, non debet conductori damnosa esse, si plus quam tolerable est laesi fuerint fructus.' Dig. xix. 2. 25. 6.

[185] 11 Geo. IV. & 1 Will. IV. c. 68.

[186] See 17 & 18 Vict. c. 31, 36 & 37 Vict. c. 48, and 51 & 52 Vict. c. 25.

party,' by which the owner is generally relieved from liability for the act of God and the king's enemies. His liability has also been limited by English statute law to the value of £8 per ton of the ship's tonnage [187], nor is he responsible for loss by fire, nor for very valuable articles unless declared and paid for specially [188]. The payment to be made by the sender of the goods to the owner of the ship is called 'freight.'

Carriers of passengers do not insure their safety, but are usually liable for injuries caused to them by neglect or unskilfulness. The liability of a gratuitous carrier would be similar to that of a gratuitous depositary.

Same—Professional service.

4. Each of the heads of service hitherto considered implies
*262 *a 'bailment,' or handing over of an object with reference to which some work is to be done. In professional and domestic services no bailment is presupposed, the undertaking being merely for the performance by one party of certain acts for the benefit of the other. Such an undertaking for reward is described in the language of Roman law as 'locatio conductio operarum.' The exercise of certain professions was thought by the Romans to be of too liberal a nature to be capable of leading to a compensation in money recoverable by judicial process. Advocates, teachers of law or grammar, philosophers, surveyors, and others were accordingly incapable of suing for their fees [189]. A similar disability attaches to barristers under English law to this day, and, so long as the Royal College chooses to maintain a by-law to that effect, to physicians also [190]. Those who thus give their aid gratuitously are, as a rule, free from liability for the negligent performance of their self-imposed task; but a professional person, employed for

[187] See now the Merchant Shipping Act, 1894, 57 & 58 Vict. c. 60, s. 503.

[188] Ib. s. 502.

[189] 'Non crediderunt veteres inter talem personam locationem et conductionem esse, sed magis operam beneficii loco praeberi: et id quod datur ei ad remunerandum dari, et inde honorarium appellari.' Dig. xi. 6. 1 pr.

[190] See 21 & 22 Vict. c. 90. s. 31, now superseded by 49 & 50 Vict. c. 48. s. 6; Gibbons v. Budd, 2 H. & C. 92.

reward, is held to guarantee that he is reasonably skilful and competent, and can recover nothing for unskilful work [191].

Same—Domestic service.

The position of a domestic servant still exhibits traces of the status of slavery out of which it undoubtedly has everywhere been developed [192]. A servant is usually entitled to his wages although prevented by sickness from doing his work. The rule of English law that a master is not in general liable for injuries which his servant may sustain in the course of his employment or which arise from the negligence of a fellow-servant has led, especially when applied to the working of large undertakings, such as railways, to a good deal of hardship, and has recently been modified [193].

*263 **Same—Agency.*

5. We have already had occasion to consider how far the rights and liabilities of contracting parties may be affected by their contract being made through the intervention of an agent [194]. The rights and liabilities in question were those of the principal contractors, as against one another, or of the agent in those exceptional cases in which, by the force of circumstances, he himself acquires the rights or incurs the liabilities of a principal. The questions which thus arise out of contracting by agency are of a wholly different character from those which arise out of 'the contract of agency,' which is the topic now to be discussed.

There is a species of contract for services, entered into, not between two principals, but between a principal and his agent. The undertaking of the agent, 'mandatarius,' is to represent his principal, 'mandans,' in dealings with third parties [195].

191 Cf. Grill v. Genl. Iron Screw Colliery Co., L. R. 1 C. P. 612.

192 A contract to serve during one's whole life a particular master is allowed by English law. Wallis v. Day, 2 M. & W. 273, 1 Sm. L. C. 361.

193 Supra, p. *138.

194 Supra, p. *240.

195 Agency, if undertaken for the benefit of the principal, is, in the language of the civilians, 'mandatum simplex'; if for the benefit of a third party, 'mandatum qualificatum.' It is then a species of 'intercessio.' Cf. Glück, Pand. xv. p. 290.

Same—Growth of agency.

The possibility of such a representation seems to be admitted only in developed systems of law. In the older Roman law a man could be represented in dealings with others only by persons 'in his power,' such as a slave or unemancipated son, and only by such of their acts as were for his advantage. The contractual agency of a stranger was only gradually introduced, and was long recognised only as a gratuitous act of friendship. 'Originem ex officio atque amicitia trahit: contrarium ergo est officio merces,' says Paulus [196]. The 'mandatarius,' though thus gratuitous, was obliged to exhibit in the execution of his voluntary promise the highest degree of care, and in default was not only liable for damages, but was also punished with infamy. His principal, on the other hand, was bound only to indemnify him for any liability incurred in, or expenses incident to, the execution of the contract.
*264 *A payment might indeed be specially promised to the mandatary for his service, but was disguised under the name of a 'honorarium,' and could be recovered only under an exceptional procedure.

The importance of agency, defined by the French Code as 'an act by which one person gives to another the power to do something for the principal and in his name [197],' has greatly increased with the development of business transactions. The presumption, according to the Code, is in favour of its being gratuitous, but English law, in the absence of evidence of a contrary intention, would imply a promise of reasonable remuneration. Under any system the principal will doubtless be held to guarantee the agent against expenses and personal liability, and the agent will be obliged to conduct the business of his principal with care, and, as a rule, not to delegate its management to another. The contract must for some purposes be entered into in a special form, as by a 'power of attorney,' or before a notary. The rights and liabilities which result from it are terminated, subject to certain qualifications, by the death or bankruptcy of either principal or agent; by efflux of time, when a period is fixed for the performance of the act to be done by the agent; by performance of the act; by revocation

196 Dig. xvii. 1. 1. 4.

197 Art. 1984; cf. Code de Commerce, art. 91.

of authority on the part of the principal; by renunciation of the commission on the part of the agent.

Same—Classes of agents.

Agents are of various classes. Among the more important classes recognised by English law are 'factors,' who are employed to sell goods for their principal. They have actual possession of the goods, and usually sell them in their own name [198]. 'Brokers' are mere mediums of communication between buyer and seller. 'Del credere' agents for the sale of goods, in consideration of a higher payment than usual, become responsible for the solvency of the person to whom they sell them. Auctioneers, al- *265 though before the goods are *knocked down they are agents only for the seller, become afterwards agents for the buyer also.

Same—Partnership.

6. When several persons unite for the purpose of carrying on business in common, which is usually done upon the terms that each of them shall be an agent for all the rest, the contract is called partnership, 'societas,' and takes various shapes, according to the business contemplated. It is defined in the French Code as 'a contract by which two or more persons agree to place something in common, with a view of sharing the profit which may result [199].' By 'the Partnership Act, 1890,' the contract is defined as 'the relation which subsists between persons carrying on business in common with a view to profit [200].' In the widest sense of the term, a partnership might be 'universorum bonorum,' relating to all the property of the partners, howsoever acquired; or 'universorum quae ex quaestu veniunt,' relating only to profits made in business dealings generally; or 'negotiationis alicuius,' relating only to the profits of a particular undertaking [201].

The contract must be in writing, according to French law if re-

[198] A factor could not pledge the goods entrusted to him, till he was empowered to do so by the 'Factors Acts,' consolidated in 1889.

[199] Art. 1832.

[200] § 1. Companies are afterwards excepted.

[201] Dig. xvii. 2. 5; cf. Code Civil, arts. 1835–42.

lating to a value greater than 150 fr., according to the English law as to contracts generally, if it is not to be performed within the year. An agreement that one partner is to have all the profits, though the other is to share in the losses, called in Roman law 'leonina societas,' is void [202]. A partnership may of course be for life or for a definite time.

It is terminated by mutual consent, or, if formed for no definite period, by the retirement of one partner even against the wish of the others, by efflux of the time for which it was formed, by the death or bankruptcy of any of the partners, and by some other causes [203]. In derogation of the ordinary rules as to survivorship in joint tenancy, English law recognises that in partnership
*266 matters 'ius accrescendi inter *mercatores locum non habet.'

Each partner is liable to account to the others and is responsible for careful management. On the other hand, he has a right of 'contribution,' 'regress,' against the other partners, to be indemnified for liabilities incurred for their common advantage.

Same—Classification of partnerships.

A classification of trading partnerships which is due to the French Code of Commerce divides them into 'sociétés en nom collectif,' i. e. carrying on business under the name of a firm with unlimited liability; 'sociétés en commandite' in which, besides the ostensible and fully responsible partners, there are others whose liability is limited to the money which they have placed in the concern; and 'sociétés anonymes,' which bear a name indicating merely the nature of the undertaking, can be formed only with the sanction of the Government, and are wholly carried on by means of a capital divided into equal shares, 'actions,' beyond the amount of which the shareholders incur no risk. They are, in effect, companies with limited liability [204]. Different views are taken of the

[202] Dig. xvii. 29. 2.

[203] Dig. xvii. 2. 63.

[204] Code de Commerce, art. 19; cf. Handelsgesetzbuch, arts. 15, &c. The German law of 1892 permits the establishment of partnerships in which the liability of all the partners is limited, and the partners have the novel power of calling up additional contributions, not for the satisfaction of creditors, but to increase working capital. See 9 Law Quarterly Review, p. 62. As to Companies, v. infra, Chapter XIV. The provisions of 28 & 29 Vict. c. 86 (see now 53 & 54 Vict. c. 39), intended to introduce into England

question whether an executory contract of partnership should be enforced by law; whether, that is to say, any one should be obliged to become a partner against his will, or mulcted in damages for refusing to become one.

For negative service.

v. Contracts for negative services, in which one party promises to abstain from certain acts, are somewhat grudgingly recognised by law, as interfering with freedom. So, although English law will recognise as valid an agreement not to marry a spec-
*267 ified person, it will refuse to enforce a *general covenant not to marry, as being against public policy. A promise whereby a man is restrained altogether, or within very wide limits, from carrying on his profession or trade has been held to be similarly void; but unless the restriction is unreasonable, or against public policy [205], the tendency of recent cases is to uphold it [206].

Aleatory.

vi. An aleatory, or wagering, contract is defined in the French Code as 'one of the effects of which, as to both profit and loss, whether for all the parties, or for one or several of them, depend on an uncertain event [207].' This description includes agreements of very different kinds.

Same—Wagers.

1. Bets and stakes are, as a rule, not enforced under modern systems of law [208]. Not long since an action could have been

something like a partnership en commandite, seem to have remained a dead letter. See Pollock's Essays in Jurisprudence and Ethics, p. 100.

[205] Cf. supra, p. *242.

[206] See Rousillon v. Rousillon, 14 Ch. D. 35; Davies v. Davies, 36 Ch. D. 359; Maxim-Nordenfeldt Gun Co. v. Nordenfeldt, '93, 1 Ch. 630, '94 A. C. 535.

[207] Art. 1964. This definition is criticised by Sir W. Anson as being wide enough to include e. g. a guarantee. He observes that, to constitute a wager, 'the transaction between the parties must wholly depend on the risk in contemplation, and neither must look to anything but the payment of money on the determination of the uncertainty.' Contract, ed. vii. p. 187.

[208] Bets on games were generally forbidden by Roman law, subject to certain exceptions ('praeterquam si quis certet hasta, vel pilo iaciendo, vel currendo, saliendo, luctando, pugnando, quod virtutis causa fiat.' Dig. xi.

maintained in England upon a wager, not contrary to public policy, or immoral, or offensive to the feelings or character of third parties; but it has been provided by a statute of the present reign that 'all contracts or agreements whether by parol or in writing, by way of gaming or wagering, shall be null and void [209].' This enactment is however expressly declared not to apply to any subscription or contribution for any plates, prizes, or sum of
*268 money to be *awarded to the winner of any lawful game, sport, pastime, or exercise. The French Code, in refusing any action for a gaming debt or the payment of a bet, makes a similar exception in favour of 'les jeux propres à exercer au fait des armes, les courses à pied ou à cheval, les courses de chariot, le jeu de paume, et autres jeux de même nature qui tiennet à l'adresse et à l'exercice du corps [210].' Some gaming contracts have been declared not only void but also illegal [211], and the difference in the character of the contract leads to different rules as to the recovery of money lent to enable it to be made, or paid mistakenly in pursuance of it.

Same—Lotteries.

2. Lotteries are illegal in England [212].

Same—Stock-jobbing.

3. Wagering contracts on the price of stock were made void and penal by an Act, now repealed, passed 'to prevent the infamous practice of stock-jobbing [213].'

Same—Annuities.

4. An agreement to pay an annuity so long as a given individual shall live, 'rente viagère,' whether the individual in question is a

5. 2), reduced by Justinian to five in number. Money paid by the loser could be recovered by him, or should he decline to sue for it, by the public authorities of the district. Cod. iii. 43.

209 8 & 9 Vict. c. 109, s. 18. By 55 Vict. c. 9, payments made by an agent in pursuance of such contracts cannot be recovered from his principal.

210 Code Civil, arts. 1965–7.

211 E. g. by 5 & 6 W. IV. c. 41.

212 By 10 & 11 W. III. and later Acts.

213 7 Geo. II. c. 8, repealed by 23 Vict. c. 28.

party to the contract or not, will generally be supported. It will be void, under the French Code, if the person on whose life it depends is ill at the time when it is made and dies of the same illness within twenty days [214].

Same—Nautica pecunia.

5. Loans to a shipowner, to be repaid only in case of the successful termination of a voyage. Of such a nature are the contracts known as 'traiectitia,' or 'nautica pecunia,' 'prêt à la grosse,' 'bottomry,' and 'respondentia.' They have always been allowed to be effected, by way of compensation for the risk run by the lender, at an extraordinary rate of interest, 'nauticum foenus.'

Same—Insurance.

6. Insurance is a contract by which one party, in consideration
of a premium, engages to indemnify another against a con-
*269 tingent loss, by making him a payment in compensation *if,
or when, the event shall happen by which the loss is to accrue.

Same—Marine insurance.

'Marine insurance,' according to an English statute, is of immemorial usage, 'by means whereof it cometh to pass, upon the loss or perishing of any ship, there followeth not the undoing of any man, but the loss lighteth rather easily upon many than heavily upon few [215].' The insurers are known as 'underwriters,' because each of them signs the contract, or 'policy,' engaging to bear a certain proportion of the whole indemnity, which may apply to the ship, to the freight which it is to earn, or to anything on board. They are usually liable in case of the loss, either total or partial, of the ship or cargo, by any peril of the sea during a given voyage, to the extent of the owner's loss, and also for any payments he may have been compelled to make on account of 'salvage,' or by way of 'general average,' 'avaries grosses.'

Same—Fire and Life insurance.

Loss occasioned by fire on land is indemnified against by 'fire insurance'; and damage of other kinds, e. g. to crops by bad

[214] Code Civil, art. 1968.

[215] 43 Eliz. c. 12.

weather or to glass by hailstones, by analogous contracts. 'Life insurance' has similarly been imitated of late years by contracts for compensation in case of illness or accident. It has been thought proper to restrict by legislation the right of insuring without any interest in the risk insured against [216], but a life insurance differs from insurances of other kinds in the amount which can be recovered under it. Policies of insurance against fire or marine risk are contracts to recoup the loss which parties may sustain from particular causes. When such a loss is made good aliunde, the companies are not liable for a loss which no longer exists; but in a life policy there is no such provision [217].

II. *Accessory contracts.*

Many contracts are entered into for the purpose of creating a right which is to be merely ancillary to another right. Of
*270 such contracts, which may properly be described *as 'accessory,' the more important species are—1. Suretyship; 2. Indemnity; 3. Pledge; 4. Warranty; 5. Ratification; 6. Account stated; 7. For further assurance.

Suretyship.

1. Suretyship, or guarantee, 'intercessio,' in French 'caution,' is a collateral engagement to answer for the debt, default, or miscarriage of another. Although thus entirely subsidiary in its nature, it is sometimes legally binding when the obligation to which it is subsidiary is merely 'natural,' in other words is incapable of being judicially enforced [218]. A promise made by a slave to his master, though it gave rise only to a natural obligation, would nevertheless, in Roman law, support a 'fideiussio'; and in French, if not in English law, a guarantee of a promise made by a minor, and therefore of no effect, may be enforced by action [219]. The contract is under some systems a formal one. In Roman law it was made by stipulation, and in England, by the Statute of Frauds, must be in writing. It is a maxim that the liability of the surety

[216] E. g. 19 Geo. II. c. 37; 14 Geo. III. c. 48.

[217] Darrell v. Tibbitts, 5 Q. B. D. 560.

[218] Supra, p. *214, infra p. *311 n.

[219] Code Civil, art. 2012.

may be less than, but cannot exceed, that of the principal debtor. Under some systems it passes, under others it does not pass, to his heirs. A contract of suretyship raises three classes of questions. As between the surety and the creditor, it may be asked, what acts on the part of the creditor, e. g. giving time to the debtor, will discharge the surety from his liability; whether the surety may insist on the creditor bringing his action in the first instance against the principal debtor, 'beneficium ordinis'; whether each of several sureties is liable for the whole debt, 'in solidum,' or only for a proportionate share of it, 'beneficium divisionis.' As between a surety and the defaulting debtor, it may be questioned how far the former is entitled to the remedies of the creditor against the latter, 'beneficium cedendarum actionum,' or to 'regress' against him on an implied contract of indemnity. As between several sureties, it is necessary to determine how far any
*271 one of them who discharges the debt *for which all are jointly liable is entitled to 'contribution' from the others [220]. The liability of a surety to the creditor terminates by a discharge either of the principal obligation by the debtor, or of the guarantee by one of his co-sureties.

Indemnity.

2. A promise to indemnify, or save harmless, may be express or implied. It is implied not only between principal and surety, and, in some systems, between one surety and his co-sureties, but also in the contract of agency. The principal promises by implication to indemnify his agent, except in the performance of illegal acts, as to which it is a maxim that 'there is no contribution between wrong-doers.'

Pledge.

3. The contract of Pledge, besides giving rise, as we have seen, to a peculiar species of right 'in rem [221],' gives rise also to rights 'in personam.' The debtor is entitled not only to have the thing pledged re-delivered to him, on the due payment of his debt, but

[220] The English doctrine of contribution between co-sureties was unknown in Roman Law.

[221] Supra, p. *201.

also to have it preserved with reasonable care in the meantime. Whether it may be used by the creditor will depend on the terms of the contract. The creditor, on the other hand, can claim to be indemnified against any expense to which he may be put in taking care of the pledge.

Warranty.

4. A Warranty has been defined as 'an express or implied statement of something which the party undertakes shall be part of the contract; and, though part of the contract, collateral to the express object of it [222].' On the one hand, it is a term added to a contract, and must therefore be distinguished from mere representations made with reference to the matter of the contract, but forming no part of the agreement of the parties. On the other hand, it is not so intimately connected with the contract as to be a 'condition precedent' to the contract coming into opera-
*272 tion. It may be broken and give rise to *a right of action for damages, without producing any effect upon the contract to which it is annexed [223].

A warranty refers most usually to title or to quality, and though most frequently accessory to a contract of sale, is also added to other contracts, for instance to a letting for hire [224].

Ratification.

5. Ratification is the adoption by a person as binding upon himself of an act previously done by him, but not so as to be productive of a subsisting legal obligation, or done by a stranger having at the time no authority to act as his agent.

The ratification of a contract barred by the statutes of limitation must in England be in writing, signed by the original con-

[222] Lord Abinger, C. B., in Chanter v. Hopkins, 4 M. & W. 404. Sir W. Anson, Law of Contract, ed. vii. p. 307 n., has distinguished no less than six senses in which this term is employed by English lawyers.

[223] For the purposes of the Sale of Goods Act, 1893, a 'warranty' is defined, s. 62, as 'an agreement with reference to goods which are the subject of a contract of sale, but collateral to the main purpose of such contract, the breach of which gives rise to a claim for damages, but not to a right to reject the goods and treat the contract as repudiated.'

[224] Cf. supra, p. *209, as to an implied warranty of authority as an agent.

tractor, or his agent duly authorised [225]. A recent Act of Parliament has made of no effect any promise made by a person of full age to pay any debt contracted by him during infancy, or any ratification made after full age of any promise or contract made during infancy [226].

The contract of a stranger can be adopted by a course of action, as well as by words or writing, but can be adopted only by one on whose behalf it was made. The agent must have intended to act for the person who by subsequent ratification becomes his principal. 'Ratihabitio,' says Julian, 'constituet tuum negotium quod ab initio tuum non erat, sed tua contemplatione gestum [227].'

Account stated.

6. Akin to ratification are the 'constitutum' of Roman law, and the promise of repayment which English law implies on an 'account stated'; as are also I. O. U.'s and promissory notes. The contract in all these cases is superadded to a preexisting con-
*273 tract by way of strengthening it; so that the *creditor may rely either upon his original claim, or upon the new claim thus created, but can in no way receive more than the sum originally due. There are cases in which the creditor can recover upon the new contract, although the old one was not legally enforceable [228].

For further assurance.

7. Conveyances of land, and other instruments, frequently contain covenants 'for further assurance,' and the like, which are strictly accessory to the principal contract in which they are inserted.

TRANSFER OF RIGHTS IN PERSONAM.

We have seen that a number of rights 'in rem' are untransferable, and this is still more usually the case with rights 'in personam.' The transfer of these, when it takes place at all, takes place either 'by act of law' or 'by act of party [229].'

225 9 Geo. IV. c. 14. s. 1; 19 & 20 Vict. c. 97. s. 13.

226 37 & 38 Vict. c. 62.

227 Dig. iii. 5. 6. 9.

228 See Chitty, Contracts, p. 589.

229 Supra, p. *141.

By act of law.

i. Certain sets of circumstances are invested by law with the attribute of effecting a transfer of rights 'in personam,' and sometimes also of the corresponding liabilities, to new persons of inherence and of incidence respectively. So in English law, most of the rights and liabilities of a woman passed on marriage till lately to her husband; those of a deceased person pass to his heir, executor, or administrator, or to a judicial functionary [230]; those of a bankrupt to his trustee in bankruptcy. On the death of one of several joint contractors his rights and liabilities pass, not to his personal representative, but to the surviving contractors. It must however be remarked that rights and liabilities arising from family relations, or which are closely connected with the personal characteristics of either party, such as those arising out of a promise to marry, or to use surgical skill, or to paint a picture, are not thus transferred 'by act of law [231].'

By act of party.

ii. The transfer of a 'right in personam' 'by act of party,' is of still more restricted application. Its possibility is indeed
*274 *flatly denied by the older theories of law. 'Obligations,' says Gaius, 'however contracted, admit of nothing of the sort [232];' and it was an axiom of the English common law that 'choses in action are not assignable.' The practical inconveniences resulting from this rule led to its gradual relaxation. It is no doubt possible by consent of all concerned to substitute a new debtor or new creditor in place of the person of inherence or of incidence as the case may be. This is however a cumbrous process, and is obviously not an assignment, but an extinction of the original right, followed by a contract creating a new right in substitution for the old one. It is an example of what the Romans called 'novatio [233].' The first step towards the assignment of an obligation was taken by allowing a stranger to it to bring an ac-

[230] 21 & 22 Vict. c. 95. s. 19.

[231] Wills v. Murray, 4 Ex. 866.

[232] Inst. ii. 38.

[233] 'Novatio est prioris debiti in aliam obligationem, vel civilem vel naturalem, transfusio atque translatio, hoc est ut cum ex praecedente causa ita nova constituitur, ut prior perimatur.' Dig. xlvi. 2. 1; cf. Inst. iii. 29. 3.

tion upon it in the name of the party entitled under it, and to retain the proceeds for himself. This was the process known in Roman law as 'cessio actionum.' The assignor was held to be a trustee for the assignee, or to have constituted the assignee his agent for the purpose of bringing actions. The English Court of Chancery, following the later Roman law [234], went so far as to allow the assignee to sue in his own name, provided that he had given consideration for the assignment, and that the debtor had had notice of it, subject however to all defences which would be good against the assignor [235]. Under the 'Supreme Court of Judicature Act, 1873,' 'Any absolute assignment, by writing under the hand of the assignor, not purporting to be by way of charge only, of any debt or other legal chose in action, of which express notice in writing shall have been given to the debtor, trustee, or other person from whom the assignor would have been en-
*275 titled to receive such claim or *debt or chose in action, shall be, and be deemed to have been, effectual in law, subject to all equities which would have been entitled to priority over the right of the assignee if this act had not passed, to pass and transfer the legal right to such debt or chose in action from the date of such notice [236].' Similar provisions are contained in several continental codes [237], and contractual rights of certain special kinds have been made assignable by statute, such as, for instance, rights arising on policies of marine and life insurance, bail bonds, and bills of lading [238]. The assignee, be it observed, in all the cases hitherto mentioned takes subject to all defences which were available against the original creditor, and sometimes subject to other drawbacks.

234 Code, iv. 39. 7.

235 See Lord Carteret v. Paschal, 3 P. Wms. 199.

236 36 & 37 Vict. c. 66. s. 25, 6.

237 E. g. in the Prussian Landrecht, i. 11. ss. 376–444; Austrian Code, ss. 1394–1396.

238 Savigny, Oblig. ii. p. 112, truly observes that ordinary shares in companies are not obligations but parts of ownership, producing therefore not interest but dividends. So it has been held by the Court of Appeal, diss. Fry, L. J., that shares before registration were *choses in action*, but afterwards property, Colonial Bank v. Whinney, L. R. 30 Ch. D. 261, reversed in H. L., 11 App. Ca. 426.

Same—Negotiable instruments.

Only one class of obligations can be said to be fully assignable. It is first heard of in the fourteenth century, and is the product of the wide extension of modern commercial transactions. What are called 'negotiable instruments,' or 'paper to bearer,' such as bills of exchange, or promissory notes, do really pass from hand to hand, either by delivery or indorsement, giving to each successive recipient a right against the debtor, to which no notice to the debtor is essential, and which, if the paper is held bona fide and for value, is unaffected by flaws in the title of intermediate assignors. It has been acutely remarked that the assignability of a negotiable instrument is due to its being in point of fact a material object, and so capable of actual delivery. The written document is thus, as it were, the embodiment of what would otherwise be an intangible, and therefore untransferable, claim [239].

*276 *Liabilities do not, as a rule, pass by voluntary assignment. Under a contract, it is, for instance, said to be only reasonable that the creditor should continue to have a right to the benefit he contemplated from the character, credit, or substance of the person with whom he contracted. It was however a rule of English common law that certain covenants between landlord and tenant, which are said to touch the land, should 'run with the land,' so that an 'assignee of the term,' i. e. a person to whom a tenant transfers his lease, can not only sue, but also be sued, upon them, as if he were the original lessee. Like rights and liabilities, in respect of these covenants, have been by statute made to attach to the person who succeeds to the rights of the original landlord, or, as he is called, 'the assignee of the reversion [240].'

EXTINCTION OF RIGHTS IN PERSONAM.

We have already had occasion to mention incidentally some of the modes in which the obligations resulting from particular contracts are dissolved. It will however be necessary to consider, from a more general point of view, the circumstances which terminate

239 Savigny, Oblig. ii. p. 99. Cf. Colonial Bank v. Whinney, u. s.

240 32 Hen. VIII. c. 34; 44 & 45 Vict. c. 41. ss. 10, 11.

minate rights 'in personam [241].' They may perhaps be classified under the following heads: i. Performance; ii. Events excusing performance; iii. Substitutes for performance; iv. Release of performance; v. Non-performance.

By performance.

i. Performance of the acts to which the person of incidence is obliged is the natural and proper mode by which he becomes loosed from the obligation of performing them [242].

Performance by a third person is sometimes permissible; so a debt was in Roman law extinguished on payment of the amount by a stranger, even without the debtor's knowledge [243].

*277 **By events excusing performance.*

ii. Events excusing performance.

1. As a general rule, at any rate in English law, 'subsequent impossibility' is no excuse for non-performance [244]; but to this there are several exceptions:

(a) When the act due is intimately dependent on the individuality of either party, the right, or liability, to its performance must necessarily be extinguished by his death. In would be obviously absurd to make the executors of the Admirable Crichton responsible for his non-performance of a contract to marry, or those of Raphael for his inability to return to life and finish the 'Transfiguration.' Serious illness may have a similar effect [245].

(b) When the performance has reference to a specific thing, its destruction, without fault of the parties, puts an end to the right.

241 'Solutionis verbum pertinet ad omnem liberationem, quoquo modo factam.' Dig. xlvi. 3. 54.

242 By performance, and by some other facts, 'etiam accessiones (i. e. sureties) liberantur.' Ib. l. 43.

243 Dig. xlvi. 3. 23; Inst. iii. 29 pr. The rule in English law is said to be otherwise. Jones v. Broadhurst, 9 C. B. 173.

244 Paradine v. Jane, Aleyn, 26, where it was held that 'when a party, by his own contract, creates a duty or charge upon himself, he is bound to make it good, if he may, notwithstanding any accident or inevitable necessity, because he might have provided against it by his contract.' For the rule in Roman law, see Inst. iii. 29. 2.

245 Robinson v. Davidson, L. R. 6 Ex. 269.

So when the proprietors of a place of public entertainment had agreed to let it on a certain day, before which it was burnt down, they were held to be free from their engagement [246].

(c) A change in the law, or the outbreak of war between the countries of the contracting parties, may operate to make performance a 'legal impossibility.'

2. Under the old Roman law all claims against a 'filius familias' were cancelled by even a 'minima capitis diminutio,' such as he sustained in passing by adoption from one family to another.

3. 'Confusio,' or 'merger,' i. e. the union in one person of the characters of debtor and creditor, is sometimes held to extinguish, sometimes only to suspend, the operation of the right [247].

*278 *4. Bankruptcy has already been mentioned more than once as one of the events which give rise to a universal succession [248]. An order of Discharge has the effect of freeing the bankrupt, either wholly or partially, according to the special provisions of the law under which he lives, from the claims to which he was previously liable.

5. The judicial rescission of a contract, or a decree of 'restitutio in integrum.'

Substitutes for performance.

iii. Among substitutes for performance, the following are the more important.

Same—Tender.

1. 'Tender,' 'oblatio,' of the precise amount due, followed by 'payment into court,' or in Roman and French law by 'depositio,' or 'consignation,' into the hands of a public officer, even before any action has been brought[249], either extinguishes or suspends the debt.

Same—Compromise.

2. 'Compromise,' 'transactio,' which may be analysed into a part payment, coupled with a promise not to claim the residue, can only

[246] Taylor v. Caldwell, 3 B. & S. 826. Cf. Dig. xlvi. 3. 107.

[247] Code Civil, art. 1300; Dig. xvi. 3. 107.

[248] Supra, pp. *142, *191.

[249] Cod. iv. 32. 19, viii. 43. 9; Code Civil, art. 1257.

operate as a discharge of the whole debt when the subsidiary promise is made in such a form, or under such circumstances, that it might equally well have been a good discharge without any part payment. So in an old English case it was resolved 'that payment of a lesser sum on the day, in satisfaction of a greater, cannot be a satisfaction to the plaintiff for a greater sum. When the whole sum is due, by no intendment the acceptance of parcel can be a satisfaction to the plaintiff [250].'

Same—Datio in solutum.

3. It was long debated but finally admitted by the Roman lawyers that a 'datio in solutum,' or giving and acceptance of something other than the thing due, and in place of it, dis-
*279 *charges the obligation[251]. So in English law it is laid down that if a debtor pays to his creditor 'a horse, or a cup of silver, or any such other thing, in full satisfaction of the money, and the other receiveth it, this is good enough, and as strong as if he had received the sum of money, though the horse or the other thing were not of the twentieth part of the value of the sum of money, because that the other hath accepted it in full satisfaction[252].'

Same—Set-off.

4. 'Set-off,' 'compensatio,' defined by Modestinus as 'debiti et crediti inter se contributio[253],' has been sometimes regarded as rateably extinguishing a claim 'ipso iure,' sometimes only as foundation for a plea, to which a Court may give regard in awarding judgment if the claim be sued upon. The French Code lays down broadly that 'la compensation s'opère de plein droit,' even without the knowledge of the debtors, and that the two debts cancel each other rateably, from the moment that they co-exist [254]; a view which was only very gradually approached by the Roman law-

250 Pinnel's Case, 5 Rep. 117. Cf. Foakes v. Beer, 9 App. Ca. 605; Good v. Cheeseman, 2 B. & Ad. 335. On the theory of 'accord and satisfaction,' the Author may perhaps refer to his Essay on Composition Deeds, Chapters ii. and iii.

251 Gai. iii. 168; Cod. viii. 43. 16.

252 Co. Litt. 212. a.

253 Dig. xvi. 2. 1.

254 Art. 1290.

yers[255]. The applicability of set-off has always been limited to debts of a readily calculable kind [256], and between the parties in the same rights. The doctrine was unknown to the English common law, upon which it was grafted for the first time by 2 Geo. II. c. 22.

Same—Substitution.

5. The substitution of a new obligation for the old one by mutual consent is a species of that mode of discharging an obligation known to the Romans as 'novatio.'

Release.

iv. The mere agreement of the parties to a discharge of the liability is not always sufficient. The principle of Roman law was that every contract should be dissolved in the same manner in which it had been made. 'Nihil tam naturale est quam eo
*280 genere quidque dissolvere quo colligatum est, ideo *verborum obligatio verbis tollitur: nudi consensus obligatio contrario consensu dissolvitur [257].' So an obligation arising out of 'stipulatio' could only be extinguished by an equally solemn 'acceptilatio,' a method which was at a later period extended by the ingenuity of the praetor Aquilius to the release of obligations of all sorts[258]. In the time of Gaius there were certain obligations which could be released only by means of a feigned payment accompanied by the ancient ceremony of the 'aes et libra[259].' A merely consensual contract, if wholly unexecuted, could be discharged by the mere agreement of the parties, but after part execution such an agreement could amount only to a 'pactum de non petendo,' which might be a good plea to an action upon the obligation, but left the obligation itself still in force.

English law requires that a contract made under seal should be discharged in like manner [260]. The effect of a mere agreement to

255 Inst. iv. 6. 30; Cod. iv. 31. 14.

256 A merely 'natural' obligation could be set off in Roman law. Dig. xl. 7. 20. 2. Cf. supra, pp. *214, *270.

257 Dig. l. 17. 35.

258 Inst. iii. 29. 2.

259 Gai. iii. 173.

260 A contract which under the Statute of Frauds has necessarily been

discharge a consensual contract depends upon the doctrine of 'consideration.' If such a contract be still executory, the mutual release from its liabilities is a good consideration to each party for surrendering his rights under it. If it has been executed on one side it can be discharged only by an agreement founded on some new consideration, or by a deed, which is sometimes said to 'import a consideration[261].' The rule does not however apply to a discharge of promissory notes or bills of exchange, which doubtless owe their immunity from it to deriving their origin from the 'law merchant [262].'

Non-performance.

v. Non-performance by one party to a contract often puts an end to the rights which he enjoys under it against the
*281 *other party. And some acts short of non-performance may have the same effect. Thus if one party by his own act disables himself from performance[263], or announces that he has no intention of performing [264], the other side is in many cases entitled to treat what has occurred as a 'breach of contract by anticipation,' and the contract as being therefore no longer binding. Since however non-performance, or breach, has also the effect of giving rise to remedial rights, its discussion may conveniently be postponed till the next chapter.

made in writing may, it seems, be rescinded absolutely without writing, but an unwritten contract superseding it by implication will be incapable of proof. See Anson, Contract, ed. vii. p. 281.

261 Supra, p. *248 n.

262 Cf. The Bills of Exchange Act, 1882, § 62.

263 Planché v. Colburn, 8 Bingham, 14.

264 Hochster v. Delatour, 3 E. & B. 678; Frost v. Knight, L. R. 7 Ex. 111; extended by Synge v. Synge, '94, 1 Q. B. 467.

*282

*CHAPTER XIII.

PRIVATE LAW: REMEDIAL RIGHTS.

Primitive remedies.

A right which could be violated with impunity, without giving rise to any new legal relation between the person of inherence and the person of incidence, would not be a legal right at all. In an anarchical state of society an injured person takes such compensa- as he can obtain from a wrong-doer, or, if strong enough, gets such satisfaction as may be derived from an act of revenge. A political society, in the first place, puts this rude self-help under stringent regulation, and secondly, provides a substitute for it in the shape of judicial process. Self-help is indeed but an unsatisfactory means of redress. Its possibility depends upon the injured party being stronger than the wrong-doer, a state of things which is by no means a matter of course; and the injured party is made judge in his own cause, often at a time when he is least likely to form an impartial opinion upon its merits. To suppress private revenge, to erect Courts of Justice, and to compel every one who is wronged to look to them for compensation, is however a task far beyond the strength of a State which is still in process of
*283 formation. *So the heroic age of Greece was characterised, according to Grote, by 'the omnipotence of private force, tempered and guided by family sympathies, and the practical nullity of that collective sovereign afterwards called the City, who in historical Greece becomes the central and paramount source of obligation, but who appears yet only in the background[1].'

Regulated self-help.

It is therefore not surprising that, as Sir Henry Maine has put it, 'the Commonwealth at first interfered through its various organs rather to keep order and see fair play in quarrels, than took them, as it now does always and everywhere, into its own hands[2].' The stages of social improvement seem to be the following. First,

[1] History, ii. p. 126.

[2] Early History of Institutions, Lect. ix.

the unmeasured, hot-blooded, and violent retaliation of the injured party is superseded by a mode of taking compensation the nature and formalities of which are to some extent prescribed by custom. 'The primitive proceeding,' says the author last quoted, 'was undoubtedly the unceremonious, unannounced, attack of the tribe or the man stung by injury on the tribe or the man who had inflicted it. Any expedient by which sudden plunder or slaughter was adjourned or prevented was an advantage even to barbarous society. Thus it was a gain to mankind as a whole when its priests and leaders began to encourage the seizure of property or family, not for the purpose of permanent appropriation, but with a view to what we should now not hesitate to call extortion[3].' This is the stage at which the seizure of pledges is so prominent, and to it belongs also the singular custom of 'sitting dharna,' according to which an Indian creditor fasts at the door of his debtor till his debt is paid. Next comes the stage when self-help, although permitted, is supervised and restrained by the political authority. Distress may still be resorted to, but only for certain pur-
*284 poses, and with many safeguards *against abuse. Life and property may be protected by force, but the force used must not be in excess of the need. Nuisances may be 'abated,' but so as to interfere with no man's rights. Last of all comes the reign of the law-courts. Legally regulated self-help is not wholly superseded, but, as a rule, redress of wrongs must be sought only from the tribunals of the sovereign[4].

The operation of law as conserving rights.

The object of a developed system of law is the conservation, whether by means of the tribunals or of permitted self-help, of the rights which it recognises as existing[5]. So long as all goes well,

3 Ib., Lect. x.

4 Cf. the edict of Marcus Aurelius: 'Optimum est ut si quas putes te habere petitiones, actionibus experiaris: . . . . . Tu vim putas esse solum si homines vulnerentur? Vis est et tunc quotiens quis id quod deberi sibi putat non per iudicem reposcit . . . . . Quisquis igitur probatus mihi fuerit rem ullam debitoris non ab ipso sibi traditam sine ullo iudice temere possidere, eumque sibi ius in eam rem dixisse, ius crediti non habebit.' Dig. xlviii. 7. 7.

5 Supra, p. *70.

the action of the law is dormant. When the balance of justice is disturbed by wrong-doing, or even by a threat of it, the law intervenes to restore, as far as possible, the status quo ante. 'The judge,' says Aristotle, 'equalises[6].' He elsewhere adopts the saying of Lycophron that the function of law is to guarantee that all shall enjoy their rights[7]. 'Hoc natura aequum est,' says Pomponius, 'neminem cum alterius detrimento fieri locupletiorem[8].'

Same—By prevention.

Sometimes the law intervenes for prevention, as by the 'injunctions' which have long been issued by the Court of Chancery to forbid a threatened mischief, and by the orders made by the Roman praetors in cases of 'novi operis denuntiatio,' or 'damnum infectum[9].'

Same—By redress.

The remedial interference of the law is however far more frequent and important. When a right is violated, the law
*285 *endeavours to prevent the person of inherence from losing, or the person of incidence from gaining. A new right is therefore immediately given to the former, by way of compensation for his loss, and a new corresponding duty is laid upon the latter, by way of make-weight against any advantage which he may have derived from his aggression. In the language of the French Code: 'Tout fait quelconque de l'homme, qui cause à autrui un dommage, oblige celui par la faute duquel il est arrivé à le réparer [10].'

In examining early systems of law we seem to come upon traces of a time when the State had to take special pains in order to insure that the new right should be as acceptable to its subjects as the indulgence of private revenge. Such is the interpretation placed upon a provision of the Twelve Tables, that a thief, if caught in the act, was to be scourged and delivered as a slave to the owner of the goods, whereas if not caught under circumstances offering to the owner a similar temptation to violence, he was

6 Eth. Nic. v. 7. 3 and 8.

7 'Εγγυητὴς ἀλλήλοις τῶν δικαίων. Pol. iii. 9. 8.

8 Dig. xii. 6. 14.

9 Dig. xxxix. 1 and 2.

10 Art. 1382.

to be liable only for twice the value of the goods. So the object of the early Teutonic legislation is well described as having been, 'to preserve the society from standing feuds, but at the same time to accord such full satisfaction as would induce the injured person to waive his acknowledged right of personal revenge. The German Codes begin by trying to bring about the acceptance of a fixed pecuniary composition as a constant voluntary custom, and proceed ultimately to enforce it as a peremptory necessity: the idea of society is at first altogether subordinate, and its influence passes only by slow degrees from amicable arbitration into imperative control [11].'

Same—Self-help.

The new right may thus be realisable by the regulated self-help of the injured person of inherence himself, as when he is al-
*286 lowed to push a trespasser out of his field, *or to pull down a wall which has been built across his path.

Same—Right of action—For compensation.

More commonly it is realisable only with the aid of the law courts, in which case it is known as a 'right of action,' 'ius persequendi iudicio quod sibi debetur [12].' The right, however realisable, we call 'remedial,' as opposed to the right from a violation of which it arises, and which we call 'antecedent [13].' Its object may be either restitution or compensation [14]. In the former case, the

[11] Grote, History, ii. p. 128. A cursory inspection of the 'Leges Barbarorum' will show how large a space in them is occupied by the topic of 'Compositio.'

[12] So Theophilus speaks of Obligations as the mothers of Actions: Μητέρες τῶν ἀγωγῶν αἱ ἐνοχαί. Inst. iii. 13.

[13] Supra, pp. *130, *148. 'Is qui actionem habet ad rem persequendam ipsam rem habere videtur,' says Paulus, Dig. l. 15. Pomponius, more truly, 'minus est actionem habere quam rem.' Dig. l. 204.

[14] 'Les actions sont des droits particuliers qui naissent de la violation des autres droits, et qui tendent, soit à faire cesser cette violation, soit à en faire réparer les effets.' Dalloz, s. v., No. 69. On the term 'cause of action,' see Cooke v. Gill, L. R. 8 C. P. 107, and Vaughan v. Weldon, L. R. 10 C. P. 47. It has been held by the Court of Appeal that 'two actions may be brought in respect of the same facts, when those facts give rise to two

aim of the law is to cancel, so far as possible, the wrongful act. It allows the injured party to remove a building which obstructs his window-light, it decrees the 'restitutio in integrum' of a minor who has entered into a disadvantageous engagement, it calls for and destroys a contract which is tainted with fraud, it orders the return of an object of which the person of inherence has wrongly been deprived, or it enforces, if need be by imprisonment, the 'specific performance' of a contract which the person of incidence is endeavouring to repudiate, a remedy which, though familiar
*287 to English Equity [15] and to German law, *ancient and modern, is opposed to the principles of Roman law and of the systems derived from it [16]. In the latter, which is also the

distinct causes of action,' per Brett, M. R., and Bowen, L. J., diss. Coleridge, L. C. J. Brunsden v. Humphrey, 14 Q. B. D. 141.

[15] The defaulter is directed to do the very thing which he contracted to do, and, if disobedient, is committed to prison for contempt of Court. Lord Justice Fry has recently shown that the Courts Christian anticipated the Court of Chancery in specifically enforcing the performance of those contracts, at least, in which there was an oath or 'fidei interpositio,' 5 L. Q. R. 235, and Specific Performance, ed. iii. p. 8. He thinks, ib. p. 14, that the remedy may have 'leaked through from the canon to the manorial law, where a Bishop was lord of a manor,' citing a case, temp. Ed. II., in a manorial court of the Bishop of Ely, from 'The Court Baron' (Selden Society), p. 115.

[16] According to the view prevalent in France, 'Nemo potest praecise cogi ad factum.' See Lord Justice Fry's Treatise on Specific Performance, ed. iii. p. 4, and the opinion of M. Renault, ib. p. 714.

The doctrine of Pothier, Oblig. § 157, 'C'est en cette obligation de dommages et intérêts que se résolvent toutes les obligations de faire quelque chose,' was adopted in art. 1142 of the Code Civil, "Toute obligation de faire ou de ne pas faire se résout en dommages et intérêts, en cas d'inexécution de la part du débiteur'; supported by M. Bigot-Préameneu ('Exposé des motifs') on the ground that 'nul ne peut être contraint dans sa personne à faire ou à ne pas faire une chose, et que, si cela était possible, ce serait une violence qui ne peut pas être une mode d'exécution des contrats.' There is nothing inconsistent with this view in arts. 1143, 1144, under which the injured party may be authorised to carry out the work agreed upon at the expense of the defaulter; nor in art. 1610, under which a purchaser may be put into possession of the thing sold if the vendor refuses to deliver it to him. Some of the older French authorities had maintained that even here the sole remedy should be in damages, but Pothier, following Paulus, Sent. vi. 1. 13. 4, and Cujas, ad. l. 1 de Act. Empt., had argued more usual, case, it gives to the sufferer a right to be compensated in damages for a wrong which cannot be undone.

Remedial right a right 'in personam.'

We have seen that while some 'antecedent' rights are available 'in rem,' others are available only 'in personam.' 'Remedial' rights are available, as a rule, 'in personam,' i. e. against the wrong-doer, who, by the act of wrong-doing, becomes at once the ascertained person of incidence of the remedial right. Such rights as
*288 those of lien and distress, *and especially certain rights enforceable in Courts of Admiralty, which are doubtless capable of being represented as remedial rights 'in rem[17],' may also be treated as being merely modes of execution, by which the true remedial right is made effective[18].

Origin of remedial rights.

The causes, or 'investitive facts,' of remedial rights are always infringements of antecedent rights, and have therefore been incidentally mentioned in the course of the discussion of such rights which has occupied the two preceding chapters. It is indeed impossible to describe what we have called the 'orbit' of a right, without at the same time mentioning the acts which break in upon it, since the extent of a right is the same thing with the power of him who is clothed with it to interfere, positively or negatively,

that the Court should authorise the purchaser himself to seize the thing sold, 'ou d'en expulser le vendeur par le ministère d'un sergent,' explaining that the maxim 'nemo potest praecise cogi ad factum' only applies 'lorsque le fait renfermé dans l'obligation est un pur fait de la personne du débiteur, merum factum, . . . il n'en est pas de même du fait de la tradition: ce fait non est merum factum, sed magis ad dationem accedit,' Contrat de Vente, § 68. I am indebted for a learned and interesting communication upon this subject to Mr. Justice Proudfoot of Toronto (now embodied in an article in the Canadian Law Times, for October, 1894), who is disposed to go further than I am able to follow him in discovering approximations to Specific Performance in Roman law and in the derivative systems. On German law, see a learned article, signed E. S., in 8 L. Q. R. p. 252, citing Dernburg, Preussisches Privatrecht, Bd. i. p. 276, and the Code of Civil Procedure, §§ 774, 775.

17 See the case of the Parlement Belge, L. R. 5 P. D. 197.

18 Supra, p. *148.

with the acts of others [19]. It will now however be necessary to consider infringements more specifically, and to classify them according to the rights which they infringe, and with which indeed, for the reason just given, they are precisely correlative.

Infringements.

Since conduct which is straightforward came to be spoken of eulogistically as being 'rectum,' 'directum' (whence 'droit'), 'recht' and 'right,' conduct of the opposite character naturally came to be expressed by the terms 'delictum,' 'délit,' as deviating from the right path, and 'wrong' or 'tort,' as twisted out of the straight line[20]. Similar conduct is less descriptively called in German 'Rechtsverletzung.'

Species of infringements—Breaches of contract—Torts.

These terms are alike employed in their respective languages to denote, in a very general sense, acts which are violations of rights. They are however usually applied only to 'wrongs independent of contract [21];' i. e. the large class of *wrongful acts which are breaches of contract are specifically so described. Certain other classes of wrongful acts also have for historical reasons specific designations which take them out of the category of delicts, or torts. Thus Roman law treated acts of certain kinds as giving rise to obligations not 'ex delicto,' but 'quasi ex delicto,' nor are breaches of trust, or such acts as are charged against a co-respondent in the Divorce Court, since they were alike unknown to the old common law, described as torts by the law of England [22].

*289

Difference between torts and crimes.

The distinction between those wrongs which are generically called 'torts' and those which are called crimes may at first sight appear to be a fine one. The same set of circumstances will, in

19 Supra, p. *134.

20 'Tam multa surgunt perfidorum compita
Tortis polita erroribus.' Prudent. in Apotheos. Hymn. 1.

'Sicut illi qui in suo ministerio tortum faciunt,' occurs in an edict of Charles the Bald. 'Tort à la leye est contrarye.' Britton, fol. 116.

21 A phrase due to the Common Law Procedure Act, 1852.

22 Although the action for crim. con. was for a tort.

fact, from one point of view constitute a tort, while from another point of view they amount to a crime. In the case, for instance, of an assault, the right violated is that which every man has that his bodily safety shall be respected, and for the wrong done to this right the sufferer is entitled to get damages. But this is not all. The act of violence is a menace to the safety of society generally, and will therefore be punished by the State. So a libel is said to violate not only the right of an individual not to be defamed, but also the right of the State that no incentive shall be given to a breach of the peace. It is sometimes alleged by books of authority that the difference between a tort and a crime is a matter of procedure, the former being redressed by the civil, while the latter is punished by the criminal courts. But the distinction lies deeper, and is well expressed by Blackstone, who says that torts are an 'infringement or privation of the private, or civil, rights belonging to individuals, considered as individuals; crimes are a breach of public rights and duties which affect the whole community, considered as a community.' The right which is violated by a tort is always a different right from that which is violated by a crime. The person of inherence in the former case is an individual, in the latter case is the State. In a French criminal trial there may
*290 *accordingly appear not only the public prosecutor, representing the State and demanding the punishment of the offender, but also the injured individual, as 'partie civile,' asking for damages for the loss which he has personally sustained [23].

The far-reaching consequences of acts become more and more visible with the advance of civilisation, and the State tends more and more to recognise as offences against the community acts which it formerly only saw to be injurious to individuals.

Possible classifications of wrongs.

Wrongful acts may be, and are, classified on five different principles at least.

i. According to the state of the will of the wrong-doer, which may conceivably be, (1) entirely absent, as in acts of innocent tres-

[23] Code d'Instruction Criminelle, art. 63. On the old English remedy, known as an 'Appeal,' abolished by 59 Geo. III. c. 46, see 4 Bl. Comm. 312.

pass; (2) such as exhibits negligence[24]; (3) such as exhibits intention, sometimes described as 'malice.'

As has already been explained, the law has in modern times substituted, in many cases, for an enquiry into the state of mind of a given defendant an enquiry into the conformity of his acts to an external standard, viz. to the conduct which may be reasonably expected from a person of his class[25].

ii. According to the state of the will of the injured party, which may conceivably, (1) fairly consent to an invasion of his
*291 right, which by being thus waived, becomes no right, *and its invasion no wrong, since 'volenti non fit iniuria[26];' and an act ab initio wrongful may lose this character by the subsequently given assent of the injured party; (2) be flatly opposed to the act, which is then of course tortious, even when an apparent assent to it is procured by duress; (3) be induced to assent by the deceit of the party injuring, the act of so procuring assent by deceit being the wrong known as 'fraud.'

iii. According to the means whereby the wrong is effected, whether, for instance, by physical violence, by words uttered, or by omission to carry out a contract.

iv. According as actual loss to the injured party following upon the act of the wrong-doer is or is not essential to its tortious character [27].

[24] Supra, p. *97.

[25] Supra, pp. *97–*101. For an interesting enquiry as to the ground of liability for torts, and especially whether or no they imply moral blameworthiness, see Holmes, Common Law, p. 79. Mr. Justice Holmes points out, in another chapter, that 'law started from those intentional wrongs which are simplest and nearest to the feeling of revenge which leads to self-redress. It thus naturally adopted the vocabulary, and in some degree the tests, of morals. But as the law has grown, its standards have necessarily become external, because they have considered not the actual condition of the particular defendant, but whether his conduct would have been wrong in the fair average member of the community whom he is expected to equal at his peril.' Ib. p. 161. Cf. also now Sir F. Pollock's work on Torts.

[26] Supra, p. *137. As to the application of this principle, and the distinction between 'sciens' and 'volens,' see Thomas v. Quartermain, 18 Q. B. D. 683; Smith v. Baker, '91 App. Ca. 325.

[27] See per Bowen, L. J., in Ratcliffe v. Evans, '92, 2 Q. B. 524.

v. According to the nature of the right invaded, whether, for instance, it be a right to personal freedom, or to a monopoly, or to the fulfilment of a contract.

Principle selected.

Writers who waver between these various points of view, subdividing one portion of the whole class of wrongful acts upon one principle, and another portion upon another principle, involve themselves in unnecessary difficulties. The last-mentioned principle of division is to be preferred. When it is once known of what right any given wrong is an invasion, its other characteristics follow as a matter of course.

List of wrongs.

A tabular view of wrongful acts, in which each is referred to the right of which it is an infringement, might easily be constructed from the data contained in the two preceding chapters.

Among rights 'in rem,' that to personal safety is violated by assault or imprisonment; family rights, by abduction of, or adultery with, a wife, by seduction of a servant, or enticing
*292 *away a slave; the right to one's good name, by defamation; rights generally available, by nuisance, and malicious arrest or prosecution; rights of possession, by trespass, conversion, detinue, and 'furtum'; rights of ownership of tangible objects by the same acts; rights of copyright, patent-right and trade-mark, by 'infringement'; rights 'in re aliena,' by 'disturbance' of an easement, or 'conversion' of a pledge; rights to immunity from fraud, by 'deceit.'

Among rights 'in personam,' family rights, and their analogues, are infringed by 'subtraction,' adultery, refusal of due aliment, ingratitude on the part of a freedman, or neglect by a vassal of his feudal duties; fiduciary rights, by breach of trust; rights of a reversioner, by 'waste'; what we have called meritorious rights, by refusal of the merited reward; rights against officials, by neglect on their part to perform their duties; rights 'ex contractu,' by breaches of contract, consisting, according to the nature of the contract in question, in such acts or omissions as non-payment, non-delivery, defective care-taking, default in marrying, non-render of services, negligent render of services, refusal to enter into partnership, doing of acts promised not to be done, breach of warranty, or non-return of pledge.

Liability for acts of servants.

With reference to these acts generally, the rule holds good that 'qui facit per alium facit per se.' The employer is responsible for acts which he has ordered to be done, or which have been done by his servant, without orders but within the scope of the servant's employment [28].

Damages for breaches of contract and torts.

The right resulting from 'wrongs independent of contract' is of a wider character than that which results from breaches of contract. In the former case only, as a rule, may mental and bodily suffering be taken into account in measuring the damages to
*293 be awarded. On the other hand, a breach of *contract is more readily established than a wrong of another kind, since it depends less on any question as to the state of the will of the wrong-doer, and some damages may be had for every breach of contract, whether or no it be the cause of any actual loss. 'Direct,' or 'general' damages are those which are the necessary and immediate consequence of the wrong, while 'indirect,' or 'special,' damages are sometimes granted in respect of its remoter consequences[29].

Transfer of Remedial Rights.

What has been said as to the difficulties attending the transfer of antecedent rights 'in personam' applies, with greater strength,

[28] Cf. supra, p. *138. On the liability of contractors as well as their subcontractors, see Bower v. Peate, L. R. 1 Q. B. D. 321. On the liability of a shipowner for the acts of his master being limited by surrender of the ship, see Holmes, Common Law, p. 30.

[29] On the 'measure of damages,' cf. 'pretia rerum non ex affectione singulorum sed communiter fungi.' Dig. ix. 2. 33. Cf. Cod. vii. 47. Does an injured person weaken his claim against the person who caused the injury, or against an insurance society, by refusing to submit to an operation suitable to his case? See F. Endemann, Die Rechtswirkung der Ablehnung einer Operation, Berlin, 1893.

to the transfer of remedial rights[30]. The non-transferability to the representatives of a deceased person of such remedial rights as arise from the violation of a right intimately connected with his individuality is expressed by the maxim, 'Actio personalis moritur cum persona[31].'

Extinction of Remedial Rights.

A mere performance of the duty antecedently owed is no discharge of the remedial right arising from its non-performance, but the right may be extinguished in a variety of other ways, including some of those which are applicable to the extinction of antecedent rights 'in personam[32].'

i. The person of inherence may formally release his right of action, for instance by deed or by the Aquilian stipulation;
*294 *or may give a covenant not to sue, 'pactum de non petendo'; or may enter into, what is called in English law, 'an accord and satisfaction' with the person of incidence, i. e. into an agreement substituting some other act for the act which has not been performed, and followed by the performance of that act. The person of inherence may also by his conduct so 'ratify' a wrong done to him as to waive his resulting right of redress, as when the owner of goods wrongfully sold treats the sale as lawful by taking part of the purchase money. The right may likewise be lost by—

ii. The bankruptcy of the person of incidence.

iii. Set-off.

iv. Merger. It has been laid down that the giving of a covenant in the place of a simple contract does not 'merge or extinguish the debt, but it merges the remedy by way of proceeding upon the simple contract. The intention of the parties has nothing to do with that. The policy of the law is that there shall not be two subsisting remedies, one upon the covenant and another upon the

30 Supra, pp. *140, *273. On the various meanings of the term 'special damages,' see Ratcliffe v. Evans, u. supra.

31 Supra, pp. *160, *273. An action for breach of promise of marriage, without damage to the estate, does not survive to the representatives of the promisee, Chamberlain v. Williamson, 2 M. & S. 408, nor against the representatives of the promisor, Finlay v. Chirney 20 Q. B. D. 494. Cf. Stanhope v. Stanhope and Adye, 11 Prob. D. (C. A.) 103, as to a decree nisi of Divorce.

32 Cf. supra, p. *276.

simple contract, by the same person against the same person for the same demand [33].' So a judgment in favour of the plaintiff is 'a bar to the original cause of action, because it is thereby reduced to a certainty and the object of the suit attained, so far as it can be at that stage; and it would be useless and vexatious to subject the defendant to another suit for the purpose of attaining the same result. Hence the maxim "Transit in rem iudicatam." . . . The cause of action is changed into a matter of record, which is of a higher nature, and the inferior remedy is merged in the higher[34].' So in Roman law an obligation was transmuted by 'litis contestatio,' and again by judgment, which was expressed by saying, 'ante litem contestatam dare debitorem oportere, post litem contestatam condemnari oportere, post condemnation-
*295 em iudicatum facere oportere[35].' An *award under arbitration does not usually extinguish a remedial right, unless followed by performance of the award.

v. 'Estoppel,' by a judgment for the defendant. 'The facts actually decided by an issue in any suit cannot be again litigated between the same parties, and are evidence between them, and that conclusive, for the purpose of terminating litigation[36].'

vi. Extinctive prescription, or limitation of actions, introduced, as it is expressed in the Act of James I, 'for quieting of men's estates and avoiding of suits[37],' by depriving the remedial right of its judicial remedy, reduces it to the position of a merely 'natural' obligation, which however still remains capable of supporting a lien or pledge[38].

The lapse of time necessary to produce this result varies very widely in different systems, and with reference to rights of different species. It begins to run from the moment when the remedial right comes into existence, in other words, when the antecedent right is violated. It may be interrupted, or prevented from running by various causes, such as the minority, imprisonment, or ab-

33 Price v. Moulton, 10 C. B. 561.

34 King v. Hoare, 13 M. & W. 494; cf. Kendall v. Hamilton, 4 App. Ca. 504.

35 Gai. iii. 180.

36 Boileau v. Rutlin, 2 Ex. 665; cf. Dig. xliv. 2. 7. 4.

37 21 Iac. I. c. 16.

38 Supra, pp. *201 n., *214.

sence from the country of the person whose right would otherwise be affected by it. On the other hand, the person who would otherwise benefit by it may keep alive his indebtedness by such acts as part payment, or payment of interest, or express acknowledgment with a promise to pay.

Suspension.

There are cases in which a remedial right is suspended without being lost. Thus a Court will refuse to try an action while an action to try the same question is pending before a Court of concurrent jurisdiction, in which case there is said to be 'lis alibi pendens.' So also it has long been said to be a principle of English law that when the fact which gives rise to the remedial right amounts also to a felony, the remedy of the injured individ-
*296 ual is postponed to the punish*ment of the crime; but much doubt has of late been thrown upon this alleged principle[39].

[39] For the history of the rule to this effect, see Wells v. Abrahams, L. R. 7 Q. B. 554, where Blackburn, J., traces all the dicta in its favour back to the case of Markham v. Cobbe, Sir W. Jones, 147, decided in 1626. In ex parte Ball v. Shepherd (1879), 10 Ch. D. (C. A.) 667, and Midland Rail. Co. v. Smith (1881), 6 Q. B. D. 561, the rule is treated as finally exploded; but see Appleby v. Franklin (1885), 17 Q. B. D. 93, and Windmill Local Board of Health v. Vint, 45 Ch. D. (C. A.) 351.

*297

*CHAPTER XIV.

PRIVATE LAW: ABNORMAL.

Normal and abnormal persons.

Among the modes in which the field of law may be mapped out, we have already explained that which divides it into 'normal' and 'abnormal'; the former kind of law dealing with rights as unaffected by any special characteristics of the persons with whom they are connected, the latter kind dealing with rights as so affected [1]. In all statements with reference to rights the standard type of personality is assumed, unless the contrary is expressed; and it is only when there is a deviation from that type that the character of the persons who are two of the factors into which, as we have seen, it is possible to analyse every right, needs any investigation. The typical person, who is thus assumed as a factor, is, in the first place, a human being, as opposed to what is called 'an artificial person[2].' In the next place, he is unaffected by any such peculiarity as infancy, coverture, alienage, slavery, and so forth.

In considering the various classes of substantive rights,
*298 we *have hitherto treated of them as normal. We are now about to treat of the effect produced upon them by abnormity of personality.

It was usual in old grammars to explain the cases of nouns by a diagram, in which the nominative case was represented by an upright line, from the base of which lines, representing the genitive, dative, accusative, vocative, and ablative, sloped off at gradually increasing angles. The accompanying figure may serve to illustrate in a similar manner the variations of juristic personality.

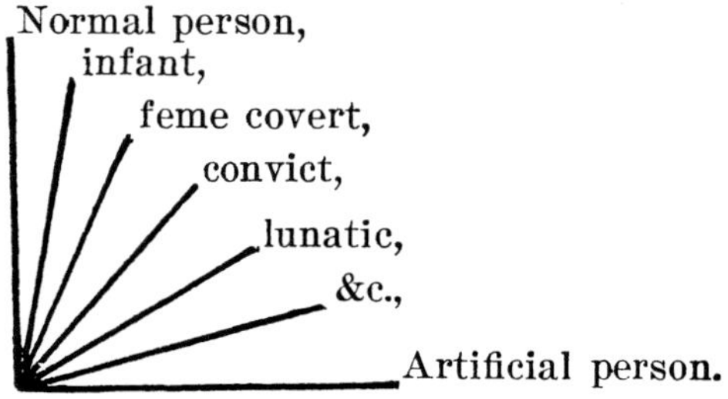

[1] Supra, pp. *118, *148.

[2] Supra, p. *85.

Natural and artificial.

The most marked distinction between abnormal persons is that some are natural, i. e. are individual human beings, while others are artificial, i. e. are aggregates of human beings, or of property, which are treated by law, for certain purposes, as if they were individual human beings[3].

I. ARTIFICIAL PERSONS.

It is by no means at the discretion of any aggregate of human beings so to coalesce as to sustain a single personality. In the words of Gaius, 'neque societas, neque collegium, neque huiusmodi corpus, passim omnibus habere conceditur: nam et legibus
*299 et senatusconsultis et principalibus constitutionibus *ea res coercetur[4].' According to some authorities, the requirement of State recognition as a pre-requisite of juristic personality was unknown under the Republic. It was certainly relaxed in favour of ecclesiastical bodies by the Christian Emperors, and was not, as a general rule, insisted upon during the middle ages[5]. Artificial persons are created by a charter granted by the executive authority in a State, or by a special statute passed by the legislature, but of late years also by virtue of general statutes, which prescribe the conditions under which voluntary associations may acquire a corporate character[6]. They may be formed wholly of natural

[3] Supra, pp. *85, *122. Order lxxi. 1, of the Rules of the Supreme Court of 1883, provides that the word 'person' shall, in the construction of the rules, unless there is anything in the subject or context repugnant thereto, include a body corporate or politic. By the Interpretation Act, 1889, s. 20, 'In this act, and in every act passed after the commencement of this act, the expression "person" shall, unless the contrary intention appears, include any body of persons, corporate or incorporate.'

[4] Dig. iii. 4. 1. pr. Cf. Dig. xxxiv. 5. 20, xlvii. 22. 'Tutti i corpi morali, legalmente riconosciuti, sono considerati come persone, e godono dei diritti civili secondo le leggi e gli usi osservati come diritto pubblico.' Codice Civile, art. 2.

[5] See on the one hand, Dernburg, Pandekten. i. p. 145; on the other, Gierke, Deutsches Genossenschaftsrecht, iii. pp. 97–208.

[6] Such as 'The Companies Act, 1862.' The Crown may delegate its power of creating corporations. 'So,' says Blackstone, 'the Chancellor of the University of Oxford has power by charter to erect corporations; and has

persons, or wholly of artificial persons, or of a mixture of artificial and natural persons. They cease to exist by no longer comprising the requisite number of subordinate persons, or by the revocation or surrender of their privileges.

The characteristics of an artificial person differ from those of a group of natural persons no less than from those of a single natural person. On the one hand, it is not merely the sum total of its component members, but something superadded to them[7]. It may remain, although they one and all are changed, 'in decurionibus vel aliis universitatibus nihil refert utrum omnes idem maneant, an pars maneat, vel omnes immutati sunt[8].' The
*300 property which it may hold does not *belong to the members either individually or collectively: 'quibus permissum est corpus habere collegii, societatis, sive cuiusque alterius eorum nomine, proprium est, ad exemplum rei publicae, habere res communes[9].' Its claims and liabilities are its own, 'si quid universitati debetur, singulis non debetur; nec quod debet universitas singuli debent[10].' Its agent, though appointed by a majority of the members, does not represent them, 'hic enim pro republica vel universitate intervenit, non pro singulis[11].' In all these respects true artificial persons are distinguishable from clubs and unincorporated trading partnerships, however large.

On the other hand, an artificial necessarily differs in many respects from a natural person. 'A corporation aggregate of many is invisible, immortal, and rests only in intendment and consideration of law. It has no soul, neither is it subject to the imbecilities of the body[12].' Its will is that of the majority of its members,

actually often exerted it, in the erection of several matriculated companies of tradesmen subservient to the students.' Comm. i. p. 474.

[7] So, says Paulus, the members of an illicit 'collegium' can take a legacy only if it is left to them individually: 'hi enim non quasi collegium, sed quasi certi homines, admittentur ad legatum.' Dig. xxxiv. 5. 20. A 'municipium,' according to Ulpian, xxii. 5, cannot be instituted heir, 'quoniam incertum corpus est.'

[8] Dig. iii. 4. 7. 2.

[9] Dig. iii. 1. 1.

[10] Ib. 7. 1.

[11] Ib. 2.

[12] The case of Sutton's Hospital, 10 Rep. 32 b.

and can be expressed only by means of an agent; there are many wrongful acts of which it is obviously incapable[13]; and its capacity for being the subject of rights, 'Rechtsfähigkeit,' and for performing legal acts, 'Handlungsfähigkeit,' is strictly limited by the purposes by which its existence is recognised.

The invention of corporations has been justly described by a high authority upon the subject as one which, 'perhaps more than any other human device, has contributed to the civilisation of Europe and the freedom of its states.' 'By this means,' says the same writer, 'municipalities were furnished with a form of government which never wore out. Charitable trusts were secured to the objects of them so long as such objects should continue to be found, the protection, improvement and encouragement of trades and arts were permanently provided for, and learning
*301 and religion kept *alive and cherished in times through which probably no other means can be mentioned that would appear equally well qualified to preserve them[14].'

Classification of Artificial Persons.

The purposes which artificial persons are intended to promote are very various, and such persons may perhaps be classified, according as they subserve one or other of them, under the following heads[15]:—

(1) Subordinately political, such as municipal corporations, generally.

(2) Administrative, such as the Trinity House or the College of Heralds.

(3) Professional, such as the College of Physicians or the Incorporated Law Society.

(4) Religious, such as the Chapter of St. Paul's or the Church Missionary Society.

(5) Scientific and Artistic, such as the Royal Society or the Royal Academy.

13 Dig. iv. 2. 9, 3. 15; cf. Metropolitan Saloon Company v. Hawkins, 4 H. & N. 87.

14 Grant, on Corporations, p. 4.

15 For a classification of juristic persons from the point of view of Roman law, see Baron, Pandekten, p. 54.

(6) For the Promotion of Education, such as the University of Oxford or the Girls Public Day School Company Limited.

(7) Eleemosynary, such as St. Thomas's Hospital, or the Corporation of the Sons of the Clergy.

(8) Trading, such as the Great Western Railway, the Lambeth Water-works Company, or the Civil Service Supply Association Limited.

'Quasi-Corporations.'

The holders for the time being of certain official positions, though not incorporated, are recognised in English law as 'Quasi-Corporations.' So the Churchwardens of a parish and their successors may hold goods but not land, as if they were an artificial person; and larger rights have been conferred by statute upon Guardians of the Poor, and Boards of Management of district Schools
*302 or Asylums. The term is *also applied to the position occupied under certain statutes by Banking partnerships and Commissioners of Sewers[16].

Older corporations.

The legal position of a corporation of the older type is comparatively simple. It exists generally for some purpose of public utility, and its members have no defined personal interest in the property which belongs to it.

Trading corporations.

The most complicated, as well as the most modern, branch of the law of artificial persons relates to those which are formed for purposes of trade. They are a natural accompaniment of the extension of commerce. An ordinary partnership lacks the coherence which is required for great undertakings. Its partners may with-

[16] There are symptoms of a tendency in England to break down the distinction between corporations and societies of other kinds. Cf. the permission given, by the Rules of the Supreme Court, of 1883, Order xvi. 14, for bringing actions in the name of and against an unincorporated firm; the definition of a 'Body unincorporated' in the Customs and Inland Revenue Act, 1885; and the attempt made in the same year to restrain the powers of 'quasi-corporations' in dealing with their property. On 'Halbcorporationen,' see Dernburg, Pand. i. p. 147.

draw from it, taking their capital with them, and the 'firm' having as such no legal recognition[17], a contract made with it could be sued upon, according to the common law of England, only in an action in which the whole list of partners were made plaintiffs or defendants.

In order to remedy the first of these inconveniences, partnerships were formed upon the principle of a joint-stock, the capital invested in which must remain at a fixed amount, although the shares into which it is divided may pass from hand to hand. This device did not however obviate the difficulty in suing, nor did it relieve the partners, past and present, from liability for debts in excess of their, past or present, shares in the concern. In the interest not only of the share-partners, but also of the public with which they had dealings, it was desirable to discourage the formation of such associations; and the formation of joint-stock
*303 partner*ships, except such as were incorporated by royal charter, was accordingly, for a time, prohibited in England by the 'Bubble Act,' 6 Geo. I. c. 18. An incorporated trading company, in accordance with the ordinary principles regulating artificial persons, consists of a definite amount of capital to which alone creditors of the company can look for the satisfaction of their demands, divided into shares held by a number of individuals who, though they participate in the profits of the concern, in proportion to the number of shares held by each, incur no personal liability in respect of its losses. An artificial person of this sort is now recognised under most systems of law. It can be formed, as a rule, only with the consent of the sovereign power [18], and is described as a 'société,' or 'compagnie,' 'anonyme,' an 'Actiengesellschaft,' or 'joint-stock company limited [19].' A less pure form of such a corporation is a company the shareholders in which incur

[17] See now Order xvi. 14, above mentioned.

[18] This requirement has been much discussed in Germany, and has been modified in the later issues of the Handelsgesetzbuch; see arts. 215, 249.

[19] The first Act for limiting the liability of members of Joint-stock Companies was 18 & 19 Vict. c. 133, passed in 1855. Speaking of the disappearance of the old Trade-guilds, M. de Laveleye says: 'Plus de corporations industrielles: les sociétés anonymes qui en tiennent lieu ne sont qu'un moyen d'associer les capitaux et non des hommes.' Formes primitives de la propriété, p. 269.

an unlimited personal liability. There is also a form resembling a partnership 'en commandite,' in which the liability of some of the shareholders is limited by their shares, while that of others is unlimited.

Subject to some exceptions, any seven partners in a trading concern may, and partners whose number exceeds twenty must, according to English law, become incorporated by registration under the Companies Acts, with either limited or unlimited liability as they may determine at the time of incorporation.

Bankruptcy of corporations.

The debts of an incorporated company of any kind are payable in the first instance only out of the corporate funds.
*304 *Should those funds prove insufficient, the company becomes bankrupt, or, as it is variously expressed, 'is wound up,' or 'goes into liquidation.' The appropriate Court investigates its affairs, and calls upon the shareholders, in the case of a limited company, for any balance which may be unpaid upon their shares, and, in the case of an unlimited company, for any further sum which may be required from their private fortunes. Out of the fund thus available, the claims of creditors which have been satisfactorily established are paid either in full or rateably, as the case may be, and the company ceases to exist.

Foreign corporations.

The existence of a foreign corporation will generally be recognised, if according to the law of the country where it was created it has attributes similar to those which are assigned to corporations by the law of the country in whose courts it is plaintiff or defendant [20].

Proprietary peculiarities.

The chief peculiarity of the proprietary rights of artificial persons relates to their tenure of land. The accumulation of estates in the hands of religious houses was directly opposed to the interests of feudal lords, who accordingly made every effort in Eng-

[20] A foreign corporation has been admitted in England to be a plaintiff since 1734, to be a defendant since 1858.

land to get rid of such tenure, which they described as being 'in mortua manu,' by a long series of enactments. These 'Statutes of Mortmain' were extended in time to the prohibition of the alienation of land to lay as well as to spiritual corporations; and this continues to be the rule of English law to the present day, when no licence in mortmain is granted by the Crown, subject to a number of statutory exceptions in the interests of religion, charity, or other definite public object [21]. The Wills Acts of Henry VIII, now repealed, in giving a general power of devise, contains an exception against devises to 'bodies politic and corporate.'

*305 *A corporation is also usually restrained from parting with its landed property, and even from leasing it for more than a certain number of years, without the sanction of a public authority.

Contractual disabilities.

The form in which, as a rule[22], an artificial person enters into a contract or otherwise performs a juristic act is, according to English law, by the imposition of its seal; unless, in the case of a trading corporation, the act is incidental to carrying on the business for which it is incorporated, and, in the case of a non-trading corporation, when the acr is of trivial importance, or of urgent necessity[23].

There are some acts of which an artificial person is obviously incapable, and there are others which the law will not recognise its capacity to perform[24]. It has long been settled in England that an assumption on the part of a corporation to do what is wholly beyond its competence may be ground for a forfeiture of the charter on which its existence depends[25], and there has been of late years much discussion as to the classes of corporate acts which

21 The enactments on this subject have been consolidated in the Mortmain and Charitable Uses Act, 1888, 51 & 52 Vict. c. 42.

22 I. e. apart from statutory provisions, such as 11 & 12 Vict. c. 63. s. 85.

23 But by 38 & 39 Vict. c. 55. s. 174, a contract the value of which exceeds £50 made by an urban authority must be under seal.

24 On the liability of a corporation for wrongs, e. g. for trespass, libel, or fraud, see Pollock, Torts, ed. iii., pp. 53, 278.

25 R. v. Mayor of London, 1 Shower 274; cf. R. v. Eastern Archipelago Co., 2 E. & B. 856.

the law will support as valid with reference to individual corporators and to third parties respectively. When railway companies were first created with Parliamentary powers of a kind never before entrusted to similar bodies, it soon became necessary to determine whether, when once called into existence, they were to be held capable of exercising, as nearly as possible, all the powers of a natural person, unless expressly prohibited from doing so, or whether their acts must be strictly limited to the furtherance of the purpose for which they had been incorporated.

The question was first raised in 1846, with reference to
*306 the *right of a railway company to subsidise a harbour company, and Lord Langdale, in deciding against such a right, laid down the law in the following terms:—

'Companies of this kind, possessing most extensive powers, have so recently been introduced into this country that neither the legislature nor the courts of law have yet been able to understand all the different lights in which their transactions ought properly to be viewed. . . . To look upon a railway company in the light of a common partnership, and as subject to no greater vigilance than common partnerships are, would, I think, be greatly to mistake the functions which they perform and the powers which they exercise of interference not only with the public but with the private rights of all individuals in this realm. . . . I am clearly of opinion that the powers which are given by an Act of Parliament, like that now in question, extend no further than is expressly stated in the Act, or is necessarily and properly required for carrying into effect the undertaking and works which the Act has expressly sanctioned [26].'

This view, though it has sometimes been criticised, seems now to be settled law. In a recent case in the House of Lords, the permission which the Legislature gives to the promoters of a company was paraphrased as follows:—'You may meet together and form yourselves into a company, but in doing that you must tell all who may be disposed to deal with you the objects for which you have been associated. Those who are dealing with you will trust to that memorandum of association, and they will see that

[26] Colman v. Eastern Counties Railway Co., 10 Beav. 13.

you have the power of carrying on business in such a manner as it specifies. You must state the objects for which you are associated, so that the persons dealing with you will know that they are dealing with persons who can only devote their means to a given class of objects[27].'

*307 *Ultra vires.*

An act of a corporation in excess of its powers, with reference to third persons, is technically said to be ultra vires[28], and is void even if unanimously agreed to by all the corporators. The same term is also, but less properly, applied to a resolution of a majority of the members of a corporation which being beyond the powers of the corporation will not bind a dissentient minority of its members[29].

Such artificial persons as have hitherto been described result from the combination of a number of natural persons for the performance of a common function, and are accordingly described as 'universitates personarum,' or, in English law, as 'corporations aggregate.' An artificial person may, however, also exist without being supported by any natural person. It may consist merely of a mass of property, of rights and of duties, to which the law chooses to give a fictitious unity by treating it as a 'universitas bonorum.' The most familiar example is a 'hereditas' before it has been accepted by the heir, which in Roman law is treated as capable of increase and diminution, and even of contracting by means of a slave comprised in it, as if it were a person[30].

It would have been quite possible to explain in the same way the devolution of the lands of the crown, or a bishopric, or of a rectory, from the sovereign, bishop, or rector, to his successor; but English law has preferred to introduce for this purpose the fiction, peculiar to itself, of a 'corporátion sole[31].' The origin of

27 Per Lord Hatherley, in Riche v. The Ashbury Carriage Co., L. R. 7 E. and I., App. 684.

28 Perhaps first in South Yorkshire Rail. Co. v. Gt. N. Rail. Co., 9 Ex. 84 (1853).

29 The Earl of Shrewsbury v. N. Staff. Rail. Co., L. R. 1 Eq. 593.

30 Supra, p. *85.

31 A corporation sole, though it may hold lands, cannot hold goods and

such a corporation is rarely traceable; but the Master of *308 Pembroke College and the Provost of Oriel *College, Oxford, were respectively made corporations sole by letters patent of Queen Anne[32].

II. NATURAL PERSONS.

The chief varieties of status among natural persons may be referred to the following causes: 1. sex; 2. minority; 3. 'patria potesta' and 'manus'; 4. coverture; 5. celibacy; 6. mental defect; 7. bodily defect; 8. rank, caste, and official position; 9. race and colour; 10. slavery; 11. profession; 12. civil death; 13. illegitimacy; 14. heresy; 15. foreign nationality; 16. hostile nationality. All of the facts included in this list, which might be extended, have been held, at one time or another, to differentiate the legal position of persons affected by them from that of persons of the normal type[33]. It may be worth while to give a few illustrations of each of the special types of status thus arising.

Sex.

1. The disabilities or privileges of women, as such, must be looked for in modern times rather in the department of public than in that of private law. It must however be remembered that even in the time of Gaius the life-long tutelage of women, 'propter animi levitatem,' had not wholly become obsolete[34], and that, by a senatusconsultum passed in the reign of Claudius, they were allowed to repudiate any liability which they might have undertaken as sureties, 'quum eas virilibus officiis fungi et eius generis obligationibus obstringi non sit aequum[35].'

chattels; because, says Blackstone, 'such moveable property is liable to be lost or embezzled, and would raise a multitude of disputes between the successor and the executor, which the law is careful to avoid.' Comm. i. p. 478.

32 See 12 Anne, St. 2. c. 6.

33 In the Tagore Lectures, 1883, Lect. xii, Dr. Jolly gives a curious account of the classes of persons incapable of inheriting, according to Hindoo law, and according to the Sachsenspiegel.

34 Inst. i. 144.

35 Dig. xvi. 1. 2.

Minority.

2. Minors are, as a rule, capable of holding and receiving property, and liable for their wrongful acts, but incapable of making a will, or of entering into a valid contract without the approval of a guardian or of some public authority[36]. The exception to this rule, in favour of upholding an infant's contracts for neces-
*309 saries, is obviously made in the interest of the *infant himself; 'ne magno incommodo afficiantur, nemine cum his contrahente, et quodammodo commercio eis interdicatur[37].' The age of full majority is differently fixed under different systems, and it may be remarked that English law, in dividing human life for most of the purposes of private law into two periods only, that which precedes and that which follows the age of twenty-one, has departed from the theory of the Roman lawyers and their followers. This theory, which postpones the date of full majority till the completion of the twenty-fifth year, distinguishes in the preceding period, infancy, proximity to infancy, and a qualified majority attained by girls at the age of twelve, and by boys at the age of fourteen years.

Patria Potestas.

3. A 'filius familias' could hold no property, except, in later times, what he acquired by way of 'peculium.' He could enter into most contracts, but was specially disabled, by the senatusconsultum Macedonianum, from borrowing money.

Coverture.

4. The effect of marriage, according to most systems of law, was to produce a unity between the husband and wife, rendering
*310 each of them incapable of suing the other[38], and *constituting a sort of partnership between them, in which the hus-

[36] Cf. the Infant Settlements Act, 1855, and the Infants Relief Act, 1874.

[37] Dig. iv. 24. It is held that things with which an infant is already sufficiently supplied, although purchased from a tradesman ignorant of the fact, are not necessaries. Barnes v. Toye, 13 Q. B. D. 410; Johnstone v. Marks, 19 Q. B. D. 509.

[38] Such is, for instance, the rule of the English Common Law, Co. Litt. 112 a. But under 45 & 46 Vict. c. 75, a married woman, subject to certain exceptions, 'has in her own name the same civil remedies, and also the same

band has very extensive powers over the partnership property, while the wife has not only no power of alienating it, but is also incapable of making a will, or of entering into any contract on her own account. The common law of England exhibits these disabilities of the wife in their strongest form. Of the several systems between which French law gives an option to persons about to marry, the 'régime de la communauté,' derived from the 'coutumiers,' is least favourable to the wife, giving, as it does, to the husband the absolute control of the common stock [39]; while the 'régime dotal,' an imitation of the dotal system of Roman law, resembles that modern creation of the English Courts of equity, a marriage settlement, in which the wife's 'separate estate' is protected not only from manipulation by the husband, but also against the possibly improvident disposal of it by the wife herself [40]. The contractual disabilities of women in England have been much modified by recent legislation, especially by the 'Married Women's Property Act, 1882 [41].'

Celibacy.

5. Unmarried and childless persons were punished under the lex Iulia et Papia Poppaea by forfeiture, either total or partial, of the 'ius capiendi ex testamento.'

remedies and redress by way of criminal proceedings, for the protection and security of her own separate property, as if such property belonged to her as a feme sole,' and the husband may similarly take proceedings, civil or criminal, against his wife. The older theory of marriage seems still to predominate in the United States. It has indeed been held in one of the appellate divisions of the Court of New York that a husband may bring an action against his wife to recover property belonging to him which has been forcibly seized and carried away by her. Berdell v. Parkhurst, 19 Hun, 358. In Schultz v. Schultz, mentioned in a former edition of this work, from information kindly supplied by Mr. Roger Foster, the supreme Court of New York held in 1882 that, in the absence of any exception as to the husband, an Act of 1860 giving to any married woman a right of action in her own name against any person for injury to her person or character included an action against her husband, and had thus 'routed and dispelled' the rules of the Common Law, which 'could not stand the scrutiny and analysis of modern civilization.' But this case has since been reversed by the Court of Appeals.

[39] Code Civil, art. 1399.

[40] Ib. art. 1540.

[41] Repealing the Acts of 1870 and 1874 on the same subject.

Mental defect.

6. A lunatic, though capable of holding property, was in Roman law incapable of any legal act. 'Furiosus nullum negotium gerere potest, quia non intelligit quid agit [42].' In modern English law a contract made by him is not ipso facto void, nor is it even
*311 voidable by him, if entered into by the *other party without notice of the lunacy, especially if it has been wholly or partly executed [43]. A somewhat similar disability has sometimes attached to persons whom a competent Court has declared to be 'prodigals.' Drunkenness cannot be said to create a status, and its effects in avoiding contracts may best be compared with the similar effects of duress.

Bodily defect.

7. Deaf or dumb persons were unable to contract by 'stipulatio.'

Office.

8. The king, according to the maxim of English law, can do no wrong. No action can be brought against him, nor indeed against a foreign sovereign as such, or his ambassador. Certain high officials are exempted from responsibility for the acts of their subordinates, and various public functionaries are relieved from liability by the Statutes of Limitation at an earlier date than other people.

Colour and race.

9. Most of the disabilities formerly attaching in the States of the American Union on account of race or colour have now been removed [44].

[42] Inst. iii. 19. 8. Cf. Dig. xliv. 7. 1. 12, l. 17. 5.

[43] Moulton v. Camroux, 4 Ex. 17; Imperial Loan Co. v. Stone, '91, 2 Q. B. (C. A.) 599. By the Indian Contract Act of 1872, §§ 11, 12, contracts entered into during lunacy or drunkenness are void. Cf. supra, p. *221. On the tort of a lunatic, see Dig. ix. 2. 5. 2.

[44] See Stimson, American Statute-law, art. 605. Though in Oregon and Nevada no Chinaman or Mongolian can be employed in public works, or in city buildings or grounds.

Slavery.

10. It may well be questioned whether a human being who is incapable of marriage, of holding property, and of contracting, can be regarded as a legal person at all. This was the position of a slave in Roman law, which declares that 'servile caput nullum ius habet,' and 'in personam servilem nulla cadit obligatio[45].' Nor was his private-law position affected, as Austin seems to think[46], by the constitutions which made it penal for his master to kill or grievously ill-treat him without cause. These were in truth analogous to the provisions in modern systems of public law
*312 for the prevention of *cruelty to animals. Since however a slave has, even for legal purposes, some of the characteristics of a human being[47], it is necessary to point out that his status is in private law abnormal to the extent of being all but non-existent.

Profession.

11. A soldier on active service enjoys, under most systems, certain exceptional testamentary privileges. By English law a barrister is incapable of validly contracting to be paid for his professional assistance; and the same disability attaches also to a physician[48].

Civil death.

12. The effects of 'entering into religion,' according to English law, have been already noticed[49]. Similar effects still follow according to the law of the Hindoos. A somewhat similar loss of legal rights resulted also from attainder for treason or felony[50].

45 Dig. l. 17. 22; although they were capable of incurring an 'obligatio naturalis,' Dig. xliv. 7. 14. Cf. Inst. iii. 20. 1.

46 Vol. ii. p. 8.

47 'Ipsi servo facta iniuria inulta a praetore relinqui non debuit, maxime si verberibus vel quaestione fieret, hanc enim et servum sentire palam est.' Dig. xlvii. 10. 15. 35.

48 Supra, p. *262.

49 Supra, p. *84; Jolly, Tagore Lectures, pp. 175, 275.

50 See now 33 & 34 Vict. c. 23.

Illegitimacy.

13. An illegitimate child is incapable of inheriting 'ab intestato' from an ascendant or collateral, because the law regards him as 'nullius filius.' Under the French Code such a child may however acquire a limited right of succession if solemnly recognised by his parents, or one of them[51].

Nonconformity.

14. Religious nonconformity has been an important cause of civil disability from the date of the imperial constitutions which are collected in the first book of the Code of Justinian, down to the laws by which a Roman Catholic was disqualified from owning a horse worth more than £5 in Ireland, or which rendered Jews incapable of holding land in Roumania.

Alienage.

15. The gradual extension of the rights of 'connubium' and 'commercium' with Roman citizens to the neighbouring Italian tribes is a well-known chapter of the history of Roman law. The
*313 Act of 1870, by which aliens were allowed *to own freehold land in the United Kingdom, marks the last step in the assimilation of their position, as far as private law is concerned, with that of British subjects.

Hostility.

16. The contracts of an alien enemy with a British subject made during the war are void, and his right to sue upon other causes of action is suspended during the war.

The incapacity by English law of the witness to a will to take a legacy under it, and of a man to marry the sister of his deceased wife; so also of a husband or wife, as a rule, to take by donation one from the other in Roman law, are instances of restrictions placed upon persons occupying for the time being certain relations to other persons, which from the limited extent of their operation can hardly be said to constitute a status.

[51] Art. 334.

*314

*CHAPTER XV.

PRIVATE LAW: ADJECTIVE.

A remedial right is in itself a mere potentiality, deriving all its value from the support which it can obtain from the power of the state. The mode in which that support may be secured, in order to the realisation of a remedial right, is prescribed by that department of law which has been called 'adjective,' because it exists only for the sake of 'substantive law [1],' but is probably better known as 'Procedure [2].' In the exceptional cases in which an injured party is allowed to redress his own wrong, Adjective law points out the limits within which such self-help is permissible. In all other cases *it announces what steps must
*315
be taken in order duly to set in motion the machinery of the law-courts for the benefit either of a plaintiff or of a defendant.

Rules of procedure occupy so prominent a place in early society, and furnish so much curious illustration of the history of civilisation, that they have attracted a share of attention perhaps in excess of their real importance. One might almost suppose from the language of some writers that an elaborately organised Procedure may precede a clear recognition of the rights which it is intended to protect. It has been said that law is concerned more with remedies than with rights. It would be as reasonable to say that a field consists in its hedge and ditch rather than in the space of land which these enclose. In point of fact, a right must be recognised at least as soon as, if not before, the moment when it

1 Supra, pp. *78, *147. See Bentham, Works, ii. p. 6.

2 The term 'Procedure' was, till the passing of the Common Law Procedure Acts, unfamiliar in English law. It is said by Lush, L. J., to denote, like 'Practice,' in its larger sense, 'the mode of proceeding by which a legal right is enforced, as distinguished from the law which gives or defines the right, and which by means of the proceeding the Court is to administer; the machinery as distinguished from the product.' Poyser v. Minors, L. R. 7 Q. B. D. 329, p. 333. Procedure is by many German writers very inappropriately called 'formal law.'

is fenced round by remedies. The true interest of the topic of Procedure is derived, first, from the close connection which may be traced between its earliest forms and the anarchy which preceded them [3], and secondly from the manner in which the tribunals have contrived, from time to time, to effect changes in the substance of the law itself, under cover of merely modifying the methods by which it is enforced.

Contents.

Adjective law, though it concerns primarily the rights and acts of private litigants, touches closely on topics, such as the organisation of Courts, and the duties of judges and sheriffs, which belong to public law. It comprises the rules for (i) selecting the jurisdiction which has cognisance of the matter in question; (ii) ascertaining the Court which is appropriate for the decision of the matter; (iii) setting in motion the machinery of the Court
*316 so as to procure the de*cision; and (iv) setting in motion the physical force by which the judgment of the Court is, in the last resort, to be rendered effectual. These rules, like those of substantive law, are primarily applicable to persons of the normal type, and only with certain modifications to abnormal persons.

Jurisdiction.

i. It is by no means the case that a remedial right is capable of being enforced everywhere. An English Court will for instance entertain an action for breach of contract quite irrespectively of the place where it was made, or broken, or in which the parties reside, but will hardly hear an application for a divorce unless the parties are domiciled in the country, nor try an action for trespass to land unless the land is within the realm.

[3] See, for instance, Sir H. Maine's Early History of Institutions, lect. ix. and x., and his interesting remarks, in Early Law and Custom, p. 364, on the prominent position occupied by Procedure in the XII Tables, as contrasted with its relegation to the last place in the Institutional writers of the Empire. 'Trial by battle' was a late survival in England of regulated self-help. After the last reported case of the kind, Ashford v. Thornton, 1 B. & Ald. 405, it was abolished by 59 G. III. c. 46.

Court.

ii. It is also necessary that proceedings be taken in the appropriate Court. Thus in England, even after the changes introduced by the Judicature Acts, it is still necessary that an administration action should be commenced in the Chancery division, and a salvage action in the Admiralty division, of the High Court of Justice. There are also matters which can only be tried in one or other of the divisions of that Court, and not in any inferior tribunal.

The action.

iii. The choice of the appropriate Court is a simple matter compared with rightly setting its machinery in motion. In this operation, which has been described by such phrases as 'legis actio,' 'l'instance,' 'la demande judiciaire,' 'action,' 'suit,' 'Verfahren,' the following stages are usually distinguishable.

Citation.

1. The summons, or citation, by which the plaintiff brings the defendant into Court.

Pleadings.

2. The pleadings, 'l'instruction de la cause,' by which the plaintiff informs the Court and the defendant of the nature of his claim, and the defendant states the nature of his defence. The de-
*317 fence may be to the effect that, even *granting the truth of the plaintiff's allegations of fact, they are in law no ground for his claim against the defendant, or it may consist in denying altogether the facts alleged by the plaintiff, or in admitting them, but alleging other facts, such as a release, or the Statutes of Limitation, which neutralise the effect which they would otherwise have had. A defence of the last-mentioned kind was called in Roman law an 'exceptio,' and in England a plea in 'confession and avoidance [4].' A plea may be either 'dilatory,' showing that the right of action is not yet available, or 'peremp-

[4] 'Comparatae sunt autem exceptiones defendendorum eorum gratia cum quibus agitur: saepe enim accidit ut, licet ipsa actio qua actor experitur iusta sit, tamen iniqua sit adversus eum cum quo agitur.' Inst. iv. 13.

tory,' showing that it is non-existent. The exchange of pleadings continues till it is clear how much is admitted and how much is denied on either side, and therefore what is precisely the dispute between the parties. This process may be carried on orally in the presence of the Court, as under the new code of Civil Procedure for the German Empire [5], or in writing or print, as in England. When well managed it gives much scope for dexterous intellectual fencing, but its tendency to over-subtlety has been a fertile theme for legal critics from the time of Gaius to that of Bentham [6].

Trial.

3. The trial, hearing, or 'audience,' at which each of the parties endeavours to establish to the satisfaction of the
*318 *Court the truth of the view maintained by him of the question at issue, whether it be one of law or one of fact; if of law, by citing authorities, if of fact, by adducing proofs.

Evidence.

Proofs may be either documentary or oral, and certain rules exist in most systems with reference to their admissibility, amounting in some systems to a body of law of no little complexity. Such a 'law of evidence' is more necessary when questions are tried by a jury than when they are decided by a professionally trained judge. Its objects are, on the one hand, to limit the field of enquiry, by the doctrine that certain classes of facts are already

[5] Civilprozessordnung für das Deutsche Reich, § 119. But in 'Anwaltsprozesse,' i. e. when professional representatives must be employed, disadvantages as to costs, and otherwise, follow, unless 'die mündliche Verhandlung' is 'durch Schriftsätze vorbereitet,' § 120: and copies of these writings are to be filed in Court, § 124. Cf. the recommendations of the Lord Chancellor's Committee on Procedure, 1881.

[6] The 'legis actiones,' says Gaius, gradually fell into disrepute, 'namque ex nimia subtilitate veterum, qui tunc iura condiderunt, eo res perducta est, ut vel qui minimum errasset litem perderet'; iv. 30: and he gives the following instance, 'cum qui de vitibus succisis ita egisset ut in actione vites nominaret, responsum est eum rem perdidisse, quia debuisset arbores nominare, eo quod lex xii tabularum, ex qua de vitibus succisis actio competeret, generaliter de arboribus succisis loqueretur'; ib. 11. Cf. Bentham, Works, ii. p. 14.

within the 'judicial notice' of the Courts, and by 'presumptions' by which certain propositions are to be assumed to be sufficiently proved when certain other propositions have been established; and on the other hand, to exclude certain kinds of evidence as having too remote a bearing on the issue, or as incapable of being satisfactorily tested, or as coming from a suspicious quarter [7]. For the last-mentioned reason certain classes of persons, or persons occupying certain relative positions, are rendered incapable of being witnesses. There are also rules regulating the right of the parties to appear in person, or to be represented by advocates, and the order in which the parties or their advocates may tender their evidence and address the Court.

Judgment.

4. The judgment, by which the Court decides the question in litigation. It may relate to a right to property, or an ascertainment [8] or a dissolution [9] of status, or an affirmation of the
*319 due execution of a legal act, or an award of damages *for a wrong, or an order for the specific performance [10] or non-performance of a certain act [11].

Costs.

The judgment usuallv charges upon the losing side the 'costs' to which the other party has been put in consequence of the suit [12].

[7] The German Civilprozessordnung is opposed to Presumptions and other so-called 'artificial' proofs; cf. § 259. The Einführungsgesetz, § 14, repeals laws restricting modes of proof. The theory of legal proof is no doubt largely due to the canonists, but it can hardly be said to have been wholly unknown to Roman law. See the opinion of Favorinus, apud Gell. Noctes A. xiv. 2.

[8] E. g. on a declaration of nullity, or under the Legitimacy Declaration Act, 21 & 22 Vict. c. 93.

[9] On a decree of divorce.

[10] Cf. supra, p. *286.

[11] As to 'tierce opposition' when the judgment affects the rights of one who is not a party to the action, see Code de Procédure Civile, art. 474.

[12] Cf. supra, p. *164. Justinian's Legislation upon the subject is contained in Cod. i. 3. 13. Costs were in England eo nomine unknown to the common law, but were given to the plaintiff by 6 Ed. I. c. 1, to the defendant by 23 H. VIII. c. 15. At one time also the judgment contained a direction "that the

Appeal.

5. The procedure on Appeal, when an Appeal is possible and is resorted to by either party [13].

Execution.

iv. Execution, whereby a successful party calls upon the officers of the Court, or other appropriate State functionaries, to use such force as may be necessary in order to carry the judgment into effect. It may be remarked that a successful defendant, except for the recovery of his costs, has obviously no need of execution, and that execution of a judgment in a civil cause is not ex officio, i. e. does not take place except on the demand of a litigant party. The constitutions of nineteen States of the United States provide that the privileges of a debtor to enjoy the necessary comforts of life shall be recognised by wholesome laws exempting a reasonable amount of his property from execution. Sixteen States have now 'Homestead laws,' exempting a homestead for the shelter and protection of the family from execution or judicial sale for debt, unless both husband and wife have expressly joined in mortgaging, or otherwise subjecting it to the claims of creditors [14].

*320 **Extraneous parties.*

Besides the original parties to an action, whose interests are directly involved in it, other persons may be brought into it by the authority of the Court. In some actions, which involve wider interests than those of the parties, notice must be given to a State functionary, who may then intervene in the proceedings on public grounds [15].

plaintiff (or the defendant) be amerced, or in mercy, "in misericordia domini regis," for his false claim (or, for his wilful delay of justice).'

13 The Sachsenspiegel gave a right of appeal to a dissentient member of the Court, as having an interest on public grounds that the law should be correctly stated.

14 See Stimson, American Statute-law, §§ 81, 83. The first 'Homestead law' was passed in 1836, by the Republic of Texas.

15 See Code de Procédure Civile, P. I. liv. ii. tit. 4, De la Communication au Ministère Public; Gerichtsverfassungsgesetz für das Deutsche Reich, § 142; Civilprozessordnung, § 568; and, as to the Queen's Proctor, 23 & 24 Vict. c. 144, s. 5.

Default.

A maximum interval may be fixed between each step in an action, on pain of a decision being given 'in default' against the party who neglects to proceed in due course.

Abnormal Adjective Law.

Adjective, no less than Substantive, law may be normal or abnormal: that is to say, artificial persons, and such varieties of natural persons as those considered in the preceding chapter, are in a different position with reference to suing and being sued from that occupied by ordinary individuals. The modifications of the rules of procedure which take place with a view to abnormal personality are of a somewhat technical character; and it may be sufficient here to refer, by way of illustration, to the rules of English law, that an alien enemy has no 'persona standi in iudicio,' that a peer is privileged from arrest, as is a clergyman on his way to or from the performance of divine service, that if one of the parties in an action for a divorce be lunatic, the suit may proceed notwithstanding his, or her, inability to plead; and to the recently abrogated rule that a husband must be joined in an action against his wife.

*321

*CHAPTER XVI.

PUBLIC LAW.

The characteristics of public law.

'I consider,' says Lord Bacon, 'that it is a true and received division of law into ius publicum and ius privatum, the one being the sinews of property, and the other of government [1].' The nature of the distinction has been already explained [2]. In private law the State is indeed present, but it is present only as arbiter of the rights and duties which exist between one of its subjects and another. In public law the State is not only arbiter, but is also one of the parties interested. The rights and duties with which it deals concern itself of the one part and its subjects of the other part, and this union in one personality of the attributes of judge and party has given rise to the view, from which we have already expressed our dissent, that the State, or, as it is expressed, the Sovereign, not only has no duties, but also has no rights properly so called [3].

The conception of public, as opposed to private, law is due
*322 *to the Romans, who say of it 'ad statum rei Romanae spectat,' 'in sacris, in sacerdotibus, in magistratibus consistit [4],' and, as a matter of fact, include in it also the law of crime. With this extended meaning the phrase has been accepted, and is in daily use, in the legal speculation and practice of the continent of Europe, but unfortunately finds no equivalent in our insular legal terminology [5]. An English lawyer, when he had been made to understand the idea, which to his foreign colleagues is at once

1 Preparation towards the Union of Laws, Works, vii. 731.

2 Supra, p. *111.

3 Supra, p. *115.

4 Dig. i. 1. 1. 2. 'Publicum ius est quod ad statum rei Romanae spectat, privatum quod ad singulorum utilitatem. Sunt enim quaedam publice utilia, quaedam privatim.'

5 The two departments were similarly confused in Old German law. Cf. Bluntschli, Deutsche Statslehre, p. 7.

rudimentary and indispensable, would probably come to the conclusion that it covers the topics which are recognised in this country as 'Constitutional law,' 'Ecclesiastical law,' 'Revenue law,' and 'Pleas of the Crown.' It is therefore somewhat remarkable that perhaps the most masterly summary of the nature of public law is to be found in the writings of an English Lord Chancellor. 'Ius Privatum,' says Lord Bacon, 'sub tutela Iuris Publici latet. Lex enim cavet civibus, magistratus legibus, magistratuum autem authoritas pendet ex maiestate imperii et fabrica politiae et legibus fundamentalibus. Quare si ex illa parte sanitas fuerit et recta constitutio, leges erunt in bono usu, sin minus, parum in iis praesidii erit. Neque tamen Ius Publicum ad hoc tantum spectat ut addatur tanquam custos Iuri Privato, ne illud violetur atque ut cessent iniuriae, sed extenditur etiam ad religionem et arma, et disciplinam et ornamenta et opes, denique ad omnia circa Bene Esse civitatis [6].'

Its parts.

The distinctions in accordance with which the field of private law has been divided and subdivided apply to public law also. In the latter as well as in the former we may detect a 'substan-
*323 tive' body of principles adopted for *the general welfare, and 'adjective' rules by which those principles are safe-guarded and reduced to practice. The distinction between rights 'in rem' and rights 'in personam' is as clearly traceable in one department of law as in the other, as is also that between rights 'antecedent' and 'remedial,' and that between rights 'normal' and 'abnormal.'

The last-mentioned distinction is indeed so strongly marked in public law as to have led to a serious misconception as to the nature of the whole subject. The reason is not far to seek. Of the two persons who are constituent elements of every right, one must always in public law be the State, acting of course through its various functionaries. Now a State is an artificial person, the often highly complex construction of which introduces numerous complexities into the rights of which it is one of the factors. Mr. Austin was so struck with this characteristic of public law as to

[6] Exemplum tractatus de Iustitia universali, Works, i. p. 804; cf. ib. vii. p. 732.

be led to identify the whole subject with those rules which define the different kinds of political status, and so to deny its separate existence, and to regard it merely as one branch of what he calls the law of persons, but we prefer to describe as the law of abnormal rights. He is thus a revolter, in the unwonted company of Blackstone, against what, according to the Roman and modern continental systems, is the primary division of the field of law. Instead of attempting a detailed disproof of a heresy which perhaps sufficiently refutes itself, by leading its apologist to conclusions which he evidently feels to be inconvenient, it may perhaps be sufficient to confront it with what we conceive to be the true doctrine, namely that among the distinctions which are traceable in public as well as in private law, that between normal and abnormal rights is among the most conspicuous.

Classification of its topics.

It by no means follows from the same principles of division being applicable both in public and in private law, that they are most conveniently applied in the same order in the two departments, or that their application produces in each case similar results.

*324 *The correlation of the parts of public law one to another is indeed far from being settled. It never attracted the attention of the Roman lawyers, and has been very variously, and somewhat loosely, treated by the jurists of modern Europe. The subject is indeed one which lends itself but reluctantly to systematic exposition, and it is with some hesitation that we propose to consider it under the heads of—I. Constitutional law; II. Administrative law; III. Criminal law; IV. Criminal procedure; V. the law of the State considered in its quasi-private personality; VI. the procedure relating to the State as so considered [7].

[7] It may be worth while to remark that what the Germans call 'Staatsrecht' deals with the topics into which we have analysed 'Public Law,' omitting Nos. III and IV.

Relations to the classification of private law.

The first four of these heads contain the topics which are most properly comprised in Public law. It would be possible, though not convenient, to arrange these topics in accordance with the classification adopted in Private law. If the attempt were made, antecedent rights would have to be sought for in Constitutional, in Administrative and also in Criminal law; remedial rights in Criminal and also in Administrative law; adjective law mainly in Criminal procedure; and abnormal law mainly in Constitutional and Criminal law. The importance of the last-mentioned topic is due, as already stated, to the fact that, whereas in Private law both of the persons concerned with any given right are, as a rule, perfectly similar, and of that normal type which requires no special investigation, the persons concerned in a Public-law right are necessarily dissimilar, one of them being always that highly abnormal person which is called a State. It may also be remarked that the majority of the rights dealt with in Public law are permanently enjoyed by the State as the person of inherence against its subjects as the persons of incidence. In Private law, on the contrary, he who is to-day the person of inherence with reference to a right of any given description may very probably be-
*325 come to-morrow the person of *incidence with reference to a precisely similar right, and vice versa.

The rules contained under the fifth and sixth heads of our arrangement are rules of Public law, because they relate to the rights of the State; but they approximate closely to rules of Private law, because they relate to the State merely as the greatest of artificial persons, and not as governing, administering, or preserving order.

It is beyond the scope of the present treatise to attempt more than a very brief indication of the topics included under each of the six heads under which we have distributed the matter of Public law.

I. CONSTITUTIONAL LAW.

The primary function of Constitutional law is to ascertain the political centre of gravity of any given state. It announces in what portion of the whole is to be found the 'internal sovereignty,' 'suprema potestas,' 'Staatsgewalt,' or, as Aristotle called it, *τὸ κύριον τῆς πόλεως*.[8] In other words, it defines the form of government.

The Sovereign power.

The sovereign part of the State, as thus ascertained, is omnipotent. Since it is the source of all law, its acts can never be illegal. As little can they be, strictly speaking, unconstitutional. The latter term is properly applied only to characterise an act of an inferior political authority in excess of its delegated powers. Thus a statute passed by the Congress of the United States may be unconstitutional, because the sovereign people has empowered the President and Congress to legislate only subject to certain reservations, and has entrusted to a Supreme Court the duty of deciding whether any given enactment is or is not made in pursuance of the restricted powers thus delegated; but the authority of the Queen, Lords, and Commons in England is fettered by no such limitation. An act is, strictly speaking, never uncon-
*326 *stitutional unless it is also illegal, and can never be either if it is the act of the sovereign power. Only in a lax sense of the term is it permissible to describe as unconstitutional acts of the sovereign power which run counter to the expectations and political usages of the inhabitants of a country.

Factors of Sovereign power.

The definition of the sovereign power in a state necessarily leads to the consideration of its component parts. The distinction between legislative, executive, and judicial functions is as old as Aristotle[9]; but it was left for Montesquieu to point out the importance of these several functions being discharged by distinct groups of persons[10]. With reference to all these questions constitutional law enters into minute detail. It prescribes the order of succession to the throne; or, in a Republic, the mode of electing a President. It provides for the continuity of the executive pow-

[8] Polit. iii. 10. 1. *Πολιτεία μὲν γάρ ἐστι τάξις ταῖς πόλεσιν ἡ περὶ τὰς ἀρχάς, τίνα τρόπον νενέμηνται, καὶ τί τὸ κύριον τῆς πολιτείας καὶ τί τὸ τέλος ἑκάστης τῆς κοινωνίας ἐστίν.* Ib. iv. 1. 1. Cf. supra, p *44.

[9] Polit. iv. 11. 1.

[10] Esprit, xi. c. 6.

er[11]. It enumerates the 'prerogatives' of the king, or other chief magistrate. It regulates the composition of the Council of State, and of the Upper and Lower Houses of the Assembly, when the Assembly is thus divided; the mode in which a seat is acquired in the Upper House, whether by succession, nomination, election, or tenure of office; the mode of electing the members of the house of representatives; the powers and privileges of the assembly as a whole, and of the individuals who compose it; and the machinery of law-making. It deals also with the ministers, their responsibility and their respective spheres of action; the government offices and their organisation; the armed forces of the State, their control and the mode in which they are recruited; the relation, if any, between Church and State[12]; the judges and their *327 *immunities; their power, if any, of disallowing as unconstitutional the acts of non-sovereign legislative bodies; local self-government; the relations between the mother-country and its colonies and dependencies. It describes the portions of the earth's surface over which the sovereignty of the State extends, and defines the persons who are subject to its authority. It comprises therefore rules for the ascertainment of nationality[13], and for regulating the acquisition of a new nationality by 'naturalisation.' It declares the rights of the State over its subjects in respect of their liability to military conscription, to service as jurymen, and otherwise. It declares, on the other hand, the rights of the subjects to be assisted and protected by the State, and of that narrower class of subjects which enjoys full civic rights to hold public offices and to elect their representatives to the Assembly, or Parliament, of the Nation. Among the circumstances which may disqualify a subject for citizenship are minority, infamy, heresy, colour, lack of settled abode, insufficiency of income,

[11] With the maxim 'the King never dies,' cf. 'Sedes Apostolica non moritur,' c. 5. de rescr. in Sext. 1. 3.

[12] Ecclesiastical is sometimes coordinated with Public and Private law. 'Nam et genera [legum] sunt tria, sacri. publici, privati iuris.' Quint. ii. 4. Cf. 'Ius triplex tabulae quod ter sanxere quaternae,

Sacrum, privatum, populi commune quod usquam est.' Auson. Id. xi. 61.

[13] M. Cogordan, La Nationalité, p. 2, points out the recent origin of this term, and that it appears in the Dictionnaire de l'Académie française for the first time in the edition of 1835.

and also sex, for in spite of the tendency of modern thought upon this subject, there are still those who say, 'die Politik ist Sache des Mannes [14].

A constitution has been well defined as 'l'ensemble des institutions et des lois fondamentales, destinées à régler l'action de l'administration et de tous les citoyens [15].' It is often, as in England, an unwritten body of custom, though, since the assertion of the 'rights of man' which preceded the French Revolution, the written enactment of such fundamental principles has been not uncommon, as well on the European continent as in America. A written constitution usually contains provisions which make innovation less easy than in the case of customary constitutions, such
*328 as that of *England, any part of which may be modified by an ordinary act of Parliament [16].

The contents of the constitutional branch of law may be illustrated by reference to a piece of proposed legislation, which enters far more into detail than is usual in such undertakings. The draft Political Code of the State of New York purports to be divided into four parts, whereof 'The first declares what persons compose the people of the State, and the political rights and duties of all persons subject to its jurisdiction: the second defines the territory of the State and its civil divisions: the third relates to the general government of the State, the functions of its public officers, its public ways, its general police and civil polity: the fourth relates to the local government of counties, cities, towns, and villages.' The Code begins with an announcement that 'the sovereignty of the State resides in the people thereof,' and the people is said to consist—'1. of citizens who are electors; 2. of citizens not electors.'

The constitutions of federal governments, such as those of the United States or Switzerland, contain provisions upon many topics

14 Bluntschli, Die Lehre vom modernen Staat, i. p. 246.

15 Ahrens, Cours, iii. p. 380.

16 Ahrens, Cours, iii. p. 381. Mr. Bryce has suggested the use of the terms 'rigid' and 'flexible' to express this distinction. See now his American Commonwealth, i. pp. 475–478. See also Professor Dicey's instructive and ingenious applications of the distinction, Law of the Constitution, ed. iv. pp. 118–128.

of private law, such as respect for property and contracts. The reason being, as has well been stated, that 'certain principles of policy or justice must be enforced upon the whole confederated body as well as upon the separate parts thereof, and the very inflexibility of the constitution tempts legislators to place among constitutional articles maxims which (though not in their nature constitutional) have special claims upon respect and forbearance [17].'

*329. II. *ADMINISTRATIVE LAW.

The various organs of the sovereign power are described by constitutional law as at rest; but it is also necessary that they should be considered as in motion, and that the manner of their activity should be prescribed in detail. The branch of the law which does this is called Administrative law, 'Verwaltungsrecht,' in the widest sense of the term. In this sense Administration has been defined as 'the exercise of political powers within the limits of the constitution [18],' as 'the total concrete and manifoldly changing activity of the State in particular cases [19],' and as 'the functions, or the activity, of the sovereign power [20].'

Its widest sense.

Different views are taken as to the topics which are included under this very wide conception. It may fairly be said to include the making and promulgation of laws, the action of the government in guiding the State as a whole, the administration of justice, the management of the property and business transactions of the State, and the working in detail, by means of subordinates entrusted with a certain amount of discretion, of the complex machinery by which the State provides at once for its own existence and for the general welfare.

17 Dicey, u. s. p. *143. Cf. Bryce, u. s. ii. p. *41. It is thus that questions such as those raised in the Dartmouth College case, supra, p. *225 n., are brought before the Supreme Court.

18 Ahrens, Cours, ii. p. 380.

19 Bluntschli, u. s. iii. p. 465.

20 Pütter, apud Holzendorff, Encyclopädie, Erster Theil (ed. i.) p. 695.

Its more specific sense.

Administrative law, as thus conceived of, is not a coherent body of doctrine, and it is convenient so to specialise the use of the term as to apply it only to two of the five above-mentioned topics. Of the rest, legislation and executive government are more fitly treated of under those chapters of Constitutional law which deal with the legislature and the sovereign; the rules for the administration of justice must be sought, so far as they provide for the organisation of the courts, under Constitutional law, so far as they govern civil procedure, under Adjective Private law, and so far as they govern crimes and criminal procedure, under those heads of Public law, namely the third and fourth, which we devote specifically to those topics; while the law relating to the
*330 *State property and its business transactions would be found in the fifth and sixth of our heads of public law.

Its functions.

Administrative law, in the specific sense of the term, which is identical with that in which some German writers employ the term 'Polizei,' deals with such topics as the following:—

Revenue.

i. The collection of the Revenue.

Armed forces.

ii. The recruitment, equipment, and control of the Army and Navy; Ship-building and Fortifications.

Dependencies.

iii. The government of Colonies and Dependencies.

État civil.

iv. The collection of statistics; the registration of births, deaths, and marriages ('état civil') [21] and of conveyances and mortgages of land; the custody of wills; the naturalisation of aliens; the granting of charters to corporations.

[21] In France this is dealt with as a matter of private law, in the Code Civil.

Material welfare.

v. The promotion of the material welfare of all the individuals of whom the State is composed, either by the prevention of evil or the production of good. Among the operations carried on by State functionaries for this purpose are the following:—

1. Measures of sanitary precaution, such as the organisation of drainage, the inspection and even destruction of unhealthy dwellings, the regulation of dangerous undertakings, such as mining, and of unwholesome trades; the inspection of ships; the prevention of the employment of women or children in certain occupations, or for more than a certain number of hours; quarantine; vaccination; the supply of pure water; the prevention of the adulteration of articles of food and drink [22].

*331 *2. The regular working of a poor-law, or the exceptional working of relief works and doles in time of famine.

3. The visitation of lunatic asylums and nunneries.

4. The protection of the coinage and the inspection of weights and measures.

5. The supervision of professions and trades.

6. The collection of information as to foreign commerce; the supervision of banks, insurance societies, and companies generally.

7. The supervision of roads, railways, canals, telegraphs, and posts.

8. The maintenance of lighthouses, harbours, sea-walls, and dykes.

9. The preservation of order, the detection of crime, and the management of prisons.

Moral welfare.

vi. The promotion of the intellectual and moral welfare of the public generally, by such measures as:—

1. The organisation of schools, and the sustentation of museums and libraries.

[22] Mr. Trail has well remarked that whenever the modern state has thought fit to depart from the system of laissez-faire, it has not been content with merely *commanding* the citizen to do certain things, but has itself seen to his doing them. Central Government, p. 158. For a thorough-going protest against government inspection, see Mr. Herbert Spencer's The Man versus the State.

2. The prevention of Sunday trading, the supervision of places of amusement, and the licensing of plays.

Self-government.

It must be remembered that much of this work, except in very highly centralised States, is entrusted to local authorities, often to the same authorities who also exercise an inferior criminal jurisdiction.

Administrative jurisdiction.

Disputed questions of administrative law, or cases of refusal to comply with its rules, are in England usually in minor matters brought before a justice of the peace. More serious questions are tried in the superior courts. Although military and ecclesiastical discipline is enforced by Courts martial and Courts christian, no person is by virtue of his official position exempted from the jurisdiction of the Common law. But it is maintained by some writers that questions affecting official persons, as such, should be exclusively decided by special tribunals, which accord-
*332 ingly exist *in many countries, with a hierarchical organisation. An appellate 'Verwaltungsgerichtshof' was, for instance, established in 1863 for the Grand Duchy of Baden. A mixed court of a similar character was created in 1847 in Prussia; and the 'conseil d'état' performs the functions of such a court in France, where questions of jurisdiction between the ordinary and the administrative Courts are decided by a 'Tribunal des Conflits [23].'

III. CRIMINAL LAW.

Perhaps the most important of the functions of the State is that which it discharges as the guardian of order; preventing

[23] See Professor Dicey's Law of the Constitution, especially ed. iv. pp. 315–323. Previously to the appearance of this work next to nothing had been written in English upon the extended meaning given upon the continent to 'administrative law.' 'Droit Administratif' is defined by M. Aucoc as regulating '1° la constitution et les rapports des organes de la société chargés du soin des intérêts collectifs qui font l'objet de l'administration publique, c'est à dire des différentes personifications de la société, dont l'état est la plus importante; 2° les rapports des autorités administratives avec les citoyens.'

and punishing all injuries to itself, and all disobedience to the rules which it has laid down for the common welfare. In defining the orbit of its rights in this respect, the State usually proceeds by an enumeration of the acts which infringe upon them, coupled with an intimation of the penalty to which any one committing such acts will be liable. The branch of law which contains the rules upon this subject is accordingly described as 'Criminal law,' 'Droit pénal,' 'Strafrecht.'

Its modern origin.

It is comparatively modern. The early tendency was to punish offences against the sovereign power by an exceptional executive or legislative act, and to treat offences against individuals, even when, like theft and homicide, they were a serious menace to the general welfare, as merely civil injuries to be compensated for by damages. The law of Rome continued to the last to treat as civil delicts acts which would now be regarded exclusively as crimes, although, by a long course of unsystematic legislation, it
*333 had also *attached penal consequences to some of them.
The merelv practical and disorderly character of the criminal law which is preserved, for instance, in the ninth books of the Codes of Theodosius and Justinian is readily explicable. The prerogative of punishment, exercised in early times by the king and the 'comitia centuriata' and in later times shared by the senate, was usually delegated in each case to a magistrate or body of commissioners. The series of statutes by which standing delegacies, 'quaestiones perpetuae,' were instituted for the trial of offences of particular kinds, whenever they might be committed, commences with the lex Calpurnia, B. C. 149, and was continued till a number of courses of conduct had been from time to time branded as criminal [24]. The legislation of the emperors, though it superseded the 'quaestiones' by the simpler procedure of the 'iudicia extraordinaria,' followed the lines of the old criminal statutes, and produced a body of rules large indeed but formless, and owing hardly anything to the great men whose wisdom had interpenetrated every doctrine of private law. The Teutonic view of even violent wrongs resembled the early Roman, in regarding them

[24] Cf. Maine, Ancient Law, ch. v.

as concerning almost exclusively the person injured, to whom therefore atonement was to be made by way of damages, 'compositio.' When the idea began to be clearly grasped by the Germans that wrong-doing might injure not merely the individual, but also the State itself, they found little assistance towards formulating it in the legal system to which they were most accustomed to turn for guidance. The criminal law of Rome, deeply tinged as it was with national idiosyncrasies, had never been prepared by juristic exposition for more general usefulness. Original legislation was therefore necessary, and the first attempt was made in the 'Constitutio Criminalis Carolina,' of the Emperor Charles V. This attempt to provide a criminal law for the whole Empire lost much of its importance from the compilation of
*334 national codes for Bavaria, Austria, and many *other German States during the latter half of the eighteenth century, but was the forerunner of the penal code for all Germany, 'Strafgesetzbuch für das Deutsche Reich,' which came into operation in 1872. Of the other great criminal codes now in force, the 'Code pénal' became law for France in 1810, and has been imitated by the Latin races of the continent; while the penal code for British India which was drafted in 1834 by Lord Macaulay was promulgated in 1860. In the mean time the whole theory of punishment and of the classification of offences has been thoroughly discussed by such men as Beccaria, Bentham, Feuerbach, Mittermaier, and Sir J. F. Stephen [25]; and the criminal branch of public law may now be said to be divided upon recognised principles, and to possess a terminology, though a somewhat loose one, of its own.

It is divided into a body of substantive criminal law and a body of criminal procedure. The former, with which alone we are concerned at present, consists of two parts, a general and a particular.

[25] The last-named in his General View of the Criminal Law, 1863; his Digests of Criminal Law, 1877, and of Criminal Procedure, 1883; his History of the Criminal Law, 1883; and his Draft Penal Code, which has been intermittently under the consideration of Parliament since 1878.

Its general part.

i. The more general part deals with such topics as the following: the nature of a criminal act [26]; the responsibility of the wrong-doer on the ground of intention or negligence [27]; facts which negative responsibility, such as tender age, compulsion, idiocy, lunacy, or drunkenness [28]; facts which may justify
*335 an act otherwise criminal, such as the consent of the *party injured, self-defence [29], lawful authority, or the public welfare; how far omission is equivalent to commission [30]; the persons by whom criminal porceedings may be instituted [31]; the list of punishments, such as death, banishment, imprisonment, hard labour, whipping, loss of civic rights, liability to police supervision, or pecuniary fine; the period of time, if any, which will be a bar to criminal prosecution [32]; the aiding and abetting of crime; criminal attempts; cumulative punishments. Here also we expect to find those distinctions between different grades of crime which occur in almost all systems. The distinction drawn by English law between 'felonies' and 'misdemeanours' is as familiar as

[26] 'Verbrechen ist die von Seiten der Gesetzgebung constatirte Gefährdung der Lebensbedingungen der Gesellschaft.' Ihering, Zweck, i. p. 481.

[27] Cf. supra, pp. *94, *97, *134, *152; Professor Clark's Analysis of Criminal Liability, 1880; Holmes, Common Law, pp. 47, 50, 75.

[28] The new anthropological school of Italian penalists finds in the habitual criminal characteristics which, on the one hand, render him irresponsible for his acts, and on the other hand forbid any hope of his reclamation. See Lombroso, Uomo delinquente.

[29] 'Vim enim vi defendere omnes leges omniaque iura permittunt.' Paulus, Dig. ix. 45. 4. But self-preservation from starvation was held no defence to an indictment for murder in the Mignonette case. R. v. Dudley, 14 Q. B. D. 273.

[30] E. g. under sect. 43 of the Indian Penal Code.

[31] E. g. according to English law not by a wife against her husband, nor v. v., except for injury to person or property; not therefore for libel, even under the Married Women's Property Act of 1882, sect. 16. R. v. Lord Mayor of London, 16 Q. B. D. 776. Cf. supra, p. *309 n.

[32] E. g. Code d'Instruction Crim. art. 637; Strafgesetzbuch, art. 65. For various periods of Prescription against the French Government, in claims for duty, see the Loi du 22 frimaire, An vii, tit. viii. art. 61, as subsequently modified. In England the rule 'nullum tempus occurrit regi' still holds good, except in so far as it has been derogated from by statute. See such statutes in Stephen, Hist. Crim. Law, ii. p. 2.

it has become unmeaning. The French Code opens with a threefold classification of wrongful acts into 'contraventions,' 'délits,' and 'crimes,' according to their being respectively punishable by 'peines de police,' 'peines correctionnelles,' or 'peines afflictives ou infamantes'; and the German Code draws a similar distinction between 'Uebertretung,' 'Vergehen,' and 'Verbrechen.' The new Dutch Code of 1886, distinguishes only between 'overtredingen' and 'misdryven'; the Italian Code of 1889, only between 'delitti' and 'contravvenzioni'; the Spanish draft Code only between 'delitos' and 'faltas.' The criminal Code Bill, which has now for many Sessions awaited the leisure of Parliament, recognises
*336 only the distinction between indictable *offences and others, expressly abolishing that between felonies and misdemeanours.

To the introductory portion of a Criminal Code belong also provisions as to the relation of the prosecution of an offence to the recovery in a civil action of damages for the injury caused by it to an individual. Such is the rule long alleged to exist in English law that the civil remedy for a wrong which also amounts to a felony is suspended till the felon has been convicted [33], and such is the article of the Code pénal which declares that 'la condamnation aux peines établies par la loi est toujours prononcée sans préjudice des restitutions et dommages-intérêts qui peuvent être dus aux parties [34].'

Its special part.

ii. The special part contains a classification of criminal acts, and specific provisions with regard to the penal consequences of each.

The list of offences.

Such acts may be, in the first place, distinguished into offences committed directly against the State, or community generally, and offences the mischief of which is primarily directed against particular individuals.

33 Wellock v. Constantine, 2 H. and C. 146. For the law as now understood, see supra, p. *296.

34 Art. 10; cf. Dig. xlvii. 10. 7.

Against the State.

The State, or community generally, is injured by:—

1. Acts tending to interrupt its friendly relations with foreign powers; whence the enactments against 'foreign enlistment,' and against libelling or compassing the death of foreign sovereigns.

2. Acts tending to the subversion of the government, such as assassination of princes, rebellion, and similar acts of High Treason.

3. Acts tending to the subversion of the liberties of the subject [35].

4. Riots and other offences against public order and tranquillity.

5. Abuse of official position.

6. Resistance or disobedience to lawful authority.

*337 *7. Obstruction to the course of justice by perjury, or falsification of documents, or rescue, or harbouring of offenders.

8. Maintenance of suits [36].

9. Omission to give information, or giving false information, as to births, deaths, and similar matters, included by the French under the phrase 'état civil.'

10. Offences relating to the coinage, or to weights and measures.

11. Cruelty to animals, though it may be doubted whether this is forbidden as brutalizing to the public generally, or as offensive to the humane sentiments of individuals, or whether it does not imply the recognition of quasi-rights in animals, analogous to the Roman prohibition of cruelty to slaves [37].

12. Acts injurious to public morality, such as bigamy.

13. Acts injurious to the public health, such as neglect of vaccination, and various forms of nuisance.

Against individuals.

Many wrongful acts, affecting primarily individuals, and therefore giving rise to remedial rights in private law, are also so harm-

[35] Cf. Code Pénal, tit. i. ch. ii.

[36] Cf. Metropolitan Bank v. Pooley, 10 App. Ca. 210, and supra, p. *164. On the lawfulness of maintenance by one who has 'an interest in the thing in variance,' see now Alabaster v. Harness, '94, 2 Q. B. 897.

[37] Cf. supra, p. *311.

ful to society as to be punished by it as crimes [38]. They may perhaps be classified under the following heads:—

1. Violence to the person, in its various kinds and degrees of homicide, wounding, rape, assault, or imprisonment.

2. Defamation of character (by English law only when in the form of a libel) [39], sometimes justifiable when shown to be true and for the public benefit [40].

*338 *3. Acts offensive to religious feeling [41].

4. Offences against family rights, such as abduction of children, or, in some systems, adultery [42].

5. Offences against possession and ownership, such as theft and arson, or other wilful destruction of property.

6. Certain breaches of contract, of a kind likely to cause social inconvenience, or for which a civil remedy would be valueless [43].

7. Fraudulent misrepresentations and swindling.

It may be remarked that offences against the property of the State are often assimilated to offences against that of individuals; and, in many instances, particular kinds of State property are, for

38 Supra, p. *289.

39 Cf. supra, p. *161: on account of its supposed tendency to arouse angry passions, R. v. Holbrook, 4 Q. B. D. 46.

40 It would seem that no proceedings can be taken for libel on a deceased person. See the charge of Stephen, J. at the Cardiff Assizes, in R. v. Ensor, 10 Feb., 1887, relying on R. v. Topham, 4 East 126, as against a dictum in 5 Rep. 125. So also the French law; cf. Dalloz, s. v. 'Presse-outrage,' art. 1128.

41 On the question whether this, or mere repugnancy to the Christian religion, be the test of a blasphemous libel, see the summing up of Lord Coleridge, C. J. in Foote's case, and Sir J. F. Stephen's History of the Criminal Law, ii. p. 475.

42 E. g. 'La femme convaincue d'adultère subira la peine de l'emprisonnement pendant trois mois au moins et deux ans au plus.' Code Pénal, art. 337. But proceedings can only be taken by the husband, and he can terminate the imprisonment by taking her home. Cf. Strafgesetzbuch, art. 171; Indian Penal Code, art. 497. On the action of the Canon law in England, see Redfern v. Redfern, '91 P. (C. A.) 139. The Penal Code of Indore punishes as adultery intercourse with a widow. 6 Law Quarterly Review, p. 89.

43 E. g. 38 & 39 Vict. c. 86. s. 5, as to malicious breach of contract, with reason to believe that the consequence may be to cause danger to life or serious bodily injury, or to expose valuable property to destruction or serious injury. Cf. the provisions in Irish Statutes against ploughing grass lands. Cf. also in Holzendorff's Encyclopädie the art. 'Vertragsverletzung.'

the purposes of the criminal law, vested by statute in certain State functionaries [44].

IV. CRIMINAL PROCEDURE.

Adjective criminal law, 'Penal procedure,' 'Instruction criminelle,' 'Strafprozess,' is the body of rules whereby the
*339 *machinery of the Courts is set in motion for the punishment of offenders.

It consists usually of two species; a simpler, 'peines de police,' 'summary convictions,' applicable, unless with the consent of the accused, only to trifling transgressions; and a more solemn, for the trial of serious crimes.

Each of these consists of several stages, having a strong resemblance to the stages of procedure in private law [45]. In the more solemn procedure we may distinguish:—

i. The choice of the proper jurisdiction.

ii. The choice of the proper Court.

iii. The procedure proper, consisting of—

1. The summons, by which the accused is called upon, or the warrant, under which he is compelled, to appear to answer the charge.

2. The preliminary investigation, terminating in the discharge of the accused, or in his being committed for trial.

3. The measures ensuring that the accused shall be forthcoming for trial, viz. either imprisonment or security given by himself or his friends.

4. The pleadings, by which, on the one hand, the prosecution informs the Court and the accused of the nature of the charge against him, and, on the other hand, the accused states the nature of his defence.

[44] Thus by 7 W. IV. & 1 Vict. c. 36, s. 40, articles sent by post are, for the purposes of the Act, made the property of the Postmaster-General. It would have been sufficient, and in accordance with fact, to declare that such articles are in his possession. This rule is peculiar to the law of England. For a comparative view of the laws of other countries upon the subject, see an art. by M. de Kirchenheim in the Revue de Droit International, xiv. p. 616.

[45] Supra, p. *316. The resemblance is stronger in England than on the continent, which is still under the influence of the 'inquisitorial' method introduced into Germany by the Constitutio Criminalis Carolina.

5. The trial, conducted on a prescribed plan and in accordance with rules of evidence which differ in certain respects from those which prevail in civil suits [46].
6. The verdict and judgment.
7. The procedure on appeal, so far as an appeal is permissible.

*340 *iv. Execution, which is carried out by the functionary to whom the force of the State is entrusted for the purpose.

The bringing of criminals to justice may be confided, as it generally is on the continent, to a 'ministère public,' 'Staatsanwaltschaft,' or left, as it generally has been in England, and was at Rome, to the industry of the injured individual [47].

V. LAW OF THE STATE AS A JURISTIC PERSON.

Besides its rights and duties as the guardian of order, in which respect little analogy can be remarked to anything in private law, the State, as a great juristic person, enjoys many quasi-rights against individuals, as well strangers as subjects, and is liable to many quasi-duties in their favour. These rights and duties closely resemble those which private law recognises as subsisting between one individual and another [48]. The State, irrespectively of the so-called 'eminent domain' which it enjoys over all the property of its subjects [49], is usually a great landed proprietor; and

[46] Supra, p. *317. On the tendency towards an assimilation of the rules of evidence in civil and criminal cases, see the remarks of M. A. Prins, étude sur la Procédure pénale à Londres, 1879, p. 4.

[47] A Roman form of indictment is preserved in the following fragment of Paulus: 'Consul et dies, apud illum praetorem vel proconsulem, Lucius Titius professus est se Maeviam lege Iulia de adulteriis ream deferre, quod dicat eam cum Gaio Seio, in civitate illa, domo illius, mense illo, consulibus illis, adulterium commisisse.' Dig. xlviii. 2. 3. The office of 'Director of Public Prosecutions' was established in England by 42 & 43 Vict. c. 22.

[48] See the remarks of Grotius upon the transactions of those 'qui summam habent potestatem . . . in his quae privatim agunt.' De I. B. et P. ii. 2. 5. 3. On the entry of the 'fiscus' into the domain of private law, see Sohm, Institutionen, § 20, Transl. p. 103.

[49] The term seems to have originated with Grotius, I. B. et P. i. 3. 6; ii. 14. 7. See Bynkershoek, Quaestiones I. P. ii. 15. It is employed by Vattel, whence perhaps imported, by the Translation of 1760, into the English language.

in respect of its land is entitled to servitudes over the estates of individuals, and subject to servitudes for the benefit of such estates. It owns buildings of all sorts, from the palace to the police-station, and a large amount of personal property, from pictures by Titian and Tintoretto to cloth for making the prison dress of convicts. It carries on gigantic manufacturing undertakings,
*341 *lends and borrows money, issues promissory notes, and generally enters into all kinds of contracts. It necessarily acts by means of agents, who may exceed their powers or act fraudulently. Its servants may wilfully or negligently cause damage to individuals. It may become a mortgagee, and in many cases allows itself a tacit hypothec by way of security for what is owed to it. It is capable of taking under a will, and succeeds ab intestato to all those who die without leaving heirs. Its rights and liabilities under many of these heads are different from those of individuals, or even of private artificial persons, especially with reference to liability for injuries done by its servants, and as to the barring of its rights by prescription, though here the modern tendency is to modify the strictness of the old rule that 'nullum tempus occurrit regi [50].'

VI. LAW OF PROCEDURE.

The substantive law affecting the State as a quasi-private juristic personality is supplemented by a body of adjective rules, prescribing the mode in which the State, as such a personality, may sue or be sued. The procedure thus provided is not, it may be remarked, as in private law, similar for both parties, but varies according as the party, plaintiff or defendant, is the State or a private individual. In other words, the procedure, as compared with the ordinary procedure between individuals, is always abnormal; and its abnormity takes different forms when the sovereign takes proceedings against one of his subjects, or a subject takes proceedings against his sovereign. The reason, of course, being that the litigation is between the sovereign, who is the source

[50] Cf. the 'nullum tempus' Act, 9 G. III. c. 16, and 24 & 25 Vict. c. 62, barring the crown as to lands and rents after sixty years. By the Code Civil, art. 2227, 'L'état, les établissements publics, et les communes, sont soumis aux mêmes prescriptions que les particuliers, et peuvent également les opposer.'

of all right, and the subject, whose rights are wholly dependent on the will of the sovereign.

*342 *The character of this procedure varies considerably in different countries.

Procedure against the State.

In England the old common law methods of getting redress from the Crown were by 'pétition de droit' and 'monstrans le droit,' in the Court of Chancery or the Court of Exchequer, and in some cases by proceedings in Chancery against the Attorney-General. It has been provided by a modern statute [51] that a petition of right may be entitled in any one of the superior Courts in which the subject-matter of the petition would have been cognisable, if the same had been a matter in dispute between subject and subject, and that it shall be left with the Secretary of State for the Home Department, for Her Majesty's consideration, who, if she shall think fit, may grant her fiat that right be done, whereupon an answer. plea, or demurrer shall be made on behalf of the Crown, and the subsequent proceedings be assimilated as far as practicable to the course of an ordinary action. It is also provided that costs shall be payable both to and by the Crown, subject to the same rules, so far as practicable, as obtain in proceedings between subject and subject [52].

Procedure by the State.

The Crown may obtain redress against its subjects by such common law actions as are consistent with the royal dignity; but much easier and more effectual remedies are usually obtained by such prerogative modes of process as are peculiarly confined to it [53], such as an 'inquest of office,' a 'writ of extent,' a 'writ of scire facias,' or an 'information' exhibited by the Attorney-General in the Queen's Bench Division of the High Court. The old exemption of the Crown from the payment of costs in proceedings with subjects has been nearly abolished by a succession of statutes.

[51] 23 & 24 Vict. c. 24. See Tobin v. The Queen, 16 C. B., N. S. 310.

[52] On the law of the United States upon this subject, cf. supra, p. *116, note 3. It is noticeable that in Egypt actions may be brought in the International Courts directly against the Government. Règlement pour les procès-mixtes, tit. i. art. 10.

[53] Blackstone, 3 Comm. 258.

*343 # *CHAPTER XVII.

INTERNATIONAL LAW.

The nature of international law.

The body of rules regulating those rights in which both of the personal factors are States [1] is loosely called 'the Law of Nations,' but more appropriately 'Ius inter gentes,' or 'International Law [2].'

It differs from ordinary law in being unsupported by the authority of a State. It differs from ordinary morality in being a rule for States and not for individuals.

It is the vanishing point of Jurisprudence; since it lacks any arbiter of disputed questions, save public opinion, beyond and above the disputant parties themselves, and since, in
*344 *proportion as it tends to become assimilated to true law
by the aggregation of States into a larger society, it ceases to be itself, and is transmuted into the public law of a federal government. The realisation of the 'civitas maxima' of which theorists have dreamed would thus be not the triumph, but the extinction, of International law, which can subsist only between States which, on the one hand, sufficiently resemble one another, and are closely enough knit together by common interests, to be susceptible of a uniform pressure of public opinion, while, on the other hand, they are not so politically combined as to be controlled by the force of a central authority. These conditions of

1 Supra, p. *117.

2 The former of these names is due to the Oxford Professor, Richard Zouch, 1650 (gallicised by the Chancellor D'Aguesseau, Oeuvres, ii. p. 337, as 'le droit entre les gens,' and by the Abbé de Saint-Pierre, in a MS. described by M. Nys, Revue de Droit International, t. xxiii. p. 428, as 'le droit entre les nations'); the latter to Jeremy Bentham, who uses it in the Principles of Morals and Legislation, first published in 1789, as appropriate to the 'mutual transactions of sovereigns as such'; adding in a note: 'the word "international," it must be acknowledged, is a new one; though, it is hoped, sufficiently analogous and intelligible. It is calculated to express, in a more significant way, the branch of law which goes commonly under the name of the law of nations.'

political independence and social sympathy have been twice realised in the history of the world. Very imperfectly, between the various cities of Hellas, which accordingly acknowledged, as in some degree obligatory on all, τὰ κοινὰ τῶν Ἑλλήνων νόμιμα.[3] More fully between the States of modern Christendom, no one of which would venture at the present day expressly to repudiate the duty of conforming to the precepts of International law in its dealings with the rest.

Just as what is not very conveniently termed 'Municipal' law is recognised as supreme over all questions of private or public right arising within the jurisdiction of any given State [4], so it is conceded that 'International law,' so far as its doctrines have been generally received, is decisive of all questions which arise between one State and another. Its true nature and functions have never been better described than in the following passage, in which they were for the first time adequately set forth in the early years of the seventeenth century. 'Ratio autem huius partis
*345 iuris est,' says Suarez, *'quia humanum genus, quantumvis in varios populos et regna divisum, semper habet aliquam unitatem non solum specificam, sed etiam quasi politicam et moralem, quam indicat naturale praeceptum mutui amoris et misericordiae quod ad omnes extenditur, etiam extraneos et cuiuscunque nationis. Quapropter licet unaquaeque civitas, perfecta respublica, aut regnum, sit in se communitas perfecta et suis membris constans, nihilominus quaelibet illarum est etiam membrum aliquo modo huius universi, prout ad genus humanum spectat, . . . hac ergo ratione indigent aliquo iure quo dirigantur et recte ordinentur, in hoc genere communicationis et societatis. Et quamvis magna ex parte hoc fiat per rationem naturalem, non tamen sufficienter et immediate quoad omnia, ideoque aliqua specialia iura potuerunt usu earum gentium introduci [5].'

[3] Thuc. iii. 59.

[4] Cf. supra, p. *118. Bentham, Principles of Morals and Legislation, ch. xvii, is mistaken in supposing Blackstone to have been the first to use 'municipal' as equivalent to 'national' or 'internal' law; a sense of the term which was well established at least as early as the sixteenth century. Blackstone expressly says, 'I call it municipal law in accordance with common speech.' 1 Comm. 44.

[5] De lege et Deo legislatore, ii. c. xix. § 9.

Although, as being concerned with the relations of States, 'international' is said to be a department of 'public' law, its analogies are rather to the private than to the public branch of law municipal. The reason being that, while in public (municipal) law the personal factors in a right are always dissimilar, in international, as in private, law they are always similar. Just as the parties in private law are two individuals, so in international law are they two States. Much confusion is occasioned by authors who, failing to grasp this essential characteristic of International law, speak of sovereigns and ambassadors as 'international persons,' or treat of States as capable of having international relations with individuals; regarding, for instance, the seizure of a blockade-runner as an exercise of authority by a belligerent State over a neutral subject.

Hence it is that the topics of this science may be most conveniently grouped in general accordance with the principles of division which were originally discovered by the analysis of private law.

There is a 'substantive' and an 'adjective' law of nations:
*346 the persons governed by this *law may be 'normal' or 'abnormal'; and their rights may be 'antecedent' or 'remedial,' 'in rem' or 'in personam.'

Classification of topics.

A distribution of the subject upon these lines, rather than in accordance with the method which, originated by Klüber, has since become traditional, especially on the other side of the Atlantic, has been elsewhere advocated by the present writer [6], in the following terms:—'The law of nations is but private law "writ large." It is an application to political communities of those legal ideas which were originally applied to the relations of individuals. Its leading distinctions are therefore naturally those with which private law has long ago rendered us familiar. In international, as in private law, we are concerned with the Persons for whose sake rights are recognised; with the Rights thus recognised; and with the Protection by which those rights are made effective. We

[6] In an Oxford lecture, a translation of which appeared under the title 'Les Débats diplomatiques récents dans leur rapport avec le Système du Droit international,' in the Revue de Droit International for 1878, p. 167.

have a law of Persons; a Substantive law which sets forth and explains the rights of those persons; and an Adjective law, which describes the procedure by which redress is to be obtained when those rights are violated. The international law of persons consists of an investigation into the nature of a sovereign State and of the deviations from it. The substantive law of nations enquires into the character, origin, and termination of the rights which States may enjoy; while the adjective law of nations describes the procedure by which redress is obtained for international wrong-doing. This last-mentioned department is subdivided into the law which regulates the relations of the belligerents to one another, and the law which regulates the relations of each belligerent with States which take no part in the war. The whole science is thus divisible into four great chapters, which may be shortly de-
*347 scribed as treating respectively of inter*national Status; of Peace; of Belligerency; and of Neutrality.'

I. INTERNATIONAL PERSONS.

The Persons known to International law are States.

The normal international person is a State which not only enjoys full external sovereignty, but also is a recognised member of the family of nations. States which vary from this type either by being defective in sovereignty, or by having no place in the family of nations, are abnormal international persons.

Normal and abnormal States.

The characteristics of a State, as distinguished from non-political societies, have been necessarily touched upon in an earlier chapter; where also will be found an explanation of the differences between a State which possesses full 'external sovereignty' and one which is 'mi-souverain,' as being 'protected' or otherwise dependent on another [7]. 'The family of nations' is an aggregate of States which, as the result of their historical antecedents, have inherited a common civilisation, and are at a similar level of moral and political opinion. The term may be said to include the Christian nations of Europe and their offshoots in America, with the addition of the Ottoman Empire, which was declared by the treaty

[7] Supra, p. *44.

of Paris of 1856 to be admitted to the 'concert Européen.' Within this charmed circle, to which Japan also has all but established her claim to be fully admitted, according to the theory of International law, all States are equal. Outside of it, no State, be it as powerful and as civilised as China or Persia, can be regarded as a normal international person.

The topics of semi-sovereignty and protection present considerable analogies to those of infancy, coverture, and tutelage in Private law. It may also be remarked that as individual human beings are born, attain the age of majority, and die, so States come into existence, obtain full international recognition, and cease to be.

*348 **Origin of States.*

A new State arises either: Originally, where no State existed previously, a case now necessarily of infrequent occurrence; or derivatively, by separation from a previously existing State, and this either by agreement with the older State, or against its wishes. It is in the last-mentioned case that other nations often feel a difficulty in deciding upon the reception which should be given to the new claimant for national honours.

Termination.

The question at what moment a State ceases to exist is the same with the enquiry as to what constitutes its identity. The identity of a State is admittedly not affected by any change of constitution or dynasty, or diminution or extension of territory, but only by the merger of one State in another, as when Poland was divided between the neighbouring Powers, or by such a dissolution of the political bond as has happened in the case of the Jews.

II. ANTECEDENT INTERNATIONAL RIGHTS.

The rights of a State, like those of an individual, are 'antecedent,' as subsisting independently of any wrong-doing, or 'remedial,' as given by way of compensation for an injury sustained [8]. Rights of the former class may be available either 'in rem,' against

[8] Cf. supra, p. *130.

all other States, or 'in personam,' against a given State only; while rights of the latter class are usually available only 'in personam.'

Rights 'In rem.'

i. Antecedent international rights 'in rem,' i. e. those which do not result from wrong-doing, and are enjoyed by a State as against all others, present many analogies to the corresponding topics of Private law [9]. They may be classified as having reference to (1) Safety; (2) Renutation; (3) Ownership; (4) Jurisdiction; and (5) the protection of subjects in foreign countries. Other classes of rights are mentioned in some books upon International law [10], which, if they ought to be treated as separate heads of right
*349 at all, would *also be species of rights 'in rem.' Such are the so-called rights of Equality, of Legation, and of Negotiation and Treaty-making; which according to our system should be rather discussed under the law of international status, being, as they are, mere corollaries from the conception of a Sovereign State as an artificial person.

(1) The right of a State to exist in safety calls for no remark. Its violation or threatened violation gives rise to the remedial right of self-preservation.

(2) Of the right to a good name, it has been well said that 'the glory of a nation is intimately connected with its power, of which it is a considerable part. It is this distinction which attracts to it the consideration of other peoples, which makes it respectable in the eyes of its neighbours. A nation the reputation of which is well established, and especiallv one the glory of which is striking, finds itself sought by all sovereigns. They desire its friendship and fear to offend it. Its friends, and those who wish to become such, favour its enterprises, and its detractors do not venture to show their ill-will [11].'

(3) International ownership, 'Dominium,' though it applies to property of all kinds, is chiefly important with reference to the 'territory,' which is, according to modern conceptions, essential to

[9] Supra, p. *148.

[10] Klüber, Droit des gens moderne, §§ 89, 141, 166; Wheaton, Elements, Pt. ii. c. 2, Pt. iii. cc. 1, 2.

[11] Vattel, i. 186.

the existence of a State. In a territory, 'universitas agrorum intra fines cuiusque civitatis [12],' are comprised the rivers which flow through it, and the ports and harbours, creeks and bays, by which its coasts are indented. The ownership of it may be acquired originally, or derivatively. In the former case, by 'occupatio rei nullius [13],' by 'accession [14],' and possibly by 'acquisitive prescription [15]'; and here difficult questions may arise as to the extent of the acquisition, for the solution of which distinctions are drawn between 'agri limitati,' 'agri adsignati per universitatem,' and 'agri arcifinii.' In the latter case [16], by cession, succession, or conquest.

*350 *Besides the 'dominium' which a State enjoys over its own territory, it may also have rights over the territories of its neighbours. Such 'iura in re aliena [17]' may be in the nature of feudal superiority, mortgage, or servitude.

(4) The right of Jurisdiction, 'Imperium,' is intimately connected with that of dominion; being, like it, exercisable only within the bounds of a given space. The rights of a nation over its territory are indeed, as Vattel says, twofold:—'1°, le domaine, en vertu duquel la nation peut user seul de ce pays pour ses besoins, en disposer, et en tirer l'usage auquel il est propre. 2°, l'empire, ou le droit du souverain commandement, par lequel elle ordonne et dispose à sa volonté de tout ce qui se passe dans le pays [18].'

The personal jurisdiction which a State claims to enjoy over its own subjects, wheresoever they may be, is a matter rather of public than of international law, but the jurisdiction which it exercises over all persons, be they subjects or aliens, in respect of acts committed by them within its territory, is legitimated only by the rule of international law which obliges the State to which such aliens may belong to acquiesce in their punishment.

Although the Dominion and the Jurisdiction of a State are both circumscribed by its territory, the two rights are not co-extensive, since by the custom of nations, 'territory' is, with a view to the exercise of the latter right, artificially extended in some directions and restricted in others. On the one hand, the Jurisdiction of a

[12] Dig. l. 16. 239.

[13] Cf. supra, p. *186.

[14] Cf. supra, p. *188.

[15] Cf. supra, p. *187.

[16] Cf. supra, p. *188.

[17] Supra, p. *193.

[18] Liv. i. § 204; cf. Grot. De I. B. et P. ii. 3. 4.

State is allowed to extend, beyond the bounds of its dominions, to all the ships that carry its flag upon the high seas, and, for certain purposes, to all ships, not being ships of war, whatever flag they may carry, which pass within three miles of its coasts. On the other hand, Jurisdiction is artificially restricted by what is known as the doctine of 'extraterritoriality,' in accordance with
*351 which certain persons and things, notably foreign *sovereigns, ambassadors and ships of war, though actually within the territory, are treated as if they were outside of it. Very extensive privileges of extraterritoriality are usually granted by Oriental nations to Christian residents by express treaty [19]; and a nation sometimes assumes, even without treaty, to exercise a Jurisdiction over its own subjects who are resident in barbarous countries [20].

A concurrent jurisdiction is allowed to all nations upon the high seas for the suppression of piracy. Since there is, as Grotius says, 'naturalis et tacita confederatio inter omnes homines contra communes societatis humanae hostes.'

(5) A State is not only entitled to the immunity from injury of its territory and of all persons therein, but may also insist that its subjects individually, wherever they may be, shall receive no harm from foreign governments or their subjects. 'Prima maximeque necessaria cura pro subditis,' says Grotius; adding, 'sunt quasi pars rectoris [21].'

Rights 'In personam.'

ii. The antecedent rights of nations 'in personam,' i. e. such as one nation may enjoy against another given nation, are almost exclusively contractual, i. e. they arise from Treaty.

It will be remembered that a contract in private law was shown to imply—i. several parties; ii. an expression of agreement; iii.

19 The grants and conventions of the Ottoman Empire to this effect are usually known as 'capitulations.' The exercise of the jurisdiction in question by Great Britain is now regulated by the Foreign Jurisdiction Act, 1890. The abolition of its exercise in Japan is provided for by the Treaty of July 16, 1894.

20 E. g. 26 & 27 Vict. c. 35, as to South Africa; and now the Foreign Jurisdiction Act, 1890, s. 2, asserts this right in the most general terms.

21 I. B. et P. ii. 25. 1.

a matter agreed upon which is both possible and legally permitted; iv. is of a nature to produce a legally binding result; v. and
*352 such a result as affects the relations of *the parties one to another; also very generally, vi. a solemn form, or some fact which affords a motive for the agreement [22]. All the elements of this analysis, with the exception of the last, are equally present in a treaty; though some of the subordinate rules under each head are incapable of transplantation from private to international law. Thus a treaty is not, like an ordinary contract, voidable on the ground of 'duress,' nor are the acts of plenipotentiaries as binding on their sovereigns as they would be under the ordinary law of agency.

Treaties, like contracts, may be divided into those which are 'principal,' which may again be subdivided, in accordance with their purpose, into treaties of peace, of alliance, of cession and the like; and those which are 'accessory,' e. g. by way of mortgage or guarantee[23].

Since a nation is obviously incapable of entering into contracts, or otherwise giving expression to its will, unless through a representative, the topic of agency occupies a large space in international law, and is sometimes added to the list of international rights, under the style of 'the right of Legation.' This is submitted to be an error. A nation cannot be said to have a right of negotiating or of sending an embassy, since it cannot insist that any other nation shall either entertain its proposals or receive its ambassador.

The law of international agency deals with the functions, privileges, and ranks of ambassadors and other public ministers; also with consuls and other agents who do not enjoy a diplomatic character. The whole question of the inviolability and extraterritoriality of diplomatic personages is naturally analogous to nothing in private law, but resembles rather that branch of public municipal law which describes the safeguards provided for the protection of government officials in the execution of their duties.

*353 *Remedial international rights vary according to the nature of the right violated; thus entitling the injured State

[22] Supra, p. *243.

[23] Cf. supra, pp. *251, *269.

to an apology, by salute to its flag or otherwise, for an insult to its dignity; to restitution of territory, or other property, of which it has been deprived; or to a money indemnity.

III. BELLIGERENCY.

The Adjective law of nations prescribes the procedure by which the Substantive law may lawfully be enforced, and corresponds roughly to what is popularly called 'the law of nations in time of war.' So far as it affects the disputant parties only, it is the law of 'Belligerency.' So far as it regulates the relations of the disputants to parties not engaged in the struggle, it is the law of 'Neutrality.'

Steps short of war.

Redress for a violated right may be obtained in a friendly manner, 'via amicabili,' by (1) negotiation, (2) arbitration, or (3) the mediation of other States. Or it may be obtained by force, 'via facti,' which is always necessarily in the nature of self-help, and liable to all the disadvantages of a procedure in which the injured party is a judge in his own cause [24].

In the latter case, if the right violated be one to acts of mere 'comity,' the remedy is what is called 'Rétorsion de droit,' i. e. a refusal to perform similar good offices. If the right be one of those which are allowed to be 'stricti iuris,' various courses of action are still open to the injured State, short of actual war. Such are 'Reprisals,' which, in their earliest form, were 'special,' i. e. exercised by injured individuals against the fellow-citizens of those by whom they had been injured; but are tolerated at the present day only in the form of 'general reprisals,' allowed by the government of a State to its subjects generally, or to its public forces. Their characteristic, in either case, being that they take place in time of peace, 'non nisi in pace represaliis locus est.' 'Embargo' and 'Pacific blockade' may be regarded either as species of general reprisals, or as coordinate examples of pre-belligerent hostility.

[24] Cf. supra, p. *282.

*354 * *War—Declaration.*

Actual war has been well described as 'the litigation of nations.' Ought it, like an action in private law, to commence with a notice served by one party upon the other, i. e. with a formal 'Declaration'? Upon this point there has been much difference of opinion and alteration of practice. According to Gentili, 'si non est bellum clandestina magis contentio quam contentio legitima fori est iudiciorum, haec primum petitio et denuntiatio fieri debet [25].'

Effect of outbreak.

When war has once commenced, the rules by which it is regulated refer in the first place to the effect of its outbreak upon the subsisting treaties between the belligerents, some of which are ipso facto abrogated, while others remain in force; and upon the rights of each belligerent over such subjects of the other belligerent and their property as may be found within its territory at the time. They refer, in the second place, to the actual conduct of warfare, on land or at sea, and to its effect upon the ownership of property.

Conduct of warfare.

Questions relating to the conduct of warfare may be considered under four heads: viz. (1) military operations, under which head will come rules as to stratagems, as to the use of certain weapons, as to sieges and bombardments, as to spies and marauders, as to quarter, ransom and prisoners of war, and as to hospitals, surgeons, and the wounded; (2) treatment of the enemy's country while occupied, and therein of property, public and private, and of requisitions and contributions; (3) 'commercia belli,' i. e. such exceptions to the rule against intercourse between enemies as truces, capitulations, safe-conducts, and cartels; (4) 'reprisals,' in the sense of the special punishments to be awarded to enemies guilty of breaches of the law of war.

The rules as to the effect of war upon ownership deal with questions of the title to conquered territory, of 'booty,' of 'prize,' of such immunity as is accorded to private property and to certain

[25] De I. B. ii. c. 1.

species of national property, of the acquisition of debts due to the enemy, and of recapture.

*355. IV. *NEUTRALITY.

It is not unusual to find in systems of municipal law prohibitions against taking up the law-suits of others by way of 'champerty' or 'maintenance,' and against interference with the course of criminal justice [26]. In international law somewhat analogous topics have come to occupy a very important place. The conduct of warfare was long discussed with reference only to belligerents, but it became clear in the course of the last century that a far more complex class of questions had arisen with reference to the rights of the belligerents towards nations which stand aloof from the war. It had become necessary to arrive at some agreement as to the mode of reconciling the right of each belligerent to carry on his warfare, with the no less undeniable right of a neutral quietly to pursue his ordinary business [27]. Attention was very early drawn to the conflict of the rights of a belligerent State with the trade of the subjects of neutral States, but the relations of a belligerent State to a neutral State were imperfectly worked out till quite modern times. The subject is most conveniently considered with reference, first, to the Rights; and, secondly, to the Duties of Neutrals.

Rights of Neutrals.

The Rights of a Neutral are the fundamental rights of a State, modified in certain respects by war; and may perhaps be enumerated as follows:—

i. To sovereignty within its territory; and so to prevent, or cancel, all belligerent acts, either in the territory itself or in the adjacent waters, to exercise there the right of asylum, and to prohibit the exercise there of any belligerent jurisdiction.

ii. To the inviolability of its public ships.

[26] E. g. Dig. xlviii. 7. 6. Cf. Cuiacius, Obs. viii. 31, 'De Ergolabis'; and supra, p. *164.

[27] The difficulty, says Grotius, had been perceived long before his time, 'cum alii belli rigorem, alii commerciorum utilitatem defenderent,' I. B. et P. iii. 15.

iii. To the security of the persons and property of its subjects, within the territory of a belligerent, subject to certain exceptions, such as the 'ius angariae.'

*356 *iv. To the continuance of diplomatic intercourse with the belligerents.

v. To recognize, under certain circumstances, a revolting population as a de facto belligerent, or even as a new sovereign State.

Duties of Neutrals.

The Duties of a Neutral may, it is conceived, be classed under three heads, of which the First consists of restraints on the free action of the State, as such; the Second, in an obligation to restrain in certain respects the acts of individuals; and the Third, in an obligation to acquiesce in the punishment of its subjects by a belligerent for acts which apart from the war would be innocent.

i. The restraints imposed upon the action of a neutral State, as such, forbid it to furnish troops, or arms, or money, or to allow passage, to either belligerent, or to open its ports so as to further belligerent objects.

ii. The State is bound to a positive interference with the acts both of its own subjects and of aliens, so as to prevent belligerent acts, or enlistments, or perhaps the equipment of war-ships, taking place within its territory, and generally to prevent its territory from being used as a base of operations by either belligerent.

iii. There are certain acts of neutral subjects with which, though detrimental to the interests of one or other of the belligerents, the Neutral State is not bound to interfere. She is however under an obligation in these cases to forego her ordinary right of protecting her subjects, and to allow them to be interfered with, and their property to be confiscated, by the belligerent who has ground to complain of their conduct.

Many commercial transactions, which in time of peace are perfectly unobjectionable, thus become in time of war punishable offences. Such are 'breach of blockade,' 'carriage of contra-
*357 band,' 'breach of the rule of the war of *1756,' and, at any rate till recently, the carriage of enemies' goods under a

neutral flag, and, according to the views of some nations, sending neutral goods under the flag of an enemy.

Most writers have been in the habit of seeing in these cases a direct relation between a belligerent State and individual subjects of a neutral State. It is submitted that such a relation should never be recognised by international law, which ought to be regarded as occupied exclusively with rights and duties subsisting between State and State.

*358

*CHAPTER XVIII.

THE APPLICATION OF LAW[1].

So long as law is regarded as a body of abstract principles, its interest is merely speculative. Its practical importance begins when these principles are brought to bear upon actual combinations of circumstances.

Three Questions.

Many questions may be raised as to the extent and mode in which this takes place, and, for their solution, rules have been laid down which, like other legal rules, are susceptible of analysis and classification. They make up that department of Jurisprudence which we propose to call 'the Application of law.' When a set of facts has to be regulated in accordance with law, two questions of capital importance present themselves. First, what State has jurisdiction to apply the law to the facts? and secondly, what law will it apply? The former of these questions is said to relate to the appropriate 'Forum,' the latter to the appropriate 'Lex.'

A third question, which, for the purpose of our present enquiry, is of less importance than these two, and may be dismissed in a few words, relates to 'Interpretation.'

*359 *It will be necessary to show very briefly how these questions arise, and in what modes they are answered, in private law; and how far the same or analogous questions have to be considered also with reference to public and to international law.

§ 1. Private Law.

The Application of Private Law.

In private law all three questions have to be answered; and first as to the 'Forum.'

[1] A translation by M. Nys of this chapter, as it stood in the first edition, appeared under the title 'de l'Application de la Loi,' in the Revue de Droit International (1880), t. xii. p. 565.

Questions of Forum.

I. Given a set of circumstances the legal consequences of which are disputed, it obviously becomes necessary to ascertain in the Courts of what country the dispute can be decided; in other words, what Court has jurisdiction to try the case ratione territorii [2].

Possible Cases.

For this purpose it is indispensable to classify on the one hand possible sets of circumstances, and on the other hand possible Courts.

The circumstances which may give rise to legal controversies have been already classified in the preceding chapters.

Possible Fora.

The Courts in which proceedings may possibly be taken are, that of the country in which the plaintiff, or the defendant, is domiciled, or to which he owes allegiance [3], or in which the defendant happens to be; that of the country in which the object in dispute is situated; that of the country in which the juristic act in question, which may have been for instance a marriage, or a sale, or the making of a will, took place; that of the country in which the wrongful act in question took place; that of the country in which a contract was to produce its results; or that in which the plaintiff chooses to commence proceedings.

*360 *It might be convenient to describe these 'Fora' respectively as the—

'forum ligeantiae,' or 'domicilii, actoris,'
'forum ligeantiae, domicilii,' or 'praesentiae, rei,'
'forum rei sitae,'
'forum actus,' including 'contractus,'
'forum delicti commissi,'

and the 'forum litis motae,' or 'fortuitum.'

2 This phrase seems better adapted than its older equivalent 'jurisdiction ratione personae' to distinguish the question stated in the text from questions as to 'jurisdiction ratione materiae,' 'sächliche Zuständigkeit,' i. e. as to the poper court, within a given territory, for the trial of a particular class of actions.

3 This exceptional forum is recognised e. g. in the Code Civil, art. 14.

Of these technical terms one only, the 'forum (domicilii) rei,' has obtained general currency, doubtless by means of the long prevalence of the maxim, 'actor sequitur forum rei.'

As examples of the questions which arise as to the 'forum,' it may be sufficient to mention that an English Court will almost always decline jurisdiction in divorce, unless the husband be domiciled in the country; and that an English Court will take cognisance of a contract, wherever made and between whatever parties, while a French Court is, as a rule, incompetent to do so unless one of the contracting parties be a French subject or domiciled in France.

The Courts of a given country have not only from time to time thus to decide on their own competence, but also occasionally to investigate the competence of the Courts of other States; the decrees of which, when duly made, they will often recognise under the technical description of 'Foreign judgments,' just as they do other foreign facts creating rights; which rights may thus continue to subsist outside of the jurisdiction which originally gave them validity.

Questions of Lex.

II. The question as to the applicable 'Lex' is far more complicated than that as to the competent 'Forum.' The circumstances which affect its solution may be enumerated as Concentricity, Time, Race, and Place.

Concentricity.

i. It often occurs that special are included in more general circles of law. A city may be governed not only by its own statutes, but also by the law of the kingdom to which it belongs,
*361 and of the empire in which that kingdom is included, *and it may be doubted whether the affairs of the citizens are to be regulated by the civic, royal, or imperial laws, where these differ from one another.

The general rule is that the nearer and narrower law is to be applied rather than the more remote and wider, 'Stadtrecht bricht Landrecht, Landrecht bricht gemeines Recht'; thus 'gavelkind' prevails in Kent rather than the general law of England as to succession to realty [4].

Time.

ii. It might be supposed that the universally admitted principle that laws have, in the absence of express provision to that effect, no retrospective operation, 'leges et constitutiones futuris dare formam negotiis, non ad facta praeterita revocari [5],' would prevent all doubt whether a given state of facts is to be governed by a new or by an old law. This is however by no means the case, since some legal relations, such for instance as acquisition by prescription or under a will, are the result of a series of facts occurring through a prolonged period. There is accordingly a literature devoted to the discussion of the 'temporal limits' of the application of law [6].

Race.

iii. There is a stage of civilisation at which law is addressed, not to the inhabitants of a country, but to the members of a tribe, or the followers of a religious system, irrespectively of the locality in which they may happen to be. This is the 'personal' stage in the development of law. The governments which the barbarians established on the ruins of the Roman empire did not administer one system of justice applicable throughout a given territory, but decided each case that arose in pursuance of the personal
*362 law of the *defendant [7]; so that, according to an often-quoted passage in one of the tracts of Bishop Agobard, it might often happen that 'five men, each under a different law,

[4] On the conflict between Federal and State decisions in the United States, see an article in the American Law Review, xvii. p. 743.

[5] Cod. i. 4. 7.

[6] E. g. Struve, Ueber das positive Rechtsgesetz rücksichtlich seiner Ausdehnung in der Zeit, 1831; Savigny's discussion of the 'zeitlichen Gränzen,' System, Bd. viii. pp. 368–540; and Chabot de l'Allier, Questions transitoires sur le Code Napoléon, 1809.

[7] Marriage was contracted according to the law of the husband, and wives married according to their own law could be dismissed at pleasure, but for such religious prohibitions as that of the council of Tibur; Mansi, t. xviii. col. 151, cited by Westlake, Private International Law, ed. 2. p. 11 n.

would be found walking or sitting together [8].' In one and the same town the Frank, the Burgundian, and the Roman lived each under his own system of law. A similar phenomenon may be seen at the present day in British India. 'The notion of a territorial law,' it has been said, 'is European and modern. The laws which Hindoos and Mahomedans obey do not recognise territorial limits. The Shasters and the Koran revealed religion and law to distinct peoples, each of whom recognised a common faith as the only bond of union, but were ignorant of the novel doctrine that law and sovereignty could be conterminous with territorial limits [9].' The British Courts, in dealing with members of the Hindoo or Mahometan communities, hold that wherever such persons go within the limits of British territory, they carry with them, as a personal law applicable to their family and possessions, Hindoo or Mahometan law respectively [10].

Place.

iv. According to modern ideas, a system of law applies not to a given race, but to a given territory. It follows from the independence of each State within its own borders that it might, without contravening any principle of international law, regulate every set of circumstances which calls for decision exclusively by its own law. This law, technically described as the 'lex fori,'
*363 may be said to be the natural law *for the Courts of each State to apply; and it is that which will undoubtedly be applied by them, in the absence of special reason to the contrary. With the development of civilisation and commerce it has however become as inconvenient as it is inequitable to apply this law rigidly to all transactions, whether completed wholly within the territory, or partly outside of it, and to acts of all persons, whether permanently settled in the country, or merely passing through it. The Law

[8] 'Nam plerumque contingit ut simul eant aut sedeant quinque homines, et nullus eorum communem legem cum altero habeat, exterius in rebus transitoriis, cum interius in rebus perennibus una Christi lege teneantur.' Adv. legem Gundobadi, c. 4, Op. i. p. 111.

[9] Cowell, Tagore Lectures, 1870, p. 40.

[10] Cf. ib. p. 5, and the First Report of the Commission for a body of Substantive Law for India, p. 80.

Courts are of course bound to apply to each case the law which the sovereign has provided for its regulation, but, as has been well observed, there is no reason to suppose that the sovereign enacted the 'lex fori' with a view to the exceptional cases in question. It accordingly became necessary to classify these 'mixed cases,' and to determine what are the categories of law by which, in accordance with equity and with the general convenience, each ought to be governed.

Possible cases—Possible laws.

The possible cases must come within the classification with which the previous chapters have familiarised us, i. e. they must be cases of status, of property, of contract, and so forth. The possible law may be that of the country to which one of the persons concerned owes allegiance, or in which he is domiciled, or in which the thing in question is situated, or in which the wrong in question was committed, or in which an act, such as the making of a will or of a contract, was performed, or in which a contract was to be carried out. These distinctions may be technically expressed by the following terms respectively:—

'lex ligeantiae,'
'lex domicilii,'
'lex loci rei sitae,'
'lex loci delicti commissi,'
'lex loci actus,' of which 'contractus' is a species.
'lex loci solutionis.'

The 'lex fori' has been previously mentioned. All of these
*364 *terms are in current use, except only the 'lex ligeantiae,' which is suggested as conveniently descriptive of the law of the country to which a person owes national allegiance; a law which, in the opinion of the school of jurists now predominant in Italy, ought to decide many of the questions which have usually been determined by the 'lex domicilii [11].' The selection from this list of the 'lex' which is properly applicable to the decision of ques-

[11] Cf. Codice Civile, arts. 6–9. This doctrine it will be observed, though presenting some analogies to that of the 'personality of laws,' explained at p. 361, is by no means identical with it.

tions of a particular class, those relating for instance to marriage, to minority, or to bankruptcy, is guided in each country by the laws of that country [12]. There is however a considerable general resemblance between the rules of different systems of positive law upon these points; and positive law is more inclined with regard to such questions than to others to pay deference both to the positive law of foreign countries, and to the theories of such experts as have written upon the subject from the point of view of propriety and convenience. The assimilation thus produced of positive systems to one another and to the theories of experts has led to an erroneous impression that there exists something like a common law of civilised nations upon the subject, instead of, as is really the case, a gradual approximation of national practice, guided to some extent by a growing body of theory [13]. Some writers have indeed been led so far astray as to assert the invalidity of any national laws which do not conform to their views upon the subject [14].

Classification of nomenclature.

The body of principles adopted in positive systems, or recommended by theorists, for the selection of the territorial 'lex'
*365 which is appropriate to the decision of any given *question of private law, has been called by many names, the variety of which attests the obscurity which has involved the true nature of the subject. They may be reduced to seven classes.

Statutes.

1. The controversy having first been raised with reference to the competing claims of the 'statuta' of different Italian cities, the whole topic was treated from this point of view. The example set by Bartolus in his comment on the code in the fourteenth century [15] was followed by a series of writers such as Halbritter, who

[12] Cf. In re Hawthorne, L. R. 23 Ch. D. 748.

[13] This error is well exposed by Lindley, L. J.: 'It is all very well to say that International law is one and indivisible,' &c., Ex parte the Union Bank of Australia, '92, 1 Ch. 226.

[14] E. g. Struve, § 9. 37. Cf. Ex parte Blain, 12 Ch. D. 522.

[15] Ad l. 'cunctos populos,' i. 1.

wrote 'De Statutis' in 1545 [16], and John Voet, who wrote in 1698 [17]. As recently as 1823 J. Henry published a 'Treatise on the Difference between Personal and Real Statutes;' and a 'Traité des statuts, lois personnelles et réelles, et du droit international privé,' by M. de Chassat, appeared in 1845.

Conflict.

2. A more descriptive name for such discussions was suggested in 1653 by Rodenburg, who prefixed to his work on the law of married people a tract entitled 'de iure quod oritur ex statutorum vel consuetudinum discrepantium conflictu [18].' Paul Voet followed, in 1661, with a treatise 'de statutis eorumque concursu;' Huber, in 1686, with his famous chapter 'de conflictu legum [19];' and Hertius, in 1688, with his tract 'de collisione legum [20].' J. G. de Meiern wrote in 1715 'de statutorum conflictu eorumque apud exteros valore;' Ham, in 1792, 'de statutorum collisione et praeferentia;' Wächter, in 1841 and 1842, 'über die Collision der Privatrechtsgesetze verschiedener Staaten [21];' Livermore, in 1828, 'on the contrariety of laws;' and Brinkmann, in 1831, 'von dem Wider-
*366 *spruche ausländischer und einheimischer Gesetze.' Story's 'Conflict of Laws' was published in 1834, and Wharton's work of the same name in 1872.

Extraterritorial effect.

3. The fact that effect is given to laws outside of the territory of the State on whose authority they depend is emphasised in the titles of such works as that of Cocceius, 'de fundata in territorio et plurium locorum concurrente potestate,' 1684 [22]; of Scheinemann, 'de auctoritate legum civilium extra territorium legislatoris,' 1696; of Seger, 'de vi legum et decretorum in territorio alieno,' 1777; also in Savigny's expressions as to 'die örtlichen

16 Ad l. 'cunctos populos,' i. 1. Tubingae.

17 In his Comment. ad Pandectas, lib. i. tit. 4, pars. 2.

18 The tract is thus referred to on the general title-page. Its own sub-title is 'De iure quod oritur ex diversitate statutorum.'

19 In his Praelectiones iuris Romani, pars ii. ad Pand lib. i. tit. 3. 1686.

20 Comm. et Opusc. i. p. 129.

21 See Archiv für civ. Praxis, Bd. xxiv. p. 230, xxv. p. 1.

22 Exercit. Curios. i. p. 680.

Gränzen [23],' and Schmid's 'die Herrschaft der Gesetze, nach ihren räumlichen Grenzen [24].'

Application.

4. The question as to the choice of the law to be applied becomes prominent in the treatise of Oerstadt, 'über die Anwendung fremder Gesetze,' 1822 [25]; in that of Struve, 'über das positive Rechtsgesetz in seiner Beziehung auf räumliche Verhältnisse und über die Anwendung der Gesetze verschiedener Oerter,' 1834; and in incidental expressions occurring in Savigny's System [26].

Comity.

5. It is of course a merely voluntary act on the part of any State when it gives effect to foreign law. In the language of Huber, 'Rectores imperiorum id comiter agunt ut iura cuiusque populi intra terminos eius exercita teneant ubique suam vim [27].' Sir Robert Phillimore accordingly entitled the volume of his Commentaries which deals with this subject (1861) 'On Private International Law, or Comity.'

*367 **International Private law.*

6. Schäffner gave to his book, published in 1841, a title apparently intended to indicate that it dealt with the mode in which rules of private law are borrowed by one State from another. He called it 'die Entwickelung des internationalen Privatrechts;' and it was followed by Pfeiffer's 'das Princip des internationalen Privatrechts,' 1851; by von Bar's 'das internationale Privat- und Strafrecht,' 1862 and (omitting Strafrecht) 1889; by Asser's 'Schets van het interna-

[23] System, vol. viii. pp. 5, 8–367.

[24] The full title of his work is 'die Herrschaft der Gesetze nach ihren räumlichen und zeitlichen Grenzen im Gebiete des bürgerlichen und peinlichen Rechts,' Jena, 1863. Cf. 'Die räumliche Herrschaft der Rechtsnormen (örtliche Statutenkollision) auf dem Gebiete des Privatrechtes,' F. Böhm, 1890.

[25] Eunomia, i. pp. 1–105.

[26] viii. pp. 15, 32, 109; cf. Sir H. Maine's definition of the topic as 'the conditions on which one community will recognise and apply a portion of the jurisdiction of another.'

[27] Prael. iuris Romani, pars ii. ad Pandect. lib. i. tit. 3.

tionaal Privaatregt;' by von Püttlingen's 'Handbuch des in Oesterreich-Ungarn geltenden internationalen Privatrechts,' and by Hamaker's tract 'het internationaal Privaatregt,' in 1878. In 1874 there appeared the 'Trattato di diritto civile internazionale' of Lomonaco; and in 1880 the first volume of the 'Droit civil international[28]' of Laurent, and the 'Droit pénal international' of Fiore, translated by C. Antoine. The 'Zeitschrift für internationales Privat- und Strafrecht,' was founded by Ferd Böhm in 1890.

Private International law.

7. In 1840 Fœlix began a series of articles 'du conflit des lois de différentes nations, ou du droit international[29],' and re-published them in 1843 as the 'Traité du droit international privé, ou du conflit des lois en matière de droit privé.' Mr. Westlake followed in 1858, 1880 and 1891 with his 'Private International Law, or the Conflict of Laws;' M. Fiore, in 1869, with his 'Diritto internazionale privato, o principii per risolvere i conflitti tra legislazione diverse in materia di diritto civile e commerciale;' M. Haus with 'Le droit privé qui régit les étrangers en Belgique, ou du droit des gens privé considéré dans ses principes fondamentaux et dans ses rapports avec les lois civiles des Belges,' 1874; M. Brocher
*368 with his *'Nouveau traité du droit international privé,' 1876;
and Mr. Foote with his 'Private International Jurisprudence,' 1878. In 1874 M. Clunet established at Paris the 'Journal du droit international privé.'

Objections to Statutes.

Objections, well and ill founded, have been urged against each and all of these phrases. The nomenclature of the 'Statutes,' an attempt to resolve a legal into a merely grammatical question, is indeed obsolete. Of the other phrases, one is distinctly misleading, while the rest are rather inadequate than erroneous.

[28] This term was first suggested by Portalis, in a report to the Académie des Sciences Morales et Politiques, Comptes rendus, 1843, t. i. p. 449.

[29] In the Revue Etrangère et Française de Législation, t. vii. p. 81. Fœlix begins, 'On appelle droit international l'ensemble des règles reconnues comme raison de décider des conflits entre le droit privé des diverses nations.' He goes on to blame Wheaton for using the term 'droit international' as equivalent to 'droit des gens,' i e. to public international law!

Objections to Conflict.

Those who deny that a 'Conflict of laws' ever really takes place are right if they mean only that the authority of a domestic can never be displaced by that of a foreign law. It cannot however be denied that, although each State is free to adopt for the decision of any given question its own or foreign law, and between various foreign laws to choose that which it prefers, yet the rival claims of these bodies of law do present themselves to the legislature or the court as competing or conflicting. There is no strife for the mastery, but there is a competition of opposite conveniences. The phrase is inadequate, because it does not cover questions as to jurisdiction, or as to the execution of foreign judgments.

Objections to Extraterritoriality.

Such expressions as seem to attribute an extraterritorial supremacy, 'Herrschaft,' to any system of law, are more obviously open to censure, as being inconsistent with the absolute sovereignty of each State within its own territory.

Objections to Comity.

When, on the other hand, the theory of 'Comity' is attacked, on the ground that a Court, in applying a particular 'lex,' is guided not by courtesy but by legal principle, it must not be forgotten that, although the Courts of each State are guided by the law of the State, the State in making that law is guided not by the law of Nations, but by general considerations of equity, accompanied by some expectation of reciprocity. 'Comity' thus expresses the truth that the adoption of this or that rule by a State is a
*369 matter of indifference to *international law. The new Italian school would indeed deny this proposition, asserting that a State, in applying foreign law to certain sets of circumstances, is but complying with an international duty of 'perfect obligation [30].'

[30] See a Report by Signor Mancini, late Minister of Justice, to the Institut de Droit International, Revue de Droit International, t. vii. pp. 333, 337, 362. Cf. von Bar, in von Holtzendorff's Encyclopädie, Syst. Theil, p. 681.

Objections to Application.

The phrase 'Application of law,' 'Anwendung der Gesetze,' is liable to no objection except that it is perhaps too wide; embracing, as it may, all the topics of the present chapter.

Objections to International Private law.

'International Private law,' though a dangerously ambiguous term, is not incapable of being understood to denote the mode in which rules of private law are borrowed by the Courts of one State from those of another.

Objections to Private International law.

The transposed version of this term as 'Private International law' is wholly indefensible. Such a phrase should mean, in accordance with that use of the word 'international' which, besides being well established in ordinary language, is both scientifically convenient and etymologically correct, 'a private species of the body of rules which prevails between one nation and another.' Nothing of the sort is however intended; and the unfortunate employment of the phrase, as indicating the principles which govern the choice of the system of private law applicable to a given class of facts, has led to endless misconceptions of the true nature of this department of legal science [31]. It has also made it necessary to lengthen the description of International law, properly so called, by prefixing to it the otherwise superfluous epithet 'public.'

It is most important, for the clear understanding of the real character of the topic which for the last forty years has been
*370 misdescribed as 'Private International law,' that this *barbarous compound should no longer be employed. Nor is its abandonment less desirable with a view to the rehabilitation of the term 'international' for the scientific purpose for which it was originally coined [32].

31 The term is thus applied, e. g. in re Queensland Co., '92, 1 Ch. 219.

32 Supra, p. *343. Mr. Frederic Harrison, in two singularly able articles in the Fortnightly Review for 1879, has suggested as a substitute for 'Private International law' the term 'Intermunicipal law.' This is surely no improvement, since 'municipal,' in accordance with established use, is either equivalent to 'national,' or relates to civic organization. 'American Inter-

The contents of the topic.

The topic in question consists of the body of rules which prevail in a given country, or given countries, or which theorists think ought to prevail generally, as to the selection of the law to be applied in cases where it may be doubted whether the domestic or a foreign law, and, in the latter case, which foreign law, is appropriate to the facts. It is a body of rules for finding rules. With this topic it is usual to combine that of the choice of the competent 'forum,' and also that of the effect to be given to a foreign judgment.

The choice of a name.

The group of topics is undoubtedly hard to name. Of the old names, 'the Conflict of laws' is probably the best, 'Private International law' is indubitably the worst. 'The Application of Foreign law,' or 'the Extraterritorial Recognition of rights,' may be suggested as at any rate not misleading, while the latter phrase might be useful as calling attention to the fact that what really happens when a law seems to obtain an extraterritorial effect, is rather that rights created and defined by foreign law obtain recognition by the domestic tribunal [33]. Thus it is that the status
*371 of marriage will be *recognised as resulting from an observance of the formalities prescribed by the 'lex loci celebrationis,' and an obligation resulting from the judgment of a competent Court in one State will be enforced by the Courts of another [34]. No name has yet been suggested which satisfactorily covers the two topics of 'Forum' and 'Lex.'

state law' is the not inappropriate title of a work by David Rorer, which appeared at Chicago in 1879 and 1893. In a syllabus of lectures for 1886, Mr. Harrison proposes to speak of the 'interterritorial application of law.'

[33] The terms 'Droit privé (ou pénal) extraterritorial,' in addition to those in the text, were suggested by the present writer in the Revue de Droit International for 1880, t. xii. p. 581. In 1883 a work appeared at Madrid, entitled 'Principios de derecho internacional privado, o de derecho extraterritorial de Europa y America en sus relaciones con el derecho civil de España,' by D. Manuel Torres Campos. Prof. Dicey, Law Quarterly Review for 1890, p. 14, seems inclined to adopt this phraseology.

[34] The theory of the text, it will be observed, assumes the foundation of this whole topic, whether it be described as 'the application of foreign law.'

Interpretation.

III. In order that the competent Court may rightly apply the appropriate law, it is necessary that the words of the law shall be properly construed. 'Interpretation' is thus a third, though a very subordinate, topic of the application of law. It is said to be either 'legal,' which rests on the same authority as the law itself, or 'doctrinal,' which rests upon its intrinsic reasonableness.

Legal.

'Legal interpretation' may be either 'authentic,' when it is expressly provided by the legislator [35], or 'usual,' when it is derived from unwritten practice.

Doctrinal.

'Doctrinal interpretation' may turn on the meaning of words and sentences, when it is called 'grammatical,' or on the intention of the legislator, when it is described as 'logical.' When logical interpretation stretches the words of a statute to cover its obvious meaning it is called 'extensive;' when, on the other hand, it avoids giving full meaning to the words, in order not to go beyond the intention, of the legislator it is called 'restrictive.'

*372 ***§ 2. Public Law.**

The application of criminal law.

It is chiefly in the criminal branch of Public law that questions of the kind now under consideration present themselves for solution.

or the 'extraterritorial recognition of rights,' to be that of 'vested rights;' a doctrine which appears to the author to remain unshaken by the numerous attacks which have been directed against it. It is well stated by Huber, 'Subjectio hominum infra leges cuiusque territorii, quamdiu illic agunt, quae facit ut actus ab initio validus, aut nullus, alibi quoque valere, aut non valere, non nequeat.' Prael. ad Pand. i. 3. § 15. Cf. Wächter, u. s.

[35] As in what are called the 'interpretation clauses' of a modern Act of Parliament, many of which are now superseded by the comprehensive Interpretation Act, 1889. Cf. Cod. i. 14. 9 and 12. Cf. also Dalloz, s. v. 'Lois,' art. 438.

The Forum.

I. The 'forum' which, ratione territorii, is properly seized of the punishment of an offence has been at different times asserted to be—that of the nation of which the offender is a subject, that of the domicil of the offender, that of the nation injured, that of the place of the arrest or detention of the offender, and that of the place where the offence was committed. These may be respectively described as the

'forum ligeantiae,'
'forum domicilii,'
'forum civitatis laesae,'
'forum deprehensionis,' or 'fortuitum,'
'forum delicti commissi.'

The last-mentioned 'forum,' which was indeed the first to assert its claims, has in recent times nearly superseded the others, as being the most compatible with modern ideas of the nature of sovereignty. Four theories as to the competent 'forum' are heard of at the present day.

The territorial theory.

i. What is known as the 'territorial theory of jurisdiction,' founded upon the competency of the 'forum delicti commissi,' asserts that each State may, and ought to, deal with all persons, be they subjects or aliens, who commit offences within its territory, or on board of its ships, against its criminal law. This proposition, though indisputably true, is as indisputably inadequate to secure the due punishment of crime. Its insufficiency to provide for the punishment of criminals who have escaped from the territory in which their offence was committed is partially redressed by
*373 treaties of Extradition, under *which such offenders are returned to the 'forum delicti;' but it still needs supplementing by other principles.

The personal theory.

ii. According to 'the personal theory of jurisdiction,' each State has a right to the obedience of its own subjects, wheresoever they may be. It follows that a subject may be tried on his return to his own country, or even in his absence, for an offence against its laws committed while within the territory of another State. This second theory, which asserts the claim of the 'forum ligeantiae,' is very variously applied in practice. England and the United States use it but sparingly, as introducing a very limited list of exceptions to the standard principle of territorial jurisdiction [36]. It is thus provided by Act of Parliament that a British subject may be indicted for murder, manslaughter, or bigamy, whether committed within the Queen's dominions or without, and may be tried 'in any place in England or Ireland in which he shall be apprehended or be in custody [37].'

The continental States agree in punishing offences committed abroad by a subject against the government or coinage of the country to which he belongs, but differ widely in their treatment of offences of other kinds. The French Code of 1808 punished offences committed abroad by Frenchmen against Frenchmen [38]. The Code for the German Empire will punish acts of its subjects which are criminal in the country where they were committed as well as in Germany [39]. The Italian Code of 1889 [40] and the Austrian draft Code of 1867 [41] contain similar provisions, with reference to offences of a certain gravity. The Bavarian Code of 1861 stated the liability of subjects without any such reserva-
*374 tion [42]; and the *French Code, as amended in 1866, provides that 'tout Français qui hors du territoire de la France s'est rendu coupable d'un crime puni par la loi française, peut être poursuivi et jugé en France [43].

This enactment is in accordance with an opinion given to the government by the Cour de Cassation in 1845 and approved by twenty-four Courts of Appeal and six Faculties of law, against

36 Cf. the Zollverein, 1 Swab. 96.

37 24 & 25 Vict. c. 100, ss. 9, 57. Cf. as to Treason, 35 H. VIII. c. 2; 5 & 6 Ed. VI, c. 11; 7 Anne, c. 21.

38 Code d'instruction criminelle, art. 7.

39 Art. 4. 3.

40 Art. 5.

41 Art. 4.

42 Inländer unterliegen den Bestimmungen der Bayerischen Strafgesetze wegen aller von ihnen in Im- oder Auslande verübten strafbaren Handlungen, art. 10.

43 Arts. 5–7.

the exclusively territorial character of penal jurisdiction. 'Ce qui est vrai,' said the Court, 'c'est que le droit de punir, au nom de la loi française, ne peut s'exercer qu'en France; ce qui est erroné, c'est que l'acte punissable, commis sur le sol étranger, ne puisse, dans aucun cas, être régi par cette loi [44].'

The 'forum ligeantiae' is not concurrent with, but excludes, the 'forum delicti' in the case of Europeans whose governments have capitulations to that effect with the governments of Oriental States.

The theory of self-preservation.

iii. What may be described as 'the theory of self-preservation' is in some continental systems considered in certain cases to confer a jurisdiction which, since it is neither 'territorial' nor 'personal,' has been called 'quasi-territorial.' It allows that the Courts of a State may punish offences although committed not only outside of its territory but also by persons who are not its subjects. Such a jurisdiction, which might perhaps be described as claimed for the 'forum civitatis laesae,' is usually asserted with reference to offences against the government of the State, or against its public credit.

The French Code, as revised in 1866, provides for the trial and punishment of any alien who, having committed abroad an offence 'attentatoire à la sûreté de l'Etat, ou de contrefacon du sceau de l'Etat,' or against the French coinage or paper currency, shall afterwards, voluntarily or by means of extradition, come with-
*375 in the French territory [45]. *The German Code of 1872 [46], and the Italian Code of 1889 [47], contain similar articles. The Bavarian Code of 1861 went further; providing also for the punishment of offences committed abroad by aliens against Bavarian subjects, 'in the absence of anything to the contrary in the treaties of the State or the principles of International law [48].'

[44] Cited by M. Brocher, Rev. de Droit Int. vii. p. 46.

[45] Art. 7.

[46] Arts. 4. 1. By the Strafprozessordnung of 1877, art. 9, the accused may be condemned though absent from German territory.

[47] Art. 4.

[48] Art. 12. A similar provision in the Penal Code of Mexico, art. 186, making a 'Delito' committed in a foreign country by a foreigner against a Mexican punishable in Mexico and according to its laws, gave rise in 1886 to

At its Brussels Session, in 1879, the 'Institut de Droit international,' after much discussion, adopted the following resolution upon this subject:—'Tout état a le droit de punir les faits commis même en dehors de son territoire et par des étrangers en violation de ses lois pénales, alors que ces faits sont une atteinte à l'existence sociale de l'état en cause, et compromettent sa sécurité, et qu'ils ne sont point prêvus par la loi pénale du pays sur le territoire duquel ils ont eu lieu.' The Institut rejected a resolution extending the right to other cases.[49].

The theory of cosmopolitan justice.

iv. The theory which may be described as one 'of general supervision,' or 'of cosmopolitan justice,' looks merely to the 'forum deprehensionis,' which we have also called 'fortuitum,' ascribing to each State the right of punishing any criminal who may come into its power.

This theory has long found favour with reference to pirates, on the ground that they have thrown off their subjection to any political authority, but some writers have claimed for it a far wider application. Vattel, for instance, makes an exception to the rule of exclusively territorial jurisdiction in the case of 'ces scé-
*376 lérats qui, par la qualité *et la fréquence habituelle de leurs
crimes, violent toute sûreté publique et se déclarent les ennemis du genre humain.' He continues: 'Les empoisonneurs, les assassins, les incendiaires de profession, peuvent être exterminés partout où on les saisit: car ils attaquent et outragent toutes les nations, en foulant aux pieds les fondements de leur sûreté commune. C'est ainsi que les pirates sont envoyés à la potence par les premiers entre les mains de qui ils tombent. Si le souverain du pays où des crimes de cette nature ont été commis en réclame les auteurs pour en faire la punition, on doit les lui rendre, comme à celui qui est principalement intéressé à les punir exemplairement [50].' The Austrian draft Code accordingly provides for the

the 'Cutting case,' on which see the official report of Mr. J. B. Moore to the U. S. Secretary of State, and Revue de Droit International, t. xx. p. 559.

49 Annuaire, iii. p. 281.

50 Droit des Gens, i. § 233. Cf. von Holtzendorff, die Auslieferung der Verbrecher, 1881, p. 7.

punishment of serious offences committed abroad by aliens, subject to the stipulations of any treaty to the contrary [51]; and the Italian Code of 1889 contains a similar provision, in case the State to which the alien belongs shall have refused to take him in extradition, with a view to punishment [52].

Combination of theories of jurisdiction.

It is obvious that the adoption by a State of one or another of the four current theories of jurisdiction, or of a combination of several of them, will determine not only the exercise of its own criminal jurisdiction with reference to a given set of facts, but also its recognition of the rightfulness of the exercise by other States of their jurisdiction with reference to the same state of facts. In cases where it recognises the concurrent competence of several States, it may or may not regard the decision of the Courts of any one of them as final, so as to give an offender the benefit of the maxim, 'ne bis in idem.' Provisions to this effect are not uncommon in continental Codes [53]. In English law
*377 *there is some authority for saying that a plea of 'autrefois acquit' or 'convict' in a competent foreign court is a good defence [54].

The readiness, or disinclination, of a State to surrender its own subjects in extradition is another result of the view which it adopts with reference to criminal competence. The continental nations, among which the doctrine of 'personal jurisdiction' is fully entertained, refuse extradition of their own subjects; while England readily surrenders its subjects because it is not, as a rule, prepared to punish them for offences committed outside of the country.

[51] 1868, art. 6.

[52] Art. 6.

[53] Code d'ins. crim. art. 7; Loi de 1886, art. 5; German Code, art. 5. 7. But cf. Austrian Code, art. 30, Italian Code, art. 8; and Fiore, Droit pénal international, i. p. 161.

[54] See R. v. Hutchinson, 29 C. II, cited in Beake v. Tyrrell, 1 W. and M., 1 Shower, 6, and in R. v. Roche, 1775, 1 Leach, 135. Cf. Bull, N. P. 245; Archbold, Crim. Pract. p. 121.

The Lex.

II. Questions as to the appropriate 'Lex' are not of frequent occurrence in criminal law. Of the four classes of such questions which may conceivably be raised, those as to (i) Concentricity, and (ii) Time [55], no doubt occasionally occur, but questions of (iii) Race, and (iv) Place, are hardly separable from the question of 'Forum.' The 'comity' which often determines a controversy in private law in accordance with rules borrowed from a foreign system has no place in the trial of crimes. No State will undertake to administer the criminal law of another, though it may sometimes go so far as to enquire into the amount of punishment to which a crime would be liable according to the law of the place where it was committed.

The topics of criminal 'forum' and 'lex' have sometimes been treated in conjunction with the analogous topics of private law, as, for instance, by von Bar in his 'Internationales Privat- und Strafrecht [56].' They have indeed much in common, and the title of von Bar's work would be objectionable only on the ground
*378 of ambiguity, if it did not seem to lend itself *to the support of statements by other writers which involve the whole subject in hopeless confusion.

It may perhaps be assumed that the reader who has followed the argument of the last few pages will at once detect the astonishing inconsistency of view which is betrayed by the following extract from a work of deservedly high authority. 'On appelle,' says M. Fœlix, 'droit international privé l'ensemble des règles d'après lesquelles se jugent les *conflits entre le droit privé* des diverses nations; en d'autres termes, le droit international privé se compose des lois civiles *ou criminelles* d'un état dans le territoire d'un état étranger [57].'

[55] E. g. German Code, art. 2.

[56] The edition of 1889 is restricted to Privatrecht.

[57] Droit International Privé, § 1. M. von Bar, who defends his combination of the two topics by the authority of R. von Mohl, Staatsrecht, 'Völkerrecht u. Politik, p. 682, endeavours to avoid the difficulties which his title raises by distinguishing between 'Internationales Recht' and 'Völkerrecht.' The former term he employs to signify a genus, of which the two species are respectively 'Völkerrecht,' by which he means Public International law,

It would not be too much to say that 'Private International law,' if thus conceived of, is neither 'private' nor 'international' in the sense in which either of those terms are usually and properly employed in Jurisprudence.

Interpretation.

III. What was said of the 'interpretation' of private, will apply also to that of public law.

§ 3. International Law.

I. No question of 'Forum' can arise in International law, of which it is an essential principle that each nation is the judge of its own quarrels, and the executioner of its own decrees.

The Lex.

II. The question of 'Lex' does indeed arise, but in a way that presents but a slight analogy to anything in either
*379 *department of Municipal law. It is merely whether a given set of circumstances comes, or does not come, within the operation of international law at all. In other words, whether the States between which a controversy has arisen are, or are not, members of 'the family of nations[58].' If not, the principles to be applied to the facts are derivable not from international law, but from views of national interest tempered by general morality. Much confused reasoning has resulted from forgetfulness of the limited area within which it is possible or desirable to apply the rules of International law, as such.

Interpretation.

III. What has been said upon the subject of 'Interpretation' with reference to municipal law, applies mutatis mutandis to International law also.

and 'Internationales Privatrecht.' Mr. Westlake, who follows Fœlix, frankly admits, in his second edition, p. 5, that he is using the term 'private' in a sense which has no relation to the division of national law into 'public' and 'private.'

[58] Supra, p. *347.

The axioms of the science and the doctrines of received text-writers will be susceptible in general only of 'logical interpretation,' but something analogous to 'authentic interpretation' would be quite possible in the case of such quasi-legislative expressions of international opinion, as, for instance, the Declaration of Paris, the Geneva Convention, or the General Act of the Brussels Conference on the Slave Trade.

INDEX.

[THE FIGURES REFER TO THE STAR (*) PAGES.]

[The figures refer to star (*) pages.]

[The figures refer to star (*) pages.]

C

[The figures refer to star (*) pages.]

[The figures refer to star (*) pages.]

D

[The figures refer to star (*) pages.]

[The figures refer to star (*) pages.]

[The figures refer to star (*) pages.]

[The figures refer to star (*) pages.]

[The figures refer to star (*) pages.]

[The figures refer to star (*) pages.]

[The figures refer to star (*) pages.]

[The figures refer to star (*) pages.]

P

[The figures refer to star (*) pages.]

[The figures refer to star (*) pages.]

Q

R

[The figures refer to star (*) pages.]

S

[The figures refer to star (*) pages]

[The figures refer to star (*) pages.]

[The figures refer to star (*) pages.]

[The figures refer to star (*) pages.]

WEST PUBLISHING CO., PRINTERS AND STEREOTYPERS, ST. PAUL, MINN.